JEWISH LITURGY

JEWISH LITURGY

AND ITS DEVELOPMENT

A. Z. IDELSOHN

SCHOCKEN BOOKS • NEW YORK

First SCHOCKEN edition 1967

Reprinted by arrangement with Holt, Rinehart and Winston, Inc.
and by permission of Hebrew Union College-Jewish Institute of Religion.

Library of Congress Catalog Card No. 67-14959

Manufactured in the United States of America

PREFACE

Jewish liturgy covers the whole range of Jewish history — a period of three thousand years — and the whole spiritual development of Judaism is reflected therein.

This book attempts to give a comprehensive presentation of Jewish liturgy in all its phases. It describes the growth and the forms the liturgy assumed during the ages. Public services and private devotions, Synagogue and Home worship, are equally treated.

Though the work was originally conceived as a companion to the author's *Jewish Music in Its Historical Development*, published in 1929, yet in its present form it stands by itself on its own ground. The author considered it essential to prepare the work chiefly as a book for students and for scholarly laymen. For that purpose, a detailed description of each individual service for the whole liturgical cycle of the most important rituals is given. The prayers in prose and liturgical poetry are characterized and analyzed, and the latest researches and findings are utilized. In order not to interrupt the description of the standard prayers and not to overburden the reader with material, we have presented the poetical insertions (piyyutim) for the special Sabbaths, the festivals and fast-days separately, in the Appendices IV–VI. For the same reason we have placed the old variants of the Hebrew texts in Appendix III. An exception, however, was made with the services of the High Holydays, in which all the poetical insertions are incorporated, for the insertions became an organic part of the services on these days.

All Hebrew quotations *within the text* have been transliterated, whereas in the appendices and in the notes Hebrew quotations are given in Hebrew characters. The Hebrew alphabetical index presents almost a complete list of the prose and poetical items of the liturgy according to the Ashkenazic, Sephardic, Italian, and Yemenite rituals.

The influence of Jewish liturgy upon the liturgy of religious movements which branched off from Judaism, as Christianity and Karaism, are treated in an appendix.

This book, too, like *Jewish Music* is printed in two types, the larger for the readers who wish to acquire a general knowledge of the subject, and a smaller one for those who are interested in a more detailed grasp of the liturgy.

The author feels indebted to all the scholars and to the publications mentioned in this book, and to several others for their pioneer works in the field of Jewish liturgy. He wishes to express his indebtedness to his friend and colleague Professor Samuel S. Cohon for his valuable suggestions, and to Rabbi Frederick A. Doppelt for his devoted assistance.

A. Z. I.

Cincinnati, O.,
December, 1931.

ABBREVIATIONS

M. — Mishna
b. — Babylonian Talmud
Jer. — Jerusalem (Palestinian Talmud)
P.d.R.E. — Pirke de Rabbi Eliezer
S.R.A. — Seder Rav Amram
M.V. — Mahzor Vitry
r. — ritual
Ber. — Berachoth
Pes. — Pesahim
R.H. — Rosh Hashana
B.K. — Baba Kama
Tos. — Tosefta
Or., or O.H. — Orah Hayim; Otzar Hatefilloth; Otzar Hapiyyut
J.E. — Jewish Encyclopedia
J.Q.R. — Jewish Quarterly Review
Ltg. — Literaturgeschichte
G.V. — Gottesdienstliche Vortraege
Ms. — Monatsschrift
Thesaurus. — Thesaurus of Hebrew Oriental Melodies

CONTENTS

INTRODUCTORY NOTES

PART I

A Survey of the Historical Development of Jewish Worship and Liturgy from Ancient Times to the Nineteenth Century

PART II

Description of the Liturgy

JEWISH LITURGY

INTRODUCTORY NOTES

The Prayer-Book

The Jewish prayer-book is unique among the rituals of all religions. Not only are the religious ideas and beliefs expressed in the Jewish prayers, but also the events, vicissitudes, and hopes of the Jewish people. It is, therefore, a reflection of both the religio-ethical ideals of Judaism and the life of the Jew as an individual and as a member of a suffering people, now scattered among the nations of the world for the last two thousand years.

The Jewish prayer-book has two basic elements: *laudation* and *petition*. On the one hand, the Jew praises the Creator of the world, and on the other, he prays unto Him for his personal needs as well as for the needs of his people. The Jew not only exalts the Supreme Being, but he also pours out his troubled heart before his Father in heaven. There are in addition some other subdivisions such as meditation, reflection, and thanksgiving.

Due to the intense group-consciousness of the Jewish people, the Jewish prayers are mostly in the first person plural. The statements (b. Sanhedrin 27b, Shevuoth 39a) — "All members of Israel are responsible for each other" — and "All members of Israel are companions" — constitute the watchword of Jewish solidarity. This sense of comradeship and responsibility the Jews learned too well during the long centuries of their sojourn among the nations throughout the tedious Diaspora. A great sage of the third century advised the people to include the entire group in one's own prayers (b. Ber. 29b). Even the first person singular often used in the Psalms is now commonly interpreted as of collective nature.

As a result of this group attitude, several prayers given in the Bible in the singular were changed to the plural. For example: "Heal me, O Lord, and I shall be healed; save me, and I shall be saved, for Thou art my praise" (Jer. 17:14) was changed to "Heal us, O Lord, and we shall be healed; save, and we shall be saved, for Thou art our praise."

The prayer-book is the mirror of the spirit of the Jewish people and its development; it reflects the spiritual, economic, political, and social history of Israel from the most ancient times up to the present. This book is the true companion of the Jew from the years of his early youth to the hour of his death. Next to the Bible, it is the most popular book in Jewish life; to a certain extent it is even closer to him, since it was at no time canonized but continued to develop and to reflect the daily occurrences of the Jewish people.

For this very reason, the prayer-book shows so many variations. Almost every country has its own variations which came as a result of the local conditions to which the Jewish group of that country was subjected. The basic elements of the prayer-book, however, remain the same throughout the Diaspora, and only those sects which broke away from the Jewish religious views and dissociated themselves from the historic house of Israel changed their ritual completely. The Karaites are a good example of such groups and sects (see Appendix II).

The greatest part of the Jewish people is known by the term "Ashkenazim." The ancestors of this major portion lived in Central and Eastern Europe for many centuries, and created a local variation in the ritual called "Minhag Ashkenaz." The members of this group still continue to pray in this ritual even after they and their fathers settled in the New World.

Next in importance to the "Minhag Ashkenaz" is the "Minhag Sepharad." This ritual was created by the Jews of Spanish extraction. The descendants of the Spanish Jews retained their ritual even after their expulsion in 1492–7. This ritual spread throughout the Orient and supplanted several existing rituals in the Oriental countries.

Other rituals, such as the "Minhag Italiani" in Italy, "Minhag Teman" in Yemen, and "Minhag Fez" in Morocco, are still used by small groups. Often individual congregations created specific "Minhagim." These "Minhagim," however, differ only in minor versions of the prayers or in the custom of reciting or omitting the one or the other section (see Chapter VII for details).

Aside from these rituals, there are several others. Some of

them are still in existence; others are now out of use, either because the followers of them died out or because they adopted another ritual.

Religious movements in Israel left a deep impression upon the prayer-book. The latest of these was the Reform Movement in Central Europe and America (Chapter XIX).

Israel may well be thankful for its great heritage of the prayer-book. In times of trials and oppressions it has served as an inspiration and as a source of strength to the oppressed members of the Jewish people.

It is because of this great religious and ethical value of the prayer-book, and because of its historical intimacy with the daily life of the Jew that we turn to it for a fuller and more complete understanding of Israel today.

The Hebrew Names "Siddur" and "Mahzor"

I. Siddur — Order. Before beginning the service, it was essential to put one's prayers in *order*.[1] Precentors and leaders in public worship were especially advised to put their prayers in order in their minds according to the set order of the service as given in the Mishnaic and Talmudic literature. In b. Rosh Hashana 17b it is stated that God showed Moses "Seder Tefilla" — the order of prayer. The first authentic compilation of prayers edited by Rav Amram Gaon in 875 was called "Seder" or "Siddur" — the Order of Amram. Since then, this name was used for any compilation of the standard prayers without additional poetry. The Hebrew title for prayer-book remained "Seder tefilloth." In Germany and among the Sephardim it is called "Tefilla" — Prayer.

II. Mahzor — Cycle. This term was originally applied to the calendar, similar to the word "Mahzarta" of the Syrian Church for "brevier." Later, it was taken over and applied to the poetical insertions in the prayers of the whole cycle of the year. The first known "Mahzor" of poetry was that of Yannai of the seventh century. Still later, customs and regulations pertaining to the ritual at large and laws pertaining to the individual Sabbaths and holidays were inserted together with the prayers. *Mahzor Vitry* is a work of that type; it was compiled in France by a disciple of Rashi (Chapter VII).

The line of demarcation between *Siddur* and *Mahzor*, however, was not always kept apart. About the time when *Mahzor Vitry* was composed, another similar compilation was written in France, in Troyes, the native town of Rashi, and was called *Seder Troyes*. This work differs from the Mahzor Vitry in that it merely mentions the order of prayers without giving their texts in full and in that it gives but abbreviated regulations of the ritual. In the later editions of the *Siddur*, there is also some poetical material inserted in the prayers.

Nevertheless, among the Ashkenazim and Sephardim the term "Mahzor" is applied only to the ritual of the holidays in which the *piyyut* is incorporated.

The Language of the Prayers

With but a few exceptions, the prayers were composed in Hebrew originally, because this was the tongue of the people. Later, when Hebrew ceased to be the spoken vernacular of the people at large and became the language of Jewish thought and sentiment, the tongue of his spirit, the sages still considered it of importance to utter prayers in Hebrew, though no objection was raised to other languages. Thus, Rabbi Jehuda Hanasi (The Prince) insisted that only Hebrew should be used, while the sages in general maintained that it is permissible to use any language for prayer (M. Sota VII, 1, b. Sota 33a). The Ten Commandments were supposed to have been announced simultaneously in seventy tongues (b. Ber. 13a; Shabbath 88b; Shevuoth 39a).

In spite of the attitude of the sages, Hebrew remained the language of Israel's prayers in public worship; in private devotion, other idioms were used, especially for those who did not understand Hebrew (see Chapter XVIII). For a time, Aramaic and Greek were employed in those countries where these languages became the vernacular of the Jews living there. After the Marranos fled from Spain and Portugal and settled in Amsterdam, the ritual was translated into Portuguese for them, because they did not know Hebrew. Their children, however, learned Hebrew and began to use the prayers in the original tongue. It was deeply felt that Israel could express his deepest emotions only in the language of his soul, in Hebrew.

The Structure of the Services

The structure of the liturgy is an artistic creation of the Jewish spirit.

Elements. Each service must consist of two elements: Praise (Shevah) and Prayer (Tefilla). In b. Ber. 32a it is stated: "Man should always first utter praises and then pray." This principle has been maintained throughout all the services.

Parts of the Services. The standard parts of the services are:

a. "Tefilla" or "Amida" is referred to the prayers recited while standing. In the services of the weekdays it consists of nineteen paragraphs (benedictions) of which the first three are praises, the last three thanksgivings, and the intermediate thirteen are petitions. This part is also called in Hebrew "Shemone Esre" — Eighteen — because originally there were only eighteen benedictions, and about 100 C.E. a nineteenth benediction was added (see Chapters III, VIII). On Sabbaths, festivals, and in the Musaf services, the Amida consists of the first three and the last three benedictions, and instead of the thirteen intermediate paragraphs, a special benediction dealing with the particular day is inserted — thus making the total equal to seven benedictions — "Bircath sheva." The Musaf service of New Year constitutes an exception; it has three intermediate benedictions instead of merely one — thus augmenting the total to nine benedictions.

The reason for cutting out the thirteen intermediate paragraphs on Sabbaths and the festivals is that no petitions and supplications are permitted to be uttered on these days, since they are days consecrated to joy and spiritual awakening (*Midrash* Tanhuma Wayyera, Warsaw, 1840, 20b). The recitation of petitions necessitates reflection on human needs which often sadden the spirit of man.

There is no service without the Amida.

In public service the Amida, with the exception of that in the evening service (see Chapters VIII, X), is first recited by each individual as a silent prayer, "Tefilla belahash," and then repeated aloud by the precentor, "Hazarath hashatz" or "Tefilla bekol." The reason for the silent Amida is in order not to embarrass people who want to seek forgiveness for their sins (b. Sota 32b). The repetition of the Amida was ordered for the benefit of those who cannot read, so that they might follow the precentor (b. Rosh Hashana, end).

b. Praise (Shevah) is also represented in every service; it does not, however, appear in such uniformity as does the element of "Prayer." The morning services of the entire year have the same sections of Praise; the evening services have their special forms of Praise; and the Minha services have their particular sections.

The Praise of the morning service is subdivided into the following sections:

1. Morning Benedictions — "Birchoth Hashahar."
2. Verses of Song — "Pesuke Dezimra."
3. Shema and its three benedictions (Deut. 6:4–9; 11:13–21; Num. 15:37–41).

Section 2 consists of praises exclusively, while sections 1 and 3 have also some petitions.

The evening service in addition to Amida contains only the Shema and four benedictions. The Ashkenazic ritual has on weekdays five benedictions.

The afternoon service has in addition to Amida Psalms 84:5 and 145 to which the paragraph "Uva letziyon" is added on Sabbaths and festivals.

c. Supplication — Tahanun — is added to the morning and afternoon services on weekdays, and is recited after the Amida.

d. Alenu — Laudation — is taken from the Musaf service of New Year and was made the concluding paragraph for every service throughout the year.

These are the standard elements in the Jewish Liturgy in all rituals, though their wording in the different rituals shows slight variations. This, too, is its standard structure. Some sections were elaborated and some abbreviated in the different rituals; fundamentally, however, all sections are retained in the various rituals.

Musaf—The Additional Service. After the morning service on Sabbaths, the festivals, and New Moon-days, there is an additional service in commemoration of the additional sacrifice offered at the Temple on these days (Num. 28:9). This additional service — called "Musaf" — used to be recited already during the days of the Second Temple (see Chapter III). The structure of the Musaf remained the same throughout the ages, with the exception of the Musaf of New Year's Day. The Musaf consists of the three introductory, the three concluding benedictions, and of an intermediate benediction.

On the Day of Atonement, there is a closing service after the Minha service; it is called *Ne'ila*. This service is derived from the service which used to be held at the Temple at the time of the closing of the gates (see Chapter III).

Only the term "Minha" occurs in the Bible; all other Hebrew names for the services are post-Biblical.

The structure, as well as the standard elements of the services were already fixed in the second century C.E. in Palestine, and were accepted by all Jewish communities in the world. Since that time, the sections of the services were enriched; at times complete parts were inserted in some of the divisions. In rare cases, however, paragraphs were omitted.

The form of a benediction — "Beracha" — must contain the formula *Baruch atta adonay elohenu melech haolam* (b. Ber. 12a). Every benediction must start and conclude with "Baruch," with the exception of the blessings over fruit and on occasions of fulfillment of commandments and those which follow another benediction (b. Ber. 46a). Those which begin and close with "Baruch" are called benedictions of "the long form" — *matbe'a aruch*, while those which only start with "Baruch" are called benedictions of "the short form" — *matbe'a katzer*. The concluding eulogy has to have the three words *Baruch atta adonay* which is taken from Psalm 119 : 12; I Chronicles 29 : 10.

On Sabbaths and festivals, the public service contains not only the element of *devotion* but also that of *instruction*. Consequently, readings from the Bible were made obligatory in the public services on these days since ancient times (see Chapter III). The reading is:

1. From the Pentateuch — "Keriath hattora" — read out of the "Sefer tora" — the parchment-roll, and

2. From the Prophets — "Haftara" — may be read out of a scroll or a printed book.

The Pentateuch is divided into sections according to the

number of Sabbaths of the lunar year, and on each Sabbath a fixed section is read. On the festivals, portions are read which deal with the different holidays. Selections were chosen from the Prophets to fit the context of the sections from the Pentateuch. In Palestine the triennial division of the Pentateuch (see Chapter IV) was used.

In addition a paragraph of the weekly Pentateuchal section is read from the Scroll on Mondays and Thursdays during the morning service and on Sabbath at the afternoon service.

The reading takes place in the morning service after the "Amida," and on weekdays after Tahanun, with the exception of Sabbaths and Fast-days on which days there is also a Pentateuchal reading in the afternoon service.

The Time of Service

There are three daily services throughout the year: in the morning — "Shaharith" — beginning with dawn and ending with noon, in the afternoon — "Minha" — beginning with a half hour after midday and may be continued until a few minutes before sunset, and in the evening — "Maariv" — beginning when at least three stars appear and ending with midnight, though, if one is prevented from uttering the evening prayers in their fixed time, he may recite them till the hour of dawn.

The idea of praying three times daily is very old, and is derived from Daniel 6:11: "And he kneeled upon his knees three times a day, and prayed, and gave thanks before his God." It is also mentioned in Psalm 55:18: "Evening and morning and at noonday will I complain and moan, and He hath heard my voice."

The reason for worshipping three times daily was originally to serve as a substitute for the daily sacrifices: the morning and daily offerings; the evening service was to substitute the parts of the sacrifices which used to be burned at night (b. Ber. 26b). Legend connects the institution of praying three times daily with the three Patriarchs, each of whom is supposed to have instituted one (*o.c.*) (see Chapter IV). Another explanation is given in Jer. Ber. IV; according to this idea, man ought to pray at every main change of the day. In the evening, one ought to pray: "May it be Thy will to lead us out of darkness into light"; in the morning: "I thank Thee, O Lord, that Thou hast led me out of darkness into light"; and in the afternoon: "May it be Thy will, O God, to let me behold the sunset, even as Thou didst merit me to see the sun shining."

These three services were made obligatory in the Academy at Jamnia, ca. 100 C.E. (see Chapter IV).

The German Jews use the term "Oren" for "to pray"; it is probably from the Italian "Orare." The East European Jews use the verbal form "davenen" for the same purpose. The source of this word is doubtful. Some derive it from the Latin "divinus"; others venture to connect it with the Arabic "da'weh"; still others believe its derivation to be from the English word "dawn," (compare *J.Q.R.*, Vol. 13, p. 219; Vol. 14, p. 85; I. B. Lewinsohn, *Toldoth Shem*, S. V.).

PART I

A SURVEY OF THE HISTORICAL DEVELOPMENT OF JEWISH WORSHIP AND LITURGY FROM ANCIENT TIMES TO THE NINETEENTH CENTURY

CHAPTER I

FORMS OF WORSHIP AND PRAYER IN ANCIENT ISRAEL

In ancient Israel there prevailed the same forms of worship as among its neighboring peoples; there was the sacrificial cult, first with altar and later with sanctuary. Scripture presents the patriarch Abraham, who, according to tradition first conceived the existence of the God Who created heaven and earth, would utter prayers on certain occasions while sacrificing, thus invoking the "One God." "And he builded there an altar unto the Lord, and called upon the name of the Lord" (Gen. 12:8), "And Abram called there on the name of the Lord" (Gen. 13:4). The same is reported of Melchizedek king of Salem who was priest of God the Most High (Gen. 14:18–24).

Abraham prays for the health of Abimelech and his court (Gen. 20:17), and his prayer is heard. He prays for Sodom and Gomorrah (Gen. 18:16–33), but to no avail. He prays for posterity (Gen. 15), and his petition is granted him. Though Abraham used the forms of worship as they were in vogue in his time, even manifesting his love and devotion to his God by being willing to sacrifice his dearly beloved son Isaac, yet at the last moment an inspiration comes upon him and it dawns upon him that his God does not want the sacrifice of human life. All God can possibly desire is to fear Him and to obey His commandments. This certainly marked a great improvement in the ancient cult. This reform became law in Israel: No human sacrifices! (Lev. 18:21; 20:2–5). When Mesa, king of Moab, "took his eldest son . . . and offered him for burnt offering upon the wall . . . there came great wrath upon Israel" (II Kings 3:27), because they were the cause of such a barbarous deed. King Ahaz, however, burnt his son as an offering (II Kings 16:3). The same is reported of Manasseh (II Kings 21:6). There existed an altar "Tofeth" in Jerusalem upon which children were sacrified to Moloch, and which king Josiah destroyed (see Chapter II).

This reform marked the beginning of improvements which tended toward loftier forms of worship, and which led to the utterance of Samuel: "Hath the Lord as great delight in burnt-offerings and sacrifices, as in hearkening to the voice of the Lord? Behold, to obey is better than to sacrifice, and to hearken than the fat of rams" (I Sam. 15:22). Influenced by his master, Abraham's servant thanks and implores the God of his lord. He repeats Abraham's blessing-prayer when saying, "The Lord, before Whom I walk, will send His angel with thee, and prosper thy way" (Gen. 24:40). Of Isaac, too, it is reported that he entreated the Lord in behalf of his wife; he blessed his son Jacob with a prayer (Gen. 27:28–29; 28:3–4). Like Abraham so also Isaac "builded an altar and called upon the name of the Lord" (Gen. 26:25). In times of distress, Jacob pours out his troubled heart to the God of his fathers, resorting neither to altar nor sacrifice, but merely praying: "O God of my father Abraham and God of my father Isaac . . . I am not worthy of all the mercies and of all the truth. . . . Deliver me, I pray Thee, from the hand of my brother . . ." (Gen. 32:10–13). His blessing-prayer to Joseph's children (Gen. 48), and his expression "I wait for Thy salvation, O Lord" (Gen. 49:18), are still used in the ritual.

Though the prayers and blessing of the patriarchs appear without sacrificial acts, none the less, the building of altars and the offering of sacrifices formed an essential part of their God worship; both were a manifestation of His presence in their midst. In one instance God even commands Jacob to build an altar. "And God said unto Jacob: Arise, go up to Beth-el . . . and make there an altar unto God. . . ." "Then Jacob said unto his household and to all that were with him: Put away the strange gods that are among you, and purify yourselves, and change your garments; and let us arise, and go up to Beth-el; and I will make there an altar unto God Who answered me in the day of my distress" (Gen. 35:1–4).

The institution of worshipping by means of words without sacrifices is therefore, according to Biblical tradition, old in Israel, reaching as far back as the patriarchs. The expression "mithpallel" — intercessor — and its verbal perfect form "vayithpallel" are already applied to Abraham; it is written, "And Abraham prayed" (Gen. 20:17).

The root "pallal" originally means to arbitrate, to judge; the reflexive "hithpallel" means to judge oneself, to cut oneself in worship (*cf.* the Arabic "falla" — notch, edge of a sword). Originally it must have implied the process of self-castigation and self-mutilation in moments of ecstasy, indicating a form of sacrifice to a god, a process which is well illustrated in the scene on Mt. Carmel between Elijah and the priests of Baal (I Kings 18:28): "And they cried aloud and cut themselves after their manner with swords and lances, till the blood gushed out upon them." This cruel practice existed even in the second century. The Greek writer Lucian relates in his treatise *On the Syrian Goddess* that "at the spring festivity in honor of Ishtar the noisy and exciting music of the double-pipes, cymbals, and drums used to stimulate the youths to such a frenzied state that they would emasculate themselves. Those emasculated servants of the Goddess Ishtar would march through the streets in procession, cut themselves with swords, and lash themselves until blood gushed forth." In Israel that barbarous practice was forbidden (Deut. 14:1): "Ye shall not cut yourselves." An emasculated individual was not permitted to enter into the assembly of the Lord (Deut. 23:2). Particularly so were the priests warned against cutting themselves (Lev. 21:5). Isaiah (56:4–5) speaks favorably of those who were emasculated by force in Babylonia (see also Dan. 1:3). There were, however, eunuchs in the courts of the Judean kings (II Kings 24:15; Jer. 29:2).

It seems that this reform occurred already in a very early period. Far back a new meaning was read into the word "mithpallel," and the term assumed the concept of prayer, implying, to intercede for something or somebody. Abraham is already accredited with the power of intercession, because "he is a prophet." As we glance over the Scriptures, we find that almost every outstanding figure in Israel was also an intercessor who would compose prayers on certain occasions. And truly, a faith which builds itself upon the stern belief in a personal God, the Originator and Guardian of everything and every living being, Who hearkens to fervent prayers, must produce devotional spirits and improvisors of prayers. It is, therefore, not a mere accident that the organizer of Israel's faith, Moses, is presented as beginning his activities not only as a redeemer and lawgiver of Israel, but also as an intercessor, interceding even in behalf of his enemy. Upon Pharaoh's request, Moses promises to entreat the Lord for him (Exod. 8:24–26; 9:27–29; 10:16–18). "He (Moses) is the great petitioner who entreats Yahve for his people. None of his compatriots stood so close to Yahve. 'With him do I speak mouth to mouth . . . and the similitude of the Lord doth he behold,' Num. 12:8. The tremendous dramatic realism that is characteristic in Christian personalities is the creation of Moses." [1]

Several prayers which are attributed to Moses remained as classical patterns in Jewish Liturgy; even a psalm (90) is ascribed to him.[2] Moses who according to tradition organized and arranged the sacrificial cult, who built the first sanctuary in Israel, and who installed the priesthood and taught the priests the regulations concerning offerings, is never recorded as having prayed during sacrifices. His prayers are always cited without any sacrifice accompanying them. "In Israel it was the great prophetic activity of Moses to offer prayers to Yahve independent of the sacrificial cult. Although later on the sacrifice occupied a large place in Israel's form of worship, yet the prayers of the great prophets and the psalmists were an approach to God without the mediacy of any sacrifices. . . . In Hellenistic mysticism, as well as in the prophetic religion of Israel, there dawned the new idea that prayer is the true and only worthy sacrifice to God. The psalmist says: 'Accept, I beseech Thee, the free-will offering of my mouth,' (Psalm 119:108); or 'Let my prayer be set forth as incense before Thee,' (Psalm 141:2)." [3]

Following the period of Moses up to that of the First Temple, we find that, alongside the priests and sanctuaries, laymen would pray in times of trouble, or the whole assembly would burst forth in a devotional outcry; at times they would resort to sacrifice, altar, and sanctuary, and at times they would not. As a matter of fact, we very seldom find that priests were asked to intervene between God and the people. Whenever there was a great man, regardless of his social standing, he would be approached to intervene in behalf of his people. Thus, we find mentioned prayers of Joshua (Josh. 7:7–9); prayers of Samson (Judg. 15:18); prayers of Hannah (I Sam. 1:11–12; 2:1–11). Following Moses, Samuel was the next great intercessor; he not only prayed for the people, but also taught them how to worship God. Thus he calls Israel to Mizpah: "And I will pray for you unto the Lord. And they gathered together to Mizpah, and drew water and poured it out before the Lord, and fasted on that day, and said there: We have sinned against the Lord" (I Sam. 7:5–6; 8:6; 12:18–25). King Saul, the zealous defender of the Yahve idea, who exterminated magic and witchcraft — a cult so much in vogue among the peoples of the Orient, especially in Assyria and Babylonia [4] — prayed occasionally to God (I Sam. 14:41; 28:10). However, none of the great men occupied so prominent a place in Jewish tradition and liturgy as did king David. No less than seventy-four psalms are ascribed to him. Furthermore, it is in his prayers as they are recorded in II Samuel 7:18–29 that we find the noun "tefilla" — prayer — coined for the first time (see also II Sam. 12:13, 16; 15:31; 24:14, 17, 25; I Chron. 16:8–36; 17:16–27; 29:10–19).

David's laudations and prayers became the foundation of Israel's worship.

Concerning fixed forms of worship in ancient Israel, it seems that in the national sanctuaries, like Beth-el, Shiloh, Gibeon, a daily service must have existed. The Book of Numbers 28 speaks of a regular daily service which consisted of a morning and an evening burnt-offering; it mentions also sacrifices on Sabbaths and holidays. It also seems that individuals would vow to make a pilgrimage to the sanctuary and sacrifice offerings annually, on which occasions they would utter improvised prayers (I Sam. 1). There were also local altars upon which communal offerings were sacrificed on certain days (I Sam. 9:12–13). Friedrich Heiler says [5] that "besides services and prayers for extraordinary events, primitive people would offer prayers at regular, fixed times: at sunrise and sunset, at changes of the moon and seasons of the year, on occasions of sowing and harvesting. Morning and evening prayer is customary not only with Christian people or with such ancient peoples as Egyptians, Greeks, and Romans, but also with primitive tribes. Every Ovambo (South Africa) appears at the gate of his den in the morning, spits toward the sun, throws a handful of leaves or grass, and expresses his desires. The Djaga Negro spits toward the sun four times every morning and says: 'O Ruwa, protect me and mine.' The Masai prays every morning as follows: 'God of my misery, give me to eat, give me milk, give me children, give me cattle, give me meat, my father.' The appearance of the New Moon is always an occasion for prayer to the Banta tribes. At sunset the Khoikhoi walk out, turn their faces toward the east, and pray: 'God of heavens, father of all.' The Ana-people in Atakpame approach with awe the holy shrine of the highest god every morning to pray and bring offerings. They bend their knees, touch the floor with their foreheads and chins, clap their hands, and say: 'Good morning, father.'"

In times of trouble, the public service in Israel would consist of prayers of repentance and burnt-offerings, accompanied by public confessions: "We have sinned, we have transgressed." The leader would pray to God for the people, or would stir the public by a sermon. Often the whole assembly would fast on that day (I Sam. 7:6; Judg. 20:26). On holidays and festal-days, peace-offerings would be sacrificed, the blood and fat and some parts of which would be burnt on the altar, other parts would be given to the priests, and the rest would be eaten by the assembly (I Sam. 2:13–15). Of Samuel it is reported that he used to "bless the sacrifice," and the people would eat of it (I Sam. 9:13). Aside from that, there is no report of any prayers or laudations having been uttered or sung on such occasions in the cult of ancient Israel, either by the priests or the public.

Some reports, however, indicate that at the sanctuaries, long before the Temple of Jerusalem, there existed the institution of Levitical singers. In II Chronicles 6 it is told that when David removed the ark to Jerusalem there was Heman the grandson of Samuel and his companion Asaph. It is stated that David left Zadok the priest and his brethren "before the tabernacle of the Lord in the high place of Gibeon . . . and with them Heman, Jeduthun, and the rest . . . to give thanks to the Lord, because His mercy endureth forever . . . to sound aloud with trumpets and cymbals and with instruments for the song of God" (I Chron. 16:37–42). Thus we see that long before David there were professional singers at the sanctuary in Gibeon, some of whom he removed to the new sanctuary in Jeruslaem.

The singing of psalms and chanting of prayers during the service dates back to the very beginnings of Israel.[6]

That there was song and instrumental music in the sanctuaries of the neighboring peoples is well known. (*Cf. Jewish Music*, Chapter I.)

CHAPTER II

FORMS OF WORSHIP AND PRAYER DURING THE FIRST TEMPLE

With the completion of the Temple in Jerusalem under the rule of King Solomon (980 B.C.E.) a new period in worship set in. Solomon's Temple was an innovation in Israel, for up to that time the sanctuaries in Israel were but high places (Bamoth), tents and tabernacles (II Sam. 7:6). According to I Chronicles 2:3, the order of the service in the Temple was as follows " . . . to burn before Him incense of sweet spices, and for the continual showbread, and for the burnt-offerings morning and evening, on the Sabbaths, and on the new moons, and on the appointed seasons of the Lord our God. . . ." "As the duty of every day required, offerings according to the commandment of Moses, on the Sabbaths, and on the new moons, and on the appointed seasons, three times in the year, even on the feast of unleavened bread, and on the feast of weeks, and on the feast of tabernacles" (II Chron. 8:13). According to I Kings 9:25, Solomon offered burnt-offerings and peace-offerings upon the altar three times a year. It seems that the institutions of the New Moon and Sabbath were very popular at the time of Elisha (II Kings 4:23). Though these reports were written down after the destruction of the Temple, they give us, nevertheless, a clue to the tradition of the forms of service at the Temple. There can be no doubt that there existed fixed times for offerings and worship. There seem to have been daily services both mornings and evenings, and special services on Sabbaths, new moons, and on the three holidays.

Solomon dedicated the Temple not only with offerings "that could not be told nor numbered for their multitude" (I Kings 8:5), but also with a wonderful prayer (*ibid.* 12–53, repeated in II Chron. 6). According to this prayer which is attributed to Solomon, but which was apparently composed centuries later, the sanctuary was dedicated "to hearken unto the prayers which Thy servant shall pray toward this place. And hearken

Thou to the supplication of Thy servant, and of Thy people Israel when they shall pray toward this place . . . and when Thou hearest, forgive" (I Kings 8:29–30). "Moreover, concerning the stranger that is not of Thy people Israel, when he shall come out of a far country for Thy name's sake . . . when he shall come and pray toward this house, hear Thou in heaven Thy dwelling-place . . ." (*ibid.* 41–42). The sanctuary is no longer considered as a habitation for the deity, as was the case in ancient Israel and among all other peoples at that time. It could no longer be imagined that God could even dwell on earth. "Behold, heaven and heaven of heavens cannot contain Thee; how much the less this house." All that Solomon asked was "that Thine eyes may be open toward this house night and day . . . to hearken unto the prayer which Thy servant shall pray toward this place" (*ibid.* 27–29).

From reports in I Chronicles 15:17–24; 16:4–43, we gather that the sacrificial cult was accompanied by the singing of psalms. This institution in Jerusalem is accredited to David. Indeed, the practice of chanting praises and prayers was an old established institution in the sanctuaries of Babylon and Egypt.[1]

The Temple dedicated to Yahve made a deep impression upon the people, both because of its magnificence and because it was consecrated to the national God; it certainly helped spread the pure God-idea in Israel. Solomon, however, did not uphold the solemn vow which he made in his prayer: to walk in the ways of Yahve and obey His laws. Later in his life "his wives turned away his heart after other gods," and he "went after Astoreth the goddess of the Zidonians, and after Milcom the detestation of the Ammonites." He built high places and altars for the deities of his foreign wives who offered and sacrificed unto their gods (I Kings 77). Together with him the people as a whole fell back to idol worship (I Kings 11:33).

After the division of the kingdom, the old and new sanctuaries scattered throughout the country began to flourish once more, especially the sanctuaries of Beth-el and Dan. Even in Judea they built "high places and pillars and Asherim . . . and there were also sodomites in the land" (*ibid.* 14:23–24). At times, a king would arise who would do "that which was right in the eyes of the Lord," and would abolish the crude cults; but the "high places were not taken away." Of King Ahab it is reported that he had introduced the Phoenician cult in Israel and had built a sanctuary unto Baal in Samaria. When the Yahve cult reached its lowest state, there arose the fiery spirit Elijah. After a successful fight with the priests of Baal, he persuaded the people — for the moment at least — to return to Yahve. This scene retains a vivid picture of the form of the Baal-worship. The worshippers of Baal would chastise themselves until blood gushed forth and would dance around the altar in halting wise, while chanting in exciting manner the words: "O Baal, answer us!" Elijah, too, approached his God with the same formula: "Answer me, O Yahve, answer me." Elijah started his service in the afternoon, at the time of the evening-offering (Minha).[2] This is further proof that the daily sacrifice was an old established institution in Israel. At that event, Elijah prayed (I Kings 18:36–37), and the people, convinced of Yahve's power, responded: "Yahve is God!" The responses of Elijah and the people became standardized in the liturgy.

Elijah who fought for Yahve's worship and teachings never refers to the Temple in Jerusalem; evidently, he did not consider this sanctuary essential toward the materialization of his ideal. Elisha, his disciple, had the same attitude to the Temple. His relation to Jehoshaphat, king of Judah, was friendly, because "he did the right things in the eyes of Yahve" (II Kings 3:14). The opposition to the sanctuaries which Jeroboam had established evidently arose not only because he had installed in them "the golden calf," visualizing Yahve, the invisible, national God, but rather due to political enmity between the northern and southern states. King Ahaz was one of the wicked kings; he introduced all sorts of cults in Jerusalem, burning even his own son as a fire-offering. His son Hezekiah, however, introduced radical reforms, abolishing the high places and exterminating all foreign cults. He even broke "in pieces the brazen serpent that Moses had made; for unto those days the children of Israel did offer to it" (II Kings 18:4). According to the report in II Chronicles 29–30, Hezekiah's activities were directed toward the purification of the Yahve cult, aiming at reforms of worship of a more basic character. For he purified the Temple, reinstated the priests and Levites in their services, and sent out a call to the people, both to Judah and to the remnants of the northern tribes, to assemble in Jerusalem in order to celebrate the Passover once more. Apparently, from that time on the Temple started to gain in reverence as the national sanctuary; for after the destruction of the Northern Kingdom, the remnants of Israel began to turn their eyes toward the only political, religious center — Jerusalem. Two prayers are retained from Hezekiah (II Kings 19:15–19; 20:3). Manasseh stood in sharp contrast to his father, for he again introduced all the abominations which his father had exterminated; but according to II Chronicles 33:19, he repented and returned to Yahve.

The idea of doing away with all sanctuaries of the country and concentrating all worship and sacrifice in one place, "in the chosen place" in Jerusalem, developed only during the reign of Josiah, about four hundred years after the building of the Temple. The cause which motivated him to purify the people of all idolatry was, as related in II Kings 22, the finding of a book of teachings by a priest. It has been suggested that this was the book of Deuteronomy which was written at that time under prophetic influence. In accordance with Deuteronomy, Josiah assembled the whole people, adults and children, into the House of Yahve and read before them this book of the Covenant, and made a covenant to obey all the statutes that were written in that book, "and all the people stood to the covenant" (II Kings 23). Then the king set out to turn all the theories of that book into actual practice. From the account given concerning his efforts we learn that up to his time several idols had been placed in the Temple: the Ashera and other crude cults, "the houses of the Sodomites" and sun-worship. There was also an altar in the Valley of Hinom around Jerusalem for the purpose of burning children to Moloch. According to the report given, Jerusalem and its surroundings were filled with altars, high places, and sanctuaries dedicated to all kinds of deities which dated back to Solomon and which the people were wont to worship. The impression one gets from this report is that the Yahve cult was merely one of the many cults even in Judah and Jerusalem. Josiah destroyed the sanctuary in Beth-el which Jeroboam had reinstituted; he also destroyed the high places in Samaria. He exterminated all forms of magic which existed in the country. He ordered the celebration of the Passover festival. "For there was not kept such a Passover from the days of the Judges that judged Israel, nor in all the days of the kings of Israel, nor of the kings of Judah" (II Kings 23 : 22). The fight of the prophets for the pure One-God idea and for the worship of One God met with success through Josiah's reforms. From that time on all pagan worship was removed from the Sanctuary of Jerusalem, as well as from among the people of Judah.

With regard to the nature of the service of the first Temple, the description of sacrifices in the Book of Leviticus may give us a true picture. The priests would offer sacrifices. After that, the priest would raise his hands and bless the people (Lev. 9 : 22). This blessing was apparently the priestly benediction (Num. 6 : 24–27). What the wording of the atonement and the confession of all sins, iniquities, and transgressions of Israel which the priest would utter on the Day of Atonement, as cited in Leviticus 16, is not at all reported. Their wording in *Mishna* Yoma is of the Second Temple. While the sacrifices were being burned on the altar, the Levites would sing psalms accompanied by instruments. Gaonic tradition goes so far as to claim that [3] the nucleus of the prayers existed already during the First Temple: the three introductory benedictions, the Avoda and the priestly benediction, the Shema and its first benediction, the Ten Commandments and the Geulah. The rest of the prayers, according to this tradition, were composed by the Men of the Great Assembly.

The services in the sanctuaries of Beth-el and Dan which Jeroboam reinstituted were probably patterned after the service of the Temple of Jerusalem. Even the same holidays were imitated, save that the dates were changed (I Kings 12 : 28–33). From Amos (6 : 5) we learn that even Davidic psalms and songs were chanted there with instrumental accompaniment.

The Psalms, created partly during the first Temple and partly during the first part of the Second Temple, though there are Biblical scholars who are of the opinion that a number of psalms are of later origin, consist of petitions, meditations, laudations, reflections, and ethical doctrines. Among the psalms are very fine descriptions of nature and of God's omnipotence and omnipresence. A number of psalms are for public worship while others are for private devotion, as evident from their form and style. There are outpourings of a noble soul next to prayers that the enemy be exterminated, fine thanksgivings for personal happiness and woeful outcries over national calamities.[4]

From a cursory classification we see that forty-eight psalms are petitional in character, that fifty-eight may be called meditations, and that the rest, only about forty-four, are laudations or hymns. This proves that the urge of prayer compelled the Levitical singers to compose more petitions and meditations than hymns and laudations.

Prayer reached its highest development in ancient Israel with Jeremiah. "He was rightly characterized as the first suppliant known in the history of religion," writes Cornill; "the father of the true prayer," says Wellhausen. The latter continues: "Under pain and tribulations the personal communion with his God dawned upon him; he gave birth to the deepest essence of piety. . . . His book contains not only speeches and prophecies, but sometimes also confessions of personal troubles and desperate struggles. . . . The thing that moved and sustained him also moved and sustained the noblest spirits of Judaism. . . . Without Jeremiah the psalms could never have been composed."

"The psalms of the Old Testament," says Friedrich Heiler, "are in their most inner substance nothing else save Jeremiah's prayerful-life transformed into prayer-poetry. The downcast Jewish community in exile and thereafter pours out its unutterable pain in songs of prayer, and likewise its imperishable faith. Like Jeremiah whose prophetic book became its gospel, the community of Israel worked itself out of fear and despair in the present to victorious confidence and to a hope in the future. . . . 'Though I walk through the valley of the shadow of death, I will not fear evil; for Thou art with me.' Jeremiah was the first to experience this, and he obtained it by his battles for himself and for the children of God after him."[5]

CHAPTER III

WORSHIP DURING THE SECOND TEMPLE

The radical reforms introduced by King Josiah had a lasting influence upon the worship of Israel. All high places and sanctuaries were abolished for all times. Through that reform some old laws were modified, as for example the priestly rule that no meat could be eaten unless the blood and some parts of the animal had been burnt on an altar or upon a high place (Lev. 17:1–10). This law was changed, because, according to Josiah's abolition of all country sanctuaries, only the one in Jerusalem remained. And in case some say "I will eat meat" and the place chosen by God "to put His name there be too far from thee, then shalt thou kill of thy herd . . . and eat within thy gates." "Only do not eat the blood; thou shalt pour it out like water" (Deut. 12:20–25). This led to a decrease in animal sacrifices. This new circumstance was likewise applied to tithes and first born which pilgrims were obliged to bring. The new law in Deuteronomy 14:24–26 reads as follows: "If the way be too long for thee, so that thou art not able to carry it . . . then shalt thou turn it into money . . . and go unto the place which thy God shall choose. And thou shalt bestow the money for whatsoever thy soul desireth. . . ."

In the worship proper too some changes apparently took place. In Deuteronomy 26:5–10, 12–15 we hear for the first time that when offering his first ripe fruit, the layman is supposed to utter a prayer by himself — not the priest, as the Priestly Code usually prescribes. This democratic attitude to permit the participation of laymen in the service of the sanctuary was evidently the fruit of consistent prophetic preaching. The prayer and praise quoted above is certainly one of the oldest Hebrew prayers; though attributed to Moses (see Chapter I) it dates back to the last century of the First Temple.

It has been generally maintained that during the Babylonian exile Israel developed a deep yearning for prayer and instruction in the word of the Divine. We gather this from numerous places in the Book of Ezekiel. It is reported that the elders of the people would gather around the prophet to ask for the word of God. In Babylon there still survived a tradition even in the Gaonic times (eighth to eleventh centuries) that since the first exile the people would assemble around the prophets and men learned in the sacred teachings and would ask them to instruct them in the words of God on Sabbaths and festivals.[1] For want of a sanctuary and its cult, they would indulge in prayer and supplication, examples of which have been retained in the books of Daniel, Ezra, and Nehemiah. Ezekiel endeavored to teach the people the laws of justice and rules of ethics which had been handed down through the long line of prophets. At the same time he taught them the priestly cult and tradition, and even outlined the structure of the future Temple to be built in Jerusalem. Ezra instructed the people in the written Mosaic laws and religious customs. Tradition has it that Ezra instituted set days for public instruction to be opened and closed with prayer and hymns, and that his Great Assembly created the pattern for benediction, prayers, sanctification, and Havdala in Israel.[2] The *Talmud* associates his name with several institutions concerning the ritual and the reading from the Pentateuch (B. Kama 83a; Meg. 31b; Soferim X, 2). The sojourn of the exiled in Babylon apparently brought about an influence of the Babylonian hymns and supplication upon the Levitical singers. A comparison of them with several psalms reveals a striking identity in content and style, as evident from the examples here given.[3] The main difference, however, is that the psalms are all addressed to the One Invisible God.

BABYLONIAN AND ASSYRIAN PRAYERS AND HYMNS:

Prayer of Nabuchadrezzar II, king of Babylon[4] (601–565 B.C.), to Marduk:

O eternal prince! Lord of all being! To the king whom thou lovest, and whose name thou hast proclaimed as was pleasing to thee, do thou lead aright his name, guide him in a straight path. I am the prince, thy favorite, the creature of thy hand; thou hast created me and with dominion over all people thou hast intrusted me. According to thy favor, O Lord, which thou dost bestow upon all people, cause me to love thy exalted lordship, and create in my heart the worship of thy divinity, and grant whatever is pleasing to thee, because thou hast fashioned my life.

Prayer by Nabuchadrezzar II: [5]

O Nabu, eternal son, exalted messenger, victorious, beloved of Marduk, do thou look with favor and joy upon my words, and a long life, abundance of offspring, a firm throne, and enduring reign, the overthrow of my foes, the conquering of the land of the enemy as a boon do thou grant me! On thy eternal tablet which defines the boundaries of heaven and earth, do thou proclaim the length of my days, do thou write my offspring!

In the presence of Marduk, the king of heaven and earth, the father, my begetter, look with favor upon my words. May Nabuchadrezzar, the king, the restorer, be ever established in thy mouth!

Incantation: [6]

O fire-god, fiery, mighty son of Anu, strongest among thy brethren art thou, who givest judgment like Sin and Shamash. Pronounce my judgment, determine my fate, burn the sorcerer and the sorceress!

O fire-god . . .
. . . burn them!
. . . roast them!
. . . overpower them!
. . . destroy them!

Incantation: [7]

O Marduk, great lord . . . by thy illustrious command, let me live, let me prosper, and let me honor thy divinity! When I plan, let me attain my plan. Establish truth in my mouth, put kindness in my heart, return and be established. May they proclaim favors to me!

May my god stand at my right hand!
May my goddess stand at my left hand!
May my god, my benefactor establish himself at my side,
To give and to command, to hearken and to show favor!
Let the word I speak, when I speak, be propitious. . . .

Incantation: [8]

Bau, mighty mistress, merciful mother, who dwellest in the brilliant heavens, I beseech thee, my mistress, stand and hearken unto me . . . since to pronounce judgments, to determine destinies, to raise to life, to grant prosperity belongs to thee; since thou knowest to protect, to benefit, and to save, I have turned to thee, I have given heed. Accept from me the *upuntu* plant and receive my supplication. To my god who is angry, to my goddess who is angry with me. . . .

Prayer to Ninib:[9]

O mighty son, first-born of Bel, powerful, perfect, offspring of Esharra, clothed with terror, filled with violence! Great storm whose attack cannot be withstood, mighty is thy station among the great gods. In Erkur, the festival house, exalted is thy head, and Bel, thy father, hath granted thee that the commands for all the gods be intrusted to thy hand.

Thou pronouncest judgments for mankind.

Thou guidest aright the hand of the weak, thou liftest up the one who is not strong.

Thou bringest back the body of him who has been sent down to the Lower World.

Thou absolvest from sin the one who has sinned.

Thou speedily bringest into favor the one with whom his god is angry. O Ninib, chief of the gods, a warrior art thou. I so-and-so, son of so-and-so, whose god is so-and-so, whose name is so-and-so, have bound for thee a card. . . . I have offered thee *tarrinnu*, a goodly odor. I have poured out for thee mead, a drink made from grain. . . .

Look with true favor upon me and hearken to my cry,

Receive my supplication and accept my prayer,

Turn with favor toward me, thy worshipper. . . . Absolve my sin, free me from my iniquity. . . . May my gods and goddesses command me and may they declare my good fortune.

Hymn to Sin, the moon-god:[10]

O Lord, chief of the gods, who in heaven and on earth is alone supreme!

Father Nannar, lord of increase, chief of the gods!

Father Nannar, lord of heaven, great one, chief of the gods!

Father Nannar, lord of the moon, chief of the gods!

Father Nannar, lord of Ur, chief of the gods!

Father Nannar, lord of Egissirgal, chief of the gods!

Father Nannar, lord of the moon-disk, brilliant one, chief of the gods!

Father Nannar, who rulest with pomp, chief of the gods!

Father Nannar, who goes about in princely garb, chief of the gods!

Suppliant:[11]

I thy servant, full of sighs, cry unto thee.

Thou acceptest the fervent prayer of him who is burdened with sin.

Thou lookest upon a man and that man lives.

O potentate of the world, mistress of mankind!

Merciful one, to whom it is good to turn, who accepteth supplication!

Priest:
His god and his goddess being angry with him, he crieth unto thee. Turn thy face toward him and take his hand.
Suppliant:
Besides thee there is no god who guideth aright.
Look with true favor upon me and accept my supplication.
Declare "how long" and let thy liver be pacified.
When, O my mistress, will thy face be turned?
Like the doves do I moan, in sighs do I abound.
Priest:
With woe and grief, full of sighs is his soul,
Tears does he weep, laments doth he pour forth!

Supplication: [12]
How long, O my mistress, will the powerful enemy consume thy land?
In thy chief city, Erech, thirst prevails.
In E-lu-bar, the house of thy oracle, blood is poured out like water.
In all thy lands hath he kindled fire and over them hath he poured fire. . . .
O my mistress, much to misfortune have I been yoked.
O my mistress, thou hast encompassed me, and into pain hast thou brought me.
The mighty enemy hath trodden me under foot like a reed.
I cannot think, I cannot plan.
Like a (wind-swept) field I moan night and day.
I, thy servant, supplicate thee.
May thy heart be at rest, may thy liver be pacified!

The service in the Second Temple as initiated by Ezra and Nehemiah, with the psalmodic song of the Levites, remained throughout the existence of the Temple. Ben Sira, Chapter L, [13] describes the cult in his time. After the sacrifices were offered, the Levites started with their songs, while the whole assembly prayed. Then the High Priest would bless the people who had prostrated themselves. In Chapter LI of the Hebrew text [14] Ben Sira gives a list of benedictions several of which remained as standard elements in the liturgy.

There is a striking resemblance to the benedictions of the Amida and to other parts of the prayers, as can be seen from the following comparisons:

Ben Sira	*Amida*
Verse:	Benediction:[15]
2. Give thanks unto the God of praises.	3. Holy ones praise Thee every day.
5. Give thanks unto *the Redeemer.*	7. Blessed art Thou, O Lord, *the Redeemer of Israel.*
6. Give thanks unto Him *Who gathereth the outcasts* of Israel.	10. Blessed art Thou, O Lord, *that gatherest the outcasts* of Thy people Israel.
7. Give thanks unto Him that buildeth this city and His Sanctuary.	14. Do dwell in the midst of Jerusalem Thy city . . . and build it an everlasting building . . . Blessed art Thou, O Lord, that buildest Jerusalem.
8. Give thanks unto Him *that causeth a horn to flourish for the house of David.*	15. Do Thou *cause to flourish the branch of David speedily, and do Thou exalt his horn by* Thy salvation.
10. Give thanks unto *the Shield of Abraham.*	1. Blessed art Thou, O Lord, *Shield of Abraham.*
12. Give thanks unto the *Mighty One of Jacob.*	1. Blessed art Thou . . . *the God of Jacob*, the great, *mighty*, and revered God.

In the same way several other benedictions can be traced:

3. Give thanks unto the *Creator of all things.*	1. (Yotzer). Blessed art Thou . . . Who makest peace and *createst all things.*
4. Give thanks unto the *Redeemer of Israel.*	3. Blessed art Thou, O Lord, Who *hast redeemed Israel.*
2. Give thanks unto the *Guard of Israel.*	4. (Evening Service). Blessed art Thou, O Lord, *Who guardest Thy people Israel.*

Ben Sira, Chapter 36:1–17, affords further comparisons to parts of the liturgy:[16]

Ben Sira	
Verses:	3. (Amida for High Holydays).
1–5. Save us O God of all and *cast Thy fear upon all the nations*. Shake Thy head against the strange people, *and let them see Thy power.*	Now, therefore, O Lord, our God, *impose Thine awe upon all Thy works, and Thy dread upon* all that Thou hast created, *that all Thy works may fear Thee. . . .* That

As Thou hast sanctified Thyself in us before them, so glorify Thyself in them before us; that they may know, as we also know that there is none other God but Thee.

they may all form a single band to do Thy will with a perfect heart, even as we know, O Lord our God, that dominion is Thine, and that Thy name is to be feared above all that Thou hast created.

12–14. *Compassionate the people that is called by Thy name, Israel* whom Thou didst surname Firstborn. *Compassionate Thy holy city Jerusalem, the place of Thy dwelling.*

2. (Grace after Meal). *Have mercy, our Lord, upon Israel Thy people, upon Jerusalem Thy city, upon Zion, the abiding place of Thy glory.*

11. *Gather all the tribes of Jacob,* that they may receive their inheritance as in the day of old.

4. (Musaf Amida for holydays). *Bring our scattered ones among the nations* near unto Thee, and gather our dispersed from the ends of the earth.

14. Fill Zion with Thy majesty, and Thy people with Thy glory.

4. Lead us with exaltation unto Zion Thy city, and unto Jerusalem the place of Thy sanctuary with everlasting joy.

17. That all the ends of the earth may know that Thou art the Eternal God.

(Alenu). Let all the inhabitants of the world perceive and know that unto Thee every knee must bend . . .

8. . . . For who may say to Thee what doest Thou?

(Ne'ila — Atta Hivdalta). . . For who shall say unto Thee What doest Thou?

A fuller description of the service in the Temple is retained in the *Mishna* Tamid V. According to Rabbinical interpretation of that report, the priests would recite every morning the benediction *Ahava* (second benediction before *Sh'ma*), the Decalogue, the paragraphs of *Sh'ma*, the *Geula*, then the third benediction of *Sh'ma*, beginning with *Emeth*, then the *Avoda* (*R'tzei*, the seventeenth benediction of the Amida), and the Priestly benediction. On Sabbaths an additional benediction was recited for the outgoing "Watch" — *Mishmar* — in which the benediction "Shalom" (*Sim Shalom*) was included (the nineteenth benediction of the Amida). On the Day of

Atonement the confession of the High Priest which is mentioned in Leviticus 16: "And he shall atone," and which is given in *Mishna* Yoma was recited. In the *Baraitha* Yoma VII, a full record is given of the service the High Priest had to recite in the "Ezrath Nashim." This service consisted of Leviticus 16; 23 : 26–32; Numbers 29 : 7–11; and concluded with eight benedictions: 1. The fourth benediction after the reading from the Scriptures, 2. The "Avoda" and "Hodaa" (seventeenth and eighteenth benedictions of the Amida), 3. For forgiveness (sixth benediction of the Amida). The other benedictions were for the Sanctuary, for Israel, for Jerusalem, for the priests, and for the acceptance of prayer which concluded with the words "Shomea T'fillah" (of the sixteenth benediction of the Amida).

In the latter days of the Second Temple there lived in Jerusalem and in other sections of Palestine pious people who were endowed with a supernatural power to make their prayers efficacious, so folk-stories recount. One of these men was called "Honi Hameagal" (the circle-drawer). This legendary personality, supposed to have lived in the first century B.C., could bring and stop rain by the power of his prayer, as the prophet Samuel did in his day. In *Mishna* Taanith III, 8, the tale of his achievements and the version of his prayer are given, and in more elaborate detail in b. Taanith 23a. Josephus, *Ant.* XIV, 2 : 1, recounts that during the fight between the two brothers Aristobulus and Hyrcanus Honi was captured by the latter's soldiers who forced him to use the power of his prayer against their enemy. But this pious man uttered the following prayer instead: "Lord of the earth, since the besieged as well as the besiegers are Thy people, I beg that Thou wilt not answer the curses which they may utter against each other." Whereupon he was stoned by the soldiers.

According to Talmudic tradition, his miraculous power was inherited by his grandchildren.

The Synagogue

During the Second Temple there developed another sanctuary in Israel — a sanctuary which was destined to replace the Temple. This sanctuary was unique in its purpose, for it was dedicated to the study of the Holy Scriptures and to prayer without sacrificial rites. Its origin seems to date back to the exilic era, when people would congregate for worship and for divine instruction. When Ezra instituted public instruction on Sabbaths and festivals, the need for a "house of assembly" — "Beith Haknesseth" — in Greek συναγωγὴ Synagogue — was strongly felt. Moreover, the Lay-representatives — "Anshei Ma'amad" — were organized. This organization, as explained in *Mishna* Taanith IV, was instituted to enable the people to participate in the cult of the Temple. Toward that purpose the country was divided into twenty-four sections. Each section would send deputies to Jerusalem twice a year for a period of one week. The duty of these representatives was to attend the daily sacrifices. They would fast four days of the week, from Monday through Thursday, pray *Shaharith*, *Minha*, and on certain days *Musaf* and *Ne'ila*. At home, the people of their section would congregate in their synagogues, and would read the first chapter of Genesis which was divided into six portions, and would perform the same devotional exercises as their representatives in Jerusalem. Here we have the nucleus for a regular daily service, though only for two weeks of the year. This practice was then extended for the whole year.

The reason for this institution was the demand of the people to share in the cult. With the increase of knowledge of the prophetic teachings among the people, it became clear to them that it is not only the priest who has access to God, but every man, the high and the simple, may approach God without any intermediator. The sages taught the people that it is even the duty of every man to pray daily, for which purpose fixed patterns of benedictions and prayers were created, which are claimed to date back to Ezra's Assembly, as cited at the beginning of this chapter.

The custom of worshipping three times daily has been treated in the Introductory Notes.

The institution of the House of Assembly spread throughout the Jewish world, so that in the last century of the Second Temple there existed in Jerusalem numerous synagogues.[17] Even in the Temple-court there was a special House of Worship where the priests and Levites would hold regular services (b. Succa 53a).

Services in the synagogues were considered long established

at the time of Jesus who, as reported in the Apostles (Mark 1:21; 6:2; Luke 4:15–20) read in the synagogues from the Scriptures during the Sabbath services.

From the old sources we learn that during the era of the Second Temple the "Shema" and the nucleus of its benedictions, the three last, the three first, as well as the intermediary benedictions, and other parts of the prayers were already well known. Furthermore, the practice of reading from the Scriptures on Sabbaths, festivals, Mondays and Thursdays was also customary then. Likewise the reading of the Book of Esther on "Purim," the chanting of "Hallel," (Psalms 113–118). On Passover eve and on the festivals and several other occasions the psalms became parts of the services. Aside from all these, several benedictions for various occasions, as Grace after meals, were also then introduced.

Alongside with the fixed formulae of the above mentioned prayers there continued to flourish the free improvised meditations. In their nature, even the fixed prayers were only patterns, frames, into which every man could pour his soul's expressions. They were transmitted orally and recited in public worship by intercessors who were learned men and well versed in the teachings and imbued with the ideals and hopes of the people; they were inspired with the religious spirit and felt human needs.[18]

The chief service, however, which absolved sins and atoned the iniquities of the individual as well as of the people at large — a service which was looked upon as a divine command without which the people Israel could not exist — was still centered in the cult of the Temple in Jerusalem. None of the prophets ever conceived the idea of doing away with the sacrificial cult, though some of them looked with disfavor upon it; and when the Temple was destroyed, one of the great spiritual leaders of that time, Rabbi Joshua ben Hananya, a Levitical singer of the Temple, broke forth in a lament: "Woe unto us that it (the Temple) is destroyed, the place where Israel's sins were atoned" (*Avoth de Rabbi Nathan*, Chap. IV). The mourners of Zion — "Aveilei Zion" — used to lament: "As long as the Temple service existed the world was blessed . . . because there is no service so precious to God as the service of the Temple (*o.c.*, ed. Schechter, Chap. IV).

CHAPTER IV

THE GROWTH OF THE LITURGY AFTER THE FALL OF THE SECOND TEMPLE UP TO THE COMPILATION OF THE FIRST PRAYER-CODE BY RAV AMRAM GAON

After awakening from the stupor caused by the terrible shock which the Jewish people suffered with the destruction of the Sanctuary in Jerusalem by the Romans, the outstanding spirits in Israel sought a way out of the confusion. Their main concern was how to reorganize Jewish religious life and institutions, and how to replace the now missing service of the sacrificial cult. On the one hand, voices full of despair were heard, as the above cited lament of Rabbi Joshua and the mourners of Zion. On the other hand, some prominent men went to the other extreme, saying that "prayer is greater than sacrifices" (Rabbi Eleazar, b. Berachoth 32a); others maintained that "the words of learning (Tora) are more valuable than burnt-offerings and peace-offerings" (*Avoth de Rabbi Nathan*, Chap. IV). Rabbi Yohanan ben Zaccai, the spiritual head of his time, answered Rabbi Joshua's lament as follows: "My son, be not worried; we have a way of atonement which is as important as these (sacrifices), and this is charity to the poor and prayer three times a day" (*l.c.*). The idea thus became prevalent that sacrifices can be replaced by prayers, if they are recited at the times when the sacrifices used to be offered (b. Ber. 26b; Bamidbar Rabba, Chap. 18). "After the destruction of the Temple," said God unto Abraham, "your children shall study the laws concerning sacrifices, and I will consider it as though they had actually offered them and will forgive their sins" (b. Meg. 31b; Taanith 27b; b. Menahoth 110a; Tanhuma, Tzav; Pesikta de Rav Kahana § 6; *Yalkut* § 776).

It thus became the duty of every man to recite the Mishnaic portions dealing with the regulations of the sacrifices both before the morning and afternoon services; these Mishnaic portions which were recited were called "Korbanoth." In addition, in the Musaf service on Sabbaths and the festivals short paragraphs describing the offerings of each of these days were inserted; a prayer was added even which embodied the petition that God speedily restore the Temple so that the sacrifices might actually be offered again. Traditional Judaism adhered to this idea throughout all ages; only the Reform Movement of the last century renounced the idea of animal sacrifices together with the hope of restoring the Temple in Jerusalem (see Chapter XIX). From the quotations cited it is evident that sacrifices were substituted by prayer temporarily only, until the Temple and its cult will be restored; they were never altogether abolished.

Following the Destruction, the sages were engaged in regulating the texts of the prayers and in making the services in the synagogue obligatory for everybody. Rabbi Gamaliel of Jamnia was the one spiritual leader mostly interested in this work. He ordered that the Amida be fixed (b. Ber. 28b; Meg. 17b), and that it be recited every day. He also ordered that a special prayer be added to the eighteenth benediction against the Sectarians (b. Ber. 28b), and that in addition to the two daily services—"Shaharith" and "Minha"—a third, the evening service—"Arvith"—be obligatory (b. Ber. 27b), which was up to that time only a service for private devotion before retiring. The explanation for this order is that this private prayer in which the *Shema* is included is bound to be neglected when people return home tired from their day's work (b. Ber. 4b). But if before going home, they attend the service in the synagogue, they cannot forego that prayer (Chapter VIII, III).

Later, the institution of the three daily services was accredited to the patriarchs. According to tradition, Abraham instituted the morning service (Gen. 19:27): "And Abraham got up early in the morning to the place where he stood before the Lord." Isaac introduced the Minha-service (Gen. 24:63): "And Isaac went out to meditate in the field at the eventide." And Jacob introduced the evening service (Gen. 28:11): "And he lighted upon the place, and tarried there all night." In the last verse the Hebrew word "wayifga" is used which, according to Talmudic explanation, means "and he petitioned" (Jer. Ber. IV; b. Ber. 26b).

Much emphasis was laid at that time upon a regular attendance at the daily services in the synagogue. Some went to the extreme by asserting that "the prayer of man is accepted only in the synagogue" (Abba Benjamin in b. Ber. 6a). Similar assertions were expressed by several other Amoras (b. Ber. *l.c.*, 7b).

This obligation to attend public services three times a day was met with opposition. We find a statement that "God said to Israel: When you pray, then pray in the synagogue; but if you cannot attend the synagogue, then pray in your field; and if you cannot worship in your field, then pray in your house. However, if you are hindered from doing that, then pray while lying in your bed; and if you are prevented from doing that, then meditate in your heart" (*Pesikta de Rav Kahana* 158a). Of Rav Kahana (third century) it is recounted that he neglected to attend the public service in the synagogue (b. Ber. 7b). Rav Hisda declared that the house of study is more important than the house of prayer. Some used to study even during the service (b. Ber. 8a). Of Rav Juda it is reported that he would pray only once in thirty days (b. Rosh Hashanna 35). Upon returning from a journey, Samuel's father would not pray for three days (b. Eruvin 65a). Rav was of the opinion that whoever is upset ought not to pray (*l.c.*). On the whole, however, the Babylonian Jews were praised for their regular attendance at public services in the synagogue.

The same difference of opinion existed with regard to fixed prayer-texts. Such men as Rabbi Joshua, Rabbi Akiva, and Rabbi Eleazar were among those who preferred a free outpouring of the soul; they believed that "whoever makes his prayer fixed, his prayers are no longer petition" (*Mishna* Ber. IV; b. Ber. 29b). Of Rabbi Eleazar and others it is reported that they used to pray every day a newly improvised prayer (Jer. Ber. IV, 4).

In fact, even the fixed forms of the prayers remained in a loose state for many centuries. In the Amida, only the first and last three benedictions were definitely fixed, while the intermediary benedictions were only frames into which the people would formulate their own prayers (b. Ber. 34a).

The custom to compose prayers *to order* never became prevalent in Jewish liturgy; the one instance cited above where Rabbi Gamaliel ordered prayers to be composed may be taken as an exception. The liturgy grew rather through the continuous improvisations of religious spirits in moments of inspiration. These men used to create prayers for their private devotion; and only after their compositions found favor in the eyes of the people, were they gradually incorporated into the public worship. It took more than nine hundred years of continuous growth for the liturgy to reach the state as presented in the first prayer-book compiled by Rav Amram (875).

In certain periods men arose who would devote their attention to collect and arrange the liturgy. At the end of the Mishnaic era, Rabbi Juda the Prince incorporated in his compendium of the *Mishna* several prayers and orders of services. He incorporated the benedictions of the "Shema" (M. Ber. I, 4), the "Amida" (*o.c.* IV, 3), benedictions over different foods and fruits (*o.c.* VI), Grace after meals (*o.c.* VII), "Havdala" for Passover evening (M. Pesahim X), the Amida for New Year (M. Rosh Hashanna IV, 5–6), Scriptural readings (M. Megilla III, 5–6; IV), and several other items.

But long before the redaction of the *Mishna* Rabbi Meyir of the second century set down the principle that every man is obliged to recite a hundred benedictions daily (b. Menahoth 43b). In this number of one hundred there are included all benedictions of the three daily services, as well as the benedictions over food and those which are uttered in Grace after meals. Rabbi Meyir's principle became the basis for the daily liturgy which was many centuries later compiled by Natronai Gaon of the ninth century at the request of a Spanish congregation.[1]

Abba Areca — Rav-and Samuel of the third century were the most outstanding exponents of the liturgy in Babylonia. They enriched it with many jewels. They composed the "Havdala" — "Watodieinu" — for the *Amida* on the eve of festivals which fall on a Sabbath (b. Ber. 33b), the introduction to the confession in the *Amida* of the Day of Atonement — "atta yodea roze" (b. Yoma 87b). Samuel composed the abbreviated *Amida* (b. Ber. 29a), and to Rav are attributed [2] the introductions and conclusions of *Malchuyoth*, *Zichronoth*, and *Shoferoth* (see Chapter XVI), called in Hebrew "Tekiatha de-be Rav" (Jer. Avoda Zara I, 2; Jer. Rosh Hashanna I, 3; Wayikra Rabba 29:1). There are other fine prayers by Rav; the "yehi ratzon" which is now used in the Ashkenazic ritual when the new month is announced was composed by him.

Just as in days of old, men with fine spiritual qualities were also sought later to function as intercessors. Poor men with heavy family obligations, men well versed in traditional lore and possessed with devotional spirits, were preferred (M. Taanith II, 2). Rabbi Juda b. Ilai added another requirement; he maintained that the intercessor ought also to have a sweet voice (b. Taanith 16a).[3] During the Mishnaic period, several pious men ranked high for their efficacious prayers; among them were Rabbi Nehunya b. Hakkana (M. Ber. IV, 2), and especially Rabbi Hanina b. Dosa (b. Taanith 24b; Ber. 33, 34).

The texts of the prayers were, as stated above, handed down orally. They were not written down in separate compilations during the Mishnaic and Talmudic periods, probably out of fear lest the Sectarians — "Minim" — under which term come heretics, Christians, and adherents to subversive doctrines — misuse the freedom of writing down prayers and insert some of their own ideas into them. Hence, the assertion: "They who write down benedictions are like unto them who burn the Tora" (b. Shabbath 115b). This assertion implied that, though benedictions include Scriptural passages, it is not permitted to save them from fire on Sabbaths; rather than desecrate the Sabbath, they may be burnt together with parts of the Tora which they include. This indicates that written prayers were not regarded as sacred books.

Due to this attitude, prayers were preserved in the memory of people. It was thus quite natural that discussions should arise concerning the correct wording of fixed prayers. Some precentors would improvise versions which were at times too long and at times too short, as reported in various instances (b. Ber. 33a, 34a). Differences in the wording of prayers gradually developed, and these became traditional with some congregations. The oldest variants known were those in Palestine and Babylonia. But in Babylonia itself there existed differences in the versions and traditions, some of which have been recorded in the *Talmud*. Rav himself, the organizer of the liturgy in Babylonia, was more than once amazed to find in the various sections of the country different liturgical customs (b. Meg. 22a; Taanith 28b).

The differences in the liturgy which existed between the Palestinian and Babylonian traditions were of a more fundamental character than mere textual variation; they touched the very principles of the liturgy. These differences were as follows: 1. In Palestine the reading of the Pentateuch was completed in three years only,[4] while in Babylonia the reading was covered in one year. Consequently, in Palestine the festival of "Rejoicing with the Tora" was celebrated only once in three years,[5] while in Babylonia it was celebrated annually.

2. In Palestine the people who were called upon to read from the Scriptures would read the portion themselves, while in Babylonia a special reader was in charge — "Korè" — and the people called upon would merely listen.[6]

3. In Palestine *Kedusha* was recited on Sabbaths and festivals only; in Babylonia every day.[7]

4. In Palestine the Amida consisted of eighteen benedictions; in Babylonia of nineteen (see Chapter VIII).

5. In Palestine seven and even six adults were sufficient to constitute a quorum for public service; in Babylonia ten adults were required (T. Soferim X, 7).

All in all, seventy-three differences are supposed to have existed in the religious customs between Palestine and Babylonia.[8]

In Babylonia the Friday evening service was furnished with the *Me'en sheva*, an abbreviation of the seven benedictions (see Chapter X; b. Shabbath 119b). There the fifth benediction for the weekdays services were also added.[9]

At the time of the redaction of the Babylonian *Talmud* the liturgy was complete in its main parts: i.e., the prayers proper without the poetry. However, even thereafter, during the period of the Saboraim, the free creation of additional prayers and benedictions continued.

They are, according to Zunz (Ltg., p. 12f.), the insertions in the *Yotzer* for Sabbaths, *Nishmath* in the verses of song, the various introductions to the *Kedusha: kether*, *na'aritzcha*, and *nakdishach*. Furthermore, the prayer *ticcanta* in the Sabbath Musaf and *atta ehad* in the Sabbath Minha, the hymn *En Kelohenu; asher heni* after the reading of the Book of Esther on Purim, *az bahataênu* for the Ninth of Av, *hanneroth* for Hanucca, *mi sheasa* and *yehadeshêhu* for the announcement of the new month, and several other prayers were also added later.

In the *Seliha* literature several Aramaic responses were retained from the old Babylonian ritual; they are: *rahamana idcar*, *mahe umase*, and *maran divishmaya*. The phrase *tithkabbal tzelothehon* in the Kaddish, *yekum purkan* after the Scriptural reading on Sabbaths, *ha lahma* the opening prayer of the *Haggada*, and *Col Nidré* are also from the Babylonian ritual.[10]

The mystics in Palestine and Babylonia developed the custom of reciting *Kedusha* in the service. These mystics were called *Yorde Mercava* (searchers of the chariot). They considered the idea of composing *Kedushas* of great importance. Some of their *Kedushas* were retained in the *Hechaloth Rabbathi*, and in the *Seder Amram* (4, 10b, 13, 14). In one of these (S.R.A., 4a), the statement is made that God has commanded the *Yorde Mercava* to recite *kadosh*, for He has no greater pleasure than when Israel raises his eyes to the heavens and sanctifies Him (Isaiah 6:3). Tradition recounts that the heavenly hosts sing *Kedusha* (b. Hullin 91b). "Israel is more beloved by God than the heavenly hosts, for while Israel sings praises to God every hour and at any time, the angels are permitted to sing in the heavens only when Israel sings here on earth" (b. Hullin 91b; *Yalkut*, 836).

In their emphasis of the *Kedusha*, however, the mystics sought to popularize the omnipotence of God and His guiding power in the world; they sought to oppose the idea current in their day that God had abandoned His creation and left it to the automatic laws of nature (see S. Baer, p. 79).

Besides *Kedushas*, the mystics composed several hymns, as *Haadereth wehaĕmuna*, *En Kelohenu*, both of which were retained in our liturgy.

The liturgy is based upon the Bible. Not only is it saturated with the Biblical spirit, with its ideas and ideals, but whole sections of the Bible are incorporated in the liturgy. There are in our liturgy the *Shema*, the verses of song, the Song of the Sea, the nucleus of the *Kedusha*, the Priestly Benediction, the Scriptural readings. Furthermore, the *Seliha* is drawn from Biblical passages. The *Malchuyoth*, *Zichronoth*, and *Shoferoth* prayers of the *Rosh Hashanna Musaf* are culled from the Bible. In almost every paragraph of the prayers Biblical phrases and expressions are worked in. The Psalms were particularly utilized in the making of the liturgy. Over fifty chapters are incorporated in the liturgy, and over two hundred and fifty passages are worked into the prayers.[11] These psalms are not only laudations, but to a large extent also meditations and petitions, as pointed out at the end of Chapter II.

CHAPTER V

THE POETRY (PIYYUT)

The poetical strain was never interrupted entirely in Israel and in its Hebrew literature. Though after the fall of Jerusalem in 70 C.E. secular songs were prohibited as a sign of mourning, yet religious songs were permitted.[1] The prayers have a simple, lucid prose style, so that they are intelligible to the average person; but alongside this prose style, poetical forms were cultivated, particularly the alphabetic acrostic and the parallelism, both of which are taken from the Biblical poetry.[2]

In the services several alphabetical selections have been retained which date back to the first century. The acrostic occurs at the first letter of each line as in *el adon* of the Sabbath morning service, or at the beginning of each word as in the *Widdui* — *ashamnu* — or as in *el baruch* and in *culam ahuvim* of the morning service. Scattered in the Talmudic literature we find several short poems in strict parallelism. They also have the Biblical word meter. One such poem is found in b. Ber. 37a; it consists of four lines, each line being divided into three parts, and each part having three accentuated words.

Out of the Greek words ποιησις and ποιητὴς the Hebrew terms *piyyut*, meaning "poetry," and *payetan*, meaning "poet," were constructed. Among many other qualities, Eleazar the son of Rabbi Simeon ben Yohai of the second century possessed the gift of poetry (Shir Rabba, Chaps. 3, 10). Though nothing is reported concerning the nature of his poetry, it is quite clear that already in the second century there were sages who occupied themselves with composing poems. The alphabetical acrostic was employed in straight or in the reversed order, as in *ticcanta shabbath* of the Musaf service for Sabbaths. Later both forms were applied simultaneously.[3] The composing of songs with alphabetical acrostic was popular among the people, and according to Ruth Rabba, 6, this custom was well known in Jerusalem before its fall.[4]

The meter in the early poetry was, as stated above, based upon the number of accentuated words. This system was taken over from the Biblical poetry. The meter employed by Ephraem Syrus (306–73) was syllabic: four, five, six, seven and eight syllables to the line.[5] He also employed the rhyme long before the Arabs.[6] Occasionally, rhyme is also found in the early Hebrew poetry, as for example in the hymn *Weye-'ethayu* of the Musaf service for the High Holydays. The oldest part of the poetry remained anonymous. The earliest name retained is *Yose b. Yose* "the orphan" who probably lived in Palestine in the first part of the seventh century.

Some poetical selections are ascribed to him, as *ahalelah* which is inserted in the Musaf of the second day of New Year divided for the *malchuyoth*, *zichronoth*, *shoferoth*. It has an alphabetic acrostic and four short (two accents) parts to the line. Furthermore, the "Avoda" *atta conanta* he based on four accents to the part, and two and three parts to the line alternating. He does not use rhyme, but employs words as rhymes. In the first section of *ahalela* the word *melucha* is the ending word and runs through all lines; in the second section *ziccaron* and in the third section *kol* serve as rhyming words.

The language used in the early poetry is of the type employed in the prayers, with but a few new conjugations which do not occur in the Bible. Some words are culled from the Mishnaic literature.

The second "payetan" whose name has been retained is *Yannai* who lived around 700 C.E. in Palestine. He was the first to introduce didactic elements into his poetry and to have created the heavy, obscure style in the "piyyut." [7] The reason for this, as suggested by I. Davidson,[8] was that in his time the study of Talmudic literature was suppressed by the Byzantine government, and in order to familiarize the people with the "Oral Laws" pertaining to the holidays and the Sabbath they were incorporated into the "piyyut." In addition to the poetical forms mentioned above, Yannai also employs the rhyme. According to I. Davidson, his poetry was neglected chiefly because he wrote in accordance with the Palestinian triennial cycle,[9] while the Babylonian annual cycle came to be generally employed by the Jewish communities in the Diaspora.[10]

Yannai wrote "Kerovoth," i.e., poetical insertions for the "Amida" of Sabbaths and festivals. In this form, as well as in language and style, he was the forerunner and, as tradition has it, the teacher of *Eleazar b. Jacob Kallir*. A legend recounts that Yannai became jealous of Kallir's success and caused his death by throwing a serpent into his shoes.[11] Indeed, Kallir was more successful than any Synagogal poet in conquering the rituals of Roumania, Rome, and Ashkenaz. He was the most prolific and most talented "payetan" of these rituals. His main activity was concentrated in the "Kerova" for the holidays, Purim, Ninth of Av, and the distinguished Sabbaths.[12] He employed the "Agada" chiefly, but together with "Agada" he also made use of "Halacha." He produced epical as well as lyrical poems; and among many obscure and difficult pieces which cannot be understood without a commentary, he composed a number of simple and delightful songs, as *Tal ten* in the Dew Prayer of the Musaf for the first day of Passover.

Kallir's poems have been retained in the above-mentioned rituals in both printed and manuscript form. They number several hundred. The forms he employed are sometimes very intricate. In addition to alphabetical acrostics, he inserts his name and the name of his father, often several times in one poem. He frequently uses Biblical phrases as refrains. Sometimes he uses Biblical phrases, words, and idioms as third and fourth lines in stanzas; sometimes, as initial words of stanzas. In using alphabetical acrostics, he selects words which start with the same letter for each line of the stanza; often he even furnishes every word of the stanza with the same initial letter.[13]

He employed the rhyme and the word accent. His meters are mostly three or four accentuated words to the line. He also uses at times two accents to the line.[14]

At times he mixes two meters in one poem, having 4 plus 3, 3 plus 4, or 5 plus 4 accents in the same poem. In rare cases, however, do we find no strict meter in his poems.[15]

Kallir drew the themes for his poetry from Bible, Talmud, and Midrash; he even presents historical events with legendary Agadic interpolations. The most interesting element in Kallir's poetry is his language. He was the first to introduce into

Hebrew poetry, in a most daring manner, not only all post-Biblical linguistic innovations in the Hebrew tongue which were created in the Mishnaic and Talmudic literatures, but he also Hebraized many Aramaic, Greek, and Latin words by giving them Hebrew grammatical forms. In addition, he coined new Hebrew forms out of stems not to be found in the Bible. Some of his artificial forms clash with the principles of Hebrew grammar.[16]

Striving after a free all-embracing form of expression, Kallir broke the fence of the Biblical style and paved the way for the Neo-Hebrew idiom. He was a fearless innovator, and in breaking this fence, he saved Hebrew from becoming a stagnant, dead Biblical idiom. Kallir himself did more for the revitalization and expansion of the Hebrew language than all the Spanish-Hebrew poets put together. His poetry was chanted and revered by millions of Jews for over a thousand years; it is still used in the Orthodox Ashkenazic ritual.

The greatest number of "payetanim" of the Roumanian, Roman, and Ashkenazic rituals imitated Kallir's style, meter, and language; and following him practically little has been created along these lines. The most prominent "payetanim" in the Ashekenazic ritual are the Kalonymites (Kalonymos): *Meshullam ben Kalonymos* of the tenth century, Moses (the old) b. Kalonymos, Yekuthiel b. Moses; *Simon b. Isaac b. Abun* of the eleventh century, *Solomon b. Juda Habavli* of Rome of the tenth century. These and other authors furnished the poetry for all the holidays and Fast-days and distinguished Sabbaths of the year. The "piyyut" flourished up to the end of the sixteenth century.[17] The Seliha poetry continued up to the middle of the seventeenth century. Sabbathai Cohen, the last Seliha writer, composed several Selihoth in commemoration of the Chmielnitzky pogroms in 1648–9, and published them in the year 1651.

Saadya Gaon of the first part of the tenth century ought to be counted among the "payetanim" of the Palestinian school. His poetry, however, was used very little; and together with his prayer-book,[18] it was finally forgotten. Only a few of his "piyyutim" were recently published.[19] Landshuth (*Amude Haavoda*, p. 286ff.) gives a detailed account of his "piyyutim" which are still known. The style of his poetry is very heavy and artificial, though his prayers show a lucid and simple language.[20]

Beginning with the tenth century, the Hebrew poetry of the Jews in the Arabic speaking countries was based upon the Arabic meters. Donash ben Labrat is the first to whom this innovation has been attributed. His opponent Menahem ben Sarug and his school fought against this innovation, maintaining that the Hebrew language does not lend itself to the Arabic meters.[21] In fact, the poets had to alter several meters in order to fit them to the nature of the Hebrew language, while some meters could not be employed at all.

The Arabic meter is based upon a number of syllables grouped according to certain formulae. Long and short syllables, as well as half or broken syllables are counted. The long syllable is marked ⊥, the short –, the half ᵕ and the broken syllable is indicated ̆. Of the sixteen meters only the following could be used, and these with alterations:

1. Wafir ᵕ – – ⊥ repeated three times in a line, and its abridged form Hazağ in which the foot is repeated only twice.
2. Rağaz ᵕ – ᵕ ⊥ repeated three times in a line; it was changed in Hebrew poetry to – – ᵕ –.
3. Mutákarib ᵕ – – repeated four times in a line.
4. Ramal ⊥ ᵕ – – repeated three times.
5. Basit – ᵕ – –, – ᵕ – repeated twice. Sometimes – ᵕ – – is changed to – – ᵕ – and the second foot is modified at the repetition to – – as in *tziyon halo thishali* by J. Halevi. Its Arabic form is ᵕ ᵕ ᵕ –, ᵕ ᵕ –. This foot is impossible in Hebrew, because there can be no three or two "Shewá mobiles" in succession.
6. Saria ᵕ ̆ ᵕ –, ᵕ ̆ ᵕ –, – ᵕ –; this was altered in Hebrew to – – ᵕ – repeated twice and to – ᵕ –.
7. Tawil – – –, – – – – repeated twice; this was changed to ᵕ – –, ᵕ – – – because of the difficulty of finding seven syllables without "Shewá mobile" between them.
8. Kafif – ᵕ – –, – – ᵕ –, – ᵕ – –.
9. Kámil ᵕ ᵕ ⊥ ̆ – repeated three times, and changed in Hebrew to ᵕ – ᵕ – because it is impossible to have two "Shewá mobiles" in succession.

Of these meters the first two are mostly employed. The poems *adon ôlam*, *yetzaw haêl*, *sheê neësar*, and *lecha eli* (Sephardic ritual before Col Nidré) are in Hazağ; while *shema koli* (*ibid.*) and *yĕiruni sĕipay* (Musaf for the Day of Atonement) are in abridged Wafir.

The hymn *yigdal* may serve as a good example of Rağaz, though the third foot is shortened.

The Arabic meters have musical time value. The musical rendition of eight meters is given in Table XVI of my *Jewish Music*, p. 115.

Besides these intricate meters, there is a simple meter consisting of seven or eight syllables to the line, not considering the "Shewa." It was easy for Hebrew poets to make use of this meter.

The most outstanding Synagogal poets of the Arabic speaking countries were:

1. Joseph b. Isaac ibn Abitur of the tenth century.
2. Solomon b. Gabirol of the first half of the eleventh century (died about 1058).
3. Isaac b. Yehuda Giyat of the eleventh century (died 1089).
4. Moses b. Ezra (ca. 1070–1138).
5. Jehuda Halevi (ca. 1085–1145).
6. Abraham b. Ezra (1093–1168).

Of these, Gabirol, Halevi, and Moses b. Ezra were the most highly talented poets. Their poetry is inspired with religious devotion, with noble expressions, and with a deep love for Israel and its spiritual values. Their style and language are culled from the Bible, revealing but few post-Biblical elements. In rare cases do they utilize Agadic or Midrashic material. Their poetry was accepted in the Sephardic, North-African, Yemenite, Southern-French, and to a certain degree in the Italian rituals.[22]

Though Halevi was opposed to the Arabic meter (*Kusari* II, § 73–78), he nevertheless wrote all his poetry, both religious and secular, in that form.

The Synagogal poetry is arranged as insertions in the various parts of the service. Accordingly, the ideas of the prayers are worked into the poetical selections. They fall into the following main divisions: *Piyyut*, *Seliha*, *Kina*, and *Hoshana*.

A. The term *Piyyut* is applied to the poetry for Sabbaths and the holidays. Its contents are laudation, historic events, Halachic and Agadic dissertations.

This type of poetry is subdivided according to its place in the services:

1. *Maarivim* or *Maaravoth* concerns itself with the evening services of the holidays. In each of the four benedictions of these services short poetical insertions are found in the Ashkenazic, Roumanian, and Roman rituals. These poetical insertions deal with the particular holiday, its history, its laws and customs. Originally, the evening services of New Year also had poetical insertions; but since pious people were wont to fast on the eve of New Year [23] (Jer. Nedarim VIII, 2), the poetical insertions were abolished in order not to prolong the services. The Roumanian ritual still carries *Maaravoth* for these evening services, as well as for the Col Nidré service. The end versions employed in the *Maaravoth* are of the Palestinian ritual. This may indicate that the custom of using such poetical insertions originated in Palestine. The Oriental and Sephardic rituals have no *Maaravoth.*

2. *Kerova* concerns itself with the poetry inserted in the first three benedictions of the Amida on the Sabbath and holidays; in some Amidas, as the Musaf of the four distinguished Sabbaths, and in the Amidas of Purim and the Ninth of Av, all the benedictions are provided with "Kerova." According to some, the word is derived from *karev* — to approach — because the precentor had to approach the ark at the Amida.[24] Others are of the opinion that it comes from the Greek word 'ακριβής, meaning, one who is well versed.[25] The plural "Kerovoth" was changed in France to "Kerovaz" by giving the word the French suffix.[26] Later, the word was interpreted to be an abbreviation of Psalm 118:15: *K̇ol ṙinna ẇishua ḃeohole ṫzaddikim.* The "Kerova" consists of the following parts:

a. "Reshuth"— an introduction; literally the word means "taking permission." The precentor takes permission to recite the poetical insertions. The preliminary formula for all such introductions is the phrase *misod hachamim.* The introduction is chanted by the precentor in solo. The introduction for the services of the High Holydays (Shaharith) have a traditional chant.[27]

b. *Magen* to the first benediction.

c. *Mehaye* to the second benediction.

d. *Meshullosh* to the third benediction.

e. In the *Kedusha* proper.

f. Usually before the "Kedusha," the *silluk* — in Arabic *charuǧ* — finale is given. This finale is a long "piyyut," leading over to the idea of "Kedusha."

The poetry in the first and second benedictions are composed of forms which enable the participation of the congregation. They have (1) refrains running through the poem which are mostly well-known Biblical phrases or single words; (2) responsive chanting where the precentor and congregation alternate; and (3) repetitions, phrases chanted by the precentor which the congregation repeats. In this manner the congregation was trained to take an active part in the poetical insertions, as it did originally in the prayers proper. Hence, congregational singing continued to develop in the Jewish service during the medieval ages.

The "Kerova" is considered the oldest part of the Synagogal poetry. In the seventh century Yannai already composed "Kerova." [28]

The Oriental and Sephardic rituals have "Kerova" only for the Day of Atonement and for the Musaf service of the first day of Passover and the eighth day of Succoth. For the New Year, they have only introductions before the *Barchu* and the *Amida*.

3. *Yotzer* concerns itself with the poetical insertions in the benediction of the *Shema;* the name is derived from the first benediction.

a. *Yotzer* in the first benediction.
b. *Ôfan* in the angelogical paragraph *wehaofanim*.
c. *Mĕora* to *yotzer hamĕoroth*.
d. *Ahava* to the second benediction.
e. *Zulath* to the paragraph ending with *en elohim zulathecha*.
f. *Mi chamôcha* to that phrase.
g. *Gĕula* before the conclusion of the third benediction. In this section, *yom leyabbasha* by J. Halevi and the three poems beginning with *berah dodi* for the first two days of Passover and for the Sabbath in Passover must be mentioned; they are highly regarded in the Ashkenazic ritual.

4. In the "Songs of Praise"—*pesuke dezimra*, there are insertions before *nishmath* called *reshuth lenishmath* in the Italian ritual. In the Ashkenazic ritual only one for the "Rejoicing with the Law" is retained; this poem praises the high values of the Tora, relates the merits of Moses as lawgiver and teacher, and laments his death.

In Arabic this insertion is also called *Muharic*—meaning, introduction.

5. *Avoda* concerns itself with the poetical insertions in the Musaf service of the Day of Atonement. This poetical rendition of the Service of the High Priest on that day is based upon the description in *Mishna* Yoma. There are several works on this same subject.

The earliest known seems to date back to Talmudic times.[29] Its form is very simple; the text follows the wording of the *Mishna*. Some fragments of that "Avoda" were recently found and published.[30]

Almost every prominent "payetan" attempted to write an "Avoda." It usually has an introduction in which Israel's history is outlined, beginning with Genesis and following the Biblical narratives. The "payetan" Yose b. Yose seems to have composed several "Avodôth." Furthermore, Kallir, Saadya, Yohanan Cohen b. Joshua, Meshullam b. Kalonymos, Solomon b. Juda Habavli, Hay Gaon, Joseph b. Isaac ibn Abitur, Solomon b. Gabirol, Isaac ibn Giyat, Moses b. Ezra, Abraham b. Ezra — all wrote "Avodoth." Even in the nineteenth century the Hebrew scholar Samuel David Luzzatto of Italy (1800–65) made an attempt to compose an "Avoda." [31]

6. *Azharoth* concerns itself with the poetical insertions in the Musaf, in some rituals in the Minha service of Shavuoth. This "piyyut" describes the six hundred and thirteen laws derived from the Bible. "Azharoth" means "warnings." The number of laws is first mentioned in b. Maccoth 23b in the name of Rabbi Simlai (ca. 200 C.E.). He divides the laws into three hundred and sixty-five prohibitive and two hundred and forty-eight affirmative commandments. Several poets have tried their talents in this type of didactic poetry; Solomon b. Gabirol was the most successful. His "Azharôth" are incorporated into the Sephardic ritual.

7. *Hoshaanoth* is a section based upon Psalm 118:25. We are told (*Mishna* Succa IV, 4) that during the Succoth festival there were processions around the altar with the four species, while the altar itself was decked all around with willows. During the procession verse 25 of Psalm 118 used to be sung. This custom was introduced into the Synagogue. Later, short poems were composed and were chanted during the procession — *hakafoth* — around the "Bema." All these poems have the alphabetical acrostic, some with initial or closing words as refrains. They are chanted by the precentor and repeated by the congregation. The lines are short, consisting of two or three words, probably to enable the people to remember and repeat them. As a rule, the word *hoshana* is repeated after each line. There is a special poem for each of the six days, and for the seventh day there are seven poems, aside from a number of poems which are recited after the procession.

"Hoshaanoth" are recited after Musaf; in some rituals after "Hallel."

These "piyyutim" consist of a prayer for salvation, for a blessed harvest, and for the redemption and restoration of the Temple.

The poetical insertion *ose shalom* is frequent in the Italian ritual for holidays and distinguished Sabbaths. It has its name from the place where it occurs, i.e., in the passage before last in the *Kaddish* after the Amida.

B. *Seliha* — more so than piyyut is the product of the Scriptures, rooted in Biblical poetry, language, meter, and form. Not only are language and style borrowed from the Bible, but also expressions, refrains, and whole phrases, even paragraphs were incorporated into the Seliha literature. Even the idea of *Seliha* and its elements are Biblical. The name *Seliha*—forgiveness—is Biblical (Psalm 130:4). In Exodus 34:9 it is recorded that while pleading for Israel Moses used the expression *wesalahta*. The verses in Exodus became the central Seliha text. According to the *Talmud* (b. R. Hashanna 17b) God taught this text to Moses and said to him: "Whenever Israel sins and recites this text in its plea for forgiveness, I will pardon . . . for this prayer will always be effective." Later, in the third or in the fourth century, the introduction to this text was composed; it is the *El melech* known as the "Thirteen Attributes."[32] Numbers 14:17–20; 15:26 are likewise inserted in the Seliha. A number of Psalms are Selihoth and are used as such.

Furthermore, II Kings 19:16; Psalm 25:11; from Solomon's prayer in I Kings 8:30–38; II Chronicles 6:21–39; Daniel 9:4–9, 15–19; Ezra 9:6–10; Nehemiah 1:5–10; 9:33, and many other passages are included in Seliha. Biblical expressions were elaborated in alphabetical acrostics, as *aneni adonai aneni* from II Kings 18:37, II Samuel 24:17 *hatathi heĕwêthi*, or as in I Samuel 7:6 *hatanu ladonai*. These and many other Biblical expressions became the patterns for alphabetical acrostics of Selihoth.

Seliha — forgiveness — presupposes confession which is *Widdui*. Since the third or fourth century, the alphabetic acrostic beginning with *ashamnu* became the standard text for "Widdui." This text too was developed out of Biblical words.

The first Selihoth, like the first "piyyutim" are anonymous. Only concerning *Avinu malkenu* does the *Talmud* (b. Taanith 25b) record that it was improvised by Rabbi Akiva. The nucleus of five lines with the initial refrain *Avinu malkenu* which he composed was later increased to twenty-nine lines in the Sephardic ritual, to thirty-eight in the Ashkenazic ritual, and to forty-four in the Polish ritual.

In addition to these simple forms, the Seliha was enriched with poetical creations during the "payetanic" era. Almost every "payetan" contributed toward the Seliha literature. Moses b. Ezra was called *Hassalah* — the supplicant — due to the wealth of his Seliha compositions. In the Selihoth there are found not only supplications concerning troubles of individuals, not only pleas for forgiveness of sins committed by individuals or the community at large, but also prayers concerning disasters and distresses which befell the communities of all Israel in various countries and different times.

Selihoth were used for Biblical Fast-days, and for special Fast-days which were proclaimed on occasions of drought or other calamities, as described in *Mishna* Taanith I–III.

In *M*. Taanith II, the Psalms 120, 121, 130, 102; I Kings 8:35–41; Jeremiah 14:1; *Zichronoth*, and *Shoferoth* are quoted as part of the service for the Fast-days. Likewise are seven lines of the Seliha *mi she'ana*.

The Seliha is developed in the following order:

a. *Pethiha* — the opening; it is followed by the

b. *Seliha* — of which two or more are given in succession at times.

c. *Akeda* deals with the sacrifice of Isaac, but is not always inserted. In some Selihoth orders, as for the day before New Year and before the Day of Atonement, the Ashkenazic ritual has three "Akedas" and two for the *Minha* service of the Day of Atonement.

d. *Pizmon*.

e. *Tehinna*.

f. *Hatanu* which consists of the martyrology of Israel.

g. *Tochaha*.

h. *Widdui*.

i. Responsive pieces.

The following poetical forms are employed:

1. *Sheniya* — two lines to the strophe.

2. *Sh'lishiya* — three lines to the strophe.

3. *Meruba* — or *Shalmonith* — four lines to the strophe.

4. *Pizmon* has four lines to the strophe at the most. It is distinguished by a set rhythmical melody according to which all stanzas are sung by the precentor and congregation responsively,[33] whereas the other Selihoth are chanted in modal form.[34]

The meters of the Selihoth are the same as those of the "piyyut," following either the verbal accents or the Arabic syllabic meters.

The Sephardic Selihoth have the Arabic Mustağib form — based upon a Biblical phrase or some Biblical word with which the rhyme continues.

Selihoth are inserted in the Italian and Ashkenazic rituals in the sixth benediction of the Amida; in the Sephardic and Polish rituals the Selihoth are recited after the Amida.

In the communities which suffered politically, socially, and religiously, the Selihoth literature was greatly developed in order to give vent to the aching hearts of the people; but in the countries where the Jews were permitted to breathe freely, the Seliha part of the liturgy shrank considerably.

The *Kinoth* are similar in form and style to the Seliha out of which they developed. The difference lies in the content. The Kinoth are restricted to the expression of deep sorrow and mourning over the loss of independence, the loss of the homeland, the fall of the Temple, and over the dispersion of Israel. In the Ashkenazic, Roman, and Italian rituals, Kallir's *Kinoth* are most outstanding, while J. Halevi's Zionide *Tziyon halo thishali* ranks as the deepest expression of the people's lament over its lost glory.

The insertion of poetry into the prayers was by no means met with favor. Many outstanding authorities opposed the "piyyut" on the ground that it brought about an interruption in the continuity of the service. Among the opponents were Nahshon Gaon, Juda of Barcelona, and Maimonides. Rabbi Nahshon said that no "piyyut" should be inserted and that a *Hazzan* who recites "piyyut" should not be permitted to officiate. A synagogue in which "piyyut" is recited, he held, the members of that congregation testify concerning themselves that they are not *students*.[35]

Juda of Barcelona opposes all insertions even such as *Haccol yoducha* in the Sabbath Yotzer and *zochrenu* in the Amida of the High Holydays, and calls the "piyyut" "compositions full of ignorance and exaggerations." [36] Maimonides rejects the "piyyut" because it causes a break in the service, because it sometimes expresses obscure and even dangerous ideas, and because we are not allowed to add prayers to those composed by the Great Assembly.[37]

On the other hand, there were men like Gershom "the Light of the Exile," Rashi, and his grandson, Rabbi Jacob Tam, who were in favor of "piyyut." Gershom considers the "piyyut" as divinely inspired. According to him, the first "payetanim," Yannai and Kallir mentioned above, lived during Mishnaic times; he identifies Kallir with Eleazar b. Shimon b. Yohai.[38] Natronai decided in favor of "piyyut" even in the Amida.[39] Mahzor Vitry 325–6 gives a long discussion with regard to the "piyyut," and quoting several authorities like Natronai, Rashi, Jacob Tam, Joseph Tov-Elem, he comes to the conclusion that it is not only permissible but even meritorious to insert "piyyut" into the first three benedictions of the Amida. In the name of Rashi several decisions are retained which speak in favor of "piyyut."[40] A man like Meyir of Rothenburg himself composed several "piyyutim." "Piyyut" became the integral part of the service in Germany, so that Maharil (Jacob Mollin) considered its recitation of great importance and ordered his disciples not to miss the "piyyut" (Maharil, chapter on Tefilla).

CHAPTER VI

THE INFLUENCE OF KABBALA UPON THE LITURGY

In its very essence, mysticism is a negation of life, an escape from its realities and hardships. "Dissatisfied and discontented with the world and its glories, the pious one feels as a stranger on this earth. He senses terrible fetters in his body, a painful dungeon, a dark grave. . . . The imprisoned soul yearns after liberation from the barriers of earthliness to the elevation into heavenly heights, to the return to the infinite Divine from which it sprang."[1] To achieve this goal the mystics of all religions turned to asceticism and ecstasy, especially in times of social and political trouble and misery and in times of cultural decline. Cool reasoning and logic were substituted by phantasy and imagination; the sense of reality was subdued, and unlimited power was given to vision.

The dark medieval ages with its barbaric treatment of the Jewish people gradually developed this type of mysticism in the soul of religious thinkers in Jewry. Mysticism increased and declined in proportion to the suffering inflicted upon the Jewish people by their Christian and Mohammedan neighbors.

The Jewish religion aims at the sanctification of life: "Be ye holy, for I Yahve your God am holy" (Lev. 19:2). Its teachings and customs are given with the purpose of purifying and sanctifying human life. The religious spirits in Israel have always yearned to come nigh to the mysterious One, to perceive "the mysteries which become more mysterious the more they are thought about," for "there will ever remain the one absolute certainty that man is ever in the presence of an infinite and eternal energy from which all things proceed" (Herbert Spencer). And when "Moses drew near unto the thick darkness where God was" (Exod. 20:21), he only succeeded to behold the reflex of Him. "Thou canst not see My face, for man shall not see Me and live" (Exod. 33:20). Only the back of God was permitted to be seen (Exod. 32:23).

Judaism, while believing in the One Mystery, the Creator, seeks to *understand* His ways and laws. Over and over again, prophets and sages advise people to search and comprehend the obvious secrets of life, and not to revere any natural phenomenon or performers of miracles, and not to veil the eye of reason. Man is advised to seek truth, for truth is the "Seal of God" (b. Yoma 69b; San. 64a).

Yet, a certain mystical element is an organic part of every religion, and also of Judaism as a religion. The central part of a belief in One Invisible God is the source of mysticism. This deeply-rooted sense in the human soul creates the sentiment of marveling at the deeds of God; it creates reverence and love for Him and in some pious souls a craving after Him, to be nigh unto Him, to petition and thank Him. As long as this sentiment remains within limits assigned by reason, it is a healthy condition of a religion. But as soon as this sentiment is exaggerated, overpowering the whole range of human spiritual activities, the mind of man falls a prey to this exaggerated mysticism which subdues and silences human reason.

Mysticism has been characterized as feminine in contradistinction to the prophetic religion which is designated masculine. "Mysticism," writes F. Heiler,[2] "is the religion of effeminate natures, eccentric devotion . . . soft passivity are characteristic of them. . . . While the prophetic religion has a distinct masculine character: ethical acridity, inconsiderate determination, and powerful activity."

As in all religions so also in Judaism mysticism had an influence upon the liturgy. Already in early times as was stated above we find mystics who occupied themselves with composing "Kedushas" and hymns; the "Yorde Mercava" in particular engaged in this activity. This influence stopped for some time, only to reappear once more with the increase of mystical tendencies which came as a result of the vicissitudes of Jewish life described above. In the sixteenth century the influence of the mystics upon the liturgy became apparent. Descendants of Spanish and other refugees settled in Safed, Palestine. They were permeated with mystical doctrines and tendencies which were now called *Kabbala*.[3] The most important protagonists of these tendencies were Moses Cordovero, his brother-in-law

Solomon Alkabetz, and Eleazar Askari. The crowning personalities, however, were Isaac Luria and his disciple Hayyim Vital.

These outstanding exponents did not change the text and order of the liturgy. Their innovations consisted of the following features:

Meditation in which both angelology and the application of the Name of God through obscure methods were emphasized.

Hymns and Songs were inserted into the prayers proper. The mystics would read secret meanings into the texts of the prayers and would count the letters in accordance with their numerical values.

New Fast-days were instituted, and the *liturgy of repentance* hitherto unknown was created by these mystics.

Cawwanoth, *yihudim* — concentrations which concerned themselves with the idea of concentration and penetration into the secrets of the Name of God by means of certain combinations.

These terms are applied to the meditations which usually start with the phrases: *lĕshem yihud*, *yehi ratzon*, *hareni muchan*, *hineni muchan*.

The idea is that no prayer should be recited, no ceremony should be observed without concentrating one's mind upon the act. Moreover, the mystics read thoughts and ideas which were unknown before into the prayers and customs. To understand the spirit of their meditations, some of them may well serve as examples:

Meditation on putting on the "Tallith":

"In order to emphasize the oneness of the Holy One, praised be He, and His divinity with awe and mercy as indicated in the *Yod Hê*— which designate judgment — and in the *Waw Hê*—which designate mercy—in a perfect unity, in communion with all Israel, I wrap my body with the fringes. May my soul, as well as my two hundred and forty-eight limbs and three hundred and sixty-five sinews, be enwrapped in the light of the 'Tzitzith'—in the spiritual enlightenment of this commandment—which is equivalent to the six hundred and thirteen commandments. And just as I cover myself with a 'Tallith' in this world, so may I merit the garment of the Rabbis, the precious 'Tallith,' in the coming world, in paradise. Through the observance of 'Tzitzith' may my soul, my spirit, my life, and my prayer be saved from all external harms—from dangerous spirits. And may the 'Tallith' spread its wings over them (soul, etc.) and save them like an eagle saves its young. And may my observance of the commandment of 'Tzitzith' be considered before the Holy One, praised be He, as though I had fulfilled it in all its details, with the proper concentration of mind, and with the six hundred and thirteen commandments related to it. Amen, Selah!"

Meditation on redeeming the first-born:

". . . May it be Thy will, O our God and God of our Fathers, that the observance of this commandment be considered in thy abundant mercy; may *peter* (firstborn) soften the judgments which amount to p.t.r. — *teref* — . . . . Mayest Thou guard my firstborn; and just as I redeemed him today from evil, so may he be redeemed from the 'left side' (the evil spirit). . . ."

Meditation on counting the "Omer":

"Lord of all worlds, Thou hast commanded us through Moses Thy servant to count the 'Omer' in order to cleanse ourselves of our filth which cleaves unto us like a shell. . . . May it be Thy will . . . that through the counting of the 'Omer' . . . I shall be purified and sanctified with the holiness from on high. And through that may all worlds be greatly influenced and our souls be improved."

Meditation on blowing the Shofar on New Year's Day; this meditation was written by Rabbi Isaac Luria:

"May it be Thy will, O God of heaven and earth, God of Abraham, Isaac, and Jacob, great and awe-inspiring God, that Thou mayest send all the pure angels, the faithful messengers, who are eager to favor Israel: *Patzpatzya* who is charged to bring to light the merits of Israel when they blow the Shofar, *Toshbash* whose duty it is to confuse Satan, and the great angels *Hadarniel* and *Tusniel* whose task it is to bring the Shofar-blasts before Thy throne of glory. Let Thy mercy over Thy people prevail, and look down upon the ashes of our father Isaac which are accumulated upon the altar. . . .

"May it be Thy will, that the blasts . . . which we blow may be embroidered (engraved) through the official *Tartiel* in Thy throne of glory, just as Thou acceptest through Elijah of blessed memory, and *Joshua* the head of the face, and the head *Matat;* and be filled with mercy over us. . . ."

Meditation on the four cups of the *Seder* service:

"I am prepared to recite 'Kiddush' over wine and to partake of the first cup which stands for the letter *Yod* of YHWH which is a shield against foolishness. . . ."

"The second cup stands for the letter Hê of the tetragrammaton; it helps understanding, and shields against whoredom. The third cup stands for the *Waw* of the Name and protects against evil desires, while the fourth cup stands for the last Hê and destroys unclean spirits."

Among the meditations there are some of a noble ethical and social spirit. The meditation on retiring is a good example:

"Lord of the world, I hereby forgive all who made me angry and caused me harm, whether they hurt my body or my honor or my property, whether purposely or unwillingly, whether in deed or in thought. May nobody be punished through or because of me . . ."

Or:

"I hereby take upon myself to observe the commandment: 'And thou shalt love thy neighbor as thyself.'"

These examples suffice to illustrate the essence of the Kabbalistic meditations which have been introduced into the liturgy since the sixteenth century.

Insertions into the prayers were introduced in various places; we shall discuss some of them here:

Moses Cordovero introduced the "Reception of Sabbath" before the Friday evening service with six psalms: Psalms 95–99, and Psalm 29. Each of the psalms stands for one of the six weekdays. The beginning letters of the psalms have the numerical value of four hundred and thirty which equals the numerical value of *nefesh*—soul. Before each psalm there is a mysterious combination of six letters. The recitation of the sixth psalm is supposed to cause a tremendous stir in the spheres above. In this psalm the tetragrammaton occurs eighteen times which stand for the eighteen benedictions of the Amida. All in all, the letters total seventy-two, corresponding to the Seventy-two-letter Name of God. This sixth psalm consists of eleven verses which equals the number of *Waw He* — the third and fourth letters of the tetragrammaton; it also contains ninety-one words which correspond to the numerical value of YHWH and ADNY together. All these calculations are the findings of Isaac Luria.

The poetical prayer *ana bechoah* consists of six words to the line; seven lines of this poem have rhyme: 1–2, 3–4, and 5–6. This poem afforded opportunity for Kabbalistic speculations. Its forty-two words are supposed to represent the Forty-two-letter Name of God which is derived from the combination of the initial letters of the words. The poem was ascribed to the Tanaite Nehunya b. Hakkana (Responses RshBA § 220).

The reason why the paragraph *berich shemê* from the *Zohar* is recited at the opening of the ark is that at that moment the gates of heaven are opened and the divine love is roused.

Hymns and *Songs* constitute one of the finest contributions of the Kabbalistic school to the liturgy. In the first place, there is the poem "Lecha Dodi" (see Chapter X), which Solomon Alkabetz composed at the request of Isaac Luria; then there are the Aramaic songs of Luria himself and the song *yedid nefesh* by Eleazar Askari; etc. They all breathe the spirit of love: the romance between God the Lover and Israel the beloved.

Man and God, as lover and beloved, is an old theme found in all ancient and primitive religions, as well as in the mysticism of Christianity and Islam. Already in the first or second century Rabbi Akiva declared that Canticles was a love song between Israel and God.[4] "The relation of the soul to God is thought of as a love and bridal affair, the ecstatic union with God as a gentle love union, and the mystical blissfulness as a love-delight."[5] "As in the primitive sexual rites so also in the love-mysticism, the soul is always the feminine part while God is the masculine principle in the love intercourse."[6] Thus Isaac Luria sings:

"Her husband (God) will embrace her (Israel) and bring her pleasure."

"He crowned the bride with the mysteries of heaven at the festivity of the holy angels."

"His love will increase to the highest degree, and He will take His mate which had been abandoned."

Askari sang in his poem *yedid nefesh* as follows:[7]

"Beloved of the Soul, merciful Father,
Draw Thy servant unto Thy will,
That swift as a hart he may run
To prostrate himself before Thy majesty,
Finding Thy love sweeter than the honey-comb
And every tempting savor.

Exquisitely beautiful is the splendor of the world.
My soul pineth for Thy love.
O God heal it, I pray Thee, by showing unto it
The delight of Thy splendor.
Then will it grow strong and be healed,
And rejoice everlastingly.

O mighty One! manifest Thy mercies,
And have compassion upon Thy beloved son.
For, oh how long, have I been consumed with longing
To behold the triumph of Thy might!
These things my heart desires;
Take pity and hide not Thyself.

Reveal Thyself, O adored One, and spread
Over me the tent of Thy peace.
May the earth be illumined with Thy glory,
And let us be glad and rejoice in Thee.
Hasten to show Thy love; and be gracious
Unto me as in the days of yore."

This song reminds one of the innumerable love songs in the Christian liturgy, as for example:

"Schmachtend um dich, muss, Lieb' ich mich verzehren und rufend geh'n umher, dich zu umfangen; Lebendig sterb' ich, willst du nicht mehr kehren, und wein'und seufz', aufs neu dich zu erlangen. . . . So wächst das Herz, das in dich aufgegangen; O stille mein Verlangen, Komm, heile meine Wunden, Lieb' hält mich so gebunden, Die letzte Kraft entschwand."

Or:

"My Jesus, be welcome, be thousand times kissed, be passionately embraced, thou my soul's desire." [8]

The Hebrew songs, however, are more abstract, and have a much nobler spirit.

In a meditation on the putting on of "Tefillin" we read:

". . . I am prepared to put on 'Tefillin' in order to fulfill the commandment of my Creator; and through the 'Tefillin' of the hand may spiritual strength be ascribed to the feminine part of the 'miniature divine presence' — *zeêr anpin* — so that the groom embrace the bride; and may it cause to lengthen my days with holy thoughts, without any thoughts of sin. May the stripes be ties of love between the groom and the bride. May the sins not cause the stripes to become ties which will fasten us to the *Samol* (evil spirit) and his mate and his whole group. . . ."

The underlying idea here is that everything in the universe has its mate; even God has a mate which is the *Shechina*.[9] Days, too, have their mates; but Sabbath, being the seventh day, has no companion. Hence, Israel becomes its mate. For this reason, Israel is called the lover — *dod* — and Sabbath the bride — *calla*. (Bĕrêshith Rabba 11:9.) [10]

At times the counting of words led to peculiarities. The custom to recite Psalm 67 during the counting of *Omer* was known already among the mystics of the thirteenth and fourteenth centuries. This psalm was read during the period of the "Omer," because it consists of seven verses totalling forty-nine words. Soon it was discovered that this psalm was engraved upon the shield of David's soldiers like a *Menora*. Whereupon this psalm was arranged and printed in the form of a *Menora* with seven branches and was embellished with different mysterious formulae. This Menora-figure of the psalm has since been circulating in all Oriental and Occidental prayer books which bear Kabbalistic tendencies.[11]

Several more items of the Kabbalistic school which were inserted into the home services of Friday evening are worthy of mention. "The Song of Peace" — Shalom Aleichem — looms among the outstanding ones. It was first printed in the "Order for Sabbath" in Prague, 1641.[12] (See Chapter XI concerning the idea of this song.) The poem reads as follows:

"Peace be with you, ye angels of service, angels of the Highest, King of Kings, the Holy One, praised be He.

"May your coming be for peace, ye angels of peace . . . etc.

"Bless me with peace, ye angels of peace . . . etc.

"May your going away be for peace, ye angels of peace . . ."

Proverbs 31 : 10–31 is another important insertion. This song, however, is not recited in order to eulogize the qualities of the "Woman of Valor," but rather in honor of the *Shechina*. The twenty-two verses of this song are supposed to be equal to the channels of blessing which come from the heavens. The woman of valor is the Tora.

The Tora is called valor — *hayil* — because the numerical value of this word is forty-eight, and that in turn equals the numerical value of the word *moah* which means brains or mind.[13]

Luria's innovation to recite the "Thirteen Attributes" at the opening of the ark before reading from the Scroll (Exod. 34 : 6) became customary in the Ashkenazic, Sephardic, and Oriental rituals of the festivals. It was originally meant for the month of *Ellul* only.[14]

All the forms of asceticism, like fasting, sleeping on the bare ground, immersions in ice-water, rolling naked in snow, being whipped the forty Scriptural lashes, exposing oneself to be bitten by insects, and so forth — all these forms which were frequent among all religious ascetics were also introduced into the Kabbalistic circles. The mildest form, fasting, was mostly resorted to. This form of repenting was much in use in ancient Israel, as pointed out in Chapter I; it remained a permanent institution in Judaism. For this reason, the innovation to fast on the eve of the New Moon which Moses Cordovero introduced and which was called "The Minor Day of

Atonement" was readily accepted by the mystics. Another institution to fast on every Monday and Thursday was later restricted to but a few days of the year. Since 1559 it has been an institution in Safed for a quorum of ten men to fast daily.[15]

In Safed there also originated the custom to rise at midnight on every weekday night, to sit on the floor, and to lament over the Destruction and the long exile.[16] Likewise, the custom to remain awake all night on "Shavuoth" and "Hoshana Rabba" and to recite "Orders"— *Tikkunim* — specially arranged for these occasions, also emanated from that Kabbalistic school.

The institution and custom to rise a few hours before sunrise, to hurry to the synagogue, and to recite supplications and chant hymns was a milder form of asceticism than fasting. Special societies were organized for that purpose in many communities. These groups called themselves *Shomerim labboker* — "Watchers of the Morning."

An elaborate liturgy was created for all these customs and institutions; part of it was newly written, but most of it was compiled from old material. First, the liturgy was compiled for each day separately. Later on, these liturgies were collected into one book called *Shaare Tziyon*, and was published by Nathan Hanover in Prague, 1662. Since the eighteenth century, these new liturgies have been incorporated into the regular prayer-book of almost every ritual. "The Minor Day of Atonement," the fast on Mondays and Thursdays, the lamenting at midnight, the reading of "Orders" during the nights of "Shavuoth" and "Hoshana Rabba" — all these became permanent institutions, though the last two rituals were not incorporated into the regular prayer-books due to their bulkiness (see Chapters XV, XVII, and XVIII).

Luria's innovations were later collected and affixed to the prayer-book and published under the name of Luria as the *Siddur Ari* (the abbreviation Ari is derived from the first letters of "Adonenu Rabbenu Isaac — our Lord, Rabbi Isaac). This prayer-book was later taken over by the "Meditators" — *mechaw'nim* — of Jerusalem in the Congregation Beth-El under leadership of Shalom Sharabi, and by the "Hasidim" under the leadership of Israel Baal Shem Tov and Shneur Zalman of Liadi (see Chapter VII).[17]

CHAPTER VII

PRAYER-CODES AND LITERATURE

The arrangement of one hundred benedictions obligatory for every individual to recite daily ascribed to Rabbi Meyir (b. Menahoth 43b), laid the foundation for a regular compendium of prayers. At the request of a congregation in Spain, Natronai Gaon (ca. 860) compiled such a list of one hundred benedictions, *me'a berachoth*, which served as the basis of several rituals later. M. V. starts with these benedictions, while others refer to them.[1]

Indeed, several authorities in Babylonia arranged parts of the ritual and gave decisions in matters of liturgy;[2] the Tractate Soferim, too (ca. seventh century), embodies a great deal of liturgical regulations and texts. Yet the first to whom a compilation of a complete order of the ritual is ascribed is none other than Amram b. Sheshna (d. 875). This work was written at the request of a Spanish congregation. It contained not only the correct wording of texts as that congregation had asked, but also explanations and regulations of liturgical customs.[3] This prayer-code spread throughout the Jewish settlements of Spain and France, and became the basis for the liturgy even in those countries where the Palestinian ritual was prevalent.

In the same manner, this prayer-code influenced both Italy and Germany.

This work was first published in 1865 by N. Koronell, and in 1912 by L. Frumkin (Jerusalem). For a thousand years it remained in MS. and was copied innumerably in different countries and at different times. It was regarded as the foundation of Jewish worship to which local traditions may be adjusted. It is quite obvious, therefore, that the copying of this work also had the purpose of including the liturgical traditions of that country or community for which the copy was being made. The MSS. retained of Rav Amram's *Siddur* vary a great deal in several points. The book is divided into two parts, part two consisting of poetical insertions by poets after Amram, as Solomon b. Gabirol, Moses and Abraham b. Ezra, and David b. Bakoda. But in the first part, too, which contains prayers, decisions and regulations regarding prayer by Saadya are incorporated. In some MS. (Oxford), Rav Hai is also quoted. A. Marx [4] and L. Ginzberg [5] made a painstaking investigation of the texts.

Siddur of Saadya Gaon (about 892–942), is to a great extent based upon the Palestinian ritual, and has in turn influenced both the Persian and Yemenite rituals. A copy of this prayer-book was found in Al-Fayyum, Egypt, the birthplace of the compiler.[6] The copy is not complete; many pages are missing. In his *Amude Haavoda* (Berlin, 1862, p. 287f.), L. Landshuth gives some variations of this *Siddur*. I. Bondi offers a thorough description of it in his *Der Siddur des Rabbi Saadya Gaon* (Frankfurt a/m, 1904). The work embodies prayers and poems by Saadya and others and a number of explanations in Arabic. The name of the prayer-book is in Arabic: *djam'a alsawath waltassabah* — A Collection of Prayers and Praises. According to Bondi (*o.c.*, p. 2), this compendium is the first and oldest prayer-book retained in its original form. Since several fragments of this *Siddur* were found in Egypt (*o.c.*, p. 9), the assumption that it was at one time in use in Egypt, at least before the time of Maimonides, is surely justified.[7]

The Persian Ritual — Nusah Paras — is chiefly based upon Saadya's *Siddur*. The MS. of this prayer-code was discovered by E. Adler, and is briefly described in his essay in the *J.Q.R.*, Vol. 10. In my *Thesaurus*, Vol. III (Hebrew ed.), pp. 39–42, I give important variants in the texts of this ritual.

The Ritual of Aleppo — Minhag Aram Tzova — has many original prayers and text-versions, apart from Palestinian elements. Of this ritual only the second volume has been retained. One fragmentary copy was in possession of Prof. A. Berliner in Berlin,[8] and one complete copy is preserved in the National Library in Jerusalem. Of the first volume only a fragment is found in the library of the Jewish Theological Seminary in New York. This ritual was printed in Venice, 1527.

In my *Thesaurus*, Vol. IV (Hebrew ed.), pp. 33–38, I give

the most striking prayers and versions of the second volume which contains the ritual for the High Holydays, Succoth, Selihoth, for some Fast-days, the benediction for circumcisions and weddings and miscellanea (benedictions over food, purchasing of slaves, funerals, etc.). This ritual, as well as the Persian and Roumanian rituals, were gradually discarded, and the Sephardic ritual was adopted in their stead.[9]

Mahzor Roumania, or the Greek Minhag is the Byzantine ritual used by the Jewish people living on the Balkan and in Constantinople. It contains "piyyutim" by E. Kallir, many of which are to be found in the Italian and Ashkenazic rituals. It has several forms of the "Kedusha" (see Chapter VIII), "Maaravoth" for Rosh Hashana and Yom Kippur evening, and the Hebrew text of "Col Nidré." The version of the prayers is similar to the Palestinian ritual. This *Mahzor* was first printed in 1510 in Constantinople, and was since reprinted several times. It was last printed in Venice, 1665.[10]

Mahzor Roma is the old Italian ritual; it was a compilation of Babylonian and Palestinian elements. Menahem b. Solomon of the twelfth century is supposed to have been the first to write down the Roman ritual.[11] His work is called *Seder Hibbur Berachoth*.[12] The first publication of the Roman ritual took place in the years 1485–6 (Soncino-Casale Maggiore). Through Sephardic influence, the Roman ritual was later varied greatly and was called the Italian ritual, several editions of which were published: Venice, 1588 and 1772. In 1856 S. D. Luzzatto edited the Italian ritual with notes and with an introduction explaining the characteristics of the poetry, giving also some data of the "Payetanim."

Maimonides (1135–1204) gives in his work *Mishne Tora*, part II, a complete order of the prayers for the entire year — *Seder tefilloth col hashana;* in a special chapter *hilchoth tefilla* he details all regulations pertaining to the ritual. In the main, his prayers are identical to the Sephardic ritual.

The Yemenite Ritual — Taclal — containing everything, is a fusion of Saadya's and Maimonides' orders. There is, however, a Sephardic influence noticeable in the prayers. Most of the "piyyutim" are Sephardic, though some of the Yemenite creations, written by anonymous writers and by their poets

Salah ibn Yahya and Yahya Aldahari, are incorporated in this ritual.[13]

This prayer-book was edited and published by Yemenite Rabbis in Jerusalem, 1894–6, in two volumes with a commentary by the grandson of the above-mentioned Salah Yahya b. Joseph.

The Fez (Morocco) Ritual — Ahavath hakkadmonim — is similar in part to the *Minhag Tripoli — Sifthe renanoth* — and to the Aleppo ritual. The prayers are only mentioned, while the "piyyutim" are given in full. Some of these "piyyutim" are compositions of local writers. This ritual was edited and published by E. Ben-Shimon in Jerusalem, 1889, according to a MS. retained in the synagogue of the native Jews of Fez known as the "Ibn Danan" synagogue.[14] There the old Moroccan ritual still survives; in the other sections of the country the Sephardic ritual prevails.

There are local prayer-codes (Tripoli, Tunis, Tlemsan, Algiers) along the North African coast which have some local versions and material.[15]

The Cochin and Sengli Ritual — Shire renanoth — has been reprinted in Bombay in 1874. It contains prayers and songs for the Sabbaths and festivals, for circumcisions and weddings. The material represents an amalgamation of various old Oriental and Occidental rituals. The poetry is culled from Syrian, Babylonian, Sephardic, and Ashkenazic poets, especially from Israel Najara. In the meditations there is a strong Kabbalistic influence noticeable.

Of the other Levantine Minhagim that of the *Island of Corfu* became known.

Minhag Sepharad — Spanish Minhag — as it became known in the last centuries, is a fusion of several rituals which prevailed in Spain at the time when the Jews still lived there. There were special rituals for Castilla,[16] Aragon,[17] Cataluna,[18] and other sections. After the Spanish Jews settled in Turkey, they continued the traditions which they had brought over from their native country; these traditions they practiced in synagogues which they organized in their new land of refuge. The continuation of the separate rituals often led to fights.[19] Finally "A General Sephardic Ritual" was compiled in which compromises were made with all traditions, even with that of the native Greek Jews, the native Arabic Jews, and the Ashkenazim. In addition, Kabbalistic material was also incorporated, especially elements of Luria's school. Thus the Oriental-Sephardic ritual was created "according to the custom of the Sephardim in Constantinople, in the East, in the West, and in Italy." The original so-called Castillian ritual was printed in Venice, 1522.

Solomon b. Isaac (1040–1105) Rashi, the great commentator of the Bible and *Talmud*, devoted himself likewise to the liturgy. His decisions and regulations were collected by his disciples; four compilations have been retained:

a. *Mahzor Vitry* by Simha b. Samuel of Vitry (in the Marne Department, France). Not only the texts of the prayers are given in this book, but also many "piyyutim," "Zemiroth" for Sabbaths and festivals, and decisions of the *Talmud* and the Codes are embodied, as well as Tractate Avoth and several Talmudic selections dealing with the religious life. The Mahzor Vitry became the basis of the Ashkenazic ritual. This work was edited with notes by S. Hurwitz and published by the Mekitzé Nirdamim (Berlin, 1893). The poetry was edited in a separate volume called *Kuntras Hapiyyutim* by H. Brody (Berlin, 1894).

b. *Siddur Rashi* contains regulations of the ritual; the texts of the prayers are not given in toto but are merely discussed. It was edited by S. Buber and published by the Mekitzé Nirdamim (Berlin, 1910).

c. *Sefer Happardes* contains responsa and regulations appertaining to the customs of the ritual by Rashi and other Rabbis. This work was first published in Constantinople in the year 1707, and was edited anew with critical notes by Rabbi H. L. Ehrenreich, Budapest, 1924.

d. *Sefer Haora* is similar in content and scope to the two works mentioned above; it was edited with notes and comparative studies by S. Buber (Cracow, 1905).

Sefer Mahkim is a short description of the French ritual by Nathan b. Juda b. Azriel who lived at the end of the twelfth century; Azriel was a contemporary of Rashi. The compiler wrote down according to the tradition he received from his father, who in turn had received it from his father; both individuals functioned as precentors. This work contains a short description of the ritual and its customs. The texts of the prayers, the "piyyutim," and Selihoth are mentioned only. It was edited and published by I. Freimann (Cracow, 1909).

Seder Troyes in France (the birthplace of Rashi) was compiled by Juda b. Eliezer according to the tradition of his teacher Menahem b. Joseph b. Juda, precentor in Troyes. Menahem was a contemporary of Nathan, the compiler of the *Sefer Mahkim;* he quotes from this book several times. The nature of this book is similar to that described above. It was edited and published by M. Weisz (Frankfurt a/m, 1905).

In Carpentras and Avignon of Southern France there survived a remnant of the old ritual of Provence. It is mainly based upon Rabbi Amram's *Siddur*, and contains "piyyutim" by the Spanish poets, notably of Moses b. Ezra and several other poets of the Provence. The ritual contains additions from the Oriental-Sephardic ritual and some local liturgical customs and prayers. It was printed in part in Avignon in the year 1767 and in Amsterdam in four volumes two volumes for the High Holydays, one for the Three Festivals, and one for the Four Fast-days (1737–56).

The so-called *French Ritual* was discarded with the expulsion of the Jews from France in the fourteenth century, and was retained only in the three Italian communities: Asti, Fossano, and Moncalvo.

The Ashkenazic Ritual, *Minhag Ashkenaz*, which is the Southwestern German ritual, was originally identical with the French ritual. As a result of local customs, however, adopted elements from the Italian and Byzantine rituals, and different prayer-versions and poetry composed by liturgists living in Germany, the Ashkenazic ritual began to branch off in the eleventh century. Men like Meyir b. Isaac, who was precentor of Worms, the Kalonymites, Gershom b. Juda, Simon b. Isaac b. Abun, Eleazar b. Nathan, Meyir Rothenberg, and later Jacob b. Moshe Mollin — called the Maharil — these men established the Ashkenazic ritual. This prayer-code was first printed about 1490; the earliest known printing, however, took place in 1512 in Prague. Important editions of this work are the *Hadrath Kodesh* printed with a commentary and notes in 1512 in Venice, and the *Maaglè Tzedek*, printed in Venice in the year 1568. Both editions give the Ashkenazic and Polish rites for the Ashekenazic congregations in Italy.

Col-bo, in four volumes, covering the Ashkenazic Polish ritual with a commentary and notes. Sulzbach, 1699, edited by Isaac ben Jacob Josevel Segal of Herlesheim, precentor in the Synagogue of Moshe Meshullam Segal, 2nd edition (Rom, Wilna, 1905). The work contains all prayers, poetry, and meditations for the entire cycle of the year, in the form of the *Hadrath Kodesh*.

Menorat Ha-maor, by Israel ibn Al-nakawa, edited by H. G. Enelow, part II (New York, 1930). This volume deals with the prayers, their sources, their Midrashic and rabbinic interpretations, and their religio-ethical values.

There is still another prayer-book of interest; it has a Kabbalistic commentary, and was written by Herz Treves, Cantor in Frankfurt a/m, and published by his son Eliezer in Thiengen in the year 1560.

In the countries east of the Danube, a special ritual has been known since the fourteenth century. In quoting that ritual, Maharil called it the *Austrian Minhag*. In the course of time, several subdivisions of this ritual developed; they are: the Bohemian, the Moravian, the Polish (the Little and the Great Polish), *Polen gadol wekaton*, the Lithuanian, and the White Russian *Reisen*. They differ from one another and from the Ashkenazic ritual in several customs, in the use of various "piyyutim," and in the variation of their orders. The Polish ritual was first published in Prague in the years 1512–22.

Mention ought to be made of the ritual compiled by Jacob Emden who is known as "Yavetz." He printed his prayer-book — *Beth Jacob* — in Altona in 1744; incorporating into it regulations and Kabbalistic meditations. The editor provided the work with a commentary and notes. He also attempted to change some established petitions, especially in the "Maamadoth" (see Chapter XVIII).

Aaron b. Yehiel Michel, of Michailishok, near Wilna (first half of the nineteenth century), compiled a commentary to the Mahzor, called *Matte Levi*, in which he gives a fairly good explanation of the text with some additional Midrashic elements. His commentary is usually printed together with several others, in some of which Heidenheim's notes are utilized. *Matte Levi* is often published in abridged form. Rom's edition (Wilna, 1876), contains the entire commentary. The same author wrote also a short explanation of the poetical texts called *Beth Levi*.

The leaders of the Hasidim [20] adopted in part the Sephardic ritual according to the arrangement and the additions of Isaac Luria — *Minhag Ari*. Shneur Zalman of Liadi [21] compiled a ritual with an elaborate Kabbalistic commentary and many meditations in the year 1800. For that work, it is stated, he consulted some sixty different rituals.[22] Among the Hasidim, this prayer-book became known as *Dem Rebbin's Siddur*.

The Meditators — *Mechawenim* — in Jerusalem published their ritual with the meditation of Shalom Sharabi (d. 1788) in Jerusalem, 1916. This ritual is the climax of mysticism; it is based upon Isaac Luria's order. It is called *Siddur tefilla leharashash*, and is composed of nine parts. Whenever the Name of God occurs, a multitude of meditations have to be read in silent devotion by the worshippers; as a result of these many meditations, the service is mostly a prolonged silent devotion.

During the medieval ages, the liturgy suffered additions and changes, partly because of the mystic movement, and partly because of the slanders — *Malshinim*. The latter were Jewish converts to Christianity who, having renounced the Jewish faith, would accuse the Hebrew religious literature and especially the liturgy of containing prayers and expressions directed against the Christians and their faith. The result of such treacherous denunciations was most disastrous to the Jewish people and to their liturgy; persecutions set in, and both innocent people and sacred books were burned at the stake. Inquisitions were established and censors were appointed by the Church to investigate the Talmudic, rabbinic, and liturgic literatures. This resulted in the extermination of all "suspicious" passages; and many texts were thus greatly corrupted.[23]

The ignorance and the arbitrary action of the printers constitute another source of corruption. On their own account, these printers introduced, omitted, or changed the texts of the prayers, often leaving mistakes.[24]

In order to reinstate the correct wording of the Ashkenazic ritual and at the same time to delete mystic material which crept into the ritual, *Wolf Heidenheim* (1757–1832) undertook the publication of a grammatically correct text according to the original pre-censored prayer-book and Mahzor with a commentary, scientific notes, and a translation in modern German (Roedelheim, 1800–5, 1812). His prayer-book passed through more than one hundred and forty editions.

L. Landshuth (1817–87) proceeded along the same lines in publishing the *Siddur* with annotations called *Hegyon lev* (Koenigsberg, 1845) and the "Haggada" with a scientific introduction concerning the sources, etc. (Berlin, 1855).

S. Baer (1825–97) took over Heidenheim's work and, utilizing his notes in MS., he edited the painstaking work — *Avodath Israel* (Roedelheim, 1868). The work contains the texts of the prayers for the cycle of the year, the "piyyut" for the distinguished Sabbaths, *Zemiroth*, and *Selihoth* for Fast-days, and psalms. These are also provided with notes, giving the sources and comparative studies of the texts according to different rituals and MSS., including also an exact explanation of the prayers and poems. Heidenheim's as well as Baer's editions became the standard prayer-books for the Orthodox Ashkenazic congregations in Central and Western Europe.

In 1914, a kind of opus magnum of the *Siddur* was published by Rom in Wilna under the title of *Otzar Hatefilloth — Thesaurus of Prayers*. Several scholars collaborated in this work. MSS. and old prints of prayer-codes and commentaries, scientific and mystic notes and comparative textual studies run along together with Midrashic and homiletical interpolations, containing also meditations and hymns and petitions from the Talmudic literature down to the works of the Hasidic Rabbi Elimelech of Lizansk (died 1786) which had hitherto never been incorporated into the *Siddur*. The work embodies a wealth of liturgic material. It was published in two editions: the Polish-Ashkenazic ritual, and the Hasidic-Sephardic ritual.

Though the first compilation of the ritual contains the prayers for the complete year, yet gradually some rituals for special occasions were singled out and edited separately. Thus, the "Haggada" for Passover evening was greatly embellished (see Sarayevo and Prague Haggadas), furnished with commentaries, and edited separately. The "Kinoth" for the Ninth of Av (only the Ashkenazic ritual) and the "Selihoth" of the same ritual were likewise separately edited. The Sephardic ritual has a separate compilation of prayers for the four Fast-days, the Tenth of Teveth, the Thirteenth of Adar, the Seventeenth of Tammuz, and the Ninth of Av. Through the Kabbalistic influence, orders — *Tikkunim* — for *Shavuoth* and *Hoshana Rabba* nights, and midnight meditations — *tikkun hatzoth* — these and many more customs came in and were likewise edited in separate books.

Translations. With thc cxception of a few prayers which were in Aramaic, the prayers were written and used in Hebrew. However, since many people and especially women did not understand Hebrew, the prayer-book has been translated in several languages. The Roman ritual has been translated into Italian with Hebrew characters in Bologna in 1538, into Spanish in Ferrara in the year 1552, into Judeo-German by Elijah Levita in Mantua in 1562, into Portuguese for the use of the Marranos in Amsterdam in 1617, into French by M. Ventura in Nice in 1772–3; into Dutch in 1791–3, into modern German with Hebrew characters by David Friedlander in 1786, by W. Heidenheim in 1800–12, and by M. Sachs in 1846; into English first by Isaac Pinto in New York in 1786. The most popular English translation of the Ashkenazic ritual is that by S. Singer in 1891, the "Mahzor" being the translation of A. Davis and M. Adler in 1901–4. The first English translation of the Portuguese ritual was done by A. Alexander in 1771–7; later in 1826 another translation by S. H. Jackson was published in New York and in 1837 by I. Leeser in Philadelphia. The best translation of the Portuguese ritual is that by A. de Sola (London, 1836–8); it was revised by M. Gaster and published in 1901–4. There are also translations into Hungarian by M. Rosenthal and M. Bloch (Pressburg, 1841), into Danish by A. A. Wolf (Copenhagen, 1845), into Polish by H.

Liebkind (Warsaw, 1846), into Bohemian (Vienna, 1847), into Mahrati (Bombay, 1859), into Roumanian (Bucharest, 1868), into Russian by J. Hurwitz (Wilna, 1870) and by A. Wahl (Wilna, 1880), into Croatian by Caro Schwarz (Agram, 1902). The "Haggada" was translated into many languages into Arabic with Hebrew characters and into English according to the Bagdad custom (Jerusalem, 1899). A *Siddur* was published in Bagdad in 1885 with an Arabic translation.

LITERATURE. In addition to the sources in the *Mishna*, *Tosefta*, *Sifré*, *Sifra*, *Mechilta*, *the Pesiktas*, the Babylonian and Palestinian *Talmuds*, the Midrashic literature, the Gaonic writings like the *She'eloth Rabbi Ahai*, the *Halachoth Gedoloth* of Jehudai Gaon and others — in addition to all these sources, an extensive literature has been created dealing with the liturgy and its regulations. Here we shall but mention the most important works hitherto compiled:

Hammanhig — The Guide — by Abraham b. Nathan of Lunel who is known as *Hayyarhi* (Lunel) of Provence was written in Toledo about 1205. The author traveled through Northern France and Spain, and he describes in his work the liturgical customs of the countries he visited. In addition, he quotes Talmudic and Gaonic sources. His work was greatly changed and abbreviated, and then printed. The Lemberg edition of 1858 is used here.

Rokeach — Pharmacist — by Eleazar b. Juda of Worms (1176–1238) deals with ethics, piety, and ritualistic laws, as well as with the liturgy and its high religious values; it is based upon the Talmudic literature. The author follows the Southwestern German tradition.[25] The Warsaw edition of 1880 is used here.

Tashbetz is a collection of decisions and customs as given by Meyir of Rothenberg; it was compiled by his disciple Simson b. Zadok about 1293. This work deals with the Ashkenazic ritual.

Shibole Haleket — Gleanings — by Zidkia b. Abraham of the thirteenth century in Italy describes the ritualistic customs of Italy and its surroundings.

Abudraham by David b. Joseph Abudraham or Abudrahim of Seville describes the Spanish ritual, giving many Talmudic quotations, and describes also the *Siddur Rav Amram*. He compiled his book in 1340, and it was first printed in Lisbon in 1489. The Warsaw edition of 1877 is used here.

Orhoth Hayyim — The Ways of Life — is the work of Aaron b. Jacob of Narbonne of the fourteenth century. Expelled from his native country, he wrote his work in Majorca. The first part of his book he devoted to the ritual. The chief value of his work lies in that it contains rich material of older sources, especially of those parts of the *Sefer Haitim* which were lost.

Col-bo — All Within It — by Shemaria b. Simha is a similar compilation. It deals with the Ashkenazic ritual; since the sixteenth century, it has been abbreviated. The edition used here is that of Venice, 1547.

Maharil embodies the customs as taught by Rabbi Jacob b. Moses Mollin (1356–1427); it was compiled by his disciples. This work contains thc ritualistic customs of the Ashkenazim. It also refers to the tunes for the various holidays. The Warsaw edition of 1874 is used here.

Haminhagim — The Customs — by Isaac Tyrna of Vienna (fourteenth century) describes the ritualistic customs of Austria, Hungary, Steiermark, and Moravia.

Turim — Rows — were compiled by Jacob b. Asher of Germany (1283–1340) who, together with his father and family, escaped persecution and settled in Spain. The first of the four parts of this code of rabbinic law contains regulations pertaining to the liturgy.

Shulhan Aruch — The Prepared Table — is based upon the *Turim* but contains additional decisions; it was compiled by Joseph Caro (1488–1575). This work considers the Sephardic as well as the Ashkenazic rituals. The latest additions to the first part were incorporated in the *Magine Eretz* by Abraham Abele Levy (1635–83).

Tzeda Laderech — Provisions for the Road — is the work of Menahem b. Zarah (died in 1385 in Toledo, Spain). He was born in Narbonne. As he states in his introduction, he wrote his work "for rich Jews who associate with princes and who, as a result of their high station and their intercourse with the non-Jewish world, are not over-rigorous with regard to the Jewish regulations" (*J.Enc.*, Vol. VIII, p. 466). The author sought to emphasize the ethical phase of the Law. He was not satisfied with stating the regulations merely. He also tried to give reasons for them. Deficient as the work is as a code, the author has succeeded remarkably well in bringing to light the religious elements of Jewish ceremonies (*l.c.*). In the first chapter, he discusses the liturgy. In the first edition of the book (Ferrara, 1554, p. 35b — used here), he discusses at length the twelfth benediction of the Amida — *Birchath hamminim* — and gives the reason for its composition. This whole paragraph was omitted in the later editions.

Matte Moshe — The Staff of Moses — is the work of Moses b. Abraham of Przemysl (sixteenth century), a disciple of Solomon Luria; it was first printed in Cracow, 1591. This work gives the Polish ritual, and quotes a great deal from the works hitherto mentioned. The edition used here is that of Warsaw, 1876.

Seder Hayyom — The Order of the Day — is the work of Moses b. Machir, principle of the Talmud School in Ain Zetun, near Safed in Palestine. He lived in the second half of the sixteenth century, and his work was first printed in 1599. This work is influenced greatly by the Kabbala of Luria. The Warsaw edition of 1876 is used here.

Pathora Dĕabba contains a selection of the customs established by Isaac Luria; it was printed in Jerusalem in 1905.

Aside from the works which contain descriptions of the liturgy in general, or deal with the ritual of various countries, there are works which give the local ritual of old communities, such as Frankfurt a/m.

Yosef Ometz is the work of Joseph Han Nordlingen (1570–1637). He finished it in 1630; it was first printed in 1723, and a revised edition appeared in 1928.

Noheg Katzon Yosef is the work of Joseph Kosman, a descendant of Joseph Han Nordlingen. This work was published in Hanau in 1718.

Divre Kehilloth is the work of Salman b. Aaron Michel Geiger, a brother of Abraham Geiger (1792–1865); it was published in Frankfurt a/m in 1862. A detailed description of the Frankfurt ritual is given in this book.

There is also the Fürth-Nurnberg ritual by Israel and Kopil b. Gumpil which was published in Fürth in 1797.

Scientific Works. 1. Wolf Heidenheim (1757–1832) was the first who started to work in the field of Jewish liturgy from a scientific point of view. His achievements are described above.

2. Solomon L. Rappoport (1785–1868) contributed valuable material in his scholarly essays in Hebrew on Kallir and other poets, and in his *Erech Millin*.

3. Leopold Zunz (1794–1886) was the pioneer in liturgical research, as well as in many other fields of Hebrew literature and history. In his works: *Vorträge des jüdischen Gottesdienstes*, 1832 (second revised and enlarged edition appeared in 1892), *Synagoggale Poesie des Mittelalters*, 1855 (second enlarged edition appeared in 1920, A. Freimann), *Ritus*, 1858, *Literaturgeschichte der Synagogalen Poesie*, 1865, and in his *Nachträge*, 1868, he discovered the paths to these hidden treasures.

4. Samuel David Luzzatto (1800–65) rendered great service by his researches into various rituals and Synagogue-poetry.

5. M. Sachs (1808–64) wrote *Die religiöse Poesie der Spanischen Juden*, 1846.

6. L. Landshuth (1817–87) rendered great service through his publications mentioned above and especially through his *Amudè Haavoda* — an alphabetical encyclopedia of the liturgical authors and poets.

7. Abraham Berliner (1833–1915) published besides several researches *Randbemerkungen zum täglichen Gebet*, Vol. I, Berlin, 1909; II, 1912.

8. Lewis N. Dembitz (1833–1911) compiled a work on *Jewish Services in Synagogue and Home*, 1898.

9. Israel Abrahams (1858–1927) wrote *Historical and Explanatory Notes*, 1914, and several essays.

10. Israel Davidson (1870–) has published, besides several studies, the *Otzar Hashira Wehappiyut* — "A Concordance of the Synagogue-Poetry"; it is in three volumes, and was published in the years 1925–31.

11. Ismar Elbogen (1874–) published several studies: *Das Achzehn Gebet*, *Studien zur Geschichte des jüdischen Got-*

tesdienstes, 1907, and the work Der *jüdische Gottesdienst in seiner geschichtlichen Entwickelung*, 1913.

12. *The Jewish Encyclopedia*, articles, liturgy, piyyut, prayer, prayer-books, Selicha, and several other subjects.

Furthermore, Hamburger's *Real Encyclopedia*, the proceedings of *The Revue des études Juives*, of the *Monatsschrift fuer die Wissenschaft des Judentums*, and of the *Jewish Quarterly Review*, Eisenstein's *Otzar dinim uminhagim*, and of the *Encyclopedia Judaica*, contains rich material on liturgy.

PART II

DESCRIPTION OF THE LITURGY

CHAPTER VIII

DAILY PUBLIC PRAYERS

The Jew prays not only on holidays, the Sabbath, and special occasions, but is also advised to strengthen himself with meditations and prayer three times each day to meet his daily tasks with firmness and courage.

I. The Daily Morning Service

Shaharith (from *shahar* — dawn) consists of the following sections:[1]

A. *Birchoth hashahar* — Morning Benedictions. The Morning Benedictions were arranged to be recited when the Jew rises in the morning, and were intended as home meditations. They consist of thanksgivings for the benefits God bestoweth upon us. Among the selections are fine ethical and social precepts and a concise declaration of the elementary ideas of Judaism, such as the unity of God who is the creator and ruler of the world, who guides man's destiny, and of the immortality of the soul. In them Israel thanks God for the privilege He has bestowed upon him to study the holy teachings. The texts are drawn especially from the *Mishna* and *Talmud* where several of them are recorded as the private meditations of prominent men.

This section was inserted in some rituals into the public service, while in others they remained as home worship.

This section contains the following paragraphs:

1. *Waani berov hasdecha* — Psalm 5:8 is recited upon entering the synagogue. The verse has ten words with which the required ten men for a public service should be counted.[2] Then there follows the verse: "Into the house of God we will walk with the throng (or with fear)," Psalm 55:15. This passage was introduced by I. Luria.[3]

2. *Ma tovu* consists of Numbers 24:5; Psalms 5:8; 26:8; 95:6; 69:14. The first verse is given in M.V. to be recited on

entering the synagogue. The interpretation of "How goodly are thy tents, O Jacob" to imply "the house of worship" goes back to b. Sanhedrin 105b. The phrase: "Let my prayer be unto Thee, O Lord, *in an acceptable time*" is explained in the *Talmud* (b. Ber. 8a) to be the proper time for public worship. The verse of Psalm 95:6 is reshaped from the plural to the singular form.

3. In older editions of the prayer-book there are also inserted at this point the following: *ani kerathicha* — a compilation of psalm-verses; *shahar avakeshcha* — a poem by Solomon b. Gabirol; and *hashti welo hith'mahmahti* — another poem by Hayyim (see S. Baer, pp. 33–34). There is also the standard hymn *Adon olam* which glorifies the supremacy of God, His Omnipotence and Providence. The author of this hymn remains unknown; but it was probably composed in the twelfth century. The poem shows Arabic meter (see Chapter V) and the style of the Spanish-Hebrew poetry. Since the fifteenth century it has been inserted in the beginning of the morning service.[4]

4. *Yigdal* — This equally outstanding hymn is ascribed to Daniel b. Juda of Rome who lived in the first half of the fourteenth century. It is based upon Maimonides' thirteen principles of faith. The Sephardic ritual has at the end of this hymn an additional line: "These are the thirteen principles of faith; they are the foundation of the divine faith and of God's Law." This hymn too is based upon the Arabic meter (see Chapter V). Though all rituals have these two hymns, only the Ashkenazic uses them for the daily service. The Sephardic, Italian, and Yemenite rituals conclude the Friday evening service with Yigdal and the Saturday morning service with Adon olam.

5. *Baruch . . . al netilath yadayim* — a blessing for the commandment of washing the hands (b. Ber. 60b).

6. *Asher yatzar* — a blessing over the physical health of the body (b. Ber. 60b).

7. *Laasok bedivrê thora* — a thanksgiving for the commandment to study the holy teachings. The Sephardic ritual has *al divre thora* (b. Ber. 11b, given in the name of Samuel of the third century).

8. *Wĕhaarev* — a prayer that the holy teachings may remain with us and with our offspring (*l.c.*, in the name of Rabbi Hamnuna of the fourth century).

9. *Baruch . . . asher bahar banu* (*l.c.*). In this benediction we have a notable reference to Israel as a chosen people. Israel is called to a special service, to testify to God's truth by its own example and by its message to the world (Abrahams).

10. *Yĕvarechĕcha* — the Priestly Benediction from Numbers 6:24–26.

11. *Elu devarim* — a paragraph composed of M. Peah I and b. Sabbath 127. In this passage various forms of charity, as well as social and religious well-doings are quoted — all being superseded by the study of the Tora.

Passages 7–11 are recited in accordance with a Talmudic injunction which enjoins everyone to read each day some passages from the Scriptures, the *Mishna*, and the *Baraitha* — all to be preceded by the benediction over the study of Tora. The readings were instituted in France (*Tosefoth* to b. Ber. 11b). In the Sephardic and Italian rituals these paragraphs are read after *laasok bedivrê thora;* they follow the S.R.A.

12. *Elohay* — a thanksgiving for the return of the soul to the body. The passage asserts also the belief in the immortality of the soul (b. Ber. 60b).

13. Here follow a series of fifteen blessings which extol God for His wondrous works and benefactions to man in general and to the Jewish people in particular. The benedictions have the short form (see above, Introductory notes; with exception of the fourteenth benediction, they are all taken from b. Ber. 60b).

Benediction 1: "Blessed . . . Who hast given intelligence to the cock to distinguish between day and night." This text is based upon Job 38:36.

Benediction 2: " . . . Who has not made me a heathen," or rather "belonging to another nation" — *goy* instead of *nachri*, which means "a stranger." [5]

Benediction 3: " . . . Who hast not made me a bondsman."

Benediction 4: " . . . Who hast not made me a woman."

These benedictions imply that non-Israelites, slaves, and women are not commanded to observe all the religious duties. They are the special privileges of the male Jew. For the second benediction the Sephardic ritual has *sheasani yisrael* . . . "Who hast made me an Israelite." The recitation of the three last benedictions is attributed to Rabbi Meyir (b. Men. 43b).

For benediction 3, Jer. Ber. IX, 2 has " . . . Who hast not made me an ignoramus."

Instead of benediction 4, women say " . . . Who hast made me according to His will." It is first mentioned in Abudarham of the fourteenth century.

Benediction 14: " . . . Who givest strength to the weary" is mentioned neither in the *Talmud* nor in the S.R.A. nor by Saadya, but in M.V., p. 57.

S.R.A. and Saadya give several more benedictions.[6] The Italian ritual retained but one benediction: " . . . Who raisest up the lowly."

14. *Wihi ratzon mil'fanecha* — a prayer that God keep us away from all evil influences and that He help us to subdue our evil inclinations and to do good deeds only (b. Ber. 60b). This prayer appears in the *Talmud* in the singular, but was changed to the plural form.

15. *Yehi ratzon* is similar in content to the previous prayer. It was the meditation of Rabbi Juda the Prince (b. Ber. 16b). This prayer was changed from the plural to the singular.

16. *Leolam* is an introduction to the following paragraph. Abrahams writes that "it is an exhortation for inward righteousness and was taken from *Tana debê Eliyahu Rabba*, chapter 21." The passage is given in S.R.A.

The original wording of this passage was *bassêser*. It is a reference to the periods of persecution when the open profession of Judaism was interdicted. It has been suggested that this passage was introduced about 452 in Babylonia. At that time the Persian king Jesdigird II issued a prohibition against the worship of any deity of a monotheistic nature. This decree came as a hard blow to the Jews. Special government officials were posted in the synagogues to watch the services. The recitation of "Shema" and the "Kedusha" was especially interdicted. Five years later the king died and his order was nullified. Since the Jews could not give free expression to the principles of their faith during that period, the spiritual leaders ordered the people to recite the phrase mentioned above. The "Shema" was reduced to but the first sentence and was placed at the beginning of the service to be recited before the arrival of the officials, while the "Kedusha" was placed in *uva letziyon* at the end of the service. On Sabbaths and holidays the first sentence of the "Shema" was repeated in the Musaf and was to be recited after the officials left the synagogue. This peculiar arrangement was retained even after the law was annulled, as a remembrance of troubled times. The shema, however, was retained here for other reasons. On some holidays or Sabbaths many insertions in the morning service cause a delay, so that when the congregation comes to the Shema in its proper place the time limited for its recitation (up to four hours after sunrise) is already passed (compare O. Ha., p. 138; Tikkun Tefilla).

17. *Ribbon col haôlomim.* The text of this paragraph is partly from b. Yoma 87a and partly from the Ne'ila service of the Day of Atonement. The end passage is taken from Ecclesiastes, 3:19. Here the problem of reward and punishment is paramount. In the Sephardic ritual there occurs the phrase "except that the pure soul which must hereafter give an account when in judgment before the throne of Thy glory" and Isaiah 40:15.

18. *Aval anahnu* is a passage from *Mechilta* on Exodus XV, 19.

19. *Lefichach anahnu* is a continuation of 18. A similar paragraph is found in the "Haggada" for Passover (M. Pes. X, 5).

20. *Shema.* The first verse of the "Shema," being the "Shema" of Rabbi Juda the Prince (b. Ber. 13b), is read in this place for fear lest by the time the congregation reaches the "Shema" in the service the time limit for its recitation shall have passed. Some rituals add the first paragraph (*Otzar Hatefilloth*, p. 145; see above).

21. *Atta hu ad . . .* is taken from the *Yalkut*[7] "as a eulogy uttered by the heavenly hosts" (Abrahams). Its content is a declaration of God's dominion and of the hope that He will sanctify His name throughout the world. For "when God

beholds the peoples of the earth indulge in pleasures while the sanctuary is destroyed, He is ready to destroy the whole world. But as soon as Israel breaks forth with the proclamation of 'Shema,' the angels respond with *atta hu ad shelo nivra*, etc. This pleases God and He decides to retain the creation of the world for the sake of Israel's 'Shema' and the angels' hymn."

22. *Atta hu* is a compilation of Biblical verses according to Jeremiah 14:22; Isaiah 44:6, 11:12; II Kings 19:15. The phrase "Our Father in heaven" is found in M. Avoth V, 23 and in b. Sota 49b. M.V., p. 61, has several more verses.

With the exception of the Ashkenazic ritual, Genesis 22 which recounts the story of Isaac's sacrifice is recited in all rituals in the morning benedictions. This custom was recommended by the *Zohar* "that it may protect Israel from all trouble." Isaac Luria and his school introduced this reading (see *Otzar Hatefilloth*, p. 135; *Seder Hayyom*, Morning Prayer).

B. *Korbanôth* — SACRIFICES. This section is composed of Biblical and Talmudic paragraphs which describe the rules and regulations pertaining to the sacrifices offered at the Temple in Jerusalem. After the Destruction, the sacrificial cult ceased in Israel. The people at large who believed that offerings were imperative for their salvation were in despair. "Woe unto us," lamented Rabbi Joshua b. Hananya, "that the place in which the sins of Israel were atoned is destroyed!" Whereupon Rabbi Johanan answered, "My son, do not worry. We have an atonement which is its equal. This is charity to the poor and whoever prays three times a day." Rabbi Simeon said, "The sayings of the Law are more precious to me than sacrifices" (Aboth de Rabbi Nathan IV); while Rabbi Eliezer said, "Prayer is greater than sacrifices" (b. Ber. 32b). Compare Chapters III–IV.

However, this view of the few could not convince the majority which had been trained for centuries in the idea that only sacrifices can atone. Consequently a ruling was issued to the effect that whoever read the Biblical and Talmudic portions dealing with the sacrifices is considered as though he himself had brought sacrifices (b. Menahoth 110a; Meg. 31a; Taanith 27b; *Tanhuma*, Tzav; *Pesikta* R. Kahana § 6; Bamidbar Rabba 18).

The portions read are as follows:

Numbers 28:1–8; in the Sephardic ritual Numbers 28:1–10. Some rituals have also Exodus 30:1–21 and Leviticus 6:1–6, 11.

Numbers 28:9–10 is recited on Sabbaths.

Numbers 28:11–15 is recited on the New Month.

M. Zevahim V. In some rituals B. Kerithuth 6a; Jer. Yoma IV, 5 are recited.

Sifra I. This passage deals with the thirteen principles according to which Talmudic discussions are conducted.

Another reason for reciting the portions dealing with the sacrifices is that they are parts of the Bible and the Talmud which everyone is enjoined to study each day (b. Kidushin 30a).

In this arrangement, the paragraphs dealing with the spices are recited first; then follow those pertaining to the daily offerings — according to the *Zohar*, Wayakhel.

In addition to these passages, the Italian ritual has M. Ber. I, 1, including also some passages from b. Ber. 1. It also embodies the Confession (Widdui) and a meditation composed of several Biblical verses and Talmudic prayers. Then there follows a compilation of Biblical verses by Nachmanides, representing the Name of seventy-two letters according to Kabbalistic doctrines.

The *tzitzith* (fringes) and *tefillin* (phylacteries or frontlets) are put on before the morning service. In some rituals they are put on before the morning benedictions; in others before "The Verses of Song." In some places it was customary to put them on at home and then walk to the synagogue. According to M.V., p. 64, they have to be put on before *yishtabbah*. The *Talmud* says that whoever recites "Shema" without wearing the frontlets is as though he testified falsely (b. Ber. 14b), because it is written "and they shall be as a sign upon your hand and as frontlets between your eyes." However, of Rav it is reported that he recited "Shema" without the frontlets and that he put them on before the "Amida" (*l.c.*). From this passage, the *Tosafoth* (*l.c.*) draws the conclusion that one may recite the "Shema" without the phylacteries and the fringed mantel — *tallith*.[8] S.R.A. has the benedictions for these ceremonials in the morning benedictions.

Baruch . . . lehithattef batzitzith — ". . . to wrap oneself in the fringed mantle" is given in b. Men. 43a.

As a result of Kabbalistic influence, the meditations *hineni mithattef*, *ma yakar*, Psalm 36 : 8–11, and *yehi ratzon* were introduced. The first meditation is quoted in the *Siddur* of Isaiah Horowitz (1555–1630); the second was inserted by Nathan Shapiro of Cracow (died 1633); and the third was first printed in N. Hannover's *Shaare Tzion*, 1662.[9]

Already in the second century some mystic meanings were read into the custom of wearing fringes. Rabbi Meyir said that the fringes are of blue — the Biblical *tĕcheleth* — "because blue resembles the sea; the sea resembles the sky; and the sky resembles the 'Seat of Glory'" (b. Men. 43b).

Baruch . . . lehaniah tefillin is the blessing over the phylactery to be put on the hand, and

Baruch . . . al mitzwathtefillin is the blessing over the phylactery to be put on the head (60b).

The meditation connected with that ceremony is taken from Horowitz's *Siddur* mentioned above. The three sentences from Hosea 2 : 21–22 were introduced by N. Shapiro, and the meditation is copied from the *Shaare Tziyon*. The recitation of the sentences from Hosea symbolizes that "the phylacteries are compared to the bridal garland, a symbol of the devotion and affection which exist between Israel and God" (Abrahams). On the mystic meaning of these and similar meditations see Chapter VI above.

Tefillin are put on for the morning service on weekdays only, because Sabbaths and festivals are symbols in themselves (b. Eruvin 96a, O.H. p. 31, 1), while Tzitzith are worn every day of the year.

C. *Pesuke dezimra* — Verses of Song. This section comprises a selection of hymns and praises from the Psalms and from other parts of the Bible. The recitation of praises was introduced before the prayer proper in keeping with the Talmudic statement that praises ought to precede prayer, as quoted above.

The Verses of Song are ushered in with a benediction:

Baruch sheamar — This benediction occurs in various rituals with different variations.[10] The number of words in this benediction was set at eighty-seven which number is in Hebrew letters *paz* — meaning "refined gold." [11] This benediction does not occur in the *Talmud*. Moses Gaon was the first who mentioned it (about 820) and it is found in S.R.A. In Saadya's

Siddur its wording is identical with that of the Yemenite ritual,[12] and is assigned for Sabbaths only. There are indications that this benediction was composed as a hymn, each line having the refrain *baruch hu* which used to be sung responsively by the precentor and congregation. At least, it was sung that way in the tenth century at the celebration of the inauguration of the Exilarch in Babylonia.[13] In the Persian ritual, this benediction is arranged according to the alphabetical acrostic.[14]

Hodu — during the morning sacrifice at the Temple, I Chronicles 16:8–22 used to be recited, and during the evening sacrifice, I Chronicles 16:23–36 was chanted (*Seder Olam Rabba*, Chap. 14; *Hamanhig*, Tefilla 2; *Col-Bo*, Venice, 1547, 1b). These passages were transferred to the Synagogue for the morning service to be recited in connection with the "Korbanoth" before "Baruch sheamar," as in S.R.A. 27a, and as it is customary in the Sephardic and Italian rituals. The Ashkenazic ritual has these passages read after the benediction "Baruch sheamar," because they belong to the "Verses of Song," (*Hamanhig*, Tefilla 19; Tur., *l.c.*).

Later several more verses from the Book of Psalms were added to this paragraph: Psalm 95:5, 9; 78:38; 40:12; 25:6; 68:35–36; 94:1–2; 3:9; 20:10; 28:9; 33:21–22; 85:8; 44:27; 81:11; 144:15; 13:6; 46:8, and 84:13.

Of the last two verses the sages said that they ought never to be removed from one's lips. This selection was not recited on weekdays (S.R.A.). Saadya, on the other hand, assigned "Baruch sheamar" for Sabbaths and festivals,[15] while *Hamanhig* (*l.c.*) says that according to the French ritual it is recited on weekdays as well as on Sabbaths.

Since the seventeenth century, Psalm 30 has been introduced into the Polish ritual to be recited before "Baruch sheamar." It was apparently taken over from the Sephardic ritual where the psalm is designated for Hanucca.

The passages of I Chronicles 16:8–22 and verses 23–30 are to be found with slight variations in Psalms 105:1–15 and in 96:1–9.

Mizmor lethoda, which is Psalm 100 is inserted because it is reminiscent of the thank-offering. "All songs will be annulled save this one." Because it refers to thank-offerings, it was not chanted in some places on Sabbaths (M.V., p. 62). However, S.R.A. 27a gives it for Sabbath, while others recited the psalm on Sabbaths only (*Shibbole Halleket*, § 76). *Rokeah* § 319 says that it used to be recited both on weekdays and Sabbaths, save that on Sabbaths the first two words were omitted. The Sephardic ritual has this psalm for both Sabbaths and weekdays.

"The appropriateness of the Psalm for daily worship is unquestionable, and its wide universalism has led to its general introduction into the daily worship," because "the service of gratitude is eternal. As the Rabbis said (Wayikra Rabba, Chap. 9), though in the time to come all sacrifices will cease, the thank-offering will never cease. In the Messianic era there will be no sin; consequently, no sorrow and no suffering. But the thank-offering will last on." "People will think less of what they lack; more of what they have. No wonder then that this Psalm became one of the most favorite in both Synagogue and Church" (Abrahams).

In the selection of psalms there is a difference between Sabbaths, festivals, and weekdays. According to Abudraham, twelve psalms are added for Sabbath. These psalms must have the contents of the creation of the world and of the Tora which was given on Sabbath. In order to honor the festivals, the same psalms are recited (*Col-Bo* 39b). The rituals vary slightly in the choice of psalms.

The following are common in all rituals:

Yehi chevod — a compilation of Scriptural verses mentioned in T. Soferim, Chap. 17 end. These verses are Psalms 104: 31; 113: 2–4; 135: 13; 103: 19; I Chronicles 16: 31. The phrase *adonai melech* is mentioned in T. Soferim, Chap. XIV, 8 and in *Hechaloth*. It is composed of Psalms 10: 16; 92: 1; Exodus 15: 18; Psalms 10: 16; 33: 10; Proverbs 19: 21; Psalms 33: 11; 33: 9; 132: 13; 135: 4; 94: 14; 78: 38; 20: 10. In addition to these verses the Yemenite ritual has Psalm 46: 12. This verse completes the five books of the Psalms out of which the compilation is made.

Ashrê is Psalm 145. The *Talmud* makes the assertion that "whoever recites this Psalm three times a day is assured of his part in the world to come, because it contains the verse 'Thou openest Thine hand, and satisfiest every living thing with favor'" (b. Ber. 4b). For this reason, two verses, Psalms 84:5 and 144:15, precede the psalm in which the *ashrê* occurs three times. The psalm is an alphabetic acrostic of which the letter "nun" is missing. It has been commented upon in the *Talmud* (*l.c.*).

Halleluya — Psalms 146–150. According to b. Sabbath 118b, Rabbi Yose says that the reason for reciting these psalms is that they conclude the Book of Psalms, and "may my portion be with those who finish the praise" (i.e., the Book of Praise—The Psalms). "The Halleluya Psalms were well chosen with their expression of putting trust in God and not in men, their elevation of moral over physical strength, yet withal with wholehearted admiration for the wonders of nature which are summoned to join in the diapason of praise — and finally the universal full-toned call to jubilant praise with which the Psalter ends" (Abrahams).

Baruch adonai leôlom — These verses are taken from Psalms 89:53; 135:21, and 72:18–19. They are the concluding verses in these psalms.

Wayvarech dawid is taken from I Chronicles 29:10–23 and from Nehemiah 9:6–11.

Wayyosha is from Exodus 14:30–31.

Az yashir is from Exodus 15:1–18; Psalm 22:29; Obadiah 1:21; Zecheriah 14:9; and Deuteronomy 6:4.

These selections have been introduced since Gaonic times.[16] Maimonides places the Song of the Sea after the concluding benediction *yishtabbah;* others, however, were of the opinion that no interruption is permissible between the Verses of Song and the Yotzer (S.R.A. 3a).

Originally the Song of the Sea was chanted in the Temple by the Levites during the Sabbath Minha sacrifice; it was divided into two parts (b. Rosh Hashana 31a). The reason for its introduction into the daily service was that the people remember the Exodus from Egypt (*Hamanhig* I, 24; Abudraham; M.V., p. 226).

On the day when a circumcision is to be performed, the Mohel chants responsively with the congregation in the synagogue from *wecharoth* up to the end of the Song of the Sea.

For the Ninth of Av the Sephardic ritual has Deuteronomy 32 instead of Exodus 15. In the twelfth century this was customary in both Palestine and Babylonia (*Hamanhig*, *l.c.*; M.V., *l.c.*).

Yishtabbah — This concluding benediction follows the Verses of Song. It is similar in style to the opening benediction. Both these benedictions are similar in style to the *bircath hashir* for Hallel (b. Pes. 118a). Some want to find in the initial letters of the second, third, fourth, and fifth words the acrostic of *shelomo* as being the name of the author of the benediction.

Sections A, B, and C do not necessarily belong to the public service; they may be recited privately without the required quorum of ten male adults.

Kaddish — The Doxology is recited after the Verses of Song. The recitation of Kaddish in the liturgy marks the conclusion of one of the sections. The Kaddish occurs in five different forms and serves as many purposes.

1. The half-Kaddish — *hatzi Kaddish* — has but two paragraphs and one response:

> I. Magnified and sanctified be His great Name in the world which He hath created according to His will. May He establish His kingdom during your life and during your days, and during the life of all the house of Israel, even speedily and at a near time, and say ye: (Congregation) Amen.
>
> II. Blessed, praised, and glorified, exalted, extolled, and honored, magnified and lauded be the Name of the Holy One, blessed be He; though He be high above all the blessings and hymns, praises and consolations which are uttered in the world; and say ye: (Congregation) Amen.

This form is used only between the sections of the liturgy.

2. The full-Kaddish — *Kaddish shalem*, *tithkabbal* — is recited by the reader after the conclusion of the main parts of each service. The full-Kaddish consists of additional three paragraphs.

> III. May the prayers and supplications of all Israel be accepted by their Father Who is in heaven; and say ye: (Congregation) Amen.
>
> IV. May there be abundant peace from heaven, and life for us and for all Israel; and say ye: (Congregation) Amen.

V. He Who maketh peace in His high places, may He make peace for us and for all Israel; and say ye: (Congregation) Amen (Singer's *Prayer-Book*, pp. 75–76).

3. The orphan's Kaddish — *Kaddish yathom* — is recited by mourners during the first eleven months, and then at each recurring anniversary of the death; it is recited after the service proper and after the Adoration. This Kaddish consists of paragraphs I, II, IV, and V.

4. The rabbinical-Kaddish — *Kaddish derabbanan* — is recited after the study or recitation of Talmudic literature, as the section of the sacrifices. It consists of I, II, and then there follows:

III. Unto Israel and unto the Rabbis and unto their disciples and unto all the disciples of their disciples, and unto all who engage in the study of the Law, in this or in any other place, unto them and unto you be abundant peace, grace, lovingkindness, mercy, long life, ample sustenance, and salvation from the Father Who is in heaven, and say ye: (Congregation) Amen (*o.c.*, p. 86).

After this, there follow paragraphs IV and V.

5. The Kaddish of Renewal — *Kaddish lĕithhadatha* — is used at funerals only by the mourners after the burial. It runs:

I. May His great Name be magnified and sanctified in the world that is to be created anew, where He will quicken the dead, and raise them up unto life eternal; will rebuild the city of Jerusalem and establish the Temple in the midst thereof; and will uproot the alien worship from the earth and restore the worship of the true God. O may the Holy One, blessed be He, reign in His sovereignty and glory during your life . . . (*o.c.*, p. 321).

This ends with the conclusion of paragraph I, and then there follow paragraphs II, IV, and V.

"Originally, it (the Kaddish) had no relation whatsoever to the prayers, and still less to the dead. It was the doxology recited by the teacher or preacher at the close of his discourse, when he was expected to dismiss the assembly with an allusion to the Messianic hope, derived especially from the Prophets and the Psalms" (Kohler). The language is Hebrew-Aramaic, the vernacular used by the Jews in Palestine during the period of the Second Temple.

In the four forms of the Kaddish there is nothing to indicate its use in the Memorial Service; [17] only in the fifth form is there a reference to the resurrection of the dead in paragraph I.

The Kaddish has as its underlying thought the hope of redemption for mankind and the sanctification of God's Name throughout the world. These ideas were so close to the hearts of the oppressed Jews in all parts of the world that they gradually began to recite the Kaddish upon occasions of personal or national distress. Whenever a member of a family died, the Kaddish was recited as a source of consolation, since it announces that God will redeem and console the whole house of Israel, yea, the whole world.

The Kaddish became a great bulwark which strengthened Judaism in the heart of Jews. No matter how far a member of the house of Israel may have drifted away from Jewish life, the Kaddish helps to bring him back to the Jewish fold.

The Reform ritual (U.P.B.) has since 1819 another insertion for paragraph III; it was first published in the Hamburg Reform prayer-book (see Chapter XIX). It runs as follows:

> Unto Israel and unto the righteous ones and unto all those who departed from this world according to the will of God, may they find great peace and a good portion in the world to come, and grace and mercy from the Lord of heaven and earth, and say ye: (Congregation) Amen.

In the Reform ritual, Kaddish is recited only once after the service by the reader and mourners.

A quorum of ten male adults is required for the recitation of the Kaddish (T. Soferim 10: 7); this is according to the Babylonian custom. According to the Palestinian custom, seven male adults are sufficient.

The nucleus of the Kaddish was the response *yĕhe shemê rabba mevarach*, which is similar to Daniel 2 : 20 and to Psalm 113 : 2; it used to be recited after a lecture. "When Israel assembles in the houses of study to hear the Aggada from a preacher, he ought to respond afterwards *Amen*, *yĕhe shĕme rabba mevarach* (b. Ber. 3a, 21b; Shabbath 119b; S.R.A. 12b, *Yalkut* § 951).

Kaddish is first quoted in T. Soferim XVI : 12; XIX : 1; XII; 21 : 6, and originated in Palestine in the last century

B.C.E.[18] A legend about Rabbi Akiva who taught an orphan to recite the Kaddish in order to save his father from Gehenna which is found in later *Midrashim* (see M.V., p. 112) would indicate that the Kaddish came to be used by mourners about the Gaonic era.

The mourner's Kaddish is furthermore mentioned in M.V., p. 74. "The boy rises and recites the Kaddish without 'Tith-kabbal.' Whenever the congregation recites some Scriptural or Mishnaic passages, Kaddish should be said thereafter." Still, Ab. b. Hiyya (died 1136 in Barcelona) rejected the idea of a mourners' Kaddish. "They busy themselves with vain hopes who reckon that the actions and prayers of their sons would benefit them after death. This too is the opinion of all good authorities." [19]

Elyakim b. Joseph (died ca. 1150 in Mayence), called "Ravya," expresses a similar view in his notes. "It is not as generally accepted," he writes, "that through the recitation of the Kaddish the son brings his father and mother to Paradise, and that he who frequently repeats the Kaddish atones by that action for the sins of his parents and helps them to enter into the future world. For there is no foundation for the view that the Kaddish is for mourners. There is no basis for it in either the Jerusalem or the Babylonian *Talmud* or in the *Tosefta*. The only source is the legend of Rabbi Akiva, and we do not base laws upon legends. . . ." [20]

And as late as the sixteenth century Abraham Hurwitz wrote: "Let the son keep a particular precept given him by his father, and it would be of greater worth than the recitation of the Kaddish. The same is true also of daughters. For the Kaddish is not a prayer for the son that the father may be brought up from Sheol, but a recognition of the parent's merit, since through its recital the child best indicates the memory of his parent by causing the congregation to respond to him with the praise, *Amen, yehê shemê rabba.*[21]

"The custom in modern times is explained as illustrating the principle that one should praise God equally for the good and for the evil that may befall one" [22] (b. Ber. 60b). It was ordered to recite the Kaddish during the first year of mourning, because "the memory of the dead begins to grow dim in the heart when twelve months have passed away" (b. Ber. 58b). "These twelve months, perhaps due to Persian teaching in origin, also correspond with the longest period of suffering in Gehenna (b. Rosh Hashana 17a; Sanhedrin 13; Shab. 33b, 152b); and as the Kaddish was largely regarded as a prayer of intercession for the departed soul, its recital during the twelve months of mourning was later curtailed to the first eleven months so as not to cast an unworthy reflection on the parent." [23]

"The use of the mourners' Kaddish was in the course of time extended also to the anniversary of the parent's death, the 'Jahrzeit' among the German Jews, although this application of it, first found in Maharil, remained strange to the Spanish and Oriental Jews, until it was adopted through a Kabbalistic explanation given it by I. Luria. The origin of the custom is perhaps to be sought in the persecutions and massacres aroused by the fanaticism of the Crusaders when thousands of Jews met a martyr's death and whole communities . . . were wiped out. The custom then developed of holding memorial services for the martyred. From a communal mourner's service, the individual naturally passes over to an individual one." [24]

In the three public services, the Kaddish is to be recited seven times daily. The number is derived from the phrase "Seven times a day do I praise Thee," Psalm 119:164 (Baer, p. 75).

D. The Shema and Its Benedictions — *shema uvirchotheha.* With this section the main public service actually begins. During the chanting of the Verses of Song, both the congregation and reader were seated. Then one of the congregants or the official reader would rise, and, approaching the desk, would recite the half-Kaddish and invoke the congregation with the phrase: "Bless ye the Lord Who is to be blessed!" — *barĕchu.* Whereupon the congregation would respond: "Blessed is the Lord Who is to be blessed for ever and ever." This custom is recorded already in Nehemiah 9:5.

The Yemenite Jews still observe this custom in its original form, while in all other communities the reader approaches the desk with the recitation of the Verses of Song. Among the Ashkenazim the reader approaches the desk when he begins the morning benedictions.

The central part of this section is the Shema — i.e., the three paragraphs preceded by two benedictions and followed by one (M. Ber. I, 4). This section contains the main principles of the Jewish faith. 1. The unity of God (Shema), 2. The love and devotion to God (first paragraph of Shema), 3. Reward and punishment in this world (second paragraph of Shema), 4. The duty of observing His commandments (third paragraph of Shema), 5. God as the continuous Creator (Yotzer), 6. His love of Israel (Ahava), 7. God as the Redeemer and Protector of Israel (Geula).[25]

1. *Yotzer* — Creator — praises creation and presents God as the Creator of both light and darkness. This was inserted as a result of the prevalent belief of Persian dualism (Ahuramazda was god of light and goodness, Ahriman was god of darkness and evil). The first sentence of the benediction was adapted from Isaiah 45 : 7 by changing the word "evil" to "all things" (b. Ber. 11b), in order to use a more reverent expression in worship. The text relates the greatness and goodness of God. "How manifold are Thy works," etc., is taken from Psalm 104 : 24. There is also an alphabetical acrostic, each word beginning with a letter of the alphabet, beginning with *el baruch* and ending with *tamid.* It also shows the poetical meter of four accents to the line. Then there follow two paragraphs the contents of which are a poetical description of the sanctification of the angels — including two sentences of the "Sanctification" (see in E). The tradition that the angels too praise God every day is based upon the vision of Isaiah 6 and Ezekiel 3 : 12–13. This tradition has been carried on by the mystics throughout the ages. The Talmudic literature has many references, for example "When the angels desire to sing praises . . . God tells them to wait until He will hear the praises and songs of Israel in their synagogues" (*Hechaloth Rabbati*, ed. Jellinek, Leipzig III, 1855, p. 161; see also b. Hullin 91b, Hagiga 13b). *Siddur R. Amram*, 4, speaks of the high value of the Sanctification in the Yotzer benediction, pointing out that while Israel recites the Sanctification, God creates the image of Jacob and kisses it. In this paragraph too there was an alphabetical acrostic, beginning with *cullam ahuvim;* of this acrostic only a few sentences were retained in

the present ritual. In some other rituals, the acrostic runs through half of the alphabet.

The concluding paragraph speaks of God's wonderful care of human needs, especially of His creation of light. In our ritual there is a later insertion speaking of spiritual light which is to shine over Zion — which insertion Saadya opposed (S.R.A. 4b; M.V., p. 65).[26]

2. *Ahava* — Love. The second benediction praises God's love which He shows to Israel in giving them His holy Tora and laws of life. We pray that He may continue to benefit us with His love, and that He may enlighten our eyes and our minds to understand His teachings, that we shall love Him and His laws. There is an insertion in the ritual which implores God to gather us from all corners of the world to our land, so that we may be enabled to sanctify His Name. The benediction concludes with the phrase "Who has chosen His people Israel in love."

The controversy in b. Ber. 11b whether *ahava rabba* or *ahavath olam* should be used was decided by the Gaonim [27] by assigning the first version for Shaharith and the second version for Maariv. The Sephardic and Italian rituals, however, use the second version only.

3. The Shema is the climax of this section. It is the watchword of Israel's faith. The first sentence (Deut. 6:4) is a declaration of God's unity. Then follows Deuteronomy 6:5–9: "Thou shalt love thy God with all thy heart," meaning, with all our inclinations, with the evil as well as with the good, "With all thy soul," meaning, even if one must give his life for his faith, "With all thy might," meaning, with all our wealth. If our wealth is at stake when we continue to observe the principles of our faith, we shall sacrifice our material belongings to preserve our spiritual life. We are further told to study the teachings and meditate on them continuously and teach them to our children. We shall make symbols of them so that we should be reminded of them (b. Ber. 12b–13a).

The second paragraph from Deuteronomy 11:13–21 teaches the doctrines of Providence and retribution. Happiness, prosperity, and long life are promised those who obey God's commandments (Jer. Ber. II, 3).

The third portion is taken from Numbers 15:37–41. It was added to the Shema in order to emphasize the necessity of religious customs in contradistinction to those who claimed that it was sufficient to think and meditate on God. This opinion was prevalent in Palestine and Egypt among the Hellenized Jews. No services or religious observance of any kind were required, according to their way of thinking. In Judaism, however, the impulse for meditation and communion is derived from acts of life. A symbol or custom is merely a device wherewith to stir the strength of man. In order to place this system of symbolism in the minds of the Jews, this third paragraph was introduced. The "Tzitzith" are the symbol in this passage.

The *Talmud* (b. Ber. 12b) explains that the reason for inserting the third paragraph was its inclusion of the five principles: Tzitzith, the Exodus, the observance of commandments, the opposition to the ideas of the Sectarians, and the warning against thinking sinful thoughts.[28]

There was furthermore an attempt to insert the portion of Balak (Num. 22–24) into the Shema, but was abandoned on the ground of *torah tzibbur* — that it would overburden the people with too long a service.[29]

In the Temple service the Ten Commandments were read before the Shema. This custom, however, was not adopted outside of the Temple, on account of the Sectarians who said that only these commandments were divinely revealed (b. Ber. 12a). In the Nash-Papyrus of about the first century C.E. found in Egypt, the Ten Commandments are given before the Shema.[30]

The Ten Commandments continued to be recited in the Palestinian synagogue in Egypt until the thirteenth century.[31]

A clearer reason is given in Jer. Ber. 1, 3c — the reason being that "they (the Minim) shall not say that only these (the Ten Commandments) were given to Moses on Mount Sinai." Kohler adds: "Only because the early Judeo-Christians claimed divine revelation exclusively for the Ten Commandments, discarding the other Mosaic laws as temporary enactments, was the recital of the Decalogue in the daily morning liturgy afterwards abolished."[32]

In order that the people shall not miss the recitation of the Decalogue, the first two paragraphs of the Shema were interpreted in such a way as to prove that the Ten Commandments are included in them (Jer. Ber., *l.c.*).

4. *Geulla* — The Redemption — (M. Tamid V, 7; b. Ber. 13a; Pes. 116b) is the third benediction recited after the Shema. The main theme of this benediction is the redemption of the people Israel from Egypt in the past, and ends with a plea for redemption in the future. According to rabbinic interpretation, the first fifteen words preceded by the Hebrew letter *waw* in this paragraph stand as reminders of the last fifteen words of the preceding third paragraph of the Shema. The benediction for redemption expresses firm belief in redemption, in Providence, and in divine protection.

A quorum of ten adults is required for the recitation of the invocation *barechu* in section D (Shema). The Reform ritual does not consider this requirement imperative.

The benedictions of the Shema (b. Ber. 11b) received their present form in the course of a millennium (see Appendix III, 1).

The Shema benedictions remained in a loose form for a long time. Saadya suggests several hymns in alphabetical acrostics.[33] The different rituals vary greatly in the wording of these benedictions.

E. *Tefilla, amida* — Prayer. This section is called Prayer because prayers and petitions find expression in it. It is also called "Amida" because it is recited while standing. It was the old Jewish custom to stand during prayer. This custom is based upon the statement in Psalm 106:30: "Then stood up Phineas and wrought judgment." According to Talmudic interpretation (b. Ber. 26b), the latter expression means "prayer." It was customary to recite the four sections thus far treated in a sitting position mostly.

The Amida has three subdivisions:

I. The first three benedictions are called "praises" (b. Ber. 34a), *shevah*. Each paragraph has the form of a benediction (see Introductory Notes, 4).

1. *Avoth* — Fathers (M. Rosh Hashana IV, 5), i.e., the three patriarchs who according to tradition recognized the eternal God; for this reason, we eulogize Him as "God of our fathers,"

as the guiding force of the history of Israel in the past and as the Redeemer of Israel in the future. The benediction concludes with the expression "Shield of Abraham" (*P.d.R.E.*, Chap. 27). The contents of the first benediction are indicated partly in Ben Sira LI, 10–12 (see Chapter III; *cf.* Appendix III, 1).

In this as well as in the following benedictions several Scriptural phrases are used. The following Scriptural phrases are to be found in this benediction: Exodus 3:15; Deuteronomy 10:17; Nehemiah 9:32; Genesis 14:19; Leviticus 26:42; Genesis 15:1.

2. *Gevuroth* — Powers (M. Rosh Hashana IV, 5), relates God's wondrous deeds in providing the needs of every living being, and expresses the belief that His lovingkindness extends even after death, and that He will "resurrect those who sleep in the dust."

"Causing the wind to blow and the rain to fall" looms among the wonders of God. It is taken from Psalm 147:18 (M. Taanith I, 1), and is recited only during the Palestinian rain-season which lasts from Tabernacles to Passover. The passage "Who causes the dew to descend" has reference to the season in Palestine between Passover and Tabernacles, and is recited during that period. This last passage is used only in the Sephardic and Oriental rituals. This second benediction concludes with "He Who resurrects the dead."

This benediction utilizes the following Scriptural phrases: Psalms 145:14; 146:7–8; Daniel 12:2; and I Samuel 2:6. The emphasis on Resurrection is possibly a result of the controversy between the Sadducees and Pharisees.[34]

During the Ten Days of Penitence which come between New Year and the Day of Atonement, *zochrenu* — "Remember us unto life" — is inserted in the benediction "Avoth," while *michamocha* — "Who is like unto Thee Father of mercy?" — is inserted in the benediction "Gevuroth."

These insertions are post-Talmudic (R. Hai).[35] T. Soferim 19:7 refers to it (S.R.A. 44b; M.V. § 326).

3. *Kedushath hashem* — The Sanctification of the Name (M. Rosh Hashana IV, 5). This benediction ends with the phrase "the Holy God." During the Penitential period, this last phrase is changed to "the Holy King" (b. Ber. 12b).

In these three introductory benedictions no petitions are to be inserted (b. Ber. 34a). An exception was later made by inserting the two sentences mentioned above for the Ten Days of Penitence.

The third benediction has some resemblance to Ben Sira LI, 2 (see Chapter III).

Kedusha — The Sanctification. In public worship, the "Kedusha" is inserted between the second and the third benedictions when the reader repeats the Amida. The reason why the "Kedusha" is recited in public only is that, as given in b. Ber. 21b, it is written "And I shall be sanctified among the children of Israel" — implying, only in the midst of the required quorum of ten male adults according to the Babylonian custom or of seven male adults according to the Palestinian ritual.

The "Kedusha" was inserted next to the third benediction which bears the same content.[36] The nucleus of the "Kedusha" consists of three Scriptural verses to which the congregation responds; they are as follows:

Kadosh — Holy, holy, holy is the Lord of hosts; the whole earth is full of His glory (Isaiah 6:3).

Baruch — Blessed be the glory of the Lord from His place (Ezekiel 3:12).

Yimloch — The Lord will reign for ever, thy God, O Zion, unto all generations; praise ye the Lord (Psalm 146:10).

To this nucleus various additions were composed throughout the first millennium. Some of these additions were adopted by all the rituals; others remained local with one or two rituals. The "Kedusha" thus took on different forms, but finally became standardized. We will first discuss the additions used in all the rituals or in the majority of them at least; then we shall treat additions and forms used in individual traditions only.

The above-mentioned three verses plus two connecting phrases between the 2–3 and 3–4 which constitute the "Kedusha" for *weekdays* are in all but the Yemenite ritual. These links are:

Leumatham baruch yomeru in the Ashkenazic ritual; *leumatham meshabehim weomerim* in the Sephardic ritual; and *uvdivre kodshecha kathew lemor* in all rituals.

The "Kedusha" was provided with three different introductions:

a. *Nakdish'cha wenaaritz'cha* — "We will sanctify and revere Thee with the harmonious utterance of the assembly of the heavenly seraphim who repeat twice a holy praise unto Thee; for thus it is written in the hand of the prophets (Isaiah 6:3): And one cried unto the other and said, Holy, holy . . . etc. . . .' "

This introduction is used in the Sephardic, the later Italian, the Persian, and the Yemenite rituals. The beginning of this version is based on Isaiah 29:23 and is used in the above-mentioned rituals for weekdays, Sabbaths, and festivals during the morning and Minha "Kedushas." A similar version is given by Saadya, Maimonides, and M.V., p. 155. Soferim 16:12 gives *naaritz'cha wenakdish'cha* [37] as the beginning of the "Kedushas" which version was retained in the Ashkenazic ritual for the Musaf of Sabbaths and festivals, as well as in the Roumanian ritual. *P.d.R.E.*, Chapter 4 end, gives the Ashkenazic version, as well as the outlines of the Ashkenazic Musaf "Kedushas," as we shall discuss later.

b. *Kether yitenu lecha* — "Unto Thee, O Lord our God, shall the heavenly angels above, with Thy people Israel assembled beneath, ascribe a crown; all shall repeat thrice with one accord the holy praise unto Thee, according to the word spoken by Thy prophets. . . ."

This is the introduction as given in S.R.A. 10b for all "Kedushas." A similar text is given in M.V., p. 175, for the Musaf "Kedusha." The Sephardic, Italian (originally also for Shaharith), Roumanian, and Yemenite rituals have this introduction for the Musaf Kedusha, while the Ashkenazic and Egyptian rituals have version (a).

This version is called *kedusha rabba* — The Great Kedusha, or *kedusha ilaa* — The Sublime Kedusha (*Zohar*, Wayakhel). Maimonides does not give this introduction, but for the Kedushas he has form (a) reading: *nakdish'cha wenamlich'cha*.

c. *Nekaddesh* — "We will sanctify Thy Name in the world even as they sanctify it in the highest heavens, as it is written in the hand of Thy prophets. . . ." M.V., p. 66, gives this as the introduction to the weekday Kedusha; it was retained as such in the Roumanian ritual. The Ashkenazic ritual, however, has it for the weekday, Sabbath, and holiday Kedushas of both the morning and Minha services. In this version there are no allusions to angels; it is not mentioned in the old sources.

In the Sephardic and Italian rituals, the Kedusha is alike for weekdays, festivals, and Sabbath morning, whereas the Yemenite, Ashkenazic and Roumanian rituals have special insertions for these days. These insertions are as follows:

a. Between the first and second response:

Az bekol — "Then with a noise of great rushing, mighty and strong, they make their voices heard, and, upraising themselves toward the Seraphim, they exclaim over against them, blessed. . . ." This insertion which is very similar to the passage of *wehaofanim* in the *Yotzer*, S.R.A., p. 10b, is also given by Saadya and in M.V., p. 156, and has been retained in the Ashkenazic and Roumanian rituals.

b. Between the second and the third response:

Mim'komecha — "From Thine place, shine forth, O our King, and reign over us, for we wait for Thee. When wilt Thou reign in Zion. . . . O let our eyes behold Thy kingdom, according to the word that was spoken in the songs of Thy might by David, Thy righteous anointed" (S.R.A.; Saadya; Maimonides; and M.V., *l.c.*). This insertion is used by the Yemenite, Persian, Roumanian, and Ashkenazic rituals.

The insertions for the Sabbath and festival Kedushas for the Musaf service are as follows:

a. Between the first and second response:

Kevodo — "His glory filleth the world, and the ministering angels inquire: Where is the place of His glory (that they may worship Him in awe) etc. . . ." This insertion is found in all rituals for the Musaf service. In the Saadya, Maimonides, Yemenite, and Persian rituals it is used for *all* Kedushas.

b. Between the second and the third response:

Mim'komo — "From His high place may He turn in mercy and be gracious unto a people who, evening and morning, twice every day, proclaims with constancy the unity of His Name, saying in love":

c. *Shema* — "Hear O Israel . . ."

d. *Ehad hu* — "Our God is One; He is our Father; He is our King; He is our Savior; and in His mercy He will let us hear a second time in the presence of all living: To be to you for a God."

Before the last passage, the Sephardic ritual has the phrase: "Behold I have now redeemed you in the latter times, as at the beginning, to be your God."

The reason for the insertion of (c) and (d) is explained in S.R.A., 11a, in M.V., p. 99, and in greater detail in a Geniza fragment.[38] The reason given in these sources is that the Jews in Palestine were forbidden to recite the "Shema" — i.e., to proclaim the oneness of God. The prohibition was issued by the Christian-Byzantine authorities. But they were permitted to assemble in the synagogues on the Sabbath morning in order to sing praises during the Shaharith service and "Kadosh" and "Shema" during the Musaf service. The fragment continues that "since the Ishmaelites (Mohammedans) conquered the kingdom of Edom, and it is again permitted to recite Shema and to pray, everything must be said in its proper place." Following this responsum which was written in Palestine in the eighth century, Saadya and Maimonides abolished the Shema including the insertions mentioned above from the Musaf Kedusha. However, in S.R.A., *l.c.*, Sar Shalom recommended that the Shema and the insertions be retained in the Musaf Kedusha as a remembrance of bygone troubles (S.R.A., *l.c.*). In some sources,[39] the same story is told of a Persian king by name of Jesdigird (see Chapter VIII: A, 16).

Hence, the Yemenite and Persian rituals which follow Saadya and Maimonides do not have these insertions; they have insertion (a) of the Musaf Kedusha and insertion (b) of the Shaharith Kedusha for the entire year. The only difference between the Shaharith and the Musaf Kedushas is that in the introduction *nakdish'cha wenaaritz'cha* is used in the Shaharith Kedusha, while *kether* is used in the Musaf Kedusha. All other rituals have the Shema and its insertions for the Musaf Kedusha.

Aside from all these insertions, the Roumanian ritual has several local variations of Kedushas.

The Kedusha is called *Kedusha daamida*, for it is recited while standing, while the Kedusha in *Yotzer* is called *kedusha dishiva* because the congregation recites it while sitting.

The Kedusha for Musaf is given in *P.d.R.E.* mentioned above. "The majestic scene is thus pictured: Two seraphs stand one on each side of the Holy One; they cover their faces in reverence and sanctify His great Name. One invokes and the other responds, saying: Holy, etc. And the 'Hayyoth' stand by, but knowing not the place of His glory, they answer and say: 'Wherever His glory is may the Name of His . . ., etc.' And Israel, a unique people on the earth for they proclaim His unity continually every day, respond and say: 'Hear, O Israel . . . etc.' And He answers His people Israel: 'I am the Lord your God who delivereth you from all trouble'" (Abrahams).

The nucleus of the Kedusha, i.e., the three responses, were apparently used as a form of sanctification during the Second Temple. The introductions and insertions were later added by the mystics. With regard to the number of times the Kedusha is to be recited, there grew out a difference between Babylonia and Palestine. According to the Geniza fragment [40] mentioned above, it was customary in Palestine to recite the Kedusha only on Sabbaths and festivals in the Shaharith service, while in Babylonia it was recited every day and on Sabbaths and the festivals in the Musaf service. It is reported that the Babylonian immigrants into Palestine introduced their custom there. It seems, therefore, that that must have introduced the introduction *kether* for Musaf which in Babylonia was used for all Kedushas, as evident from S.R.A. Accordingly, the statement in T. Soferim, Chap. 20:7, that on the days on which no Musaf is recited there is no "Kadosh" — with the exception of Hanucca and Purim — is based upon the Palestinian custom.

Whenever Kedusha is said, the third benediction is changed to read as follows: *ledor wador* — "Unto all generations we shall declare Thy greatness, and to all eternity we will proclaim Thy holiness, and Thy praise, O our God, shall not depart from our mouths for ever, for Thou art a great and holy God and King. Blessed . . ."

This version is used in the Ashkenazic and Italian rituals, and is found in M.V., p. 66 (*cf.* Appendix III, 1.)

II. *Emtzaïyoth* — Intermediary Benedictions include benedictions 4–16; they are also called *bakkashoth* — petitions (b. Ber. 34a). Though the *Talmud* says that the intermediary benedictions have no order (*l.c.*), and that they should remain in a loose form suited for man to pour out his troubled heart through them, they were nevertheless arranged according to a certain order (Jer. Ber. 14, d; b. Megilla 17b), for which order reasons are given (*l.c.*).

4. *Bina* — Wisdom is the first benediction of this subdivision (b. Ber. 34a). Just as king Solomon asked for wisdom (I Kings 3:7–9), so also does the Jew place above all things the value of the mind — to understand the wonders of God.

Atta honantanu — "Thou has favored us with a knowledge of Thy Law . . ." is inserted in this benediction for the Saturday evening service (M. Ber. V, 2; b. Ber. 33a). This prayer embodies the petition that the coming week may begin for us with peace, and that we may be withheld from all sin, and that we fear God. It is likewise called "Havdala" — Separation (*l.c.*), because it marks the distinction between Sabbath and the weekdays. Only some sentences of the wording of this prayer are found in Jer. Ber. V, 2. S.R.A. and Maimonides have a text which varies from the Ashkenazic ritual as given with slight variations in M.V., p. 180. The Sephardic, Yemenite, and Italian rituals follow S.R.A. with slight variants (*cf.* Appendix III, 1).

5. *Teshuva* — Repentance (b. Meg. 17b; Jer. Ber. *l.c.*). It is a prayer that God may cause us to return to His Law and to His service (*cf.* Appendix III, 1).

6. *Seliha* — Forgiveness. On Fast-days, the "Selihoth" are inserted in this benediction. The idea is taken from Isaiah 55:7 (*cf.* Appendix III, 1).

7. *Geulla* — Redemption (b. Meg. 17b; Jer. Ber. *l.c.*). The phraseology of this benediction is derived from Psalm 119:153–4 and from Jer. 50:34; the singular is changed to the plural. According to Zunz[41] and Landshuth,[42] this benediction was composed in times of national distress, during the time of Antiochus IV or Pompey. The Palestinian version is about the same as

in the prevailing rituals. In *Sifré*, Deuteronomy § 343, the version for the conclusion is: "He Who looseth the captives."

Anenu is inserted in this benediction on Fast-days. The prayer reads: "Answer us, O Lord, answer us on the day of this fast . . . for we are in great trouble. . . ." Its original text is to be found in Jer. Ber. IV, 3, and in b. Taanith 13b. The text of this prayer occurs with some variations in the different rituals. The Aruch S.V. *Kaval*, however, gives us a version which is different from those of the rituals.

8. *Refua* or *bircath haholim* is a prayer for the sick. The first sentence is taken from Jeremiah 17:14, the singular being changed to the plural. An old version of the first century B.C.E. reads in the conclusion as follows: "He Who healeth the sick." [43] This is also the version in the *Sifré* (*l.c.*) and in Jer. Ber. II, 4; [44] while b. Shab. 12a reads: "He Who healeth the sick of His people Israel."

9. *Bircath hashanim* (M. Ber. V, 2; b. Meg., *l.c.*) is a prayer which "goes back to the period when Israel still dwelt in Palestine, and agriculture was the staple occupation of the people" (Abrahams). The insertion of the phrase "Give dew and rain as a blessing" is said in winter from the sixtieth day after the autumnal equinox — the third or fourth of December — up to the first day of Passover (Abrahams).

The wording of the text of this benediction varies in the different rituals.[45] The most striking difference, however, is that of S.R.A. which has been adopted in the Sephardic and Yemenite rituals for the winter-season. The translation thereof is as follows: "O Lord, our God, bless this year for us; bless its every kind of produce for our benefit; and bestow dew and rain for a blessing upon the face of the earth, and water the surface of the earth; and satisfy the world with Thy goodness, replenish our hands with Thy blessings, and with the rich gifts of Thy hands. Protect and guard this year from all manner of evil, and from every form of calamity and destruction. Cause our hope therein to be good, so that it may end peacefully. O have pity and mercy thereon, and on all its produce and fruits, and bless it with pleasant, blissful, and liberal showers, so that it may close with life, peace, and plenty, as the good years which were for a blessing."

The text of the prayer for the summer-season runs as follows in the European-Sephardic and Yemenite rituals: "Bless us, our Father, in all the works of our hands, and bless this year with beneficial dews, with blessings and prosperity; and may it close with life, plenty, and peace, like the good years which were for a blessing. For Thou, O God, art good and beneficent, and blessest the years."

The versions given by Maimonides are similar to these two versions (*cf.* Appendix III, 1).

K. Kohler [46] is of the opinion that this prayer was originally for the New Year or for the Day of Atonement (Jer. Yoma V, 3). It was taken over into the Fast-days service when it was embodied into the daily prayers.

Benedictions 4–9 are personal petitions.

10. *Kibbutz galuyoth* (b. Meg., *l.c.;* Jer. Ber., *l.c.*) is a prayer for the gathering of the exiled Jews from their dispersion to Palestine. The idea and the wording are borrowed from Isaiah 27 : 13; 11 : 12; Ezekiel 20 : 34; 37 : 21; 39 : 2. The idea of gathering the exiled is expressed also in Ben Sira 36 : 11 and 51 : 11. In the latter as well as in Isaiah 56 : 8, the eulogy of this benediction is given. "Throughout the period of the Second Temple there was a vast Diaspora, or scattering of Israel in various lands. . . . Such settlements were a cause of pride to some. . . . But to others the same fact bore a different aspect, and the concentration of Israel and its reunion on the sacred soil were regarded as an object of prayer" (Abrahams; *cf.* Appendix III, 1).

The wording of this benediction is similar to that of the concluding paragraph of the "Shoferoth" for the New Year's Musaf (see Chapter XVI).

11. *Hashiva shofĕtenu* or *bircath mishpat* (b. Meg., *l.c.;* Jer. Ber., *l.c.: Shofĕtenu betzedek*). This is a prayer for the domination of righteous judgment; it is taken from Isaiah 1 : 26–27. The wording: "Restore our judges as at first, and our counsellors as at the beginning (remove from us grief and suffering); reign Thou over us, O Lord, Thou alone . . ." may indicate the expression of protest against foreign judges and dominion, most likely against the Romans toward the end of the period of the Second Temple. The sentence in parenthesis is not

found in S.R.A. nor in the Palestinian version. The Palestinian version of the eulogy is *ohev hamishpat* without *melech;* it is taken from Isaiah 61 : 8.[47]

The three benedictions 9–11 seem to have close relation to one another. "They deal with three aspects of the restoration of Jewish independence: the Redemption, the Gathering of the Dispersed, and the Restoration of the Judges. As such, they could have developed only in a time of great nationalistic enthusiasm. . . . We know from the *Talmud* that for about forty years before 70 (b. San. 41a), the jurisdiction of the Jewish courts was limited. We may therefore assign the prayer for the restoration of Jewish judges to that time" (Finkelstein).[48]

K. Kohler,[49] however, refers the benediction to the "Kingdom of God" — "the Malchuth Shomayim," and quotes the Baraitha (b. Meg. 17b; Jer. Ber. 11, 4) which says "When the exiled have been gathered, judgment is held, and the wicked are humbled and the righteous are made to rejoice." Kohler comes to the conclusion that though this was the original idea of the benediction following Ezekiel 20: 34–36 and 39 : 2f., "in all likelihood the misrule under the late Maccabean and Herodian rulers led to a change of the prayer to make it refer rather to the time being instead of the Messianic future."

During the Ten Days of Penitence, the eulogy is changed to *hammelech hammishpat* (b. Ber. 12b) — The King of Judgment. A similar change is made in the third benediction: *hammelech hakkadosh* — The Holy King. Concerning the exceptional use of the article (it should be *melech hammishpat*) Rashi (*l.c.*) remarks and quotes similar usage of the article in the Bible, as in Joshua 3 : 14; II Kings 16 : 17; Jer. 31 : 39.

12. *Bircath hamminim* or *hatziddukim* also *hazzedim* (b. Ber. 28b; Jer. Ber. IV, 3; Tanhuma, Korah end; M. R. Bamidbar 18, 17). This benediction or "malediction," as Kohler calls it, [50] was composed according to Talmudic sources (*l.c.*) by Samuel the Younger about 100 C.E. at the request of Rabbi Gamaliel and against sectarians and heretics among the Jewish people. However, Kohler is of the opinion that this prayer was composed before the Destruction.[51] "The hostile kingdom spoken of in such fierce terms can only refer to the fourth world

kingdom of Daniel, either that of Syria or of Rome." The expressions "the uprooting, the crushing and the hurling down of the kingdom of arrogance. . . . Who breakest the enemies and humblest the arrogant" — all these point to the hostile and arrogant rule of the Romans. "But then," Kohler concludes, "when these Christian maligners in the very midst of the Synagogue had become a menace to the Jewish people, and Rabbi Gamaliel called for some of his disciples to formulate a prayer against the 'Minim' or heretics, Samuel Hakatan rose and gave the prayer against the hostile Roman power a new implication by changing the words at the beginning by a direct reference to the 'Minim.' As it was, however, merely a casual change of words, he failed, as we are told, in the following year to remember exactly the words he had used before. . . . Since then the various versions present different terms for the initial words, while the rest retained the old form" (*cf.* Appendix III, 1).

The text underwent several changes due to the attack of the Church which claimed that this prayer was directed against Jewish converts to Christianity. Consequently, the first word *lameshumadim* was changed to *Welammalshinim* — to the slanderers. Likewise was the word *lannotzerim* — the Christians — removed. The word "to the converts" has been retained in the Yemenite ritual. The meaning of *lameshumadim* is "to the baptized" according to some scholars, and is derived from *lameshuamadim*, using the "Shafil" form of the Syrian root *amad*, as *meshuabadim* from *avad*. This refers to the followers of John the Baptist (see Yuhasin ed. Fil., p. 15). Hence, in the prayer were specified the "Meshuamadim" who were the followers of John the Baptist, the "Minim" who were the heretics, and the "Notzrim" who were the followers of Jesus and who antagonized the disciples of John. Later the source of the word was forgotten, and was identified with *shamad* — to exterminate — to which it really has no relation. R. Hai Gaon still knew the source of the word.[52]

13. *Bircath hatzaddikim* (R. Hananel to b. Meg. *l.c.*) is a benediction for the righteous and for the pious and for the true proselytes and the remnant of the Scribes. This prayer is a logical consequence of benediction twelve. The terms "tzadikim," "hassidim," "soferim" recall an earlier time

during the Second Temple. "The remnant of their scribes" may refer to the Pharisaic leaders who escaped the persecution of Alexander Jannaeus (103–76 B.C.E; *cf.* Appendix III, 1).

14. *Bonê yerushalayim* is referred to in Jer. Ber. II, 3: "Build the House." This prayer probably dates back to the pre-Maccabean times. Ben Sira 36: 12 has the old formula retained in the earlier versions:[53] "Have mercy upon Thy holy city Jerusalem, the place of Thy dwelling; fill Zion with Thy majesty and Thy Temple with Thy glory." The wording of the eulogy too is found in Ben Sira 51 : 11, as well as the eulogy of benediction fifteen: "Who choosest Zion, Who buildest the city and His sanctuary, Who causest the horn of David's house to sprout forth." The first is found in Jer. Yoma 7: 1: "Who dwellest in Zion." This benediction suffered changes after the Destruction. According to the new conditions, it was reshaped into a prayer for the rebuilding of Jerusalem. The original form of this benediction has been retained in the third benediction of *bircath hammazon* (see Chapter IX).

On the Ninth of Av, a special prayer is inserted in this benediction; it begins with the word *nahem* — comfort: "Comfort, O Lord our God, the mourners of Zion. . . ." It describes the devastation of Jerusalem by the Romans. Some rituals, as the Sephardic, Italian, Yemenite, and Maimonides read: *rahem* — "have mercy" (Jer. Ber. IV, 3).

15. *Bircath dawid* (b. Ber., *l.c.*, com. R. Hananel, not mentioned in Jer. Ber., *l.c.*) is a prayer for the reinstatement of the dynasty of David. Jer. Ber. IV, 3 and Tos. Ber. IV end, state that after the *bircath hamminim* was introduced in the Amida, benedictions fourteen and fifteen were combined in order not to exceed the number of the eighteen benedictions of the Amida. The Midrash Thil. 18 : 31 (also b. Pes. 117b) explains that this prayer was then inserted in the Haftara benedictions (see Chapter X), as S.R.A. in fact gives the wording of the benediction (2ab). The eulogy has "The Shield of David." Concerning the change of the eulogy, b. Pes. points out that the latter version should be used for the Haftara, while the version "Who causest a horn of salvation to sprout forth" should be used for the Amida.

In fact, in the Kerova of the Palestinian "payetanim," as

Yuda b. Mastia (17th of Tammuz, Ital. ritual) and E. Kallir (Purim) there is no poetical insertion for the fifteenth benediction; whereas the fourteenth benediction closes with *elohê dawid uvone yerushalayim* which points to the fact that both benedictions were included in the fourteenth [54] (Jer. Ber. IV, 3).

The Babylonian ritual retained the benediction separately, disregarding the number of eighteen benedictions in the Amida (b. Meg., *l.c.*). The first sentence is based upon Psalm 132 : 17.

Elbogen [55] entertains the idea that the fifteenth benediction is the last one introduced into the Amida, but Landshuth [56] and later Kohler [57] brought proofs that this benediction is very old. However, the question still remains unsettled. There can be no doubt concerning the antiquity of the text, but this does not answer the question why this benediction was omitted from the Palestinian ritual. The insistence on number eighteen, as given in Jer. Ber., *l.c.*, has Midrashic character only. In all likelihood, the Babylonian ritual never abolished the benediction, as seen from the abbreviated Amida *havinenu* (b. Ber. 29a and Jer. Ber. IV, 3). Both the fourteenth and fifteenth benedictions occur in the Haftara benediction and in the "Bircath Hamazon" with some variations.

Benedictions 10–15 are called the nationalistic prayers, for they deal with national-religious aspirations.

16. *Shomea tefilla* (b. Meg., *l.c.;* Jer. Ber., *l.c.*) is the concluding benediction of the second, petitional section, and utilizes Psalm 65 : 3.

Originally, part of the High Priest's prayer on the Day of Atonement (Jer. Yoma VII, 1) was incorporated into the Amida. The oldest known version read thus: *shema adonai bekolenu werahem alenu baruch. . . .*

This version seems to be pre-Maccabean.[58] Later, different variations developed in the rituals. The eulogy is also given in b. Ber. 29b.

III. *Běrachoth aharonoth* (b. Ber. 34a; Jer. Ber. II, 4) are the last three benedictions. Thanksgiving is their underlying thought (*l.c.*). These benedictions were part of the Temple service (M. Tamid, *l.c.*) but have been altered after the Destruction to suit the new conditions.

17. *Avoda* (M. Tamid V, 1; b. Ber., *l.c.*) is a prayer for the

acceptance of the service in the Temple (Jer. Sota VII end, Yoma VII, 1). The old version has been retained partly in Wayyikra Rabba, 7:2; it reads as follows: *retzê elohenu shochen betziyon yaavducha vanecha.*

The eulogy for this benediction we find in Jerushalmi (*l.c.*) and runs as follows: *sheothecha nira wenaavod* or *sheothecha levadecha beyira naavod.*

Rashi to b. Ber. 11b gives a similar version. This version was used in the old pre-Maccabean rituals too.[59] The *Midrash* (Shoher Tov 17) says that since the Destruction, the Hasidim Harishonim ordered that the version *anna hashev shechinathecha letziyon weseder haavoda lirushalayim* be recited three times daily. This is still used in the Ashkenazic ritual on the festivals when the Cohanim bless the congregation with the conclusion as cited above from Jeremiah. The eulogy *hammahazir shechinatho letziyon* is formed according to M. Thil. 9., M.V., p. 67, however, gives both versions for the daily prayers.

Yaale weyavo — On the day of the New Moon, this prayer is recited for the prosperity of the new month. It is inserted in this benediction, and has reference also to Jerusalem, Messiah, and Israel. This same prayer is recited also on the Three Festivals in all the services. The *Talmud* (b. Ber. 29b) merely mentions the necessity of remembering the new month in the seventeenth benediction; whereas T. Soferim 19:11 quotes this prayer in the "Bircath Hamazon."

18. *Hodaa* (M. Ber., *l.c.;* b. Meg., *l.c.;* Jer. Ber., *l.c.*) is called thanksgiving, and like the preceding benediction was part of the service at the Temple. The first phrase is taken from I Chronicles 29:13. Originally, this benediction was recited after the sacrifice, while the congregation prostrated itself (Ben Sira 50:16–21; M. Tamid VII:3). In the synagogues, the people bow their heads; and while the reader recites the benediction, they say the *modim derabbanan* — the "Modim" of the Rabbis — which is quoted in b. Sota 40a. The eulogy of this benediction is taken from Jer. Ber. I, 7.

The old Palestinian version of the eighteenth benediction [60] is much shorter than that in S.R.A. which, in turn, is shorter than that in the rituals.

On "Hanucca" and "Purim," paragraphs which recount the story of these days are inserted in this benediction. They are preceded by *al hannissim* — "Concerning the miracles" (Soferim 20, 8).

The passage for Hanucca begins with *bimê mattithyahu*. Mattathias was called "High Priest," though only his son Simon was later honored with that title. Some hold that his father Johanan was a High Priest (S. Baer, p. 101). The text for Purim begins with *bime mordechay*. Both texts occur for the first time in S.R.A. 35b, 36b.[61] At the conclusion, both of them have in S.R.A. the sentence "Just as Thou didst perform a miracle for them, so also mayest Thou perform miracles and wonders for us at this time." This sentence also appears in M.V., p. 68, as well as in Saadya and Maimonides. Of this sentence Abudraham says that M. Rothenberg ordered to omit it. Following him, the Sephardic and Ashkenazic rituals abolished this phrase, while the Italian, Persian, and Yemenite rituals retained it.

Uch'thov "O inscribe all the children of Thy covenant for a happy life . . ." is inserted in this benediction and is recited during the Ten Days of Penitence. Like the two mentioned in the first and second benedictions, it became customary to recite this passage since Gaonic times.

19. *Bircath cohanim* (M. Tamid IV, 1; Sota VII, 2). The Priestly Benediction is the oldest liturgical text (Num. 6:22–27), and was recited by the priests at the conclusion of the daily sacrifice. Ben Sira L:19–20 describes the Priestly Benediction. Already during the Second Temple, the Priestly Benediction was transferred to the Synagogue (M. Sota VII, 6; *Tosefta*, Sota VII, 8). The Priestly Benediction had to be recited in Hebrew only (M. Sota VII, 2, b. Sota 38a), though other parts of the service were permitted in any other language (b. Ber. 13a; Tosefta, Sota VII, 7).

The introductory passage has the phrase *baberacha ham'-shulesheth* — "in the three-fold blessing" — which refers to the three verses of the Priestly Benediction. The phrase "the children of Aaron Thy holy people" is found in M. Yoma IV, 2.

Sim shalom (b. Meg., *l.c.*). This prayer for peace is culled from the last word of the Priestly Benediction. The *Mishna* cites the Priestly Benediction as the last benediction, but apparently a short prayer for peace was attached to it. Kohler (*l.c.*), maintains that the prayer for peace was not known in the Temple service and that it was composed by the "Hasidim" "who would not recognize the mediatorship of the priesthood." The prayer does not mention the Temple service and the priests at all. Neither can this prayer be identified with the Priestly Benediction as was already noted by Asheri to Tamid 5. He, however, mentions the prayer for peace as being a part of the Temple service; while Dr. Finkelstein [62] doubts whether this prayer for peace was introduced into the Temple service.

A similar prayer is given in b. Ber. 55b: *addir bammarom* — Glorious on high, abiding in might, Thou art peace and Thy Name is peace; may it be Thy will to grant unto us peace." This prayer with the inserted phrase "and unto Thy people Israel, life and blessing" is still recited after the blessing of the Cohanim (*cf.* Appendix III, 1). Later on, the prayer underwent a series of changes, and finally received the form as given in S.R.A. with the eulogy "Who blesses His people Israel with peace." [63] The original eulogy (Lev. Rabba 9 end; Derech Eretz Zuta end) has been retained in the Ashkenazic ritual for the Ten Days of Penitence [64] (M.V., p. 384).

Shalom rav is another version of the prayer for peace. It is now used in the Ashkenazic ritual for the Minha and Maariv services. It is first mentioned in the eleventh century, and was first introduced by M. Rothenberg. However, as Dr. Finkelstein rightly points out, the fact that Provence, Avignon, and Carpentras have only this version for all services would indicate that it is very old.[65]

Besêfer hayim. This passage was inserted in Gaonic times, and is recited during the Ten Days of Penitence. It first appeared in S.R.A. and is used in some rituals with variations.

Before the Amida the verse of Psalm 51 : 17 is recited (b. Ber. 4b), while after the Amida *elohai netzor* — a meditation composed by Mar the son of Ravina — is added. This was his prayer after the services (b. Ber. 17a); of this only one sentence has been omitted, while the sentence "Do it for the sake of Thy Name" has been inserted in accordance with Samuel (Rokeah § 327; *Hamanhig* 1, 62). In some rituals, this prayer is still more extended (S. Baer, p. 104). The verse of Psalm 19:15 has been added according to a Talmudic explanation (b. Ber. 9b). The last verse "Who makest peace" is from Job 25:2, while the first phrase "Guard my tongue from evil and my lips from speaking guile" is taken from Psalm 34:14, with the change of the second person to the first singular.

The verse, "Then shall the offering of Juda . . . be pleasant . . ." is taken from Malachi 3:4, and the preceding meditation "that the Temple be speedily rebuilt" is from Avoth 5:23. The last paragraph is used in some rituals only.

S.R.A. adds the prayer of Rava (b. Ber. 17a) which is now used on the Day of Atonement only.

Havinenu — The Shortened Amida. In cases of emergency, it was permitted to abridge the intermediary benedictions. Such an abbreviated version was composed by Samuel and is given in b. Ber. 29a and with some variations in Jer. Ber. IV, 3. The Babylonian version, however, was introduced into the rituals. Besides these, many abridged forms were composed within a period of several centuries, some of which are in poetical forms.[66]

The question concerning the date of the composition of the benedictions of the Amida and the time when they were canonized in their present successive form is very intricate and very difficult to answer because of the lack of sources. In the last decades, different opinions appeared, but none of them seems to be acceptable without hesitancy.[67]

To summarize the various views we may assume that the nineteen benedictions were all composed during the second half of the era of the Second Temple, that they were originally created individually and only gradually arranged in a certain succession, and that this succession seems to have been different at the time of Ben Sira. Tradition has it that the first and the last three benedictions were arranged in the days prior to the Destruction. There are evidences, however, that the intermediary benedictions were also known at that time. The oldest report of the number eighteen dates back to the first century C.E., when Rabbi Gamaliel definitely fixed this number and made it obligatory to recite each day.

Why the Babylonian ritual has a separate benediction for the Davidic dynasty, making a total of nineteen, and why the Palestinian ritual did not have this separate prayer cannot be definitely ascertained. Various motives are given. The only plausible reason seems to be that such an emphasis upon the reëstablishment of the glorious dynasty would have been dangerous in Palestine during the Hasmonean and Herodian rulers at first and later during the rule of the Romans. It was wise not to have such an ambitious prayer inserted in order not to make the Roman authorities suspicious and hurt thereby the house of the Prince which was of Davidic descent, but which the Romans considered only the religious head of Israel. On the other hand, in Babylonia the hope for a political rule of the house of David was cherished, because the Exilarchs had already some power over the Jewish community and because there was naught to fear from the Persian government, since the Jewish aspiration was connected with Palestine. It seems, therefore, that the statement in Jer. Ber. IV, 3 that there were originally seventeen benedictions and that they were fixed in Jamnia to eighteen by adding the benediction concerning the "Minim" is quite true and in keeping with our discussion. The statement further adds that there are no nineteen benedictions, because the benediction of the Davidic dynasty was united with the prayer for Jerusalem. This does not imply that the sixteenth benediction is a new product. As Kohler rightly points out, "the language of the prayer speaks in favor of its ancient character," [68] but it was omitted in Palestine out of political considerations, while it was retained in Babylonia.

F. *Tahanun* — THE PETITION. This section follows the Amida on weekdays on which no festal-days or days of historical commemoration occur. It is omitted on days on which a festivity — a circumcision or a wedding — takes place in the congregation where the participants are present.

The custom of reciting individual petitions after the public prayers seems to date back to the Temple service. M. Tamid VII, 3 and Ben Sira L: 16–21 relate that after the sacrifice the people would prostrate themselves in prayer. This act was called *nefilath appayim* — "falling on the face," and was carried over into the Synagogue to be enacted after the Tefilla which now replaced the sacrificial cult. However, the custom of prostration was abandoned, and was substituted by reclining on the left side (b. Meg. 23a; Jer. Avoda Zara IV, 1). Prostration on the floor was looked upon with suspicion, because it was identical with pagan worship (*l.c.*). For this reason, no Jewish community uses this custom, with the exception of the Ashkenazim who prostrate themselves once on New Year and four times on the Day of Atonement (see Chapter XVI). The Karaites, however, still resort to this custom in their daily services up to the present day.[69]

At first the content of the Petition was free. S.R.A. 12a, gives five different paragraphs to choose from. Saadya and Maimonides likewise provide short passages. M.V., p. 68f., has already the whole text as it is used in the Ashkenazic ritual. Gradually, a set text was introduced in all rituals.

There are two Tahanunim in all rituals: a short one for Sundays, Tuesdays, Wednesdays, and Fridays, and a long one for Mondays and Thursdays. The ideas for the Tahanun were drawn from Daniel 9:3f.; Ezra 9:6f.; and Nehemiah 1:4f. — i.e., confession of sins, self-accusation and humiliation, and a plea for repentance and salvation.

In the Ashkenazic and Sephardic rituals the short Tahanun consists of Psalm 25 (M.V., p. 70), preceded by the sentence: "Merciful and gracious God, we (I) have sinned before Thee; have mercy upon us (me), and receive my supplications (save us)." The Ashkenazic ritual has this sentence in the singular, while the Sephardic and Italian rituals have it in the plural. With the beginning of the eighteenth century, the Ashkenazic ritual changed to Psalm 6,[70] and with the end of the seventeenth century the verse from II Samuel 24:14 was added, because of the expression *nipĕla na*. This addition came through the influence of the Kabbalistic "Shaare Tziyon."[71] In the Italian ritual, an alphabetic acrostic precedes the Psalm. When reciting the Psalm, the people recline on their left sides.

Following the S.R.A. 19b, and the *Zohar*, *Bo* 41a Isaac Luria introduced the recitation of the Widdui and the Thirteen Attributes. This custom was adopted in the Sephardic-Oriental, the Italian, and Yemenite rituals for Mondays and

Thursdays only, while the Hasidic ritual has it for every day. *Col-Bo* 19 has this custom for Mondays and Thursdays only.

Shomer yisrael is a poem three stanzas of which are used in the Ashkenazic ritual for the daily Tahanun, while the Sephardic, Yemenite, and Roman rituals use the poem for the Seliha of the Ten Days of Repentance. The Sephardic and Yemenite rituals have a fourth stanza *shomer goy rabba* and the Roman ritual has a fifth stanza *shomer berith avothenu*, while the Tripoli ritual has a sixth stanza *shomer goy baruch*.[72] It seems that the poem was originally extended to an alphabetic acrostic of which the first two *baruch*, *ehad* and the two before the last *rabba*, *kadosh* have been retained. The content of the poem consisted of a rehearsal of the most important phrases of the prayers. The use of the poem in the daily prayers of the Ashkenazic ritual is but of late date. *Col-Bo*, *l.c.*, says that it is customary to recite one of the poems — without specifying which one.

Mithratze berahamim is to be found in the Roman ritual with some variations.

Waanahnu lo neda is mentioned in M.V., p. 71.

The closing paragraph is found in all the rituals and is given in S.R.A. It is a compilation of Biblical verses: II Chronicles 20:12; Psalms 23:6; 33:22; 79:8; 123:4; Habbakuk 3:2; Psalms 103:14, and 79:9.

In the Ashkenazic ritual *the long Tahanun* consists of seven paragraphs, as in M.V., p. 68f. In the Sephardic and Yemenite rituals the fifth paragraph is missing, while the others are shortened. The reason why a long Tahanun was arranged for Mondays and Thursdays is that on these days the people would assemble in the cities from the suburban hamlets to attend the markets. For this reason, Scriptural readings were instituted and special petitions were assigned.

Concerning the composition of this Tahanun, a number of stories are circulated. *Hamanhig* I, 69 reports that three sages of the Jerusalem exiles composed it; one compiled the first three paragraphs, the other four and five, and the third six and seven. A similar story is related in *Col-Bo* 18, and a third variation of the story is cited by S. Baer, p. 112. Zunz suggests that it was written during the Gothic and Frankish persecutions of the seventh century.[73]

The paragraphs consist largely of Scriptural verses: Psalms 78 : 38; 40 : 12; 106 : 47; 130 : 3–4; Jer. 14 : 7; Psalms 26 : 6; 20 : 2, 10; Daniel 9 : 15–19; Isaiah 64 : 7; Joel 2 : 17; Psalms 103 : 10; 38 : 22; Jer. 14 : 9; Exodus 32 : 12; Daniel 9 : 7; Gen. 41 : 16; Lam. 3 : 40; and Psalm 118 : 25. The Italian ritual uses but a few verses of this Tahanun, while the Sephardic ritual has three Selihoth inserted here.

After these seven paragraphs, Psalm 6 or 25 is recited, following which the Ashkenazic ritual has a poem of four stanzas with the refrain "O Lord, God of Israel." This refrain is cited in M.V., p. 71, with a fifth stanza. The refrain is also found in the Sephardic ritual but with two other poems, one having "Abraham" and the other "Samuel" as acrostics.

The Ashkenazic ritual continues with "O Guardian of Israel." The concluding paragraph is then used in all the rituals, as in the short Tahanun. *El erech appayim* is given in two versions. The Sephardic ritual has two similar passages. They are cited in Abudraham, p. 70; while M.V., p. 71, gives one for the reader and the other for the congregation.

The half-Kaddish is recited before these paragraphs.

G. The Reading from the Scriptures. In the morning service on Mondays and Thursdays, readings from the Pentateuch were ordered to follow Tahanun. The custom is very old; it goes back to the time when the Jewish people still lived in Palestine and used to gather in the towns from villages and hamlets on these days because they were "market-days." According to tradition (Jer. Meg. IV, 1; b. B. Kama 82a), it was instituted by Ezra in order to remind the people of the current portion of the week to be read on the Sabbath (see Sabbath Service), and in order not to let three days go by without Scriptural instruction. The reading on Mondays and Thursdays consists of the first section or "parasha" of the weekly portion known as "Sidra" — order. This part is divided into three subdivisions, each of which must consist of a minimum of three verses. An adult is called upon for each division. Originally, each person had to read the division apportioned to him. This custom still prevails among the Yemenite Jews. Gradually, however, due to a lack of proper training, this custom was abandoned, and a Reader of the Scriptures — *baal korê* — was appointed. The people called upon recite the benedictions pertaining to the Law before and after the reading (see above A). The people are called upon in a fixed order: first a "Cohen" i.e., a descendant of the Aaronites, then a "Levi" i.e., a Levite, and then an "Israelite" i.e., a Jew who is neither a "Cohen" nor a "Levi." In case there is no "Levi," the "Cohen" takes the "Levi's" part too, in which case the "Cohen" recites the benediction twice. The same procedure is followed if there is no "Cohen"; the "Levi" substitutes for the "Cohen." If neither are present, three Israelites are called upon (b. Gitin 59–60). The portion is read from the Scroll only; no other book, whether printed or written, may be used. In case there is no Scroll, the portion is not read. (For further details, see Chapter X, B.)

Before the reading the ark is opened with the recitation of Numbers 10:35 and Isaiah 2:3; this recitation appears first in *Col-Bo*. It became customary since 1541. Following this recitation, a paragraph from the *Zohar* (Wayakhel) "Blessed be His Name" which Isaac Luria introduced (1534–72) and which became generally used in the Ashkenazic ritual since about 1600 is recited.[74] The reader then takes the Scroll, and turning toward the congregation he recites: "Magnify the Lord with me . . . etc." from Psalm 34:4; whereupon the congregation recites I Chronicles 29:11 and Psalm 99:5, 9. The reader then recites "May the Father of mercy . . . etc." (Singer 67), and while unrolling the Scroll he reads "May His Kingdom be revealed soon . . . etc." which is taken from Tractate Soferim XIV, 12. He then calls the Hebrew name of the person and the name of his father. Every person is called to the reading from the Pentateuch by his and his father's Hebrew name.[75] The congregation and reader recite "And ye that cleave unto the Lord your God are alive every one of you this day" (Deut. 4:4). The person called upon recites the benediction: "Blessed art Thou . . . Who givest the Law" — a benediction already recited in the morning blessings. After the reading, he recites: "Blessed art Thou . . . Who hast given us the Law of truth. . . . Who givest the Law" (Singer 68). When called upon, persons who have been in danger of their lives recite the benediction: "Blessed art Thou . . . Who doest good unto the undeserving, and Who hast also rendered all good unto me." Whereupon the congregation responds with "He Who hath rendered Thee all good, may He do only good unto thee for ever." This text is quoted in the *Talmud* (b. Ber. 54b).

After the reading, the Scroll is lifted — *hagbaha* — as it is rolled open partly to show the congregation the place read, while another person proceeds to roll, bind, and dress the Scroll — *gelila*. When the Scroll is raised up, the congregation recites: "And this is the Law . . . etc." — a selection of Biblical verses from Deuteronomy 4:44; Proverbs 3:18, 17, 16; and from Isaiah 42:21.

On the days when Tahanun is recited, a prayer of five paragraphs for the welfare of Israel and its sages, for redemption and the restoration of the Temple (Singer 69–70) is recited in the Ashkenazic and Italian rituals after the reading from the Pentateuch. In the Sephardic ritual this prayer is recited only on those Sabbaths on which the New Month is announced.

When the Scroll is returned to the ark, Psalm 148:13, 14 and a selection of Biblical passages: "And when it rested he said, Return, O Lord . . . etc." (Singer 71), are recited (Num. 10:36; Psalm 132:8–10; Prov. 4:2; 3:18, 17; Lam. 5 end). These selections are according to the Ashkenazic ritual; the Sephardic ritual has other Biblical verses for the opening of the ark. Before the reading, the verse "And this is the Law . . . etc." is recited; it is repeated when the Scroll is lifted.[76] The benediction over the Law and the verse "O magnify . . . etc." are the same in all rituals.

H. The Concluding Parts. This section consists of Psalms 84:5; 144:15, and 145. The recitation of these Psalms three times daily is recommended in b. Ber. 4b. Psalm 20 is added for the days on which Tahanun is recited. Then there follows a long paragraph beginning with "And a redeemer shall come to Zion" — *uva letziyon goel*. This recitation is called the "Kedusha" of the Biblical portion — *kedusha desidra* (b. Sota 49a). It consists of a repetition of the Kedusha in Hebrew and Aramaic with several Scriptural verses: Isaiah 59:20–21; Psalm 22:4; I Chronicles 29:18; Psalms 78:38; 86:5; 119:142; Micah 7:20; Psalms 68:20; 46:8; 84:13; 20:10; 30:13; Jeremiah 17:7; Isaiah 26:4; Psalm 9:11; and Isaiah 42:21.

There is also a prayer that God may open our hearts to understand and observe the Law, so that we shall inherit life ever lasting. It concludes with a trust in God and in His providence

Various reasons are given for the inclusion of this paragraph. One holds that it was inserted after the service for late-comers who missed the Kedusha and that it was given in Aramaic for those who are ignorant of Hebrew. The arrangement of the preceding Psalms with this paragraph and the ideas expressed therein may serve as a substitute for the regular service (Abudraham). For this reason, this paragraph is not recited on Sabbaths nor on festivals, because everybody is supposed to be present and on time at the service on holidays.

Another opinion is that after the service a lecture or a rabbinical discourse used to take place; whereupon this conclusion would follow since it consists of the "Sanctification" and of a prayer for the observance of the Law. This custom was very popular in Talmudic times; it was later abandoned due to changes of conditions. Indeed, whenever special recitations from the Bible and Talmudic literature are obligatory in the service, this paragraph is read, as for example: on Sabbath afternoon and evening, on Purim and the Ninth of Av (Rashi to b. Sota 49a; S.R.A. 14–15; M.V., p. 25; *Hamanhig* I, 76).[77]

The text of this paragraph is given in S.R.A.; while Saadya gives only the part beginning with *baruch elohenu* for the individual, because the paragraph was originally intended for public service. M.V., p. 73, gives the full text.

This section is in all rituals; after its reading, the Kaddish "Tithkabbal" is recited.

Alenu is taken from the Musaf service of New Year. As a daily prayer, we first find the Alenu in M.V., p. 75. The Sephardic ritual has only the first paragraphs; all others have both paragraphs.

The keynote of the Alenu is a proclamation of God as King over Israel and over the universe, concluding with Zechariah 14:9: "On that day the Lord shall be One and His Name shall be One" (*cf.* Appendix III, 1).

After the Alenu, the so-called "Mourner's Kaddish" is recited (see Kaddish).

Shir shel yom — The Psalm of the Day is recited at the end of the morning service in the Ashkenazic ritual, while in all other rituals it is recited before the Alenu. This custom was taken over from the Temple service during which the Levites would sing a special psalm each day (M. Tamid VII, 4; b. Rosh Hashana 31a given in the name of Rabbi Akiva). Besides the daily psalms, every holiday or distinguished day has its specific psalm the content of which has either some direct bearing with reference to the day or else expresses an idea related to it. In addition, the Ashkenazic ritual has Psalm 83 which is quoted in M.V., p. 74; while the other rituals add other psalms.

En kelohenu. Following S.R.A., the Sephardic and Yemenite rituals have this hymn for weekdays too, while the Ashkenazic ritual has it only for Sabbaths and holidays. According to M.V., p. 106, Rokeah 319, and *Col-Bo* 37 end, the reason why this hymn is recited on these days is that it completes the one hundred benedictions which every man is supposed to recite each day — since on Sabbaths and holidays the Amida is abbreviated from eighteen to seven benedictions and several benedictions are thus lacking. The hymn has in its acrostic the words "Baruch, Atta, and Amen" repeated four times. It occurs for the first time in Hechaloth,[78] and was recast in the rituals in order to obtain the acrostic *amn.* It has been retained in its original form in S.R.A. 14a. Already M.V., p. 176, however, gives it in its present version. M.V., p. 74, has this hymn for the weekday service.

A portion describing the "Spices" used in the Temple service from the *Baraitha* Krithuth 6 is recited after this hymn. This paragraph is not used in the Sephardic ritual; while in the Italian and Yemenite rituals only "Spices" is recited and not "En Kelohenu."

The concluding paragraph "Says Rabbi Eleazar" is from b. Ber. 64 end. It also occurs in other places in the *Talmud.* The Italian ritual does not have it. After these recitations the "Rabbinical Kaddish" is said. In some Ashkenazic congregations, the "Song of Unity" — *shir hayihud* — is recited responsively; it is divided into seven parts, and each day one part is recited (see Chapter X).

This concludes the public morning service. The private prayers, devotions, and readings which follow we shall treat in Chapter XVIII.

II. Minha — The Afternoon Service

The name "Minha" is taken from the afternoon sacrifice at the Temple. Before the service, portions dealing with the sacrifice of the daily burnt-offerings and of the "Spices" are read. These portions are as follows: Num. 28 : 1–8; Exodus 30 : 34–36; and b. Krithuth 6. The Italian ritual has Exodus 30 : 34–36 only.

The Minha service starts with "Ashrê," on account of the statement in b. Ber. 4b to read this psalm twice daily (see Verses of Song). Then there follows the Amida, which is repeated in the public service including the Kedusha. The short Tahanun and Kaddish "Tithkabbal" are recited, while Alenu with the Kaddish conclude the service.

If one is prevented from praying the Minha service, he is to recite the Amida twice in the evening service. If the following day happens to be a festival or a Sabbath or a day on which no Tahanun is recited, then Tahanun is omitted from the Minha service.

On a Fast-day, the Scroll is taken out before the Amida, and Exodus 32 : 11–14 and 34 : 1–10 is read. In the Ashkenazic ritual, the last sentence of Exodus 32 : 12 and 34 : 6–7 up to the word *wenakke* and the last sentence of verse 9 are chanted according to the Pentateuch Mode for the High Holydays.[79]

In some congregations, Minha is recited just before the evening service.

III. Arvith, Maariv — The Evening Service

The morning and afternoon services correspond to the morning and afternoon sacrifices at the Temple and act as their substitutes. The "Maariv" service has no equivalent in the ancient Temple service.

There was an old custom to recite the Shema and some prayers at home just before retiring, in accordance with the Scriptural advice (Deut. 6: 7): "And thou shalt . . . speak of them . . . when thou liest down . . . " (M. Ber. I, 3).

Rabbi Gamaliel of Jamnia ordered that the evening prayer shall be recited in the Synagogue and that this service be obligatory (b. Ber. 27b). The reason for this arrangement is given in b. Ber. 4b: "Upon returning home in the evening from his day's work, let no person say: 'I will go home, eat and sleep a little and then I will recite the Shema and pray,' for the result will be that he will be overcome by fatigue and will sleep throughout the whole night without having prayed. Therefore, before he returns home, every person shall go to the Synagogue, first study and read a little, and then recite the 'Shema' and pray, and after that go home and have his meal."

There was, however, strong opposition to this innovation; some claimed that it placed too heavy a burden upon the people. As a compromise, it was agreed that the Amida shall not be repeated twice in the evening service (Abudraham, p. 77).

Though the evening service became obligatory, the custom to read the Shema, at least the first paragraph, before retiring remained (b. Ber. 4b).

The evening service consists of two main sections:

I. *The Shema* and its benedictions, and

II. *The Amida.*

There are four benedictions in all rituals: two before and two after the Shema (M. Ber. I, 4). They are similar in their contents to the Shema benedictions of the morning service, with emphasis on the change of day and night, light and darkness.

Before the first benediction, the invocation *barechu* — "Bless ye the Lord" etc. — is recited, as in the morning service. Before the invocation, different Scriptural verses are read, according to the customs of the various rituals. The Sephardic and Ashkenazic rituals have Psalm 134 and several other verses, followed by *wehu rahum* — "And He being merciful, forgiveth iniquity . . . etc." from Psalms 78:38; 20:10. The reason for reciting these last two verses is given in M.V., p. 77, in *Hamanhig* I, 83, and in Abudraham, p. 75. In the Ashkenazic ritual, they are not said on Sabbaths and holidays (*Hamanhig, l.c.*).

1. *Asher bid'varo* — "Blessed art Thou . . . Who at Thy word bringest on the evening twilight . . . etc." (b. Ber. 11b). The eulogy concludes with *hammaariv aravim* (*l.c.*, 12a). This benediction corresponds to the Yotzer in the morning service. There, the creation of light is praised; here, the change of day and night is declared and praised.

2. *Ahavath olam* — "With everlasting love hast Thou loved the house of Israel . . . etc." (b. Ber. 11b). This benediction, too, corresponds to the "Ahava" benediction of the morning service.

Then the Shema follows as in the morning service.

3. *Gĕulla*, beginning with *emeth weĕmuna* — "True and trustworthy," has the same idea as the "Geula" in the morning service.

The Palestinian eulogy was *melech tzur yisrael wegoalo* — "King, Rock of Israel and his Redeemer" — as in the Palestinian morning service.[80]

4. *Hashkivenu* — "Cause us to lie down in peace . . . etc." — is a night prayer given in b. Ber. 4b and 9b. The wording varies in the different rituals. The *Talmud* considers this benediction a prolongation of the "Geula." The eulogy is *shomer ammo yisrael la'ad* — "Who guidest Thy people Israel for ever." The Palestinian version was *pores succath shalom alenu wĕal ammo yisrael wĕal yerushalayim* (Jer. Ber. IV, 5) which has been retained for Sabbaths and the holidays (see Chapter X).

5. *Baruch adonai lĕolam* — "Blessed be the Lord for evermore . . . etc." is a post-Talmudic addition composed in Babylonia probably (M.V., p. 78). According to some, it was inserted because the synagogues were placed outside of the city limits, and the people, being afraid to remain till after the evening service, would recite this prayer which contains the Name of God eighteen times and which thus replaced the Amida. Another reason given is that since *Maariv* used to be optional, this benediction served to replace the Amida. Only the Ashkenazic ritual has this benediction; while in the Italian and Yemenite rituals only the first paragraph is given in a shortened form. The Palestinian and Sephardic rituals do not have this benediction at all (M.V., *l.c.;* Abudraham, *l.c.*).[86]

Then the Amida follows.

On certain days, special psalms are recited after the service. In the month of Ellul up to Hoshana Rabba, Psalm 27 is recited both in the evening and the morning. This recitation was recommended by Sab. Rashkower in 1788.[81]

During Gaonic times, the recitation of Tahanun was customary in the evening (S.R.A. 19a).[82] M.V., p. 79, gives the recitation of the "Spices."

The Alenu and the Kaddish conclude the evening service.

CHAPTER IX

DAILY HOME PRAYERS

Prayer is not restricted to the Synagogue nor to the three daily services. In every act of his life the Jew is taught to give thanks and lift up his soul toward God. It thus became an obligation to utter words of devotion before and after partaking of food. These words of devotion are called

1. *Grace* before and after meals:

Before a regular meal, as before praying, the washing of the hands became obligatory. The Psalmist says, "I will wash my hands in innocency; so will I compass Thine altar, O Lord" (Psalm 26:6). According to a rabbinic interpretation, not only the Sanctuary is called altar, but also the dining-table.

When washing the hands a benediction is recited:

I, a. "Blessed . . . hast given us a command concerning washing of the hands." This benediction is also the first morning benediction. The expression *nĕtilath yadayim* for *rĕhitzath* is explained by the custom of lifting up the hands after washing and is the Aramaic translation of *sĕu yedêchem* — lift up your hands (Psalm 134:2; Baer, p. 36; K. Kohler). This benediction is given in b. Ber. 60b.

The custom of washing the hands as a sign of purification before divine services and before meals was enforced by the Pharisees against their opponents, the Sadducees, and especially against the early Christians to such a degree that if somebody neglected the custom he was suspected of heresy.[1]

b. Then the benediction: "Blessed . . . Who bringest forth bread from the earth" is said over bread; it is cited in M. Ber. VI, 1, and is based on Psalm 104:14.

II. The Grace after meals, *bircath hammazon*, is introduced, with Psalm 137. On days on which no Tahanun is said, Psalm 126 is recited instead. In some Eastern European communities Psalm 23 is recited. In other communities it is said before washing the hands. This custom is first mentioned in 1603.[2]

The source for the reciting of Psalm 137 is to be found in the *Zohar*, Teruma, where we read as follows: "Whoever enjoys his meal has to remember the desolation of the Holy Land and of the Temple, and express his grief and sorrow." This was limited to the weekdays, while on the Sabbath and festivals on which cheerfulness is prescribed, the Psalm 126 is ordered instead.

The *Talmud* traces the institution of saying Grace back to the patriarch Abraham. In b. Sota 10a Resh Lakish interprets the passage "And Abraham planted a tamarisk in Beer Sheba" (Gen. 21 : 33) that the patriarch made a garden and planted therein all kinds of precious things for the entertainment of wayfarers. "And he called there on the Name of the Lord." Abraham had the name of God proclaimed by all passers-by. How? After they ate and drank, they would rise to thank Abraham. But Abraham asked, "Was the food you have eaten mine? You have partaken of the bounty of the God of the universe. Now praise, glorify, and bless Him Who spoke and the world was" (Abrahams).

According to the testimony of the *Book of Jubilees*,[3] the first three benedictions of Grace were known long before the Destruction. In the Christian prayers of the first century as retained in the Didache, these three benedictions are reworked.[4]

According to b. Ber. 48b, the fourth benediction was added by the sages in Jamnia.

Josephus (II *Wars* VIII, 5) testifies to the custom of thanksgiving after meals, and goes back to the time of Simon ben Shetah (Jer. Ber. VII, 2), about 100 B.C.E. In the *Talmud* b. Ber. 48b it is stated that the first benediction was composed by Moses (Deut. 8 : 7–10), the second by Joshua, and the third by David and Solomon. The fourth was added by the sages after the Fall of Bar-Cochva.

a. *Hazzan* — "Blessed . . . Who givest food to all." This idea is found in Psalms 136 : 25 and 145 : 15–16. The thought is that God feeds all creatures.

b. *Bircath haaretz* — The blessing for the land. Some phrases of this benediction are based on Jeremiah 3 : 19; Exodus 2 : 2, and Deuteronomy 7 : 8. Ideas pertaining to the liberation from Egypt, to the covenant, and to the inheritance of the *land* are given expression in this benediction. On Hanucca and Purim, paragraphs which recount the miracles that happened to Israel in those days are included in this benediction; these paragraphs are the same as those found in the Amida of the morning service (Singer, pp. 51–52). It also embodies the petition that we may not be in need of gifts from flesh and blood — from human beings.

c. *Bone yěrushalayim* — The Rebuilding of Jerusalem. On Sabbaths, the paragraph "Be pleased, O Lord . . . etc." (b. Ber. 48b) is inserted; on holidays or half-holidays the paragraph "May our remembrance . . ." is added here. This benediction is similar to the fifteenth benediction of the Amida.

d. *Hattov wehammetiv* — "He Who is kind and deals kindly." This benediction ends with "of no manner of good let us be in want." The part beginning with *Harahaman* — "All Merciful" — is a later addition in which are included petitions for sustenance, redemption, and blessing for the host and his household and for one's own parents and family; it ends with "O fear the Lord" which is a compilation of Biblical verses.

If three male adults eat together, one of them begins the Grace as follows: "My lords, let us bless!" Whereupon the others respond: "Blessed be the Name of the Lord from this time forth and forever." Then he continues: "With the permission of my lords, we will bless Him of Whose bounty we have partaken;" and the others respond: "We will bless . . . and through Whose goodness we live."

In case there are ten adults present, the leader says: "We will bless *our Lord*."

Then he recites the entire Grace, while the others respond with "Amen" after each benediction and after each "The All Merciful."

Often the leader takes a cup of wine into his hand during Grace and drinks it afterwards. The whole procedure is described in b. Ber. 45, 49; Pesahim 103b.

The versions of several paragraphs vary in the different rituals. Maimonides gives an abbreviated wording, while the Sephardic ritual has a still longer form than the Ashkenazic ritual. The Yemenite ritual has a very short form similar to that of Maimonides, but it has a long benediction for the host which the guests are to recite; it begins with "And furthermore may God bless and guard and support and make to blossom and multiply and plant and enrich and strengthen and give long life to our lord the host. . . ."

Besides these, the Ashkenazic ritual has a short form of Grace in cases of emergency (Singer, p. 286; Baer, p. 562) which contains the nucleus of the four benedictions (*cf.* Appendix III, 2).

2. Blessings on various occasions:

I, a. Over wine: "Blessed . . . Who createst the fruit of the vine" (M. Ber. VI, 1).

b. Over food prepared of wheat, barley, rye, oats, and spelt, mixed with milk, butter, oil, or eggs: "Blessed . . . Who createst various kinds of food" (*l.c.*).

c. Over fruits which grow on trees: "Blessed . . . Who createst the fruit of the tree" (M. Ber., *l.c.*).

d. Over fruits which grow in or on the ground, as herbage, etc.: "Blessed . . . Who createst the fruit of the earth" (M. Ber., *l.c.*).

e. Over water, liquor (except wine), fish, meat, eggs, milk, and cheese: "Blessed . . . by Whose command all things come into being" (*l.c.*).

II, a. After partaking of any of the aliments referred to in the last three benedictions of I (c–e), the following short Grace is recited: ". . . Who createst many living beings and their wants. . . . Blessed be He Who is the life of all worlds" (b. Ber. 37a; Baer, p. 567; Singer, p. 290).

b. After the first two benedictions of I (a–b), the following is recited: "Blessed . . . (after wine) . . . for the vine and the fruit of the vine," and after foods mentioned in b: ". . . for the sustenance and the nourishment," "for the produce of the field" (Baer, p. 566; Singer, pp. 288–289).

III, a. On smelling fragrant trees or barks: "Blessed . . . Who createst fragrant woods" (b. Ber. 43b).

b. On smelling odorous plants: "Blessed . . . Who createst odorous plants" (b. Ber. 43b).

c. On smelling odorous fruits: "Blessed . . . Who createst a goodly scent to fruits" (*l.c.*).

d. On smelling fragrant spices: "Blessed . . . Who createst divers kinds of spices" (*l.c.*).

e. On smelling fragrant oils: "Blessed . . . Who createst fragrant oil."

f. On seeing lightnings, falling stars, great mountains, or other wonders of nature: "Blessed . . . Who hast made the creation."

g. On hearing thunders: "Blessed . . . Whose strength and might fill the world" (*l.c.*).

h. At the sight of the sea, ocean: "Blessed . . . Who hast made the great sea" (*l.c.*).

i. On seeing beautiful trees or animals: "Blessed . . . Who hast made such as these in Thy world" (*l.c.*).

j. On seeing the rainbow: "Blessed . . . Who rememberest the covenant, art faithful to Thy covenant, and keepest Thy promise." This benediction is based on Genesis 9: 12–17 (b. Ber. 59a).

k. On seeing trees blossoming for the first time in the year: "Blessed . . . Who hast produced therein goodly trees . . . to give delight unto the children of men" (b. Ber. 43b).

l. On seeing a distinguished sage, one learned in the sacred Law: "Blessed . . . Who hast imparted of Thy wisdom to them that fear Thee" (b. Ber. 58a).

m. On seeing a wise scholar in secular knowledge: "Blessed . . . Who hast given of Thy wisdom to flesh and blood" (*l.c.*).

n. On seeing a king or ruler of the country: "Blessed . . . Who hast given of Thy glory to flesh and blood" (*l.c.*).

o. On seeing strangely deformed creatures: "Blessed . . . Who variest the forms of Thy creatures" (b. Ber. 58b).

p. On fixing a Mezuza: "Blessed . . . Who hast sanctified us . . . and commanded us to affix a Mezuza" (Jer. Ber. IX, 3).

q. On tasting any fruit for the first time in the season, or on entering into the possession of a new home, or on observing a festival: "Blessed . . . Who hast kept us in life . . . and hast enabled us to reach this time" (b. Ber. 54).

r. On hearing good tidings: "Blessed . . . Who art good and dispensest good" (M. Ber. 9, 2).

s. On hearing evil tidings: "Blessed . . . the true Judge" (*l.c.*).

There are some more benedictions (see Baer, pp. 568–571), for various occasions. All these blessings are mentioned in the *Mishna* and *Talmud*.

3. Prayer before retiring at night.

The custom of reading the Shema with some prayers before retiring has been mentioned in Chapter I in connection with the evening service. The main text to be found in all rituals with some variations is as follows:

a. "Blessed . . . Who makest the bands of sleep to fall upon mine eyes . . . Who givest light to the whole world in Thy glory." This text is taken from b. Ber. 60b with some abbreviations.

b. The first paragraph of the Shema according to the Ashkenazic ritual; the Sephardic ritual orders the recitation of the whole Shema.

c. Psalms 91 and 3.

d. "Cause us, O Lord our God, to lie down. . . . " which is the same as the fourth benediction of the evening service without the concluding eulogy.

e. "Blessed be the Lord by day . . ." which is an abbreviation of the fifth benediction of the evening service (Ashkenazic ritual), also without the concluding eulogy.

f. A selection of Biblical verses, beginning with "The angel who hath redeemed me from all evil . . . " (Gen. 48:16), (Baer, p. 575; Singer, p. 296).

g. "In the name of the Lord, the God of Israel, may Michael be at my right hand, Gabriel at my left, before me Uriel, behind me Raphael, and above my head the Divine Presence of God." Bamidbar Rabba II, 9 gives some information concerning the four angels mentioned in this prayer. There, Michael is placed at the right, Uriel at the left side, and Gabriel in the front. They are created to correspond to the four directions of the wind.

h. Psalms 128; 4:5, and the hymn "Adon Olam."

i. Isaac Luria introduced a number of supplications and confessions to be recited before the first paragraph (a).

The Sephardic ritual mentions the first paragraph of the supplication in paragraph i. It then follows with the prayer "May we lie down in peace" which we mentioned in paragraph d, after which paragraph a is given with some variations. The Shema then follows as in paragraph b, and then Psalm 91 preceded by some Biblical verses which we mentioned in paragraph f. Whereupon Psalm 51 follows, concluding with a selection of Biblical verses.

CHAPTER X

THE SABBATH SERVICES

1. *Kabbalath shabbath*—The Inauguration of Sabbath. I. Friday before sunset, the Jewish woman kindles the Sabbath lamp consisting of a seven branched candelabra or of a minimum of two candles (M. Sabbath II: 6). Light and joy are a natural association with the Sabbath.[1] While kindling the Sabbath lights, a blessing is recited: "Blessed . . . and commanded us to kindle the Sabbath light." Preceding and following the kindling, meditations are recited (Singer, p. 108; Baer, p. 173). Shortly before the inauguration of the Sabbath—"Kabbalath Shabbath"—the Song of Songs used to be chanted. The mystics in Israel conceived the Sabbath as the beloved of Israel to whom he ought to sing a love song. Rabbi Akiva and other sages said that if the books of the Scriptures are holy, then the Song of Songs is the holy of holies (M. Yadayim III, 5; Midrash Sh. H. Sh. I, 11). The *Zohar*, Teruma, 143a, and Noah 62b explains the high value of chanting the Song of Songs on the eve of the Sabbath.[1a] The *Talmud* (b. Sabbath 119a), relates that the sages would clothe themselves in fine garments and would receive the "Sabbath Bride" or the "Sabbath Queen."

II, a. Since about 1600,[2] the service starts with Psalms 95–99, 29. Moses Cordovero, a Kabbalist of Safed and of Isaac Luria's school, introduced the recitation of these psalms. These six psalms stand for the six work-days (*cf.* Baer, p. 178 and *Otzar Hatefilloth*, p. 590). The Italian ritual has none of these psalms, while the Sephardic ritual has Psalm 29 only (see Chapter VI).

Anna bechoah is a mystical meditation with an alphabetic acrostic; its origin is obscure (see Chapter VI).

b. "Come, my friend, to meet the bride . . ." —*Lecha Dodi*—is a poem by Solomon Alkabetz (1505—died after 1572); he was a brother-in-law of Moses Cordovero, lived in

Safed, and was encouraged by Isaac Luria to compose this poem about 1571 (*Hemdath Yamim*, Leghorn, 1763, 1, 41; *Seder Hayyom*, *l.c.*).

This poem spread to all Jewish communities and became a favorite text for Synagogal composers, so that over two thousand settings were composed to it.

The name of the author is to be found as an acrostic at the beginnings of the stanzas: *Shelomo hallewi.*

The poem starts out with a refrain based on b. Sabbath 119a. In the first stanza: "Observe and Remember," the author refers to the Midrashic explanation (b. Shevuoth 20b) of the discrepancy between the two versions of the fourth Commandment in Exodus 20:8 and Deuteronomy 5:12, according to which God uttered both words simultaneously.

In the second stanza, the sentence "last in the making, first in thought" means that, though Sabbath came after the creation of the world (Gen. 2:3), it was nevertheless the aim of the entire creation (Breshith Rabba X:10). According to another explanation, the author refers to the Tora which was created before the world (b. Pes. 54).

The second stanza begins with "Come, let us go out to meet the Sabbath." In fact, under the leadership of Isaac Luria, the Kabbalists used to go outside of the city limits into the open fields; there they would chant psalms and songs and would thus receive the Sabbath. This custom, however, was later abandoned; and the Sabbath was received in the Synagogue-court in the open air (*Shivhê Ari; Seder Hayyom*, Sabbath).

While the first two stanzas deal with the value of the Sabbath, stanzas 3–8 deal with the hope of rebuilding Jerusalem, the coming of the Messiah, and the redemption of Israel.

In the last stanza, the poet turns to Sabbath again, calling it the crown of the husband. In the Sephardic, Italian, and Yemenite rituals, there is an additional phrase "Come, O Bride, Sabbath Queen" which is repeated in some places three times. While reciting the last stanza, the congregation turns toward the door, as if to welcome an entering guest.

The poet utilized several Biblical phrases: Isaiah 52:2; 51:17; 60:1; Jud. 5:12; Isaiah 60:1; 54:4; Psalm 42:12; Isaiah 14:32; Jer. 30:18; 30:16; Isaiah 49:19; 62:5; 54:3, and 25:9.

If Friday or Saturday is a festival, then the six psalms and the poem are omitted, in order not to overemphasize the Sabbath above the festival.[3]

c. After "Lecha Dodi," Psalms 92 and 93 are recited. Psalm 92 was sung by the Levites in the Temple on Saturdays (M. Tamid VII, 4; b. Rosh Hashana 31a). Neither S.R.A. nor M.V. nor *Hamanhig* nor even *Col-Bo* mention the reading of this psalm. Only Maimonides (Resp. "Peêr Haddor" § 116) says that its recitation on Friday evening was an ancient custom.

Bamme madlikin (M. Sabbath II), is read in some Ashkenazic congregations; it concludes with "Rabbi Eleazar said" (b. Ber. end). This reading is mentioned in S.R.A. 26a. In Italy and Germany this reading is postponed until after the service. The Sephardic ritual gives it before "Lecha Dodi" and the concluding paragraph after the poem.

Following "Lecha Dodi," the Yemenite ritual has *Bar yohay* — a well-known poem among the Oriental Jews; it was written by Simon Labi who lived in the first half of the sixteenth century. When a New Month falls on a Sabbath, an additional poem is chanted: *Shiru laêl nĕvonay.*

The Yemenite ritual does not have Psalm 93.

In the Ashkenazic ritual there is a custom that in the first week of their mourning mourners come to the Friday evening service and remain at the entrance of the synagogue. After Psalms 92 and 93 are recited, the reader walks up to them and says: "May God console you among the Mourners of Zion and Jerusalem" (Baer, p. 182). In some places, this is done before the Psalms are recited. This seems to be an old custom, for already in Jerusalem a special gate to the Temple was built for mourners. After the Destruction, the custom was transmitted to the Synagogue, where, so Soferim XIX, 12 states, after the Sabbath Musaf service the reader would meet the mourners at the entrance and would recite a benediction and the *Kaddish.*

In the Hasidic ritual, the Talmudic selections are recited after the service, while selections from the *Zohar: Kegawna* and *raza deshabbath* are read after "Lecha Dodi."

III. Then the regular evening service follows: i.e., the "Shema" and its four benedictions. The fourth benediction has the eulogy for Sabbaths and festivals (S.R.A. 25a): " . . . Who spreadest the tabernacle over us and over all Thy people Israel and over Jerusalem" (see Chapter VIII : III). This ending is mentioned in Jer. Ber. IV, 5. In Seville and Toledo it was customary to recite the same eulogy as on weekdays (Abudraham, p. 79).[4] The reason for the change may be that, in a religious sense, Sabbath itself is the guardian of Israel; hence the wording "Who guardest Thy people Israel for ever" is changed to embody the idea of peace which falls upon the Jewish home with the evening of the seventh day (Abrahams; see *Hamanhig*, II, 3; *Col-Bo* 34). The wording of the fourth benediction is abbreviated in the Sephardic ritual for Friday evening by cutting out the passage: "And remove from us enemies . . . from before and behind us;" this passage is cut out because on Sabbaths no mention of trouble ought to be made (*Hamanhig*, *l.c.*).

After the fourth benediction, Exodus 31:16–17 is recited. This is not mentioned in S.R.A. M.V. gives it as a silent reading. However, this reading was sanctioned already in Gaonic times,[5] probably due to the high value of the ideas expressed in the passage. The fifth benediction is not recited;[6] in some rituals, however, as in the Persian, the last paragraph of the fifth benediction is recited.[7]

The Amida of the Friday evening service consists of the three first and three concluding benedictions. A benediction dealing with the significance of the Day — *Kedushath hayyom* — is inserted between them. The Hebrew term for the benediction of the Day appears in M. Rosh Hashana IV, 5. The Amida is called *bircath sheva* (Tos. Ber. III, 12), because it has seven benedictions. In b. Ber. 29a, a reason is given for the number seven. *Tanhuma* Wayyera, beginning, says that the intermediary benedictions of the Amida ought not to be recited on Sabbaths, because they are petitions; when one recited them, he is reminded of his troubles, and on Sabbaths one ought rather to forget his sorrows and not be sad.

The benediction of the Day consists of an opening which used to be *umêahavath'cha* as quoted in Tos. Ber. III, 7 and in a longer from in S.R.A. 25a. This passage is also given by Saadya,[8] in *Hamanhig*, and in the Roman and Italian rituals.

The other opening passage is *atta kiddashta* which is now generally used; it first appeared in M.V., p. 143. *Hamanhig*, Sabbath 5, says that this opening passage was used in France and Provence, and remarks that it is more fit. Maimonides, too, gives this passage. The source of this text is unknown. It seems, however, that the first passage is Palestinian, while the second is Babylonian.

The next passage is Genesis 2: 1–3. This text does not occur in S.R.A. in the Amida; it is given for the reader to recite after the Amida. It was inserted in the Amida due to the statement in b. Shabbath 119b which maintains that even the individuals have to recite it. Hence, from M.V. down, with the exception of the Roman and the Yemenite rituals, all rituals give this passage in the Amida.

There is a Midrashic comment that *way'chulu* be recited three times: once in the Amida, once thereafter, and once at the *Kiddush*.[9]

The Sephardic ritual adds the paragraph *yismĕhu* (Abudraham) — "May they rejoice in Thy kingdom, they who observe the Sabbath . . . etc." This passage appears in the Sabbath morning service. The idea of rejoicing is mentioned briefly in the concluding paragraph, in the version given in S.R.A. and M.V.

The concluding paragraph, "Our God and God of our fathers . . . Who hallowest the Sabbath . . . etc." — *mekaddesh hashabbath* — (b. Pes. 117b) appears in all rituals with slight variations.

After the Amida, the reader and congregation repeat Genesis 2: 1–3 aloud (b. Pes. 106a). Then the reader recited the *meên sheva* — an abbreviation of the Amida. This repetition is for the late-comers (Rashi to b. Shabbath 24b). The first sentence seems to be the original wording of the "Avoth" (see Chapter VIII, E). The seven benedictions are included in the *magen avoth* as follows:

1. With His word He was a shield to our fathers — *Avoth.*
2. By His bidding He will quicken the dead — *Gevuroth.*

3. The holy God, like unto Whom there is none — *Kedushath Hashem.*
4. Who giveth rest to His people on the holy Sabbath day — *Kedushath Hayyom.*
5. Him we will serve with fear and awe — *Avoda.*
6. We will give thanks unto His Name — *Hoda'a.*
7. He is the Lord of peace — *Shalom.*

Following these benedictions, the Amida then turns to the significance of the Sabbath; whereupon the concluding paragraph is repeated. *Hamanhig*, Sabbath 7, reports that the "Magen Avoth" used to be chanted in a sweet tune. This chant is called "Mogen Avoth" mode.[10]

Following this, the reader recites the *Kaddish.*

Kiddush (b. Pes. 106; Ber. 20b). The santification over wine in the synagogue is an old institution; it was instituted as an accommodation to wayfarers who used to lodge and eat in the synagogue premises, as explained in b. Pes. 101a. Originally, it was arranged for the home to be recited before the evening meal. This custom survived in the Ashkenazic ritual only (M.V., p. 146), though according to Natronai Gaon "Kiddush" should be recited in the synagogue even if there are no wayfarers present (S.R.A. 25b).

The text of the *Kiddush* consists of Gen. 1:31 and 2:1–3. Then there follows the blessing over wine and the closing paragraph "Blessed . . . Who hallowest the Sabbath" (b. Pes. 117b). In the home, the benediction over bread follows (see Chapter IX). The text is given in S.R.A. 26a.

Before the blessing over wine, the sentence "Listen to me my lords and teachers" is recited, and all present respond with "To life." This is based upon *Tanhuma*, Pekude (Warsaw, 1840, 117a) which states that the response "To life" by the people present in the synagogue removes the suspicion which one might have concerning the presence of poison in the wine.

The use of wine for "sanctification" is first derived from the place wine occupies in the Scriptures. "Wine maketh glad the heart of man" (Psalm 104:15); "yea, it cheereth even God" (Jud. 9:12–13). For this reason, wine was offered at the sacrifices in the Temple, and from there the sanctification over wine was introduced into the home as a symbol of joy to usher in all holidays (M. Ber. VIII, 1). "It has been very plausibly maintained that such a custom as this is sanctified by use and degraded by abuse. Judaism is not a form of austere discipline; it not only admits, but also emphasizes the joyous side of life" (Abrahams).

At the conclusion of the Friday evening service, Alenu and the Mourner's Kaddish follow, and then the hymn Yigdal is chanted.[11]

2. The Sabbath morning service — *shaharith.*

a. In the morning, the "Bircoth Hashahar" are read as on weekdays.[12] In the Ashkenazic ritual, Psalm 100 of the "Verses of Song" is omitted, because there was no thank-offering on Sabbaths, and Psalms 19, 34, 90, 91, 135, 136, 33, 92, and 93 are inserted instead (M.V., p. 62). In the *Talmud* (b. Ber. 4b; Pes. 118a), Psalm 136 is called "The Great Hallel" — *hallel haggadol* — to distinguish it from the "Egyptian Hallel" — *hallel hammitzri* — (Psalms 113–118) which is sung on festivals, New Moons, and on Hanucca. The reason for these additional readings is given in *Col-Bo* (quoted by Baer, p. 62); the reason is that on Sabbaths praises ought to be given which deal with the wonders of God and His creations.[13]

b. Through the Song of the Sea the order of the "Verses of Song" is the same as on weekdays. Then, the praise *Nishmath* — "The breath of every living being shall bless Thy Name. . . ." (Singer, pp. 125–127), follows and concludes with "Praised be Thy Name for ever" which is recited also on weekdays as the concluding benediction of the "Verses of Song." The idea of this hymn is that there is no means by which to describe the greatness of God. S.R.A. gives a much shorter form of that praise. In the *Talmud* (b. Ber. 59b; Taanith 6b) it is quoted as part of the service for rain, while in b. Pesahim 118a it is recommended for the closing of the "Haggada" service on Passover night. This praise is called the Benediction of the Song — *bircath hashir* (*cf.* Appendix III, 3).

Many Biblical phrases have been utilized in the *Nishmath.*[14]

The half-Kaddish follows the "Verses of Song."

c. The Shema and its benedictions:

(a) The *Yotzer* benediction has the same beginning as on weekdays, but after the first sentence, special phrases are inserted: "All shall thank Thee . . . by Thy attribute of mercy. . . ." Then the weekday text follows: "In mercy Thou givest light. . . . Thou stronghold of ours. . . ." Here another insertion follows: "There is none to be compared unto Thee . . . for the resurrection of the dead." The Sephardic, Yemenite, and Roman rituals have some variations in this insertion.

El adon — "God the Lord over all works. . . ." It is an alphabetical hymn; its meter is four accents to the line. This poem was most likely composed by "Searchers in the Chariot" — *Yorde mercava.* To this group the paragraphs in the Kedusha and in the *Yotzer* are attributed.

The hymn is a praise to God for the creation of the heavenly hosts: the sun, moon, and the stars. The phrase: "He looked, and ordained the figure of the moon" may refer to b. Hulin 60b which interprets Genesis 1:16 where first the sun and the moon are called "two great lights" and then the sun is referred as being "the greater light" and the moon as "the lesser light." The initial words of each line present the poem for the weekday Yotzer which is *El Baruch.*

The paragraph "To the God Who rested from all the works . . . and on the earth beneath . . ." is also inserted. The sentence *tifereth ata lĕyom hamĕnuha* is translated in two ways: "With honor did he robe the day of rest" (De Sola, Heidenheim, and Sachs), or "Who robed Himself with glory on the day of rest" (Singer).

From "be Thou blessed" and on up to the end of the fourth benediction "Who hast redeemed Israel" there follows the same text as on weekdays.

d. The Amida for the morning service consists of the first three and last three benedictions of the weekday Amida. The intermediate benediction is devoted to the significance of Sabbath similar to that of the Friday evening service.

In public worship, the "Kedusha" is recited between the second and the third benedictions (see Chapter VIII, E). There is a special Kedusha for the morning service of Sabbaths and festivals. In the Ashkenazic ritual, the Kedusha starts with the same introductory passage as on weekdays:

I. "We will sanctify Thy Name," recited by the reader, and the congregation responds:
II. "Holy, holy, holy, etc. . . ."
III. Reader: Then with a noise of great rushing . . . etc."
IV. Congregation: "Blessed be the glory . . . etc."
V. Reader: "From Thy place shine forth . . . etc."
VI. Congregation: "The Lord shall reign . . . etc."
VII. Reader: "Unto all generations . . . etc."

Passages I, II, IV, VI, and VII are also used in the weekday Kedusha. Passages III and V are special insertions. Passage III is based on Ezekiel 3:12–13, and V is rather a prayer for the restoration of Zion and Jerusalem. S.R.A. gives the same two passages in abbreviated forms. In S.R.A. this Kedusha is used for all services with the introductory passage "Kether" (see Chapter VIII). For the morning service of Sabbath, the Sephardic and Italian rituals have the same Kedusha as on weekdays. The Yemenite and Persian rituals have *nakdishach wenaaritzach* at the beginning, and then III and V with some variations follow (on details about the Kedusha see Chapter VIII, E).

According to the Ashkenazic ritual, the intermediate benediction has the following paragraphs:

I. "Moses rejoiced in the gift of his portion. . . ." in which Exodus 31:16–17 is included.
II. "And Thou didst not give it. . . ." in which the contents of Jubilee 11:16 are echoed (Abrahams). For *arelim*, the Italian ritual has *arlê lev*. Maimonides gives this passage for the Musaf. The Sephardic ritual has the beginning of the passage: "The people that hallow the seventh day. . . ." namely, "May they rejoice." The Yemenite ritual has the first part only: "May they rejoice," until "The people who hallow the seventh day."
III. The closing paragraph is the same as in the evening service.

e. If the New Moon and half-holidays occur on Sabbath and Hanucca, the Hallel is recited after the Amida (Psalms 113–118). For the differences in the forms of the Hallel (see Chapter XII).

f. The Order of Reading from the Pentateuch and the Haftara (Prophetical selections):

A. Before taking out the Scroll, the following verses are recited: Psalms 86 : 8; 145 : 13; a compilation of 10 : 16, *adonai melech;* 93 : 1, *adonai malach;* Exodus 15 : 18, *adonai yimloch lĕolam waed;* Psalms 29 : 11, and 51 : 20. The reading of these verses is given in T. Soferim XIV : 8. Then there follows "Father of mercy." The passage: "And it came to pass when the ark set forward . . . etc." is the same as on weekdays; likewise the paragraph from the *Zohar:* "Blessed be the Name of the Sovereign . . . etc."

The reader then takes the Scroll and chants: "Hear, O Israel. . . ." "Our God is One. . . ." and "Magnify the Lord with me. . . ." Whereupon, the congregation joins with the recitation of "Thine, O Lord, is the greatness. . . ." and with "Magnified and hallowed. . . ." given in T. Soferim XIV : 12.

The Scroll is then placed upon the desk, and the reader recites: "And may He help. . . ." He then names the person who is called to the reading of the portion. The benedictions are the same as on weekdays.

The Sephardic ritual inserts other Biblical verses; it has no "Shema" save "O Magnify the Lord. . . ."

B. The reading from the Pentateuch in public is an old institution. Talmudic tradition refers public readings on Sabbaths, holidays, New Moons, and half-holidays to Moses, and the readings on Mondays and Thursdays to Ezra (Jer. Meg. IV, 1; b. B.K. 82).

Traces of readings in public are found in Exodus 24 : 3; Deuteronomy 5 : 1; 27 : 11–26; 31 : 11–12. In the latter, it was ordered that the Tora should be read before the whole assembly of the people at the Sanctuary on Succoth at least every seven years (Deuteronomy 31 : 19, 28; II Kings 23 : 2; Nehemiah 8 : 2–8). *Mishna* Megilla II, 4–5 knows it as an old established custom. From the Scriptural quotations we see that originally the readings took place on festivals. Ezra read on every day of the Succoth week (Nehemiah 8 : 18); the High Priest had to read on the Day of Atonement (M. Yoma VII, 1). But evidently, this custom was extended to all Sabbaths and festivals as well as to the days of Hanucca and Purim at an early date, probably about the third century B.C.E. Philo (De Opificio Mundi, p. 48), Josephus (Contra Apionem II, 17), and the Apostles (Acts 15:21) speak of it as an old institution. The reason for the institution of this custom was to instruct the people in the Law and its regulations concerning the ways of Jewish life in general and in the laws pertaining to the holidays in particular, as evident from the quotations cited above.

The reading takes place in accordance with a fixed order. For the festivals, the portions dealing with each holiday were ordered to be read. For Sabbaths, the Pentateuch was divided into small portions: *parasha*, *seder*, or *sidra*. In Palestine, the reading of the Pentateuch was covered in three or in three and a half years; the Pentateuch was thus divided into about one hundred and seventy-five portions. In Babylonia, the reading was completed in one year; the Pentateuch was thus divided into fifty-four larger portions (b. Meg. 29b). The Palestinian custom continued up to about the ninth or tenth centuries. The Babylonian custom finally came to be generally used (see Chapter IV).

The portions are subdivided into seven small sections on Sabbaths. For each section a person is called upon to read (see Chapter VIII, G). The division of fifty-four portions was arranged for leap years which have an additional month. Furthermore, if a festival falls on a Sabbath, the regular portion is substituted by the portion for that festival. Due to these two circumstances, there are several superfluous portions during the year. In order to complete the reading of the Pentateuch by the end of the year, two portions are read on some Sabbaths (*cf.* Appendix III, 3).

Aside from the regular portions, additional paragraphs are read on some Sabbaths. For instance, when a New Moon falls on a Sabbath, Numbers 28:9–15 is read. Furthermore, on the four distinguished Sabbaths: 1. *Shekalim* which falls on the Sabbath on which the month of "Adar" is announced or on which the New Moon of this month occurs, 2. *Zachor* which falls on the Sabbath before Purim, 3. *Para* which comes on the Sabbath after Purim, and 4. *Hahodesh* which falls on the Sabbath on which the month of *Nissan* is announced.

On these four distinguished Sabbaths the following additional portions are read respectively: Exodus 30:11–16; Deuteronomy 25:17–19; Numbers 19; and Exodus 12:1–20.

The additional readings for these four Sabbaths are given in Tos. Meg. (3) 4 (ed. Zuckerm., p. 225).[15]

On the Sabbath which falls on the week of Hanucca, the portion from Numbers 7 is read.

A special Scroll is taken out for the additional readings. If there is no extra Scroll, both readings are taken from the same Scroll.

At times, two special readings are added. For example, if the sixth day of Hanucca which is the New Moon day of the month "Teveth" falls on a Sabbath, then there is one additional reading for Hanucca and another for the New Moon (b. Meg. 29b). The same procedure is followed when "Shekalim" and a New Moon come together on a Sabbath. For this purpose, three Scrolls are taken out, one for each reading.

C. The reading from the Prophets is called *Haftara*, meaning, the conclusion. The custom of reading from the Prophets is supposed to be younger than that of reading from the Pentateuch. It was considered an established custom at the time of Jesus (Luke 4:17; Acts 13:15). In the Scriptural reading of the morning service, the readings from the Prophets became obligatory on Sabbaths and festivals. The readings from the Prophets may have been instituted to emphasize the great value of these books to the Pentateuch and to show that they contain ideas parallel to those in the Pentateuch. This was done to oppose the Samaritan viewpoint which maintained that only the Pentateuch is sacred and which did not recognize the Prophets at all. In fact, the portions read from the Prophets are selected in such a way as to make the ideas parallel to the ideas, events, or laws expressed in the Pentateuchal portion (b. Meg. 29b). This, however, holds true only of some of the *Haftaras;* in several others the relation between them and the Pentateuchal portion is very loose — unless there was some reason for their reading which is no longer known. Abudraham, p. 93, states that the reason for the institution of the Haftara is that a prohibition against the reading of the Pentateuch was once issued by Antiochus Epiphanes and the reading from the Prophets was then substituted.[16]

The Haftara is usually read from a printed book. No Scroll is necessary. In some congregations a Scroll is used. The person who is to read the Haftara is called *maftir;* he recites the benediction of the Tora, and the last few verses of the seventh part are repeated to him. He then says the second benediction. The Scroll is then lifted toward the people who recite "And this is the Law," which Moses set before the children of Israel, as on weekdays (T. Soferim XIV: 14). Whereupon the person called on recites the first benedictions which are mentioned in T. Soferim XIII: 9–14 together with the second benedictions.

There are altogether five benedictions. One is recited before and four after the Haftara. Some of them are quoted in the *Talmud* and have much in common with the benedictions recited by the High Priest on the Day of Atonement (M. Yoma VII, 1). The third and fourth benedictions bear similarity to the weekday Amida (see Chapter VIII, E). The contents of the benedictions are as follows:

1. "Blessed . . . Who hast chosen good prophets."
2. "Blessed . . . Who speakest and fulfillest . . . Who art faithful in all Thy words."
3. "Have mercy upon Zion. . . ."
4. "Gladden us, O Lord our God, with Elija the prophet . . . and with the kingdom of the house of David."
5. "For the Law, for the divine service, for the prophets . . . Who sanctifiest the Sabbath."

Since the person called to read the Haftara is not included in the *seven*, a minor, a boy less than thirteen years old, may read it.

In the subdivisions of the Pentateuchal portions as well as in the Prophetic selections there are differences between the various rituals.

On the four distinguished Sabbaths, on Sabbaths on which a New Moon occurs, and on Sabbaths on which Hanucca falls special Prophetic selections are read: For "Shekalim," II Kings 11: 17–20 and 12: 1–17 is read; for "Zachor," I Samuel 15 is read; for "Para," Ezekiel 36: 16–38 is read; for "Hahodesh," Ezekiel 45: 16–25, and 46: 1–18 is read; for New Moon, Isaiah 66 is read; for Hanucca, Zachariah 2: 14–17; 3; and 4: 1–7 is read on the first Sabbath, and I Kings 7: 40–50 is read on the second Sabbath of Hanucca.

Concerning the Modes according to which the Pentateuch and the Prophets are chanted compare *Jewish Music*, Chapter III.

D. After the reading of the Haftara and its benedictions, prayers for the welfare of the scholars and academies in Palestine and Babylon, as well as for the welfare of the communities, are recited. There are two paragraphs in Aramaic, both beginning with *yekum purkan* — "May salvation from heaven." In all likelihood, they were composed in Babylon where Aramaic was the vernacular of the Jews, though S.R.A. does not have them. M.V., p. 99, mentions only one paragraph. Following these, there is a Hebrew paragraph the content of which is similar to the second Aramaic passage. It singles out those who donated to the Synagogue and its upkeep and those who give to charity.

The other rituals have no Aramaic paragraphs. Only the Sephardic ritual inserts into the Hebrew an Aramaic passage.

On Sabbaths on which the New Moon is announced, the Ashkenazic ritual has an introductory prayer *yĕhi ratzon* — a petition composed by Abba Arecca (b. Ber. 16b). In order to fit this prayer to the occasion, the sentence "to renew unto us this coming month for good and for blessing" is inserted. In the first part of the eighteenth century, this prayer was introduced into the Polish ritual. The Ashkenazic ritual carries it since one hundred years ago. It is not recited in most of the Southwestern congregations. M.V., p. 58, has this paragraph in the daily morning benedictions.

Following this prayer, there is *mi sheasa* — "He Who wrought" — and then the name of the month and the day on which the New Moon occurs are announced, and this part is concluded with "May the Holy One . . . renew it . . . etc. — *yĕhadĕshehu*.

In these two passages the hope for redemption and for the renewal of the coming month for blessing and salvation is voiced.

The other rituals differ in the order of announcing the month. The Sephardic ritual has those petitions which the Ashkenazic ritual, following S.R.A., has for Mondays and Thursdays after the reading from the Pentateuch; then the second and concluding paragraphs follow with but slight variations. The Italian ritual has only the second paragraph, and closes with the concluding passage of the petition mentioned in the weekday reading.

A prayer for the welfare of the government is recited every Sabbath after the Haftara. This custom is based upon Jeremiah 29:7 and M. Avoth III:2: "Pray for the welfare of the government." Several Biblical phrases are utilized in this prayer. It closes with the verses from Jeremiah 23:6 and Isaiah 59:20 — which are a prayer for Israel's and Zion's redemption. The Sephardic ritual has the same prayer, but the Italian and the Yemenite rituals do not have it.

In the Sephardic and also in the Ashkenazic rituals, a prayer is offered before "Ashre" for those who will fast on the public Fast-days: the Tenth of Teveth, the Seventeenth of Tammuz, the Fast of Gedalia which falls on the third of the month of Tishri.

Then "Ashre" — Psalm 145 — is recited.

On Sabbaths on which no holidays nor New Moons nor announcements of New Months nor any of the distinguished Sabbaths occur, the paragraph "May the Father of mercy . . ." — *av harahamim* — is recited in the East European congregations. In the Southwestern German congregation this prayer is recited only on the Sabbath before Shavuoth and the Fast of the Ninth of Av. This prayer does not appear in any other ritual. It was seemingly composed during the first Crusade in 1096. This elegy over the persecuted Jewish communities utilizes several Biblical passages, as: II Samuel 1:23; Deuteronomy 32:43; Joel end; Psalms 79:10; 9:13, and 110:6–7.

On returning the Scroll to the ark, the same Biblical verses are recited as on weekdays, with the addition of Psalm 29 concerning which the rituals vary.

3. *Musaf* — The Additional Service. When the Scroll is replaced in the Ark, the half-Kaddish is recited, and then the Amida of the additional service is read, first in silent devotion, and then repeated by the reader aloud. As already mentioned above (see Structure, etc.), this service was instituted to replace the additional sacrifice in the Temple which used to be offered in accordance with Numbers 28:9 (b. Ber. 26). The Hebrew name does not occur in the Bible, save in *Mishna* Taanith IV, 1, 4. According to Tosefta Ber. III and b. Succa 53a, this service was in use at the time when sacrifices were still offered: "If somebody prayed Musaf even before the

morning burnt-offering was sacrificed, he also fulfilled his duty." The form of the Musaf, i.e., seven benedictions, is given in the Talmudic literature (Tos. Ber. III, 10).

The additional service consists of the three first and the three last benedictions of the Amida, with an insertion for the sanctification of the day. There is a difference of opinion concerning the contents of this intermediate benediction with regard to the necessity of adding some new material (Jer. Ber. IV, 6).

The nucleus of the intermediate benediction is the passage in Numbers 28:7. An introductory paragraph precedes it. According to the Ashkenazic, Persian, Roman,[17] Italian, and French (M.V.) rituals, this paragraph is: *ticcanta shabbath* — "Thou didst institute the Sabbath"; it has a reversed alphabetical acrostic. It has been suggested that this paragraph is of Palestinian origin. The old Sephardic, Yemenite, and Portuguese rituals (Abudraham; Maimonides; Gaster I, p. 117) have another introduction: "On Mount Sinai didst Thou command Moses. . . . " — *lemoshe tziwwitha*. In the Sephardic-Oriental ritual both paragraphs are given. The sentence: "May it be Thy will . . . to lead us up in joy unto our land, and to plant us within our borders where we will prepare . . ." is found in all Musaf services.

Landshuth, pp. 319, 467 holds that the Sabbath version is the oldest and served as a nucleus for the version of the festivals and New Moons.

The two closing paragraphs follow the Biblical passage. The last paragraph is the same as in the morning service, while the passage: "May they rejoice" which occurs in the morning service of the Ashkenazic ritual in part is given in the Musaf in full.

If the New Moon falls on Sabbath, another introductory paragraph is recited; it is *atta yatzarta* — "Thou didst form Thy world of old. . . ." This passage utilizes several Biblical phrases and is given in S.R.A. and in all the rituals. The Ashkenazic ritual has some variations in the sentences.

The closing paragraph is likewise changed and elaborated with ideas appropriate for the New Moon. The plea for the forgiveness of iniquities is based upon b. Shevuoth 9a–b; it speaks of hidden sins committed during the month that are bound to be known. M.V., p. 197, has a longer version.[18]

The Kedusha for the Musaf has the following:

I. Reader: "We will revere and sanctify Thee. . . ."
II. Congregation: "Holy, holy, holy, etc."
III. Reader: "His glory filleth the universe. . . ."
IV. Congregation: "Blessed be the glory. . . ."
V. Reader: "From His place may He turn in mercy . . ."
VI. Congregation: "Hear, O Israel. . . ."
VII. Reader: "Our God is One. . . ."
VIII. Congregation: "I am the Lord your God . . ."
IX. Reader: "And in the holy words. . . ."
X. Congregation: "The Lord shall reign. . . ."

S.R.A., Sephardic, Aleppo, Italian, and Yemenite rituals and Abudraham have another version for I: "Unto Thee, O Lord, a crown. . . ." — *kether*. The Ashkenazic passage is similar to the first passage in the Kedusha of the morning service, according to the Sephardic ritual discussed in Chapter VIII, E. Both passages draw upon *Pirke d. R. Eliezer*, Chapter IV, where a scene of angels chanting to the Lord is presented. The idea of making a crown for God is often expressed in the Talmudic literature (*cf.* b. Hagiga 13b). Passages II–IX are found in all rituals with the exception of the Yemenite and Aleppo. These rituals have II–IV and IX; for V–VIII, they have only one long paragraph which is V of the Shaharith Kedusha.

The reason for reciting the Shema in the Kedusha we explained in Chapter VIII, E.

After Musaf, the Kaddish-*tithkabbal* is recited; then follows the hymn "En Kelohenu" (see Chapter VIII, H), after which come *pittum haketoreth* a paragraph from b. K'rithuth 6a, one from M. Tamid, end *hashir shehalĕwiyim*, and one from b. Ber., end *amar rabbi ĕliezer*. After these recitations, the rabbinical Kaddish follows, whereupon Alenu and the Mourner's Kaddish are recited. Then the seventh part of the "Song of Unity" and the "Song of Glory" and the "Song of the Day" (Psalm 92) are recited.

The "Song of Unity" is attributed to Samuel the Pious of the twelfth century, Samuel b. Kalonymos of Germany. In a pleasant style and simple form the author expresses some philosophical ideas of Saadya Gaon's *Emunoth Wedêoth*.

The "Song of Glory" is ascribed to Juda b. Samuel the Pious, a son of the former Samuel. He lived in Regensburg. The poem is identical in style and form to the previous.

Both these forms are chanted in the traditional mode of "Akdamuth" in responsive form.[19]

4. The Afternoon Service, *Minha*. The Sabbath Minha service begins with "Ashre" — Psalm 145 — and "a redeemer shall come to Zion. . . ." The reason why the latter is recited in the afternoon instead of in the morning service as on weekdays is (as given in *Rokeah* § 362 and *Col-Bo*), not to prolong the morning service. Since before the service on Sabbath afternoon, it was customary to lecture as it was on weekdays after the morning service, it was found fitting to recite this prayer which embodies the petition for the retention of the Tora in our midst, as well as a glorification of God (Abudraham, p. 68).

The half-Kaddish is then recited and is followed with Psalm 69:14. Whereupon the Scroll is taken out according to the same ritual as on weekdays.

The reading from the Pentateuch is the same as that on Mondays and Thursdays, namely, the first ten verses of the next Sabbath portion subdivided into three parts to which three persons are called upon: Cohen, Levi, Israel (b. Meg. 31b). The replacing of the Scroll takes place in the same manner as on weekdays. M.V., p. 179, gives the reading of the petitions for Mondays and Thursday which are not used in the Ashkenazic ritual (see Chapter VIII, G).

In Babylonia and in some other places it was customary to read a prophetic portion (*Haftara*) even during Sabbath Minha service. (b. Shabbath 24a and Rashi's commentary there.)[20]

Then the Amida follows. It consists of the three first and the three last benedictions and of a special intermediate benediction which has two paragraphs:

I. *Atta ehad*— "Thou art One and Thy Name is One . . ." is used in all rituals. The idea is taken from a Midrashic interpretation of I Chron. 17:21 (Tosafoth to b. Hagiga 3b). The old Roman ritual, however (A. Schechter, *o.c.*, p. 114), has another paragraph: "Let us rest, O our God. . . ." S.R.A. 30a gives both prayers.

The sentence: "Abraham was glad, Isaac rejoiced, and Jacob and his sons rested thereon" is based on a Talmudic tradition which maintains that the patriarchs observed the Sabbath (b. Yoma 28b; Breshith Rabba § 11, 7–9).

II. This paragraph is the same as in the other Sabbath Amidas.

After the silent devotion, the reader repeats the Amida, and the weekday Kedusha is recited.

After the Amida, three verses from Psalms 119:142; 71:19, and 36:7 are recited. These verses occur in the same order in S.R.A., while in M.V. in the Sephardic and Yemenite rituals the verses appear in the reversed order. The reason for reciting the acceptance of the "Divine Judgment," as these three verses are called — *tzidduk haddin* — are manifold. One reason is that Moses died on Sabbath afternoon, as tradition recounts (*cf.* Baer, p. 265, and S.R.A. 30a).

The full-Kaddish is recited, and then Alenu and the Mourners-Kaddish.

Between Tabernacles and Passover, a selection of Psalms is read after the afternoon service. This custom is not mentioned in S.R.A. nor in M.V. (Baer, p. 266, quotes several reasons for this custom). According to the Ashkenazic ritual, Psalms 104, 120–134 are recited (Abrahams, pp. clxxi–clxxii, gives various opinions for the selection of these Psalms). The Italian ritual has Psalm 119 instead of 104 and concludes with Psalm 90. The Yemenite ritual has none at all; the Sephardic ritual has Psalms 119, 120–134, 16, and 75.[21] Landshuth, p. 347, quotes the *Levush* § 669 who says that Psalm 104 was originally ordered to be recited on the Sabbath on which Genesis 1–2 is read, because it deals with the creation of the world.

Mishna Avoth is recited between Passover and New Year (in some congregations only up to the Seventeenth of Tammuz and in others up to Ellul or only to Shavuoth); one chapter is read every Sabbath. This custom is mentioned in S.R.A., *l.c.*, and in M.V. § 141; and from § 424 on the *Mishna* is given with an elaborate commentary. This custom is also mentioned in b. B.K. 30a. The Sephardic and Italian rituals, however, do not have this custom. Each reading is preceded by a short sentence from M. Sanhedrin X : 1: "All Israel have a portion in the world to come. . . ." and concludes with another passage from *Mishna* Maccoth III : 16: "Rabbi Hananya . . . the Holy One . . . was pleased to make Israel worthy. . . ."

Originally, the custom of reading *Mishna* Avoth was instituted for the whole year, as M.V. has it, to instruct the people in the Ethics of the Fathers. Later on, changes were introduced, and readings from the Book of Psalms were substituted. The exact reason for this substitution is not certain.[22]

5. Evening Service for the outgoing Sabbath — *arvith lemotzaê shabbath.* Preceding this service, Psalms 144 and 67 are chanted in the traditional tune.[23] Abudraham, p. 98, states that the reason why these psalms are chanted between the afternoon and evening service is that the outgoing Sabbath ought to be accompanied with song, in the same manner that the Sabbath is received. In the Sephardic ritual, therefore, these two psalms constitute the closing of the psalms recited in the afternoon. They are all chanted before the evening service.

This service starts later than the usual time of the evening service, so that the people rejoice with the Sabbath as long as possible (b. Shabbath 118b). In the Ashkenazic ritual the chanting of these two psalms became customary about the beginning of the seventeenth century.[24]

The evening service is the same as on weekdays, save that in the Amida a paragraph is inserted in the fourth benediction: "Thou hast favored us. . . ." (b. Ber. 33; Pesahim 104a). The version in our Ashkenazic ritual differs somewhat from that in M.V., p. 180. S.R.A. has another version which is to be found in the Italian ritual too. Again, the Sephardic ritual has a different version. The Yemenite ritual which follows Maimonides has other variations. All, however, express the main idea — that of distinguishing the Sabbath from other days and Israel from other nations. The rule in the *Talmud* (Pesachim, *l.c.*) states that a minimum of three distinctions must be expressed: between sacred and secular, between light and darkness, and between Israel and other peoples; and a maximum of seven such distinctions.

After the Amida, half-Kaddish is recited, and then Psalms 90: 17; 91, and the part of "And a redeemer shall come to Zion" beginning with "But Thou art holy . . ." to the end of that prayer.

S.R.A., 31a, says that these readings have to be chanted in a sweet tune and their recitations have to be prolonged in order to give the wicked a little more rest. During the Sabbath the wicked are believed to be freed from Hell, but as soon as Israel finishes the evening service they have to return to their ordeal. These paragraphs are not recited if the outgoing Sabbath falls on a holiday.

The paragraphs inserted in the fourth benediction are called *Havdala*—"Separation." In addition to these, there is another *Havdala* over wine. The recitation of both is compulsory (b. Ber. 33a–b). Tradition has it that like the benedictions and prayer, *Kedusha and Havdala* were arranged by the Men of the Great Assembly (b. Ber., *l.c.*). Great emphasis was laid upon the recitation of "Havdala" over wine (b. Pes. 113; S.R.A. 32). This recitation consists of the following:

I. A benediction over wine.

II. A benediction over the kindling of fire: "Blessed . . . Who createst the light of the fire" (M. Ber. VIII, 5; b. Ber. 51b–52a).

III. A benediction over spices: "Blessed . . . Who createst divers kinds of spices."

IV. "Blessed . . . Who makest a distinction between the holy and the profane" (b. Ber. 33; Pesahim 104). The wording of this benediction is practically the same as the insertion in the Amida.

The Talmud orders the recitation of these four benedictions, while the introductory paragraph: "Behold, God is my salvation. . . ." consisting of Isaiah 12: 2–3; Psalms 3: 9; 46: 12; Esther 8: 16; and Psalm 116: 13 is a late addition.

S.R.A. and the Yemenite ritual have no introduction at all. The Sephardic, the Sephardic-Oriental, and the Roman rituals have different introductions. The Italian ritual has the same version as the Roman plus additional sentences. M.V., p. 116, gives several more verses in addition to our version.

The reason for saying the benediction over spices is given in M.V., p. 117. With the outgoing of the Sabbath, the additional soul is believed to depart from us. Joy then leaves us. For this reason, we are ordered to invigorate ourselves with the perfume of spices.

The reason for the benediction over light is given in S.R.A. 32; it is to marvel at God's creation of the light of fire at night when we see it. It became customary to look at the fingers while reciting this benediction, in order to distinguish by the light of fire between the color of the nails and the color of the fingers. Baer, pp. 311–312, gives another Midrashic reason.

The "Havdala" is recited by the reader in the synagogue and again at home by everybody.

Preceding the "Havdala" — in some communities following it — a selection of Biblical verses is recited. It begins with *weyitten lecha* — "And God give thee of the dew of heaven. . . ."; it consists of eight paragraphs. The first seven are from the Bible; the eighth is from b. Meg. 31a. The Sephardic, Italian, and Sephardic-Oriental rituals have parts of it with some other selections. M.V. has almost the same version as the Ashkenazic ritual, while the Yemenite ritual does not have such a selection at all.

These passages give assurance of the divine blessing, deliverance, consolation, and peace, selected for meditation at the conclusion of the Sabbath and at the commencement of the new week (Abrahams; see Tur Or. H. § 294).

THE POETICAL INSERTIONS FOR DISTINGUISHED SABBATHS. Several Sabbaths of the year were embellished with poetical insertions into the service explaining their significance. Such insertions are found in those rituals which cherished "piyyut," such as the Roman, Italian, Roumanian, and Ashkenazic rituals (Appendix IV).

The poetical insertions for the distinguished Sabbaths — and there are about twenty-eight of them — lend both color and content to these Sabbaths. The material is usually taken from the Jewish lore and the history appertaining to these days.

In this manner, religious regulations as well as pleasant and sad historic events are kept fresh in the mind of the Jew, especially if they are presented in poetical forms and are chanted in Jewish traditional tunes.

The special liturgical elements for Sabbath voice the idea of rest, cessation of labor, the idea of spiritual elevation, of instruction in religious and ethical principles. It is their purpose to purify heart and soul from the daily toil and to lift up the spirit from the pettiness of weekday life. The angels of peace relieve the Jew from the grasp of the angels of battle, and elevate him to the realm of peace and bliss.

The prayers breathe into the heart of the Jew a hope in a brighter and better future when his redemption will come and when the eternal Sabbath will dawn upon him and upon all mankind.

Thus the Sabbath liturgy achieved its purpose. Throughout the ages it strengthened religious-ethical ideals and Jewish consciousness.

CHAPTER XI

SABBATH MEDITATIONS AND SONGS FOR THE HOME

The main ideas of Sabbath: physical and spiritual rest and joy, spiritual elevation and instruction in Jewish religious and ethical principles, so wonderfully expressed in the Sabbath service, received additional emphasis in the meditations arranged for the home and in the "Table Songs" — *Zemiroth* — sung during the meals. These were instituted with the purpose of extending the Sabbath atmosphere from the synagogue to the home, so that Jewish life be filled with the Sabbath-spirit throughout the Sabbath-day. In addition to these, several ceremonies for the home were created during the ages, which ceremonies also helped to permeate the Jewish family with the lofty ideals of the Sabbath and Judaism.[1]

1. FRIDAY EVENING. The blessing over the light has been explained at the beginning of Chapter X.

Upon reaching his home on Friday evening, it is customary for the father to bless his children. When blessing his sons, he says: "God make thee as Ephraim and Manasseh"; to daughters, he says: "God make thee as Sarah, Rebekah, Rachel, and Leah." Then he recites the Priestly Benediction. Sometimes, the father or the rabbi performs this ceremony of blessing in the synagogue.

Then the family sings the hymn *Shalom alêchem* — "Peace be with you, ye angels of peace." This hymn was introduced by the Kabbalists, and is not more than three hundred years old (see Chapter VII). It is based upon b. Shabbath 119b the Agada of which speaks of two angels accompanying every man home from the synagogue: one good angel and one evil angel. When, upon entering the home, the good angel finds the lights kindled and the table set and the house well arranged, he says: "May it be God's will that the next Sabbath be as this one," while the evil angel is compelled to say: "Amen!"

If it is otherwise, the evil angel says: "May it be this way next Sabbath too," whereupon the good angel is forced to say: "Amen!" (see Yavetz, p. 306; Baer, p. 196; *Otzar Hatefilloth*, p. 625).

The Oriental-Sephardim sing this hymn also.

Then there follows Proverbs 31:10–31 — the wonderful eulogy on the woman of valor, which was interpreted by the Kabbalists as referring to the Shechina (see Chapter VI).

The Kabbalists and Hasidim sing in addition two songs by Isaac Luria: *Athkinu sĕudatha* — "I shall arrange the meal" — and *Azammer bishvahin* — "I shall sing praises." Following the hymn "Peace be with you, ye angels of peace," Hasidim also recite the meditation: *ribbon col haolamim* — "Master of all worlds" — which is attributed to Rabbi Joseph of Rashkov.

Then the Kiddush is chanted in a traditional mode.[2] At home Genesis 1:31 through 2:3 is chanted as an introduction to the Kiddush, as explained in Chapter X, 1. Kiddush is to be said over wine; the reasons for the use of wine are given in the Talmud (*cf.* M.V., pp. 84–85). If there is no wine, the Kiddush may be recited over bread (*l.c.*), in which case the blessing over wine is omitted and that over bread is said.

It is customary to have two loaves of bread in commemoration of the double portion of Manna the children of Israel used to find on Friday, one portion being for Saturday (Exod. 16:22–27).

Sabbath is also to be distinguished by special food, notably by fish (b. Shabbath 118b).

Between courses "Table Songs" — *Zemiroth* — are sung at the meals.

On Friday evening, the Ashkenazic ritual begins the "Table Songs" with the hymn:

a. *Col mekaddêsh shĕvii* — "Whoever sanctifies the seventh day as it befits it. . . ." The author of this song is Mose; his name is inserted as an acrostic in the second word of the first three lines. This song has four lines to the stanza with rhyme. The last line is Scriptural. Many Biblical phrases are utilized here. The author also used Talmudic material, as well as non-Biblical words and forms.

This song has an alphabetical acrostic. In the Ashkenazic ritual the acrostic runs up to "צ" only, while M.V., p. 147, has the entire acrostic. This song is chanted either in the "Adonoi Moloch" or in the "Mogen Ovos" mode.[3]

b. *Menuha wesimha* — "Rest and Joy" — is likewise the work of Mose. The structure of this poem is similar to the preceding song. An English rendition of this poem by A. Irma Cohon is printed in my *Jewish Songbook*, p. 105.

c. *Ma yafith* — "How beautiful and sweet . . ." is the work of Morechai b. Isaac. The song has four rhymed lines to the stanza. The content of this song is largely taken from Halachic material pertaining to the laws of Sabbath. Midrashic material, particularly the idea "Sambation rolls out" which is based on Gen. Rabba XI, was likewise utilized. Furthermore, the idea: "He placed His light into the world. . . . He then wanted to hide it . . . thou (Sabbath) prayest . . . and he hid it (the light) for those who fear Him. . . ." is based upon Gen. Rabba XII.

This song became very popular in Germany and in Poland, and received a set tune.[4] "To the Polish 'Pans' this song was a symbol of Jewish song, and they used to delight themselves urging their Jews to sing it accompanied by dances and comical gestures." [5]

d. *Yom ze leyisraêl* — "This day to Israel. . . ." is ascribed to Isaac Luria because some editions have the full acrostic of his name, though in the Ashkenazic ritual only five stanzas with the acrostic Isaac are given. This song has a refrain repeated after each stanza. Each stanza consists of six lines, and each line has two accentuated words with a rhyme. The song describes the delight of Sabbath and the reward for those who keep it according to Rabbinic interpretation. It is known among the Oriental as well as among the Occidental Jews. There is no known traditional tune to this song. An English rendition of the poem by A. Irma Cohon is printed in my *Songbook*, p. 103f.

e. *Ya ribbon alam* — "God Lord of the world . . ." is the work of Israel Najara (Safed, 1550 — lived in Damascus and died in Gaza about 1620). Although in Aramaic, this song gained widespread popularity throughout the Jewish world. After relating the wonders of God's creation, the poet concludes with a prayer that God may redeem His people and lead them to His chosen sanctuary where the souls will rejoice with songs and meditations. This song was set to innumerable tunes.[6]

f. *Tzur mishelo achalnu* — "Rock from whose store we have eaten." This song has no bearing upon Sabbath; it is rather an introduction to Grace. The four stanzas have the contents of the four benedictions of the Grace in an abridged form. It is also sung by the Oriental communities.

There are a few more songs which are little used, as *Ma yediduth* — "How lovely is thy rest," *Yom shabbath*, "This day is a holy Sabbath. . . ."

The Oriental Jews have several more songs by Abraham ibn Ezra, Jehuda Halevi, and Israel Najara. In general, there is no limit nor fixed order to the Table Songs; everybody may select as many religious songs in Hebrew as he desires.

After the meal, Psalm 126 is chanted for which the Ashkenazim have traditional tunes.[7] Then Grace is recited as on weekdays, save that there is a special insertion for Sabbath in the third benediction: "Be pleased . . . to fortify us by Thy commandments."

2. SABBATH NOON. After the morning and additional services, the "Great Kiddush" — *Kiddusha rabba* (b. Pesahim 106), is recited over wine or any other beverage before the meal. This Kiddush consists of the following:

a. Exodus 31 : 16–17; Exodus 20 : 8–11.

b. A benediction over wine or other beverage.

c. A benediction over bread.

The Kabbalists and Hasidim first chant two Aramaic songs by Isaac Luria: *Asadder lis'udatha*, *Athkinu sĕudatha*. Preceding it (a), they recite Psalm 23 and Isaiah 58 : 13–14.

Between the courses,[8] "Zemiroth" are sung again:

a. *Baruch adonai yom yom* — "Blessed is the Lord daily" — a poem by Simon bar Isaac bar Abun of Mayence of the eleventh century (died in 1096). M.V., p. 117, has some slight variations in the text.

This song has five rhymed lines to the stanza. The name of the author is to be found in the acrostic.

Baer, p. 254, considers the part beginning with *baruch hu elohenu* a separate song, and is of the opinion that it was written with the aim of reciting it after Grace, because it has reference to that prayer. However, M.V. gives the first two stanzas as second and third stanzas after the beginning of the song *baruch adonai yom*, *yom*. The present form with an additional stanza seems to be a later arrangement.

The material is Biblical with Midrashic interpretations. Both the style and language are obscure.

b. *Baruch el elyon* — "Blessed be the Most High God" — is a poem by Baruch ben Samuel of Mayence (died 1221, Zunz, *Lit. ges.*, p. 306). The song carries the name of the author as an acrostic, and has four lines to the stanza with a cross rhyme and a refrain. It lays emphasis upon the observation of Sabbath.[9]

c. *Yom ze mechubbad* — "This day is honored above all days" — is a poem by Israel and was printed already in 1545.[10] The song is also found in the Oriental-Sephardic ritual.

The stanzas have four rhymed lines with an end rhyme running through the stanzas and with a refrain.

d. *Yom shabbath en lishcoah* — "The day of Sabbath shall not be forgotten" — is the work of Jehuda Halevi. It has eight syllables to the meter, and the acrostic "Jehuda." The Sephardic-Oriental ritual has this song also.

e. *Ki eshmera shabbath* — "If I will observe the Sabbath" — is a poem by Abraham ibn Ezra. His name "Abraham" is in the acrostic. The meter is the abridged Rağaz (see Chapter V). The stanzas have four lines and a refrain. This song is also found in M.V., p. 178, as well as in the Oriental rituals.

f. *Shim'ru shab'thothay* — "Observe ye my Sabbaths. . . ." has the name of Solomon in the acrostic. It is also found in the Sephardic-Oriental ritual.

Ul'wu alay — "and borrowed on my account" — is based upon b. Betza 15b. The poet urges that Sabbath be celebrated with fine garments and dishes, because the observance of Sabbath hastens redemption (b. Shabbath 118b).

g. *Dĕror yikra* — "He will announce freedom" — is a poem by Donash ibn Labrat, a Moroccan poet and scholar of the tenth century. This song is given in M.V., p. 178, and is known among the Oriental Jews.

Besides these quoted songs, other songs are printed in the various prayer-books and songsters, but they did not gain popularity.

After the Zemiroth, Psalm 126 and Grace are chanted.

Between the *Minha* and the evening services a light meal, known as the "Third Meal," ensues. At this meal, the Kabbalists and Hasidim sing two songs by Isaac Luria: "I shall arrange the meal . . ." and "The children of the palace. . . ." *Bĕne hechala;* both are in Aramaic.

After the meal, Grace is chanted.

In addition to the Zemiroth hitherto described, it is customary among the Hasidim to sing at the Sabbath meals tunes without words or with texts of their own creation.[11]

Following the "Havdala," Zemiroth are sung again:

a. *Hammavdil* — "May He Who maketh a distinction between holy and profane" — is an acrostic with the name "Isaac Hakkaton." This song is used by all the Jewish communities. Mahzor Vitry presents it on p. 185 (Baer, p. 312). In his commentary to b. Yoma § 1233, Mordechai says that this poem has to be recited at the concluding service of the Day of Atonement, because it is of a penitential character. Indeed, the Tlemsan, Cochin, and other rituals have a "piyyut" which has the only refrain of this song, and whose author is also Isaac.[12]

There are several tunes known for this text. In Eastern Europe the tune in *Jewish Music*, p. 401, is familiar; in Mesopotamia, the tune in *o.c.*, p. 373, 6, is known; and among the Oriental-Sephardim, *l.c.* 7 is used. The Portuguese have another tune.[13]

b. *Eliyahu hannavi* — "Elijah, the prophet. . . ."

"Already in the eleventh century there were songs of Elijah sung by all Jewish communities on the outgoing of Sabbath. The oldest part of this group is the refrain 'Elijah, the prophet, Elijah, the Tishbite, Elijah, the Gileadite, may he speedily come to us with the Messiah the son of David.'"[14] This is based upon Malachi 3 : 23–24. According to Talmudic interpretation, Elijah will announce Israel's redemption on the outgoing of Sabbath (b. Eruvin 43b; Shabbath 118b; compare M.V., p. 184, and Baer, p. 310).

In the Ashkenazic and Sephardic rituals, the song has an alphabetic acrostic and another version from the text in M.V., p. 184. Both recount the activities of the prophet. The Roman ritual (ed. Schechter, p. 115) has an Elijah song by Anan HaCohen. The Babylonians have still another song; it is also used by the Oriental-Sephardim (*Jewish Music*, 372, 2; *Sefer Hashirim*, # 51). The Oriental-Sephardim sing a text written by David ben Aaron Hasin (*Sefer Hashirim*, # 54).

Two tunes are the most popular among the East European Jews.[15] The Babylonian and Sephardic tunes are also well known in the Near East.[16]

c. *Bemotzaê yom menuha* — "At the outgoing of the day of rest" — is the work of Jacob Manui (Menu) who, according to Zunz (*o.c.*, p. 485), lived in the thirteenth century. The song carries his name in the acrostic. However, in the version in M.V., p. 185, the acrostic shows the name of Jacob Min Jericho (of Jericho).

The content of this song is a plea for redemption through the appearance of Elijah.

This song is known in the Orient as well as in the Occident.

d. *Amar adonai leyaakov* — "God spoke to Jacob. . . ." — is a compilation of Biblical phrases in alphabetical order with the refrain "Do not fear, my servant Jacob." M.V., pp. 190–191, has a somewhat different version. This song is known to the Ashkenazim only. Its tune is given in *Jewish Music*, p. 402, 4.

e. *Haddesh sesoni* — "Renew my joy" — is an acrostic giving the name "Shiloh." Zunz, *o.c.*, p. 490, suggests "Hassan" derived from the acrostic of the first four words. This song has five lines to the stanza, and is a plea for redemption through Elijah. M.V., p. 188, has it already, and so does the Oriental-Sephardic ritual. It seems to be of Oriental origin.

f. *Ish hasid haya* — "A pious man there was. . . ." is the work of Jesse ben Mordechai; it occurs already in M.V., p. 184. This song relates the legend of the events of a pious man.

g. *Addir ayom* — "Mighty, revered, and awe-inspiring. . . ." is an alphabetic acrostic; it, too, appears in M.V., p. 186.

h. *Eli hish goali* — "My God, hasten my redeemer. . . ." is an acrostic giving the name "Nahman" as the author. According to Zunz, *o.c.*, p. 364, it is Nahman ben Moshe Hassan.

i. *Elohim yisadenu* — "God will support us. . . ." is an acrostic giving the name "Abraham." It has four rhymed lines to the stanza.

After the songs, a meditation is recited. It is based upon Jer. Ber. V, 1, and begins with "Lord of all worlds, Father of Mercies. . . ." (Baer, p. 313). S.R.A. has a different and shorter form of this meditation. Abudraham gives still another version and says that its recitation is not customary in some places. The Oriental-Sephardic ritual has still another version which is recited before the "Havdala."

Aside from these songs and meditations for the meals, there are several more to occupy the people during the Sabbath. There is the chanting of the weekly portion; each verse is repeated twice while its Aramaic translation is cited but once [17] (b. Ber. 8a). There is also the study of *Mishna Shabbath* and several other Talmudic and Midrashic selections. In addition to these, the Kabbalists recite portions from the Zohar.

Literature of a religious purport was also provided for the women. The Pentateuch mixed with Midrashic interpretations and rabbinical legends has been translated into the Yiddish-German language of the seventeenth century. This work is generally known by the name *Tze'ena Ur'ena*. Furthermore, meditations for Sabbath and all festivals and for various occasions have been compiled in the same vernacular; these are called *Tehinoth* (see Chapter XVIII).

Among the Oriental and Levantine communities, there is an old custom to rise before sunset on Saturdays, to assemble in synagogues, and to sing religious songs. These songs are called *Bakkashoth*, *Shevahoth*, and *Pizmonim*. The authors of these songs are Jehuda Halevi, Abraham ibn Ezra, Israel Najara, and many other Oriental poets who lived between the seventeenth and nineteenth centuries.

CHAPTER XII

PRAYERS FOR DISTINGUISHED DAYS

The daily services and the prayers for the home are provided with special insertions and additions for distinguished days. These days and insertions are:

1. *Rosh hodesh* — New Moon. With the exception of the New Moon of Tishri on which New Year occurs and which has a ritual of its own, there are according to the Jewish calendar eleven, and in a leap year twelve, New Moons.

As all Jewish Sabbaths and festivals, the New Moon begins with the preceding evening.

In the evening, morning, and afternoon services the paragraph: *Yaale weyavo* — "Our God . . . may our remembrance. . . ." is inserted in the seventeenth benediction of the Amida. Instead of "Tahanun," "Hallel" is recited after the Amida in the morning service; it is composed of a benediction, of Psalms 113, 114, 115:12–18; 116:12–19, 117, and 118, and closes with a concluding paragraph and a benediction.

This "Praise" was also called "Song" (b. Pes. 117b; Eruvin 10b) and the "Egyptian Hallel" (b. Ber. 56b).

This form of the "Hallel" is called "Half Hallel," because Psalms 115 and 116 are recited in part only. According to b. Taanith 28b; b. Arachin 10, Rabbi Yohanan explains that the "Whole Hallel" is to be recited only on full holidays on which no work is permitted and on those days on which separate sacrifices are offered. There are eighteen such days in Palestine and twenty-one in the Diaspora: eight (resp. nine) days of Tabernacle, eight days of Hanucca, the first (resp. second) day of Passover, and the day (or two days) of Pentecost. In the "Hallel," the first four and the last five verses of Psalm 118 are repeated. In ancient times, there were three forms of reciting the "Hallel": "In form A the leader intoned the first half verse, whereupon the congregation repeated it. Then the leader sang the succeeding line, the congregation always repeating the same half-line which thus became a refrain throughout the entire song. . . . In form B the leader sang a half-line at a time, and the congregation repeated what he had last sung. . . . Form C was responsive in the real sense, i.e., the leader would sing the whole first line, whereupon the congregation would join with the second line of the verse." [1]

The repetition of the verses mentioned was customary in Mishnaic times (M. Succa III). In the *Talmud* (b. Succa 38b), the custom is explained (see Rashi and Tosefta to that).

The custom of reciting "Hallel" was well established in the days of the Second Temple (M. Succa III; b. Taanith 28b). Rashi still recited it without introductory benedictions (M.V., p. 192).

If the whole Hallel is read, the first benediction ends with the phrase: "to complete the Hallel" (S.R.A.; Sephardic). The Yemenite ritual has this phrase also, while the Ashkenazic ritual has the version "to recite the Hallel" for both forms, basing itself on Rabbi M. Rothenburg (see Baer, p. 328).

The concluding paragraph is mentioned in b. Pes. 118a, and is similar to the concluding benediction of the "Verses of Song" (see Chapter VIII).

Following the Hallel, the whole Kaddish is recited. Then the Scroll is taken out and the passage from Numbers 28:1–15 is read. This passage is subdivided into four parts for which four persons are called upon (M. Megilla IV, 2). There is no *Maftir* on the New Moon.

Then "Ashre" (Psalm 145) and *uva letziyon* are recited; the Tefillin are then taken off and the half-Kaddish is said.

The additional service — Musaf — is recited.

This service consists of the first three and the last three benedictions of the Amida, the weekday Kedusha in which the Sephardic ritual has "Kether" at the beginning, and of an intermediate benediction — *roshê hodoshim* (see Chapter XV).

The intermediate benediction consists of an introductory paragraph which runs as follows:

"The beginnings of the months Thou didst assign unto Thy people . . ." It is based upon Numbers 28:11. The phrase "for a season of atonement" is based upon the explanation in b. Shevuoth 9b that the sacrifice on the New Moon atones the sins committed during the month, especially for the sin of partaking of unclean foods.

The wording of this paragraph has variations in the different rituals. The Ashkenazic and Sephardic is the nearest to that given in S.R.A. and M.V. Maimonides and the Yemenite ritual have some inserted passages, as the phrase, "On account of our sins were we exiled," which occurs in the intermediate benediction of the Musaf for the festivals (see Singer, p. 234).

The second paragraph is taken from Numbers 28:11. The Yemenite ritual does not have this paragraph.

The third paragraph concludes the benediction. Its version is identical to that of S.R.A., while M.V. has an additional phrase. The Sephardic and Yemenite rituals have another insertion: "O may this month be the end . . . of all our troubles, and an opening and beginning of the redemption of our souls." The twelve pleas for comfort and forgiveness are for the twelve months. There is a thirteenth phrase for the leap year; it speaks of the atonement of transgressions. This interpretation, however, is of a very late date (see Baer, p. 240).

After the additional service, the Kaddish, Alenu, the Mourner's Kaddish, and the Song for the New Moon which is Psalm 104 are recited.

2. THE SANCTIFICATION OF THE NEW MOON — *Kiddush levana.* There is an old custom to have a short service in the open on a clear night on every New Moon when seeing the new moon. The time for this service is from the third or fourth night up to the night when the "moon gains its half size." No quorum is compulsory for this service. The service, however, must be recited by at least two adults together. This service cannot be held on Friday and holiday evenings.

The rabbinical explanation for this service is that on account of its monthly appearance, the new moon is considered the emblem of Israel; like the moon, Israel goes through several phases of persecution without being destroyed. For this reason, the appearance of the New Moon is sanctified (*J. Enc.* VIII, p. 679); and furthermore that "the periodical reappearance of the moon, like the reappearance of everything that is of benefit to mankind, such as fruits in their respective seasons, should be recognized by praise and gratitude to the Creator" (*J. Enc.* IX, 244).

The *Talmud* (b. Sanhedrin 42a), says: "One who recites the benediction of the moon at the proper time is like one who is received in audience by the *Shechina.*"

In the Ashkenazic ritual, the service of the Sanctification of the New Moon starts with Psalm 150; then a benediction follows the text of which is given in b. Sanhedrin 42a and in Soferim XX:[2] "Blessed . . . Who createst the heavens by His word and the stars by His command. He implanted in them fixed laws and times. . . . He ordered the moon to renew itself, as a crown of beauty over those He sustained from childhood (Israel), and as a symbol that they likewise will be regenerated in the future. . . . Blessed. . . . Who renewest the months."

Then follow several Biblical verses, each repeated three times. In these verses the desire for Israel's redemption is voiced.

The formulae of mutual greeting "Shalom Aleichem" "Aleichem Shalom" and "David king of Israel liveth and existeth" are repeated three times. The idea of the first is probably based on the belief that with the renewal of the moon everyone ought to feel reborn and ought to look upon himself as a regenerated person. The idea of the second phrase is based on the belief that Messiah is a descendant of David, so that the hope for the reappearance of the Messiah necessitates the statement that the Davidic dynasty is still in existence.

A Talmudic passage (b. San. 42a) with a prayer that the deficiency of the light of the moon caused by the moon's complaint against the sun (b. Hullin 60b) be readjusted is then recited. The service closes with Psalms 121 and 67. In case a quorum of ten adults is present, the rabbinical Kaddish is said.

3. *Hanucca* — The Feast of Dedication (or the Feast of Lights). The *Talmud* (b. Shabbath 21b) gives the story of the purification of the Temple and of the cruse of oil, as well as the reason for the kindling of the lights and the customs connected with it (see my *Ceremonies*, p. 29f.).

The lights are kindled in the Synagogue after the Minha service. In the home they are kindled about a half hour after the setting in of darkness. The order of the number of candles is followed in accordance with the custom of Hillel (b. Shabbath, *l.c.*), i.e., one candle on the first night and then increasing the number of candles by one each successive night till the eighth night.

Two benedictions are recited before kindling the lights:

a. "Blessed. . . . and commanded us to kindle the light of Hanucca."

b. "Blessed. . . . Who wroughtest miracles for our fathers."

On the first night, the benediction "Blessed. . . . and enabled us to reach this season" is recited.

These benedictions are quoted in b. Shabbath 23a where the reason for saying "and commanded us" is also explained.

Then the paragraph "we kindle those lights on account of the miracles . . . which Thou didst work for our fathers. . . . During all the eight days of Hanucca these lights are sacred . . . but we are only to look at them, in order that we may give thanks unto Thy Name for Thy miracles" — this paragraph is recited. The text is given in T. Soferim XX: 6.

Whereupon the hymn *Maoz tzur* — "Rock of Ages" — is sung. The song recounts the wonders of the Exodus from Egypt, of the Babylonian exile, the fall of Haman, and the conquest of the Syrian Greeks by the Maccabees. The text is the work of Mordechai, an Ashkenazic poet of the thirteenth century. The Ashkenazim have a tune for this song which became traditional since the sixteenth century.[3]

In the service, the story of Hanucca is inserted in the seventeenth benediction of the Amida: "In the days of the Hasmoneans" which is preceded by the passage: "We thank Thee also for the miracles" (see Chapter VIII).

These two paragraphs are also inserted in the second benediction of Grace (see Chapter IX, II).

After the Amida, the whole Hallel is recited, and Numbers 7 is read (M. Megilla III: 6). This Pentateuchal portion is divided into eight sections for the eight days of Hanucca, and on each day three persons are called upon to the reading.

During Hanucca Psalm 30 is recited, because it was written in commemoration of the dedication of the Temple and because it speaks of deliverance.

On the Sabbaths which fall on Hanucca special poetical insertions are recited in the *Yotzer*, according to the Ashkenazic and Italian rituals (see Chapter X).

4. *Purim* — The Feast of Lots. This Feast occurs on the fourteenth of the month of *Adar* and is celebrated in commemoration of the events related in the Book of Esther. In the service of that day and in the preceding evening service, this Feast is marked by the insertion of the paragraph "In the days of Mordechai and Esther" and by the same introductory passage "We thank Thee also for the miracles" which introduced the Hanucca insertion. The text of this special paragraph is given in S.R.A. and in M.V. where the same closing phrase is added as in the Hanucca insertion.

This paragraph is also inserted in Grace after meals.

In the evening service, the Book of Esther is chanted from a Scroll after the Amida according to a traditional mode.[4] The reading of the Book of Esther, or as it is called in the rabbinical literature "The Scroll" — *mĕgilla* — is a very old custom (M. Megilla Iff.). Prior to the reading, three benedictions are recited:

a. "Blessed . . . commanding the reading of the Megilla."

b. "Blessed . . . Who wroughtest miracles for our fathers."

c. "Blessed . . . Who hast preserved us . . . to reach this season."

The last two benedictions are the same as on Hanucca.

After the reading of the Megilla, a benediction is recited: "Blessed . . . Who hast pleaded our cause . . . Who deliverest Thy people Israel from all their adversaries, O God, the Redeemer!" The whole text of these benedictions is given in b. Megilla 21b.

They are to be found in all the rituals.

The Ashkenazic ritual has a "piyyut": "Who broughtest the counsel of the heathen to naught"; it is an alphabetic acrostic given in M.V., p. 214. With poetical embellishments it recounts the story of *Purim* and closes with a eulogy on Esther and Mordechai, called the "Lily of Jacob"— *Shoshannath yaakov.*

The Sephardic and Italian rituals have only a few phrases: "Accursed be Haman's memory; blessed be Mordechai . . .

and may Harbonah also be remembered for good" (Jer. Megilla III end; b. Megilla 7b).

These rituals, on the other hand, have Psalm 22 before and Psalm 124 after the reading of the Megilla. M.V. and the Sephardic-Oriental ritual have several poems, one of which *Korêê mêgilla* is generally sung.[5]

Then the paragraph: "Thou art holy" which appears in the morning service as part of "Uva letziyon" is recited.

In the Amida of the morning service poetical insertions by Eleazar Kallir are recited with each benediction; these insertions are based upon the story of Esther embellished with Midrashic interpretations. The custom of reading these insertions prevails in the Ashkenazic ritual.

Kerova — wayyeĕhav omen. With the exception of the fifteenth, there are insertions for each benediction of the Amida (see Chapter VIII). The insertions are short, consisting of six lines to the stanza. Aside from these insertions, the twelfth benediction has an elaborate poem consisting of five alphabetical parts. At the beginning of each stanza a word from Esther 2:17 is used, and a word from Esther 8:15 precedes the sixth line. The poet inserted his name in a fivefold alphabetical acrostic, the acrostic of the name appearing on the second word of the sixth lines.

After the Amida, the Scroll is taken out and the passage of Exodus 17:8–16 is read; to this passage three persons are called upon. The reading is ordered in M. Megilla III:6. The passage consists of nine verses only; but since, according to b. Megilla 21b, the minimum Pentateuchal reading must be of ten verses, the last verses are repeated. The reason for reading this passage is that it relates the war with Amalek, and according to Talmudic tradition, Haman was a descendant of Amalek (*cf.* Chapter X).

After the reading the Scroll is replaced in the ark, and the reading of the Megilla follows in the same way as on the preceding evening.[6]

5. The Counting of the Omer — *sĕfirath haomer.* Beginning with the second evening of Passover, the custom of counting the "Omer" starts immediately after the evening service. The word "Omer" means "sheaf." In Leviticus 23:15 we

read: "And ye shall count unto you . . . from the day that ye brought the sheaf of the wave offering, seven Sabbaths shall be complete." At the time when the Temple existed in Jerusalem, a sheaf of barley was cut in the field from the ripe crop every day during the seven weeks from the second day of Passover to the Feast of the Weeks. A handful of this sheaf was burned on the altar, and the rest was consumed by the priests. No member of Israel was allowed to partake of the new barley harvest before he brought this offering. In commemoration of this custom, the counting of the "Omer" was introduced (M. Menahoth X; b. Menahoth 61–62, 65–66a).

Before counting the "Omer" a meditation is recited: "Lo, I am about to fulfill the affirmative precept of the counting of the Omer."

Then there follows a benediction: "Blessed . . . concerning the counting of the Omer."

On every evening the number of days is announced. On the first evening it is announced: "This is the first day of the Omer"; a week later the formula reads: "This is the seventh day, making one week of the Omer"; and so on. The formula of the last day is: "This is the forty-ninth day, making seven weeks of the Omer." [7]

The formula in the Sephardic ritual is as follows: "This is the eighth day of Omer, making one week and one day."

The formula in the Italian ritual is: "This day of the Omer is the first day."

Then a prayer follows: "May the All-Merciful restore the service of the Temple to its place. . . ." Psalm 67 is then recited. The Ashkenazic ritual adds the mystic meditation: "We beseech Thee, release Thy captive nation." This meditation is also to be found in the Friday evening service just before "Lecha Dodi." The Ashkenazic ritual closes the service with another meditation: "Lord of all worlds, Thou hast commanded us through Moses Thy servant to count the Omer, so that we may be cleansed from our sins. . . ." (see Chapter VI).

CHAPTER XIII

PRAYERS FOR SPECIAL OCCASIONS

1. *Brith mila* — Circumcision. A service developed in connection with the command in Genesis 17:9–14. (Abraham circumcised Isaac eight days after his birth, Gen. 21:4.) This service is held in the presence of a quorum either at the home or in the synagogue.

When the child is brought in for circumcision, the people present rise and say: "Blessed be he that cometh."

The father then says: "I am herewith ready to perform the precept of circumcising my son . . . as it is written in the Law."

The *Mohel* — Circumciser — places the child upon the "chair of Elijah" and recites: "This is the chair of Elijah," and a few Biblical verses; whereupon the assembly responds: "O let us be satisfied with the goodness of Thy house, Thy holy Temple."

The reason for having a chair of Elijah is given in *Pirke de Rabbi Eliezer*, Chapter 29 end. The prophet complained to God that Israel was neglecting his covenant (I Kings 19:10–14). In consequence of this accusation, God ordered him to be present at each circumcision that he may witness Israel's loyalty to his covenant.[1]

The child is then placed upon the knees of the "Sandik," or godfather, and before operating, the Mohel says: "Blessed. . . . Who hast given us the command concerning circumcision." Immediately thereafter, the father says: "Blessed . . . Who . . . commanded us to introduce him into the covenant of our father Abraham." Then the bystanders respond with:

"Even as he has entered into the covenant, so may he enter into the Law, the nuptial canopy, and into good deeds."

The texts of the benedictions are given in b. Shabbath 137b; *Tosefta* Ber. VI (VII): 12–13).

Then the Mohel recites the benediction over wine and another benediction: "Blessed . . . Who didst sanctify the beloved from the womb. . . . Therefore . . . give command to deliver from destruction the dearly beloved of our flesh. . . ."

The service then closes with a prayer for the child as a name is given him and with a prayer for the well-being of the parents.

The Sephardic, Oriental, and Yemenite rituals have several songs before and after the circumcision.

A meal is served after the ceremony. The partaking of this meal is considered so meritorious that it is even permissible to break a fast for it — with the exception of the fast of the Day of Atonement. The meal is arranged in a manner that it expresses joy for the possibility afforded to fulfill this principal commandment as did Abraham of old (Gen. 21 : 8).[2]

The Grace is introduced with a song: "We will give thanks unto Thy Name." This song consists of four stanzas, each stanza beginning with the phrase "With the sanction of God, of the Law, of the priests, of all present."

At the closing of Grace a poem by Abraham ben Isaac HaCohen is inserted (eleventh century, Zunz, *Ltg.*, p. 153). Each stanza of this poem begins with "May the All Merciful — *harahaman* — ; and contains a prayer and a blessing for the child and his parents. It closes with the plea for the coming of Messiah for the sake of the new members of the covenant.

The insertions in Grace are not found in other rituals. M.V., p. 628, has a different text with the same beginning: "May the All Merciful."

A custom prevails in many communities to assemble on the eve of the eighth day and to recite prayers and sections from the Bible and Rabbinical literature. This custom is called "Ben Zachar" or "Shalom Zachar." A special ritual for this purpose was published; it is called *Berith Yitzchak* (Bombay, 1891).

2. *Pidyon habben* — The Redemption of the First-Born. Originally, the first-born son (of the mother) was to be sanctified to God (Exod. 13 : 2). This law was modified to the effect that the child be redeemed on payment of five "Shekels" to the priest (Num. 18 : 16).

The ritual for that ceremony consists of presenting the child at the age of a month to the "Cohen" with five "Shekels." The formula which the father has to recite varies in the different rituals. The Ashkenazic ritual has two versions. One is short and reads as follows:

Father: "My wife gave birth to a boy, a first-born."

Cohen: "What do you prefer, your son or the five 'Shekels.'"

Father: "I desire rather my son; here, take the value of his redemption."

The dialogue is given in Hebrew or Aramaic.

The other version is the same in content but is longer, having additional passages from the Pentateuch which refer to the law.

Following this, the father says: "Blessed . . . concerning the redemption of the son," and "Blessed . . . and enabled us to reach this season."

Holding the money over the child's head, the Cohen recites: "This instead of that. . . . May this child enter into life, into the Law and the fear of Heaven. . . ." While placing his hand upon the head of the child, the Cohen utters the Priestly Benediction, and with this the ceremony closes.

Other rituals have a slightly different text for the Cohen. Abudraham, *Caftor Waferah*, Chapter 16, and *Col-Bo* have a long benediction which is quoted by Baer, p. 584.

A meal is served after the ceremony.

The first two benedictions recited by the father are given in b. Pesahim 121b.

After the last benediction by the Mohel, the Yemenite ritual has two Aramaic passages; they are given in S.R.A. 52b.

There is also a special benediction for the circumcision of proselytes, and one also for slaves (S.R.A. 53a).

The Sephardic ritual has a prayer for the naming of a daughter. At first, Canticles 2:14 is recited, and then: "May He Who blessed Sarah . . . bless this beloved child, and may her name be called. . . ." and there follows a prayer for the child and the parents.

In case a girl is the first-born child, Canticles 6:9 is read.

3. *Bircath êrusin wenisuin* — The Marriage Ritual. This service is introduced with a short passage usually sung by the

Cantor: "He Who is mighty. . . . may He bless the bridegroom and the bride."

The couple is then placed under a canopy — *Huppa* — "which is now a symbolic reminiscence of the marriage-chamber" (Abrahams).[3] Then the rabbi, or any prominent person, takes a cup of wine and says the benediction over wine.

The first benediction is called the "Betrothal Blessing" — *bircath êrusin* — and is recorded in the *Talmud* (b. Kethuvoth 7b). In olden times this benediction was recited at the engagement. This custom still prevailed in the eleventh century (M.V., pp. 587–588). The benediction praises God for laws of chastity and for the institution of marriage. There are slight variations in the wording of this benediction.

Then the groom takes a ring which has no stone and places it upon the bride's forefinger of the right hand and says (in Hebrew): "Behold, Thou art consecrated unto me by this ring, according to the Law of Moses and of Israel."

The use of a ring was not known in Talmudic times; coins were used instead (M. Kidushin I, 1). Abudraham, p. 195, still says that a stoneless ring or a coin or any object equivalent to a small coin may be used. Shulhan Aruch, *Even Haezer*, 27 : 1, 31, 2 is of the same opinion, saying, "Some use a ring." The Yemenite ritual still has the formula: "Behold, thou art consecrated unto me with this coin."

The wedding contract — *kethuva* — is then read in Aramaic; whereupon the "Wedding Benedictions" — *bircath nissuin* — are chanted.

In b. Kethuvoth, *l.c.*, seven benedictions are cited. First comes the benediction over wine, and then follow:

a. "Blessed . . . Who hast created all things in His glory."

b. "Blessed . . . Creator of man."

c. "Blessed . . . Who hast made man in Thy image . . . and hast prepared unto him, out of him an everlasting establishment. . . ." (*Cf.* Gen. 2 : 21–25.)

d. "May she who was barren (Zion) be exceeding glad, when her children are gathered within her in joy. . . ."

This allusion to the joy of Zion is based upon Isaiah 62 : 5: "As the bridegroom rejoices over the bride, so shall Thy God rejoice over Thee." It is furthermore in keeping with the vow of the Psalmist — 137 : 6 — to remember Jerusalem on the occasion of one's greatest joy.

e. "O make these loved companions greatly to rejoice, even as Thou didst gladden Thy creation of old in the Garden of Eden. . . ." (Gen. 2 : 15.)

f. "Blessed . . . Who hast created joy . . . bridegroom and bride . . . love, brotherhood, peace, and fellowship. Soon may be heard in the cities of Judah . . . the voice of joy. . . . " This benediction again refers to Psalm 137 : 6 and Isaiah 62 : 5 mentioned above.

In addition to these benedictions, the Yemenite ritual has several Biblical selections and psalmodies which are sung in unison; it also has a very rich collection of wedding songs in Hebrew and Arabic.[4] M.V., pp. 593–596, has several wedding songs, S.R.A. 53 cites a poem in which "Israel" is the rhyming word. The Persian, Babylonian, and Sephardic-Oriental communities also have a rich treasure of wedding songs.[5]

The wedding benedictions are sung according to a traditional mode.[6]

A wedding-meal is served after the service. A poem by Dunash ben Labrat ushers in the Grace: "Banish, O Lord, both grief and wrath." The invocation reads: "With the sanction of those present we will bless our God in whose abode is joy."

Following Grace, the wedding benedictions are repeated.

4. The Funeral Ritual. The *Talmud* says that when on his death-bed, man should utter confession (b. Shabbath 32a), because "there is not a righteous man upon earth that doeth good and sinneth not" (Eccles. 7 : 20). It was believed that "all who die expiate their offences by death" (*Sifré* 33a).

a. The confession reads as follows:

"I acknowledge unto Thee, O Lord my God and God of my fathers, that both my cure and my death are in Thy hands. May it be Thy will to send me a perfect healing. Yet, if my death be fully determined by Thee, I will in love accept it at Thy hand. . . . O may my death be an atonement for all the sins . . . of which I have been guilty against Thee. . . . Thou Who art the father of the fatherless . . . protect my beloved kindred with whose soul my own is knit. Into Thy hand I commend my spirit; Thou hast redeemed me, O Lord God of truth."[7]

And when the end is approaching: "The Lord reigneth; the Lord hath reigned; the Lord shall reign for ever and ever"; this is repeated three times. Then there follows: "Blessed be His Name Whose glorious kingdom is for ever and ever"; this too is repeated three times. Then: "The Lord is God" which is repeated seven times; and following this: "Hear, O Israel, the Lord our God, the Lord is One." [8]

b. The Burial Service is called *tzidduk haddin* — The Justice of the Judgment. The Jew firmly believes that God's ways are ways of righteousness and that His deeds are deeds of Judgment (Deut. 32 : 4).

A selection of Biblical verses is recited which begins with: "The Rock, His work is perfect, for all his ways are judgment, a God of faithfulness and without iniquity, just and right is He."

The first sentences are recorded in b. Avoda Zara 18a.

Then Psalm 16 is read.

When the coffin is lowered into the grave, the following sentence is said:

"May he (she) come to his (her) place in peace."

The mourners then tear their upper garment about three inches and say: "Blessed be the Judge of Truth" (b. Ber. 58a based on Genesis 37 : 34; I Samuel II : 11).

All present wash their hands and say:

"He will destroy death forever; and the Lord God will wipe away tears from off all faces; and the rebuke of His people shall be taken away from off all the earth: for the Lord God hath spoken it" (Isaiah 25 : 8).

The funeral Kaddish is then recited (see Chapter VIII).

People who did not visit the cemetery for thirty days say the following benediction (b. Ber. 58b):

"Blessed . . . Who formed you in judgment . . . Who brought death on you in judgment . . . and Who will restore you to life in judgment. . . ." (S.R.A.)

The whole service with the regulations and meditations is printed in separate volumes: *Ma'bar Yabok* and *Totzoth Hayyim* by S. Baer.

For seven days services are held for the mourners in the house of the deceased individual. On these days, Psalm 39 and a prayer for the soul of the deceased are recited. In the fourth benediction of the Grace a special passage is inserted for the mourners; it is cited in S.R.A. 55a, Baer, p. 558.

The Sephardic ritual has a different wording of the confession, a very short *tzidduk haddin* — Justice of the Judgment — and an elegy consisting of seven stanzas for the seven circuits around the bier in the Mortuary Hall.

As the coffin is being lowered into the grave, Psalm 91 is recited.

There are also special prayers to be recited while washing the corpse.

The Sephardic ritual has separate prayers for deceased men, women, and children; they are called *Hashcava.*

5. Prayers When Going on a Journey — *tefillath haddere̲ch.* The *Talmud* (b. Ber. 29b) advises those who are setting out upon a journey of a distance of one "Parsa" at least — a Persian mile [9] — to recite the following meditation:

"May it be Thy will . . . to conduct us in peace . . . unto the haven of our desire. . . ."

Several Biblical verses are then recited: Genesis 32:2; 35:5; 48:16; 49:18; Exodus 23:20; Numbers 6:24; and Psalms 91 and 121.

Upon entering a city, the following is to be recited:

"May it be Thy will to lead me into this city in peace" (b. Ber. 60a).

A similar formula is said upon leaving a city. After having left the city, one is to continue with the following:

"Just as Thou hast led me out of this city so mayest Thou lead me in peace . . . and save me from enemies and ambush on my way."

CHAPTER XIV

THE HAGGADA FOR PASSOVER

The "Seder" is celebrated on the evening of the fourteenth of Nissan in commemoration of Israel's exodus from Egypt, as told in Exodus 12. It became a home-celebration par excellence. The ceremonies observed therein are intended to remind the Jewish people of the great event when God redeemed them from bondage and made them a free people, dedicated to serve the eternal God only. All customs are therefore attuned to the aim of stirring in both young and old, the spirit of liberty, of spiritual and physical freedom. The story and songs implant within one the conviction of the ultimate victory of individual freedom, of light succeeding darkness, and of ethical relations superseding tyranny.

This memorable celebration has retained its value for our days as in days of old, and has exercised a great pedagogical influence upon the children for which purpose it was chiefly instituted. It was introduced so that the father teach his child the religio-ethical doctrines deduced from that event and from its underlying lofty ideals that the child may be permeated with them and draw strength from them to carry on the fight for justice and righteousness and spiritual liberty with the firm belief of ultimate success.

The story tells of suffering, of sorrow and pain, of struggle with the iron yoke of slavery, of afflictions which penetrate to the very core of life; it also speaks of hope for deliverance and of idealistic devotion to the cause of humanity as evinced by the illustrious leader, Moses, who created a free people out of slaves and gave them laws of the highest ethical value.

On the occasion of this celebration every Jewish home receives the atmosphere of a sanctuary in which each member of the family is a priest and the house-master—the high-priest — a sanctuary to serve the purest human ideals and the living God.

In the *Seder* (literally, Order of the Service) there are blended in happy combination the influences which have contributed so much toward inspiring the Jewish people which is scattered throughout the world with a feeling of kinship. Year after year, the Seder has thrilled them with an appreciation of the glories of their past . . . and quickened within them the enthusiasm of high idealism of freedom.[1]

The *Haggada* — which is *the narrative* of Passover is not purely devotional. It has intensely spiritual tones mingled with bursts of good humor . . . and lofty poetry with playful ditties for the entertainment of the children. . . . The assignment of a prominent part in the service to the child is consonant with the Biblical ordinance: "And thou shalt tell thy son on that day, saying: It is because of that which the Lord did for me when I came forth out of Egypt" (Exod. 13 : 8). Parent and child are thus brought into a union of warm religious sympathy — their souls are fired with the love of liberty, the keynote of the *Haggada*.[2]

THE SEDER AND ITS IDEAS. The exodus from Egyptian bondage became a powerful lever of spiritual progress. "Ye have seen what I did unto the Egyptian and how I bore you on eagle's wings, and brought you unto Myself" (Exod. 19 : 4–5).[3] Israel's experience was unique from the very first moment when it departed from Egypt. Again and again races have been subjugated, reduced to slavery; but does history know of another horde of slaves that recovered itself, regained freedom, reëstablished its own civilization, its own government? It is eminently proper, therefore, that in the prophetic as well as the rabbinic cycle of ideas, the exodus from Egypt should occupy a prominent place. Its importance had been recognized still earlier — in the code, the Tora. The most exalted moral statutes concerning the treatment of strangers are connected with the exodus, and are, from a psychological point of view, impressively inculcated by means of the reminder: "Ye know the heart of the stranger, seeing ye were strangers in the land of Egypt" (Exod. 23 : 9). It is remarkable how even the law of the Sabbath rest, on first sight unconnected with the story of Israel's slavery and redemption, is brought into relation with and illuminated by it. The fourth commandment in the second version of the Ten Commandments in Deuteronomy disregards the dogmatic reason attached to it in the first version: "For in six days the Lord made heaven and earth and rested on the seventh day." It emphasizes rather the ethical motive, that the servant should be granted a day of rest and employs the memory of the Egyptian experience to urge consideration for such ordinances. This method, characteristic of the Bible and still more of the Rabbis, which strives to establish a connection between the most important moral laws and the history of Israel in Egypt the Prophets and Psalmists employ to give reality chiefly to the religious idea of God's providence and grace. The Rabbis finally deduce from it the two fundamental elements of man's ethical education: the idea of liberty and the idea of man's ethical task.

Political and even civil freedom was lost. If the Roman Pharaohs did not exact labor, they the more despotically exacted property and blood, and aimed at the annihilation of the ideal possessions — the Law, its study, and its practice. Yet the idea of liberty, of inner moral and spiritual liberty, was cherished as a pure exalted ideal possible only under and through the Law and was associated with the memory of redemption from Egyptian bondage the memory of which was connected with symbolic practices accompanying every act, pleasure, and celebration.[4]

The "Seder" and its service and its liturgy, the *Haggada*, developed during the time of the Second Temple and in the first century thereafter. In earlier times, the observance of the "Pesah-offering" and the "Matza-festival" was not very much in vogue. The Bible records only a few celebrations: Joshua 5:10–11; King Hezekiah ordered to celebrate the festival (II Chron. 30:2, etc.); King Josiah did likewise (II Kings 23:21–22; II Chron. 35). The Bible emphasizes that "there was not kept such a passover from the days of the Judges (II Chron. 35:18 reads 'from the days of Samuel the prophet'), nor in all the days of the kings of Israel, nor of the kings of Judah." When the Babylonian exiles returned to Jerusalem with Ezra, they celebrated the festival again (Ezra 6:19–22).

But "during the centuries of Roman oppression, when the Jewish people groaned under the crushing burden of the Caesars, even as did their forefathers in Egypt, the ancient Feast of Freedom was charged with new vitality. Its annual occurrence came like a summons to new life and to liberty, making each Israelite feel as if he personally had shared in the Exodus."

During the latter part of the period of the Second Temple this festival became one of the most outstanding Jewish holidays on which occasion hundreds of thousands of people would assemble in Jerusalem, as Josephus, an eye-witness, relates.[5]

From that time on the *Haggada* ritual dates, as described in *Mishna* Pesahim V and X. While sacrificing the Pascal lamb, Hallel was chanted by the Levites, the people participating with "Halleluya" or responding with the first sentence of the chapter after each half-verse.[6]

The meat of the lamb sacrificed was then brought home, was roasted and eaten as Hallel was sung and the nucleus of the Haggada text was recited (M. Pes. X; b. Pes. 114a ff.).

After the destruction of the Temple, the "Seder" received greater emphasis and the "Haggada" was elaborately furnished with texts of symbolic meanings and homiletical interpretations, with fervent prayers and with symbolic and didactic songs for children. The "Seder" and its ritual became a strict home ceremony and service and remained as such to the present day.[7]

Bedikath hametz — Searching for Leaven. This practice is prescribed in M. Pes. 1:1–3; it is done on the evening preceding the fourteenth of Nissan.

While engaged in this ceremony, a benediction is recited: "Blessed . . . and hast commanded us to remove the leaven" (b. Pes. 7b).

After the remnants of leaven have been collected, the following declaration in Aramaic is made: "All manner of leaven that is in my possession, which I have not seen or removed, shall be as naught, and accounted as the dust of the earth" (b. Pes. 6a–b; She'iltoth § 73).[8]

On the morning of the fourteenth of Nissan, the collected remnants have to be burned at the beginning of the sixth hour which is about 11 A.M. (M. Pes. 1:4).

a. Order of the *Seder:*

The abbreviated order was known since the eleventh century.[9]

Kaddesh — Recite the Kiddush.

Urĕhatz — Wash the hands.

Carpas — Partake of parsley dipped in salt water (M. Pes. X: 3).

Yahatz — Break the middle Matza and hide one part which is to be eaten at the end of the meal as the *Aphikomon* (M. Pes. X, 8 b. Ber. 39b).

Maggid — Tell the story of Israel's deliverance from Egyptian bondage.

Rahatza — Wash the hands for the meal (b. Pes. 115b).

Motzi, matza — Recite the blessing over Matza and over bread (b. Pes. 115a).

Maror — Partake of the bitter herb, and recite the benediction.

Corech — Combine Matza, Maror, and Haroseth and eat them together (b. Pes. 115; Zevahim 79).

Shulhan orech — Partake of the meal.

Tzafun — Conclude the meal by eating the hidden Aphikomon — ἐπικώμιον — is the Greek for dessert.

Barech — Say Grace.

Hallel — Recite the remainder of Hallel.

Nirtza — Pray for the acceptance of the service.

The following things are placed upon the table:

I. Three Matzoth covered. Two represent the "double portion" (Exod. 16: 22), while the third symbolizes the "Bread of affliction" (Deut. 16: 3).

II. A roasted shank-bone of a lamb — *zeroa* — in commemoration of the Pascal lamb.

III. A roasted egg, commemorating the festival offering — *hagiga.*

IV. A piece of horseradish — *maror* — and a dish of cut horseradish.

V. *Haroseth* — made of fruit, nuts, cinnamon, and wine, symbolizing the clay in Egypt (M. Pes. X, 3; b. Pes. 115–116).

VI. Parsley or watercress — *carpas.*

A cup of wine is placed at each plate, and a large goblet of wine in the center of the table — called the "cup of the prophet Elijah."

Cushions are placed on each seat in order to recline on the left side — a custom practiced by free men in the Roman period. "Even the poorest Israelite shall not eat without reclining" (M. Pes. X, 1).

Everybody "even the poorest who subsist on charity shall drink four cups of wine (M. Pes., *l.c.*). Wine, symbolizing the climax of joy on other festive Jewish occasions,[10] as on Sabbaths, the festivals, marriages, circumcisions, was prescribed for the *Seder* in a special measure. This number (four) the *Talmud* (Jer. Pes. X, 1) determines by the four promises of redemption made to Israel (Exod. 6:6–7): *Wehotzhethi*, *Wehitzalti*, *Wegaalti*, and *Welakahti* — that is, Bringing out of bondage, Deliverance from servitude, Redemption from all dependence on Egypt, and Selection as the people of God.

The reason for the cup of Elijah is that on Passover eve Elijah is supposed to announce the redemption. Originally, however, the fifth cup was ordered for Elijah to decide its legality, since he will decide all doubts in religious matters. In the *Talmud* (b. Pes. 117b, Tosafoth), a fifth cup was demanded for the recitation of the "Great Hallel" — Psalm 136 (S.R.A. 41a).[11]

b. The Haggada is ushered in with the "Kiddush" — *Kaddesh* — for the festivals (M. Pes. X, 2).

The benediction over wine is said first and then: "Blessed . . . Who hast chosen us from all peoples, and exalted us above all tongues, and sanctified us by Thy commandments. And Thou hast given us in love . . . appointed times for gladness, festivals and seasons for joy: This day of the Feast of Unleavened Bread, the season of our Freedom, an holy convocation, as a memorial of the exodus from Egypt. . . ."

This paragraph closes with: "Blessed . . . and enabled us to reach this season (M. Pes., *l.c.*). If the festival occurs on a Friday evening, references to Sabbath are made. If it happens to fall on a Saturday evening, a "Havdala" is inserted with the blessing over the light (see Chapter X).

The text is fully discussed in the *Talmud* (b. Pes. 105–107) and is given in S.R.A. 38a. The Yemenite and Aleppo rituals have a long text for Kiddush in which Israel's qualities and God's wonderful deeds with Israel are highly praised.[12] Abudraham, however, rejects this version, because it is not the traditional Kiddush.

Rehatz — the hands are washed but no benediction is uttered.

Carpas — some parsley dipped in salt water is taken,[13] and the benediction: "Blessed . . . Who createst the fruit of the earth" is then recited.

Yahatz — the master of the house breaks the middle Matza and, leaving one half, he hides the other half for the *Aphikomon*.

The second cup of wine is then filled and the recitation of the Haggada begins.

Maggid — Recitation. *Ha lahma* — "Behold! this is the bread of affliction which our fathers ate in the land of Egypt: let all those who are hungry enter and eat thereof; and all who require, come and celebrate the Passover. At present, we celebrate it here, may we celebrate it next year in the land of Israel. This year we are here subdued, but next year we hope to be free men."

The Yemenite ritual has at the beginning the sentence: "In haste did we leave Egypt."

This paragraph is in Aramaic, the vernacular spoken in Babylon and Palestine during the Second Temple and thereafter. With this announcement it was customary to invite the poor to partake in the Seder service in the language spoken. This paragraph is not quoted in the *Mishna*.[14]

Here follows the recitation of the "four questions" which the child asks the father:

Ma nishtanna — "Wherefore is this night distinguished from all other nights?" The questions are according to M. Pes. X:4. "Why do we eat only unleavened bread?"; "Why *Maror* — bitter herbs?"; "Why roasted meat only?", and "Why do we dip twice?"

When the Pascal lamb was abolished, the question about roasted meat was omitted and was replaced by the question: "Why do we have to eat in a reclining position?"

The questions were created in accordance with the Biblical statements (Exod. 13 and 14) which were intended to provoke queries in the minds of the children, so that the opportunity may arise to instruct them concerning Israel's history. The *Mishna* (*l.c.*), recommends a narrative which "begins with reproach and ends with praise." The *Talmud* (b. Pes. 116a) quotes the paragraph to begin as follows:

Avadim hayinu — "We were slaves unto Pharaoh . . . and God brought our ancestors out of Egypt. Had He not redeemed us, we, our children, and our children's children would still have continued in bondage. . . . And though we all know the lore, it is still our duty to recount the story of the Exodus. . . ."

This beginning follows the form prescribed by Samuel (b. Pes. 116a).

Maase berabbi — A story is then related about the sages Rabbi Eliezer, Rabbi Joshua, Rabbi Eleazar ben Azaria, Rabbi Akiva, and Rabbi Tarfon who once continued to recount the story of the exodus throughout the night. A similar story is quoted in *Tosefta* Pes. end about Rabbi Gamaliel and the elders.[15]

Amar R. Eliezer — "Rabbi Eleazar ben Azaria said: 'Verily, I am about seventy years old, and I have hitherto not been able to prove that the history of the Exodus ought to be told at night . . .' " Ben Zoma derived it from the Biblical verse: "Remember thy going out from Egypt *all* the days of your life" (Deut. 16:3); the word "all" includes nights. The sages derived from this expression that it includes the Messianic Era — that is, even in the Messianic Era the story of the Exodus ought to be recited.

This passage is taken from M. Ber. I, 5, and occurs also in *Sifré*, Re'e § 130. *Mechilta*, Bo, 16.

Baruch hammakom — In this paragraph the idea that one should be provided with four answers for four types of men is developed:

a. The wise man who asks concerning the statutes of *Pesah*. This man ought to be taught all the laws concerning Passover, even the rule that no Aphikomon — dessert — should be eaten after the partaking of the Pascal lamb, so that the taste of its meat shall remain (b. Pes. 119b). Now, since the Matza substitutes the Pascal lamb, it is not allowed to eat any desert thereafter.

b. The wicked man who asks: "What does this service mean to you?" — to you and not to him! He is to be answered with Exodus 13 : 8.[16]

c. The simple man who asks: "What is this?" He is to be enlightened with Exodus 13 : 14.

d. But he who is not yet able to ask you must start to teach with the narrative of Exodus 13 : 14–15, explaining also why the celebration does not occur on the New Moon of the month of Nissan but only on the fourteenth of Nissan, as given in Exodus 12 : 2f., when Matza and Maror are eaten.

This passage occurs in a varied version in Jer. Pes. X : 4 and in the *Mechilta* 17, 18 end.

Mit'hilla — Here the narrative starts as indicated in b. Pes. 116a in the name of Rav. Joshua 24 : 2–4. This paragraph tells that our ancestors were idol worshippers, and that God took Abraham and led him to Canaan and caused him and his descendants to settle there. But Jacob and his children went to Egypt (*Mechilta*, Bo, Wehiggadta).

Tzê ul'mad — In this passage the story of the belief in God is recounted. Abraham demonstrated his belief in God when he was told concerning the redemption of his descendants from Egypt after four hundred years of slavery (Gen. 15 : 13–14). From Abraham's trust in God the following deduction is drawn:

Wehi sheameda — "And it is this same promise which hath supported our ancestors and us; for not only hath one risen up against us, but in every generation there are some who have risen up against us to destroy us; but the Holy One, blessed be He, hath always delivered us from their hands" (M. Pes. X : 4).

Bimthê mĕat — Here the narrative of Deuteronomy 26 : 5–8 is read in accordance with M. Pes. X : 4; the story is embellished with Midrashic and legendary material as found in the *Mechilta* and *Sifré* where the passages of Exodus 1 : 7; 13 : 8f.; Deuteronomy 26 : 5f. are interpreted in accordance with the special Agadic hermeneutics. These are as follows:

"The Aramean intended to *destroy* my father (Onkelos' Aramaic translation).

"He went down into Egypt" — compelled thereto by the word of God (b. Shabbath 89b).

"And there he became a great nation. . . ." They were noted because they did not change their names and language (not even their clothing); they did not use slanderous words and lived in chastity (Wayyikra Rabba, Chap. 32:5).

"And He saw the afflictions. . . ." This refers to the forcible separation of husband and wife from married life (b. Yoma 77b, 74b; Wayyikra Rabba, Chap. 19). *Wayyeda* is also used for married relationships (Gen. 4:1; 24:16).

This exhortation continues up to the counting of the ten plagues. Out of the initials of the Hebrew words for the plagues Rabbi Juda formed three mnemonic words in order to facilitate remembering the order in which the plagues succeed one another.[17]

Wayyotziênu — Here follow the three passages which try to deduce in a Midrashic style from the Exodus 8:15 and 14:31 that if there were ten plagues in Egypt, the Egyptians were stricken with five times as many on the Red Sea; and if there were in Egypt forty, every plague being equivalent to four, then there were two hundred on the Red Sea; and if every plague in Egypt consisted of five plagues, making a total of fifty, then there were two hundred and fifty on the Red Sea (*Mechilta*, Bo. 7; Beshallah, Chap. 6; *Yalkut*, Beshallah, 240; Shemoth Rabba, Chap. 8; *Yalkut*, Shemoth, 173).

Camma maaloth — This is a summary of the kindnesses which God extended to Israel since the exodus up to the building of the Temple (*Sifré*, Ha'azinu, 337).

R. Gamaliel — This passage is given again in the *Mishna* (Pes. X:5) in an abbreviated form: "Rabban Gamaliel said: Whosoever did not explain these three things on Passover has not acquitted himself of his duty; these three things are concerning the Pascal lamb, the unleavened bread, and the bitter herb. Pesah? Because the Lord passed over our fathers' houses in Egypt. Matza? Because our fathers were redeemed from Egypt. Maror? Because the Egyptians embittered the life of our ancestors in Egypt." For each of these three, our Haggada has additional quotations from the Bible.

Bechol dor — "It is therefore incumbent upon each one in every generation to regard himself as if he personally had gone forth out of Egypt, as it is said (Exod. 13:8). . . ." Later additions have: "Not our ancestors alone, but us also did He redeem with them. . . ." (M. Pes. X: 5). The *Mishna* then continues:

Lĕfichach — "We therefore are in duty bound to thank . . . Him Who wrought us these miracles . . . from darkness to a great light; and therefore let us sing before Him 'Halleluya.'"

Psalms 113 and 114 are recited.

Baruch . . . asher gĕalanu — The conclusion then follows according to the wording in the *Mishna* (*l.c.*): "Blessed . . . Who hast redeemed us and our ancestors from Egypt . . . enable us to enjoy in peace other solemn feasts . . . rejoicing in the rebuilding of Thy city. . . ." The wording is ascribed in the *Mishna* (*l.c.*) to Rabbi Akiva who must have composed it after the fall of Jerusalem.

Thus far the text of the *Haggada* is of Mishnaic times.

After the reading, the second cup is drunk. The Ashkenazic, Italian, and Yemenite rituals, following S.R.A. 39a and M.V., p. 296, have the benediction over wine recited here, while the Sephardic ritual does not have the benediction.

The Yemenite ritual has a long form of the benediction; it is an alphabetical acrostic beginning with "Thou hast redeemed our fathers," telling the story of the Exodus in brief, and closing with the same wording of the *Mishna*.

Rahatza — Then wash your hands and say the benediction: "Blessed . . . and commanded us to raise [18] (to wash) our hands."

Motzi, *Matza* — The upper Matza is taken and the benediction over bread is said, and then the benediction: "Blessed. . . . Who commanded us to eat unleavened bread."

Maror — Bitter herbs, the size of an olive is dipped in Haroseth and the following benediction is recited "Blessed . . . and commanded us to eat bitter herbs."

Corech — Break the third Matza, take two pieces of it, and put between them some bitter herbs with Haroseth and say: "This is to commemorate the practice of Hillel in the time of the Temple who thus used to eat in fulfillment of the Biblical statement: 'Together with unleavened bread and bitter herbs they shall eat it' — the Pascal Lamb" (Num. 9: 11; b. Pes. 115a).

Shulhan Orech — The meal is then served.

Tzafon — The hidden piece of Matza is produced and eaten as the Aphikomon — dessert. The reason for eating Matza instead of any dessert is in order to retain the taste of the Matza after the meal (see b. Pes. 119b and Rashi's explanation).

Barech — Before Grace, the third cup is filled. In the third benediction of Grace, "Yaale Weyavo" is inserted in which the particular festival is named.

After Grace, the third cup is taken for which the benediction over wine is said.

The fourth cup is filled, the door is opened, and the following is recited:

Shefoch — "Pour out Thy wrath upon the heathen that know Thee not and upon the kingdoms that call not upon Thy Name" (Psalm 79:6). The Italian ritual has only this one sentence. S.R.A., the Sephardic, and Yemenite rituals add: "For they have devoured Jacob, and laid waste his beautiful dwelling" (Psalm 79:7). The Ashkenazic ritual adds Psalm 69:25 and Lamentations 3:66. M.V., p. 296, adds several other Biblical verses.

While this paragraph is recited, the door stands open to indicate the spirit of freedom. Later on, this custom was interpreted, making it symbolic of the coming of the prophet Elijah who will bring the good tidings of the redemption.

Hallel is now completed with Psalms 115–118. In addition, the Great Hallel — Psalm 136 — and the "Benediction of the Song" — *bircath hashir* — which begins with "the breath of all living shall bless Thy Name" (see Sabbath morning service, Chapter X) are recited.[19]

After this recitation the fourth cup is taken with the benediction over wine, and after the drinking another benediction is said (Chapter IX).

This is the text of the Haggada according to Talmudic sources. It is also the text given in S.R.A. and in the old Sephardic and Yemenite rituals. M.V., p. 298, adds a poem by Isaac which according to Zunz (*Ltg.*, p. 168) is Isaac ben Samuel.

The Italian and Ashkenazic rituals add several songs and "piyyutim":

a. A poem with the refrain "And it came to pass at midnight" written by Yannai about the seventh century; it is also for the Sabbath before Passover (see Appendix IV). The poem begins with: *az rov nissim* — "At that time Thou performest many miracles at night. . . ." It is an alphabetical acrostic and is based upon Bamidbar Rabba 20:11. The author recounts all the miracles God performed for Israel on that night. According to Midrashic interpretation, Abraham's victory over the kings (Gen. 14), Laban's dream (Gen. 31:24), Jacob's wrestling with the angel (Gen. 32:25–31), the plague of the Egyptians' first-born, Israel's victory over Sisera (Judg. 4), the disastrous plague in the Assyrian army (II Kings 19:35), Daniel conceived the prophecy of Nebuchadnezzar's dream (Dan. 2), Belshazzar was killed (Dan. 5), Haman was doomed (Esther 6) — all these took place on this night, and the last redemption, too, will occur on this night (b. Rosh Hashana 11a; *Tanhuma*, Balak, 214a).

b. *Ometz gĕvurothecha* is a poem with the refrain: "And ye shall say: It is the sacrifice of the Lord's passover"; it is in the same form and along the same lines as the previous poem. It occurs also in the morning service of the second day of Passover, and is ascribed to Eliezer Kallir (see Chapter XV).

Both poems were chanted already in the time of the Maharil in the fourteenth century.

c. *Addir bimlucha* is a song known already in the times of Rabbi M. Rothenberg in the thirteenth century.[20] It is an alphabetic acrostic, and the text is sung to certain tunes.[21]

It has been suggested that Kallir is possibly the author of this hymn (O.H., p. 1011).[22]

These three poems occur also in the Italian ritual.

According to the Italian and Ashkenazic rituals, the fourth cup is taken and the benedictions before and after the wine are recited only after the singing of these three songs.

The Ashkenazic ritual has three more songs:

Addir hu — a poem which used to be sung also in the German translation, the tune of which became popular since the beginning of the seventeenth century.[23] According to Zunz, *Ltg.*, p. 20, the text originated in the sixth or seventh centuries, and is a jingle in alphabetic order. The central idea of the poem is "build Thy Temple speedily." The Hebrew and German versions are printed in the Prague Haggada, 1527.

e. *Ehad mi yodea* — "Who knows one?" This riddle-jingle was composed for children in order to keep them alert during the service. Starting with the question: Who knows one? the poem runs up to thirteen.

Both songs (d and e) are also found in the Southern French ritual — Avignon and Carpentras.

f. *Had gadya* — "An only kid. . . ." With this allegorical song the Haggada comes to an end in the Ashkenazic, Oriental-Sephardic, and the Bagdad rituals. This song was also used in the sixteenth century in the Southern French communities in the Provencal dialect;[24] the oldest print is the one of Prague in the year 1590.

Folksongs of a similar content are found in various languages.[25] Rabbinical sources gave this song Midrashic and allegorical interpretations:

One kid — This is the Temple.

My father bought for two Zuzim — David paid for the Temple place twenty-four Zuzim, collecting from each tribe two Zuzim.

"Then came the cat" — This is Nebuchadnezzar, king of Babylon, and destroyed the Temple.

"Then came the dog" — This is Cyrus, king of Persia, who conquered Babylon.

"Then came the stick" — This is Alexander the Great who subdued Persia.

"Then came the fire" — This refers to the Maccabees who burnt the stick — and won a victory over the Greeks.

"Then came the water" — This is Rome; and quenched the fire — destroyed the power of the Maccabees.

"Then came the ox" — This is Ismael, or the Islam, and drank the water — and conquered (eastern) Rome.

"Then came the slaughterer and killed the ox" — This is Messiah, son of Joseph, who will destroy the mighty ox.

"Then came the angel of death and killed the slaughterer" — According to Rabbinic tradition, this Messiah will fall a victim in his fight.

"Then came the Holy One, blessed be He, and killed the angel of death" — In the future God will abolish death and destruction, and humanity will enjoy eternal life and peace.

Before the poem "Addir Hu," the order of the Pesah service is completed with the following recitation: "As we have been privileged to celebrate this Pesah, so may we live to celebrate it again. O Pure One Who dwellest on high, establish Thy congregation, lead them speedily unto Zion in joy and song." [26] This is a closing passage of a "piyyut" for the Great Sabbath (i.e., of the Sabbath before Passover) by Joseph Tov-elem (see Appendix IV).

CHAPTER XV

THE SERVICES FOR THE THREE FESTIVALS

The services for the Three Festivals: Passover — *Pesah*, the Feast of the Weeks — *Shavuoth*, and Tabernacles — *Succoth* — have one and the same structure and the same elements with the exception of distinctive references to each Festival.

This is true of the old liturgical material fixed during the Talmudic period and first arranged in the S.R.A.

In post-Talmudic times, the services for the Festivals were enriched with poetical insertions and prayers for each of the Festivals. In these insertions and prayers the ideas and laws pertaining to these days were described in "payetanic" style and method.

The liturgy of the Festivals voices the main ideas for which they were instituted, namely: seasons of joy and thanksgiving in commemoration of the kind deeds God did to our ancestors in redeeming them from Egyptian bondage, in giving them the Tora, and in settling them on the Promised Land and teaching them the true ways of life. Though we have lost our land and are dispersed throughout the world because of our sins, yet we fervently pray and hope that we shall again be redeemed and brought back to our sacred home where we shall serve God in joy and exaltation.

These Festivals are based upon the experiences of the Jewish people and have Jewish nationalistic aspirations. They are at the same time imbued with universal human hopes and religious ideals, with the ideals of liberty (Passover), Revelation (Shavuoth), and thanksgiving (Succoth).

The basic structure of the services is retained in the liturgy of the Three Festivals. The daily services remain as they are, with the exception of certain omissions and additions.

A. Material Common for All Festivals. I. The evening service to the Amida is in the same form as on Friday evening. After the fourth benediction, the verse: "And Moses declared the set feasts of the Lord unto the children of Israel" is recited (Lev. 23:44).

The Amida consists of seven benedictions: the three regular introductory and concluding and one intermediary benediction.

This latter benediction consists of:

1. *Atta vehartanu* — "Thou hast chosen us from all peoples . . . and brought us near unto Thy service, O our King, and hast called us by Thy great and holy Name. . . ." It is cited in b. Yoma 87b.

2. *Wattodiênu* — On Saturday night a "Havdala" is inserted which is called in the *Talmud* (Ber. 33b) "The Pearl" and is attributed to Rav and Samuel. The *Talmud* (*l.c.*) gives the wording without the sentences: "Thou hast given us, O Lord our God, righteous judgments, true laws, good statutes and commandments." "Thou hast made a distinction between holy and profane, between light and darkness, between Israel and other nations, between the Seventh day and the six working days." S.R.A. has the same version as in the Ashkenazic and Sephardic rituals with an additional sentence which the Italian ritual follows. Other variations are to be found in M.V. and Maimonides. The Yemenite ritual keeps closer to the Talmudic version.

3. *Wattiten lanu* — "And Thou hast given us in love (if it is Sabbath) Sabbaths for rest, appointed times for gladness . . . the day (here the particular festival is mentioned) on Passover: The Feast of Unleavened Bread, the season of our Freedom; on Pentecost: The Feast of Weeks, the season of the Giving of our Law; on Tabernacles: The Feast of Tabernacles, the season of our joy — on the Eighth Day of Succoth and on the Rejoicing of the Law: The Eighth-day Feast of Solemn Assembly, the season of our joy, an holy convocation, as a memorial of the departure from Egypt."

4. *Yaale weyavo* in which mention of the individual Festivals is also made (Soferim XIX:7).

5. *Wehassiênu* — O Lord our God, bestow upon us the blessing of Thy appointed times for life and peace, for joy . . . and may Israel, Who hallow Thy Name, rejoice in Thee. Blessed . . . Who hallowest Israel and the seasons."

This paragraph is mentioned in Jer. Ber. IX: 3. The closing formula is cited in b. Ber. 49a; Betza 17a; Soferim XIX: 7.

In the closing paragraph Sabbath has to be mentioned, if the day is the Sabbath (see b. Betza, *l.c.*).

In Hebrew the Festivals are also called *rĕgalim* (*regel*—foot). The passage in Exodus 23: 14, is explained to mean that the people would make pilgrimages on foot (b. Hagiga 3a).

6. The Kiddush over wine is the same as in the Haggada (Chapter XIV). On the first two nights of Passover, no Kiddush is recited in the synagogue, because everybody is expected to recite it at the "Seder" service.

7. *Alenu*, and Kaddish.

II. The morning service is the same as on Sabbaths, with the exception of the Sabbath insertions in the Yotzer benediction. Instead of these insertions, the weekday formula is used, save when the Festival occurs on Sabbath. In such case, the Sabbath insertions are recited (see Chapter X).

The Amida is the same as in the evening service (see I). At the repetition, the "Kedusha" of Sabbath Shaharith is used.

After the Amida, the Hallel (Psalms 113–118) is chanted (see Chapter XI).

The ritual for the taking out and replacing the Scroll is the same as on Sabbath, save that before the "Shema" the Thirteen Attributes (Exod. 34: 6–7) are recited three times, and then a meditation beginning with "Lord of the universe, fulfill the wishes of my heart for good . . ." is recited. Both recitations were introduced as a result of mystic influences.[1] They are late insertions used only in the Ashkenazic [2] and in the Sephardic-Oriental ritual. In his *Siddur* (Altona, 1745) Rabbi Jacob Emden remarks that these insertions were introduced by Isaac Luria (see Chapter VI). The Sephardic-Oriental ritual has special meditations for Passover, for the Seventh day of Passover, for Pentecost, for Tabernacles, and for *Shemini Atzereth*.

III. The Additional Service, too, has the same structure as that of Sabbath, i.e., the three introductory, the three concluding benedictions, and the Kedusha. The intermediate benedictions consist of:

1. "Thou hast chosen us" and "Thou hast given us in love" — both paragraphs as they occur in the evening and morning services.

2. Then follows the paragraph *Umipĕne hataênu* — "But on account of our sins we were exiled from our land . . . and we are unable to go up in order to appear . . . before Thee . . . have mercy upon us and upon Thy Sanctuary, and mayest Thou speedily rebuild it and magnify its glory. . . . Do Thou speedily make the glory of Thy kingdom manifest upon us . . . bring our scattered ones among the nations near unto Thee. . . . Lead us with exaltation unto Zion Thy city . . . and there we will prepare before Thee the offerings."

Here the quotations from the Pentateuch are given in which the sacrifices for each Festival are enumerated. For Passover: Numbers 28 : 16; for Pentecost: *ibid.* 28 : 26; and for Tabernacles: *ibid.* 29 : 12, 17f.

The part from "But on account of our sins . . . by the mouth of Thy glory, as it is said . . ." is to be found with some variations in the Musaf for the day of the New Moon if it falls on Sabbath. Some scholars hold that the first paragraph of the intermediary benediction for the Amida of the Festivals was taken from that of the day of the New Moon (see Landshuth, p. 319).

Preceding these verses, Numbers 28 : 9 is recited, and following them, the passage "They that keep the Sabbath" is said.

3. *Melech rahaman* — "Our God and God of our fathers, merciful king, have mercy with . . . build Thy house . . . and establish Thy sanctuary upon its site . . . restore the priests to their service, the Levites to their song and Israel to their habitations: and there we will go up to appear . . . at the three periods of our festivals. . . ."

Some sentences of the last two paragraphs are mentioned in Soferim XIX : 7. S.R.A. (Ed. Frumkin) gives their entire texts with slight variations which is common to all rituals. Some scholars (Rappaport, Zunz) hold that the intermediary paragraphs were composed by Rav out of the Sabbath Musaf (see Chapter X; Landshuth, p. 467; Zunz, S.V., p. 313).

4. The paragraph "Bestow upon us . . ." is repeated, and this closes the intermediary benediction.[3]

5. The Priestly Benediction—*nesiath cappayim.* The old custom that the priests should bless the people, as given in Numbers 6:22–27, has been transplanted into the synagogue (M. Sota VII:6) in the public service. Originally, it was arranged for every morning service, for the Musaf of Sabbaths and holidays, and for the Minha service of Fast-days. On the Day of Atonement, the Priestly Benediction used to be pronounced at the "Ne'ila" service instead of at the Minha (M.V., pp. 99–100). This procedure prevails still in Jerusalem. In the Diaspora, however, the custom was limited to the Three Festivals and the High Holydays for their Musaf services.[4]

Originally, the Priestly Benediction was uttered by the Aaronites at every public service (M. Taanith IV, 1), but soon its use was restricted to the morning service only (b. Taanith 26b), with the exception of the Day of Atonement on which Day the Ne'ila service also had the Priestly Benediction. It was further restricted to the Musaf service of the Three Festivals and the High Holydays, while in Jerusalem the custom to recite the Priestly Benediction in the daily morning service and in all Musaf services still prevails.

The Priestly Benediction is recited in the synagogue by the reader, while the Cohanim repeat each word.[5] This custom seems to have been introduced to enable those who are not familiar with the text to participate in the Benediction. In accordance with Leviticus 9:22, the Cohanim have to stand up and raise their hands. In the Temple they are to raise their hands over their heads; in the provinces, up to their shoulders (M. Sota VII:6, b. Sota 38a). The priests ascend the platform before the ark; they take off their shoes, raise their hands, cover themselves with the "tallith" and face the congregation.[6] Then they pronounce each word in responsive form, after the reader,[7] and stop after each of the three verses. The reader calls out: "Priests," and they reply: "Thy holy people, as it is said." Then they recite the benediction given in b. Sota 39a: "Blessed . . . Who hast sanctified us with the sanctity of Aaron and hast commanded us to bless Thy people Israel in love." Prior to the Priestly Benediction, the Cohanim have to recite a benediction given in b. Sota 39a, and to read a meditation after the ceremony (*l.c.*). They have to face the congregation; they have to take off their shoes before the ceremony (*l.c.*) and wash their hands (*l.c.*, 39a). The *Talmud* advises the people not to look at the Cohanim while they bless them (b. Hagiga 16a), at least not in the Temple service. Later on, the custom developed for the Cohanim to arrange their fingers in such a way that five openings be distinguished (M.V., p. 105; Maharil) thus interpreting the verse in Canticles 2:9: "He peereth through the lattice" in such a way as to divide the word *ha-harakkim* to mean "five lattices." It was also advised that whoever has had a dream should recite a meditation during the Priestly Benediction (b. Ber. 55b). In addition, there were inserted Biblical passages to each word of the Priestly Benediction to be recited by the congregation.

In the seventeenth benediction, the reader closes with: "And may our prayer be acceptable unto Thee as burnt-offering. . . . Blessed . . . Whom alone we serve in awe" [8] (see Chapter VIII).

The priests say the following meditation: "May it be Thy will, O our God, that the benediction which Thou hast commanded us to bless Thy people Israel be a perfect one, and no sin shall interfere with it." This meditation is cited in b. Sota 39a. There are variations of this meditation (*cf. Otzar Hatĕfilloth*, p. 944).

When the priests stop at the end of each verse, the congregation responds with "Amen" or "May it be the will of God" and recites a silent prayer: "I am Thine and my dreams come from Thee . . . turn all my dreams to good. . . ." This meditation is from b. Berachoth 55b.

At the end another meditation is recited which is suggested in "Shaare Tzion."

After the Priestly Benediction, the priests offer a short prayer which is quoted in b. Sota 39a; while the congregation recites: "Mighty on high. . . ." (b. Ber. 55b).

The platform on which the Cohanim perform their ceremony is called *duchan* — estrade. The name is borrowed from the Temple. It was an elevated place upon which the Levites stood when they sang the sacred music (M. Arachin II, 6). This term was later applied to the function of the Cohanim while reciting the Priestly Benediction in the synagogue (b. Shab. 118b).

In case there are no Aaronites in the synagogue, the reader recites the Priestly Benediction with an introductory passage already cited in S.R.A. 12a.

In the course of centuries various traditional chants developed for the Priestly Benediction sung by the Cohanim; there grew up different chants for the different festivals of the year.

B. ADDITIONS FOR THE INDIVIDUAL FESTIVALS. I. The Evening Services. The ASHKENAZIC ritual[9] has poetical insertions for the Shema-benedictions of the evening services. It has separate insertions for the first and second, the seventh and eighth evenings of Passover and Tabernacles and for the first and second evenings of the Feast of Weeks.

These poetical insertions are called *maaravoth*. In M.V., p. 565f., this type of poetry is called *maarivim*.

The oldest compositions date back to the eleventh century.[10]

The insertions are placed before the closing sentence of each benediction or paragraph. There are six of them; the third is usually a long one. A seventh poem is added on the first and second evenings of Passover and on the first evening of Shavuoth (*cf.* Appendix V, *a*).

Hakafoth. On Simhath Tora eve after the service it became customary among the Ashkenazim beginning with the sixteenth century to take out all the Scrolls from the ark and make a procession with them around the "Bema" seven times.[11] This procession is repeated during the morning service. The Oriental-Sephardim have it on Simhath Tora after Minha. The Hasidim, however, make "Hakafoth" even after the evening service of "Shemini Atzereth."[12]

This custom aims to display the Jews' rejoicing with their Tora and to endear it to their children.

In the Ashkenazic ritual the service for the *Hakafoth* is the same as cited in M.V., p. 456f.

1. Before taking out the Scrolls a selection of Biblical verses is recited responsively; these verses are: Deuteronomy 4:35; Psalms 136:4; 86:8; 104:31; 113:2; I Kings 8:57; I Chronicles 16:35; *adonai melech* as in the morning service (Chap-

ter I); Exodus 15:18; Psalm 29:11; Numbers 10:35; Psalm 132:8–10; Isaiah 25:9; Psalm 145:13; Isaiah 2:3. Then "Father of mercy" is recited as on taking out the Scrolls for reading; it is followed by Psalms 51:20 and 118:25. M.V. has Psalm 24:7–10 instead of Isaiah 25:9 and Psalm 145:13. Then follow two poems: *ohavê adonai zera avadaw* and *yedidê êl adath* which are also quoted in *Sefer Hamahkim.*

2. Then the circuits are made, while chanting an alphabetic litany with the alternating refrains: "We beseech Thee save us"; "We beseech Thee make us prosper." This recitation is interspersed with meditations.

3. When the circuits are over, the reader chants "Shema," "Our God is One," and "Magnify," according to the tune used on High Holydays.[13]

In the German communities, *al haccol* is then chanted in responsive form (Maharil; Mahkim). In some congregations, some passages are read from a Scroll.

4. *Sisu wesimhu* — "Rejoice in the Law" — is then chanted. This hymn underwent several changes. There is a German and a Polish version of it. Both drew their material for the second part from M.V., § 421–422, while the first section does not occur in that source. This seems to have been taken from an alphabetical acrostic, *ahalela elohay* — "I shall praise my God with the refrain: 'Let us rejoice with this Tora'" — *nagil wênasis*. Only the stanzas *alef-hê* were taken.

The Italian ritual has the passage *ashrechem yisrael* with variations, as in M.V. only up to *heth;* then it has *mi ala lammarom* (*cf.* Appendix V, b).

II. The Morning Services — *shaharith.* According to Maharil and M. Rothenburg,[14] the paragraph *nishmath* is divided. The second part starts on Shavuoth with *haêl bethaatzumoth*, on Succoth with *haggadol bich'vod*, and on Passover with *haggibor lanetzah.* The Polish ritual, however, always starts with *haêl bethaatzumoth*, save on the High Holydays when it starts with *hammelech yoshev.*

The reason for this arrangement is that on Shavuoth we proclaim Him as "God," on Succoth as "The Great One," on Passover as "The Mighty One," and on the High Holydays as "Sovereign Ruler." [15]

The poetical insertions usually occur in the first benediction of Shema after the introductory benediction: "Blessed . . . Who formest light and createst darkness, Who makest peace and createst all things"; they also occur in the third benediction.

The Italian ritual has poetical insertions before *Nishmath* and *barechu* only. The Polish ritual has only once an introduction to *Nishmath* on Simhath Tora.

Of all rituals the Ashkenazic is the richest in poetical insertions. It has "Yotzer" and "Kerova" for all the festivals, mostly compositions by E. Kallir, Solomon b. Juda of Rome, Meshullam b. Kalonymos, and Simon b. Abun of Mayence. Outstanding are the selections of the "Geula" for the first two days of Passover and the Sabbath which occurs during the Passover week. They start with "Flee my beloved" and fervently plead for redemption and springtime for Israel. The initial words are taken from Canticles 2:17. Another poem elaborately sung is the "Yotzer" for Passover, "Go out and see," in which too are utilized phrases of the Song of Songs, which came to be considered the spring-song of Israel's rejuvenation. It is also found in the Italian ritual. Its theme is a call to God to behold the sufferings of Israel and God's answer that Israel through his suffering should become aware of his sins.

Most interesting is the "Nishmath" and "Yotzer" for Simhath Tora, which elaborates on Moses' life and his struggle with approaching death. This theme is used in the Italian ritual for Simhath Tora to a more extensive degree than in the Ashkenazic.

The Sephardic, Italian, and Yemenite rituals have neither "Yotzer" nor "Kerova" for the morning service (Shaharith). All of the rituals have poetical insertions for the prayer for "Dew," *Tal,* inserted in the Musaf service on the first day of Passover; and for "Rain," *Geshem,* in the Musaf of the eighth day of Succoth. The poems used in the Sephardic and Yemenite rituals are by a certain Solomon, and have a fluid and pleasant style. The poems in the Italian ritual are by local composers, and those in the Ashkenazic ritual are attributed mainly to Kallir, some being simple and charming, while the others are heavy and obscure.

The source for the Prayer for Rain is to be found in the *Mishna* Taanith I : 1. The original form was "Who makest the wind to blow and causest the rain to descend." This formula is still said in the Amida after the first benediction from *Shemini Atzereth* to Passover.

The Ashkenazim have a special tune for the half-Kaddish before the Musaf of the first day of Passover and the eighth day of Succoth. In the same tune, the first benediction of the Amida and the insertions 1 and 2 are chanted.[16] The Sephardim, too, have special tunes for the insertions 1–6.[17]

Among other poetical insertions the "Azharoth" should be mentioned. They are to be found in all the rituals either before or in the Musaf, or also after the service. They give an account of the six hundred and thirteen laws, which the Rabbis found in the Bible, and were worked out in verse by several didactic poets. The one used in the Sephardic and Yemenite rituals is ascribed to Solomon b. Gabirol, whereas the Italian composition, which is in part used also by the Ashkenazim, seems to be very old and anonymous. The Ashkenazim have also a poem in Aramaic, which is a glorification of the Tora, by Meyir b. Isaac of Worms (*cf.* Appendix V, d).

The poetical insertions helped to create the special atmosphere of each festal day, and to recreate for the Jew the glory of his past. They aroused in him enthusiasm for the lofty ideals of his heritage, and a yearning for his national rehabilitation.

III. ORDER OF THE READINGS FROM THE PENTATEUCH AND THE PROPHETS. ON PASSOVER. First day: The Sephardic ritual reads Exodus 12 : 14–51. This is in accordance with S.R.A. Abudraham says that this is the custom of most congregations in Spain. The Ashkenazic, Italian, and Yemenite rituals read Exodus 12 : 21–51 in accordance with b. Megilla 31a. From the second Scroll, Numbers 28 : 16–25 is read. For the *Haftara*, Joshua 5 : 2–15; 6 : 1, 27 is taken. The Sephardic and Italian rituals do not read the last verse, but conclude with the verse "Our Redeemer! the Lord of hosts is His Name, the Holy One of Israel."

The Ashkenazic and Polish rituals start with Joshua 3 : 5–7 and then continue as above. However, b. Megilla, *l.c.*, gives the first custom.

Second day: Leviticus 22 : 26 and through 33. From the second Scroll the same passage is read as on the first day. For Haftara, II Kings 23 : 1–9 and 21–25 are read (Abudraham). The Italian ritual gives II Kings 23: 21–30, while the Yemenite ritual has II Kings 22 to 23: 25.

Third day: Exodus 13: 1–16; from the second Scroll: Numbers 28: 19–25.

Fourth day: Exodus 22: 24–30; 23: 1–19.

Fifth day: Exodus 34: 1–26. If this reading falls on a Saturday, the reading begins from Exodus 33: 12–23 and continues to Exodus 34: 1–8.

Sixth day: Numbers 9: 1–14.

The reading from the second Scroll is the same as on the third day.

On the Sabbath that falls during the Passover week, Exodus 33: 12 through 34: 16 is read. From the second Scroll: Numbers 28: 19–25 is read. The Haftara is taken from Ezekiel 37: 1–14.

Seventh day: Exodus 13: 17 to 15: 26. From the second Scroll, the same is read as on the third and sixth days. The Haftara is taken from II Samuel 22.

Eighth day: Deuteronomy 14: 22 to 16: 17, if it falls on Sabbaths; on weekdays, the reading starts from Exodus 15: 19. From the second Scroll, the same is read as on the previous days. The Haftara is taken from Isaiah 10: 32 to the end of Chapter 12.

b. Megilla 31a gives the following order of readings: *meshech*, *tura*, *kadesh*, *bcchaspa*, *pĕsal*, *bemadbara*, *shelah*, *buchra*.

The reasons for the selection of these sections are given in the *Talmud* and have been collected in M.V., p. 303. The readings for the first, second, seventh, and eighth days relate the Exodus, the crossing of the Red Sea, and the laws pertaining to Passover. The reading for the third day explains the law concerning the first-born; this portion is read in commemoration of the saving of Israel's first-born during the plague of the Egyptian first-born. The readings for the fourth and fifth days are to remind the people of the observance of the holidays, while the reading for the sixth day contains the law that people who were not levitically clean on Passover should observe a second Passover — *pessah sheni* — on the fourteenth of the month of "Iyyar" — a month after the first Passover.

On Shavuoth. For the first day: Exodus 19 and 20. From the second Scroll, Numbers 128: 26 to the end of the chapter is read. For the Haftara: Ezekiel 1 and 3: 12.

For the second day: The same reading as on the eighth day of Passover. From the second Scroll, the same section is read as on the previous day. For the Haftara: Hab. 2: 20 to the end of Chapter 3.

The reason for the reading of the first day is obvious, since the section relates the revelation on Mount Sinai and contains the Ten Commandments. The section read on the second day gives instruction as to the observance of the holidays.

ON SUCCOTH. For the first day the same reading is used as on the second day of Passover. From the second Scroll: Numbers 29 : 12–16 is read. For the Haftara: Zechariah 14 is read. The Yemenite ritual starts with Zechariah 3 : 9.

For the second day: The same section as on the first day. From the second Scroll, the same passage is also read as on the first day. For Haftara: I Kings 8 : 2–21. The Yemenite and Italian rituals read I Kings 7 : 57; 8 : 1–15.

For the third, fourth, fifth, sixth, and seventh days the section Numbers 17–24 is read. On each day three paragraphs are read: Cohen, Levi, and Israelite. For the fourth Israelite called upon the first two paragraphs are repeated. On the third day, the reading begins from "And on the second day"; on the fourth day: "On the third day"; on the fifth day: "On the fourth day"; and on the sixth and seventh day: "On the fifth day."

For the eighth day — "Shemini Atzereth" — the same portion is read as on the eighth day of Passover and as on the second day of Shavuoth. The Italian ritual starts from Deuteronomy 15 : 12. From the second Scroll, Numbers 29 : 35 to 30 : 1 is read. For the Haftara: I Kings 8 : 54–66 is read. The Italian and Polish rituals add 9 : 1.

For the ninth day — *Simhath Tora* — Deuteronomy 33 is read. From the second Scroll: Genesis 1 and 2 : 1–4 is read. The Italian ritual reads only Genesis 1 : 1–6.[18] From the third Scroll, the same passage is read as on the eighth day. For the Haftara: Joshua 1. The Sephardic ritual reads only Joshua 1 : 1–9.

Aside from the readings from the Pentateuch and the Prophets, the three books: Song of Songs, Ruth, and Ecclesiastes are read.

The Song of Songs is read on the Sabbath which falls during Passover week; if the Sabbath falls on the seventh day of Passover, the Book is read on that day. This reading on Passover is based upon the Rabbinic interpretation that Canticles 1, 9 refers to the Exodus (M.V., p. 304).

Ruth is read on Shavuoth, because, according to Chapter 1 end, the episode took place at the "season of barley harvest," i.e., Shavuoth (*o.c.*, p. 344).

Ecclesiastes is read on the Sabbath during the week of Succoth; or, if Sabbath falls on the eighth day, it is read then. This reading is mentioned in *Hamanhig*, Succa § 59. There the author says that it is a French custom and gives some Midrashic reasons for the reading. The Sephardic and Italian rites do not read the Book of Ecclesiastes.

In the Sephardic and Italian ritual, the Book of Ruth is divided into two instalments for both days of Shavuoth: Part 1 consists of Chapters 1 to 3 : 8; part 2 of Chapters 3 : 8 to the end of the Book.

The Song of Songs is also read in the Sephardic-Oriental and Italian rituals before Minha in two instalments: on the seventh and eighth days of Passover. In the Yemenite ritual, this book is read on the seventh day.

These readings occur in the above-mentioned rituals before the Minha service, and in the Sephardic-Oriental ritual they are translated into Ladino (Spanish-Jewish vernacular).

In the Ashkenazic and Yemenite rituals, Ruth is read on the second day. Ecclesiastes is read in the Ashkenazic ritual only. All the three books are read in the Ashkenazic ritual at the morning service before the reading from the Pentateuch.

Hamanhig, Succa § 55, says that this reading became a general custom. T. Soferim XIV : 3, mentions the reading of Canticles and Ruth, without specifying when they are to be read.

For the Sabbath which falls during the week of Succoth the reading is the same as for the Sabbath of the Passover week. From the second Scroll, the same is read as on *hol hamoed.* For the Haftara: Ezekiel 38 : 18, 39 : 1–16. The Italian and Yemenite rituals read Ezekiel 38 or 39 : 1–10 (*cf.* Appendix V, c).

IV. *Yizcor* — the Memorial Service (see Chapter XVI, par. 5). The Italian ritual has a memorial service only on the eighth day of Passover. The Polish ritual, however, and also some Ashkenazic congregations, have this service also on the second day of Pentecost and the eighth day of Succoth. The Italian ritual combines with this service prayers for resurrection and for annulment of vows and oaths.

The Ashkenazic ritual calls for donations — *matnath yad* — on the eighth day of Passover and Succoth and on the second day of Pentecost, because the Scriptural reading on these days closes with a call for the donations for the sanctuary (Deut. 16 : 16–17). The Italian ritual has this custom for the eighth day of Passover.

The other rituals have neither the Memorial Service nor the call for donations on these days.

After the Haftara, the Memorial Service is recited.

V. *Succoth.* On the first to seventh day, with the exception of Sabbath, the four plants are taken before Hallel, as prescribed in Leviticus 23:40. A meditation is read: "Lo, I am prepared . . . to fulfill the command of my Creator. . . . While I wave them, may the stream of blessing flow in upon me, together with holy thoughts, which tell that He is God. . . ." This meditation is taken from *Shaare Tzion* by Nathan Hannover; it is mentioned on several occasions (see Chapter VI).

On the first day, the benediction: "Blessed . . . and enabled us to reach this season" is uttered.[19]

The names of the four plants are: *Lulav* — palm-branch; *Ethrog* — citron; *Hadasa* — myrtle; and *Arava* — willow-branch.[20]

In b. Succa 37b the form of the waves is given. The wavings are directed toward the four winds, the heavens, and the earth. They symbolize the stream of abundance which comes from these directions. The wavings take place in the Hallel while chanting the verses 2 and 3, 25 and 29 of Psalm 118.

For the eighth day the Italian ritual has the same *en camocha* as for the eighth day of Passover. On Simhath Tora, Psalms 6 or 12 are recited. For the "Hathan Tora" — i.e., the person who is called upon to finish the reading in the first Scroll — the same prayer is offered as in the Ashkenazic ritual.

Then several hymns follow (*cf.* Appendix V, d).

VI. *Hosha'anoth* — Prayers for Salvation. *Mishna* Succa IV, 5 tells us that on each of the six days of the Succa festival the people and priests would circle the altar, while chanting "I beseech Thee, O God, save us; I beseech Thee, O God, cause us to prosper" — Psalm 118:25. On the seventh day, they would make seven circuits.[21] While making the circuits, they would carry the willows brought from a nearby place — "Motza" (in Latin: Colonia). The *Talmud* (b. Succa 43b) says that during the procession the priests would carry the four plants.[22]

This custom was transplanted into the synagogue, and was executed after the Musaf service.

A Scroll is taken out and placed upon the reading desk (Almemor), while the precentor makes a circuit around the Almemor. He is followed by all who have a bough of the four plants.

The verse cited was first chanted during the procession. Gradually, prayers were composed, using the psalm-verse as a refrain. The compositions grew in abundant numbers already at the time of Saadya Gaon—at the end of the tenth century. Every gifted precentor would compose prayers for these processions, writing separate prayers for each day. All have the alphabetical acrostic. Because the way around the Almemor was short, the prayers are likewise short. As a rule, they consist of as many words as there are letters in the alphabet. Sometimes, they have two words to the line, or an initial key-word to the line.

On Sabbath which falls during the Succoth week, no circuit is made, because it is forbidden to carry the four plants to the synagogue on Sabbath.

In addition to the verse of Psalm 118, the obscure sentence, *ani wahu hoshia na*, mentioned in *Mishna* (*l.c.*) used to be chanted and is now greatly utilized in the *Hosha'anoth* liturgy.

The selections used in the liturgy vary greatly, although they have the same contents.

In the Italian and Ashkenazic rituals the prayers are mostly the same, while the Sephardic and Yemenite rituals have each different selections.

M.V., again, has a set of prayers of which only a few were taken over into the Ashkenazic ritual.

In general the contents run along the same lines: We pray Thee, save us, for Thy sake, or for the sake of Thy sanctuary, or for the sake of the patriarchs and heroes of Israel. Save Thy people which, though tormented, clings to Thee and to Thy teachings.

In the Ashkenazic ritual, the greatest part of the *Hosha'anoth* is ascribed to Kallir, while the Sephardic selections are compositions by Joseph and Isaac.

The seventh day is called "Hoshana Rabba"—The Great Salvation—or "Yom Arava"—The Day of the Willow (Italian). On this day, seven circuits are made. Each circuit is made in the name of Abraham, Isaac, Jacob, Moses, Aaron, Phineas, and David. In the Sephardic ritual, special prayers are recited, recounting the merits of the heroes.

After the completion of the seven circuits, the four plants are put aside. The willow [23] is then taken and several selections are recited, at the conclusion of which "May the messenger announce good tidings" is said three times, and the willow — a bough of five twigs — is beaten against the bench or against the floor several times.[24]

The seventh day is considered the day of sealing the decree of judgment (Jer. Rosh Hashana IV, 8). For this reason, some customs of the High Holydays are used on this day.

The Sephardic and Yemenite rituals have several supplications before the *Hosha'anoth*. As well as the Ashkenazic and Italian rituals, they have several phrases from the "Ne'ila" service. In some congregations, the Shofar is blown, basing themselves upon the Jer. *Talmud* quoted above.

In Rome "Un'thanne Tokef" is recited in the Musaf service of this day.[25]

Several tunes from the High Holydays services are also used.

In the Verses of Song, the psalms for Sabbaths and Holidays are recited.

In the Musaf service of this day, the Sabbath and holiday Kedusha is chanted according to the High Holyday tunes.

On the other half-holidays — *hol hammoêd* — of Passover and Succoth, the weekday services are read with the insertions for the holidays. After the morning Amida, Hallel is recited. Then follow the reading from the Scriptures and the holiday-Amida for the Musaf service.

VII. *Ushpizin* — is the Aramaic term for "Guests." The Kabbalist Isaac Luria introduced the custom of reciting an invitation to the four patriarchs, to Joseph, Moses, Aaron, and David, inviting them to be the guests at the meals in the Succa. The idea was taken from the *Zohar*, Emor: 103–104, "When one sits in the Succa, the Shechina spreads its wings over it, and Abraham and five righteous men with David come and sit with him. For this reason, one is to be joyous on these days in the presence of such guests. . . . Therefore, everyone shall try to invite an equal number of poor people for the meals in the Succa; otherwise, Abraham and the other righteous men rise and say: 'Let us leave the tents of these wicked people.' But if one entertains poor people in his Succa, then not only do the above mentioned seven righteous men rejoice, but even God partakes of their joy and in the joy of the poor."

Isaac Luria assigned one of the seven righteous men for each of the seven days of Succoth. A special invitation is recited for each of them. Standing at the entrance of the Succa, one has to say (in Aramaic): "O enter ye sublime and holy guests! Come, O ye Fathers lofty and holy to sit in the shadow of the sublime faithful, in the shadow of the Holy One, blessed be He. May Abraham, and with him Isaac . . . enter."

On the first day, the following invitation is spoken: "I invite for my meal the lofty guests. . . . I pray thee Abraham my sublime guest to sit with me."

On the second day Isaac is invited in similar manner; on the third day Jacob is invited; and so forth.

In addition to this invitation, two meditations are recited. They express the following hopes: "May God spread over us the tabernacle of peace for the sake of the Succa (the Succa being the symbol of peace); may He surround us with His holy and pure glory; may He bestow His blessings upon the hungry as we did to the poor; and may we merit to sit in the holy land (Palestine)."

CHAPTER XVI

THE SERVICES FOR THE HIGH HOLYDAYS

The services for the High Holydays may well be considered the climax of Jewish worship. In them the most important Jewish ideals are expressed: The sovereignty of God over all creatures, the brotherhood of the human family, the revelation of the divine spirit to man, the providence of God, the concept of reward and punishment, the restoration of the Jewish people and the sanctuary in Zion where a center for enlightenment for mankind shall be created. In addition to these ideas, the idea of renouncing one's own sins, seeking forgiveness, and vowing to lead a clean life is emphasized on the Day of Atonement.

On these days, it is the desire of the Jew to elevate himself above his daily routine and to draw near to God. For this reason, these days are dedicated entirely to worship and meditation. For this purpose, the service was elaborately built up of laudations and prayers, hymns and poems, meditations and petitions. The *Talmud* already calls attention to the length of the prayers on these days (Tosefta Ber. 1 : 6; b. Rosh Hashana 35a).

In accordance with this outline, several prayers are common for both holydays: New Year and the Day of Atonement; while several others are especially for the one or the other day.

The New Year falls on the first and second day of the month of Tishre, while the Day of Atonement falls on the tenth of Tishre. These and the intermediate days are called the season of penitence — *asereth yĕme tĕshuva.*

A. New Year — *Rosh Hashana*

I. Standard Prayers. The Hebrew name occurs in Ezekiel 40 : 1 but has no reference to the holyday. The Biblical name for the day is *yom tĕrua* — "Day of blowing the horn" — or *zichron tĕrua* — "A memorial with the blast of horns" (Lev. 23 : 24; Numbers 29 : 1). In the prayers the day received the name *yom hazziccaron* — "A day of memorial." The *Mishna* speaks of this holyday as an old established institution, and devotes to it a whole Tractate. It, therefore, appears that at least during the second part of the period of the Second Temple the New Year was well fixed. Already in the time of Ezra and Nehemiah this day was held to be "holy to the Lord" (Nehem. 8:9).

Originally, there was only one day set aside for this holyday, for the Bible speaks of but one day. But for some reason, it was extended to two days toward the end of the Second Temple, making it "one long day." [1] Since that time, it is observed for two days even in Palestine where the other holydays are observed but one day.

New Year is designated in the *Mishna* Rosh Hashana 1:2 as a day on which all creatures pass in judgment before God. For this reason, this day is called *yom haddin* — "the Day of Judgment."

The standard prayers are elaborated with special insertions in the Amida and with the blowing of the Shofar.

1. The Evening Service. a. The Shema and its benedictions is the same as on Friday and the Festival evenings. In the Sephardic and Yemenite rituals, Numbers 10:10 is inserted before the Amida; in the Italian ritual, Leviticus 23:4; and in the Ashkenazic ritual, Psalm 81:4–5.

The half-Kaddish is then recited in which the Ashkenazic ritual reads *lĕela ul'ela.*

b. In its structure, the Amida is similar to that of Sabbath and the Festivals; that is, it has seven benedictions of which the three introductory and the three concluding are the same. It has the following insertions:

In the first benediction: *zochrenu lĕhayim* — "Remember us unto life (O God), the King! Who delightest in life: inscribe us in the book of life, for Thy sake, O God of life."

In the second benediction: *mi chamocha* — "Who is like unto Thee, O merciful Father, Who in mercy rememberest Thy creatures to grant them life."

In the third benediction: The following short paragraphs are inserted:

Uv'chen ten pahdecha — Proclaiming man's recognition of God's sovereignty.

Uv'chen ten cavod — God's restoration of Israel in Zion and the reinstitution of the Davidic dynasty.

Uv'chen (weaz) tzaddikim — Proclaiming the ultimate victory of righteousness when wickedness and tyranny will vanish.

Wethimloch atta — Only God will rule over mankind from His sanctuary in Zion.

Kadosh atta — There is only One God and none other.[2]

The five passages are important enough to have their translation reproduced (S. Singer, p. 239):

"Now, therefore, O Lord our God, impose thine awe upon all thy works, and thy dread upon all that thou hast created, that all works may fear thee and all creatures prostrate themselves before thee, that they may all form a single band to do thy will with a perfect heart, even as we know, O Lord our God, that dominion is thine, strength is in thy hand, and might in thy right hand, and that thy name is to be feared above all that thou hast created.

"Give then glory, O Lord, unto thy people, praise to them that fear thee, hope to them that seek thee, and free speech to them that wait for thee, joy to thy land, gladness to thy city, a flourishing horn unto David thy servant, and a clear shining light unto the son of Jesse, thine anointed, speedily in our days.

"Then shall the just also see and be glad, and the upright shall exult, and the pious triumphantly rejoice, while iniquity shall close her mouth, and all wickedness shall be wholly consumed like smoke, when thou makest the dominion of arrogance to pass away from the earth.

"And thou, O Lord, shalt reign, thou alone over all thy works on Mount Zion, the dwelling place of thy glory, and in Jerusalem, thy holy city, as it is written in thy Holy Words, The Lord shall reign for ever, Thy God, O Zion, unto all generations. Praise ye the Lord.

"Holy art thou, and dreaded is thy name, and there is no God beside thee, as it is written, And the Lord of hosts is exalted in judgment, and the holy God is sanctified in righteousness. Blessed art thou, O Lord, the holy King."

The last paragraph used to be recited daily in the old Palestinian ritual,[3] at least the first sentence; while the Babylonian ritual adopted it for the High Holydays only.

This benediction concludes with *hammelech hakkadosh* — "The holy King" — instead of with "The holy God" as in the daily prayers (b. Ber. 12b; see Chapter VIII, e).

The three paragraphs beginning with *uv'chen*, though not found in the *Talmud*, are ascribed to Abba Areca (Rav).[4]

In the Italian and Yemenite rituals, the first sentence of *Kadosh atta* is missing. This version follows that of Maimonides.

The Sanctification of the Day consists of:

Atta vehartanu, wattitten lanu — Maimonides, the Sephardim, and Yemenites have *yom tov;* while the Ashkenazic and Italian rituals do not insert these two words.[5]

Yaale weyavo — The same paragraph as in the Amida of the Festivals, save that the references are changed to New Year.

Meloch is the concluding paragraph of the intermediary benediction; it summarizes the ideas expressed in the insertions of the third benediction. In this paragraph, the Italian ritual has the sentence *Wĕhasiênu* from the Festivals which sentence was omitted for the reasons explained above (*cf.* M.V., p. 368). Abudraham gives this sentence. M.V., p. 360, relates that it has been eliminated in Worms by Rabbi Isaac (the teacher of Rashi in the eleventh century), and that it used to be said in Palestine. On the other hand, *Meloch* was recited in the old Palestinian ritual at every Festival.[6]

In the second concluding benediction, the Sephardic and Ashkenazic rituals have *uch'thov* — "And inscribe all the children of Thy covenant for a happy life." S.R.A., M.V., Maimonides, the Italian and Yemenite rituals have *zechor rahamecha* (the Yemenite ritual having only the first phrase) in addition; this the Ashkenazic ritual uses for Musaf only.

In the last benedictions, all rituals have *bĕsefer hayim* — a short prayer that God inscribe us for life, peace, and prosperity. According to M.V., the Ashkenazic ritual has a change in the seal of the benediction: *ose hashalom* — "Maker of peace" — which was in use in the old Palestinian ritual.[7]

Kiddush is the same as on the Festivals, with the exception of a change made in the last sentence which reads: "For Thou hast chosen us and hast sanctified us above all nations; and Thy word is truth and endureth for ever. Blessed . . . Who sanctifiest Israel and the Day of Memorial."

Whereupon "Alenu" is recited and "Yigdal" or "Adon Olam" is sung.

On Sabbath, the same insertions are read as on Festivals which fall on Sabbath.

At home, there is a custom to dip bread or apple in honey and to say: "May this coming year be a sweet and pleasant one." This custom was derived from Nehemiah 8:10 (see O.H. § 583, Abudraham, Maharil, Rosh Hashana).

2. The Morning Service — *shaharith.* a. It is the same as that of Sabbaths and the Festivals. In the Ashkenazic ritual, *hammelech* is emphasized in the *Nishmath* (see Chapter XV) — a custom introduced by M. Rothenburg who also introduced the manner in which this passage should be sung.[8]

But though there is no difference in the texts from those of Sabbaths and Festivals, there is a marked distinction in the way they are sung. The same texts are set to modes and tunes especially composed for the High Holydays.[9] The same is true of the evening service.

The Amida as outlined in the evening service is repeated in the morning service.

After the repetition of the Amida by the precentor,[10] the supplication *avinu malkenu* is recited; it is in place of Hallel which is recited on the Three Festivals. The explanation as given in b. Ber. 32b is that on this day God judges everybody, and it is therefore more fitting to recite supplications than Hallel.

The ritual for the taking out the Scrolls is the same as on the Three Festivals, save that another meditation is inserted which is to be said after the Thirteen Attributes. It is a petition for forgiveness of sins and for sustenance, and was taken from *Shaare Tzion.* Only the Ashkenazic ritual has the Thirteen Attributes; in some Oriental-Sephardic congregations it is also recited.

b. The Scriptural reading for the first day is from Genesis 21; for the second from Genesis 22 (b. Megilla 31a), because, according to the *Talmud* (b. Rosh Hashana 10b, 11a; *Midrash* Pesikta Rabbati 40), the conception of Isaac and his attempted sacrifice took place on New Year's Day.[11] For the same reason, the Haftara of the first day is read from I Samuel 1 and 2:1–10, because Samuel was conceived on New Year's Day (*l.c.*). On the second day, the Haftara is read from Jeremiah 31:2–20 because of the prophecy of salvation expressed therein (*l.c.*).

From the second Scroll Numbers 29:1–6 is read.

For the reading from the Pentateuch, the Ashkenazic ritual has a special Mode of chanting.[12] This Mode is used for both New Year and the Day of Atonement in the morning services.

On Sabbath, seven people are called to the reading; on weekdays only five, the sixth being called for the Haftara.

c. *Tekiath shofar* — The Blowing of the Horn. Although the blowing was prescribed for all festivals and New Moons while the sacrifices were being offered (Numbers 10:10: "And on the day of your gladness, and in your solemn days, and in the beginnings of your months ye shall blow with the trumpets over your burnt-offerings, and over the sacrifices of your peace-offerings; and they shall be for you a memorial before your God") the New Year received the name of the "Day of the blowing the ram's horn"; for on this day a ram's horn must be used (M. Rosh Hashana III:3). In the *Talmud* (b. Rosh Hashana 16a) it says that the reason for using a ram's horn is that it serves to remind the people of the sacrifice of Isaac and of the substitution of a ram in place of Isaac. The blowing of the Shofar was introduced into the Synagogue.

On Sabbaths the Shofar was blown in the Temple only. After the fall of the Temple, Rabbi Johanan ordered that on Sabbaths it be blown only in places where there was a Court (M. Rosh Hashana IV:1). Later on, it was forbidden entirely (b. Rosh Hashana 29b).

The Jewish philosopher Saadya Gaon gave the following reasons for the blowing of the Shofar (quoted in Abudraham, p. 145):[13]

1. To proclaim the sovereignty of God on the anniversary of the creation, for according to Rabbi Eliezer in b. Rosh Hashana 10b–11a, 27, the world was created on this day — on New Year.
2. To stir the people to repentance.
3. To remind the people of the revelation on Mount Sinai.
4. To remind us of the messages of the Prophets.
5. To remind us of the destruction of the Temple.

6. To remind us of Isaac's sacrifice.

7. The sound of the Shofar causes the human heart to tremble.

8. To remind us of the Day of Judgment.

9. To remind us of the blasts of the Shofar of redemption which Messiah will sound.

10. To remind us of the resurrection.

Out of these motives Maimonides emphasizes only 2, 7, and 8 (Hilchoth Teshuva 3, 4).

According to the Ashkenazic ritual, Psalm 47 is recited seven times before the blowing. The Italian ritual prescribes that it be recited but once before the Scriptural reading.

The Sephardic, Italian, and Yemenite rituals contain several Biblical verses referring to the powers of the Shofar, the first of which is verse 6 of Psalm 47. The recitation of this verse and of Psalm 89:16 is based upon Lev. Rabba § 29:3.[14]

There are several meditations to be read before and after the blowing; they were introduced by Isaac Luria. They are found in the Ashkenazic and Sephardic-Oriental rituals (see Chapter VI).

There are two series of blowing of the Shofar. One is called *tĕkioth mĕyushav* — The blowing while seated, i.e., after the Scriptural reading; the other is called *tĕkioth mĕumad* — the blowing while standing, i.e., during the Amida of the Musaf service. The blowing while seated has the following order:

1. *Tekia* — a long stretched sound; *shevarim* — three broken notes; and *tĕrua* — a tremolo or nine staccato notes. Then *tekia* is repeated. This set is repeated three times.

2. *Tekia*, *shevarim*, *tekia* repeated thrice.

3. *Tekia*, *tĕrua*, *tekia* repeated thrice.

In the Bible only "tekia" and "tĕrua" are mentioned. In the third century, however, doubt arose as to the correct execution of "tĕrua." There were those who said that it is like a sigh — *genuhe ganah* — while others interpreted the sound to be like the vibrating voice of weeping — *yĕlule yalal*. Finally Rabbi Abuhu ordered that both forms be used, calling the first *shevarim* and the other *tĕrua* (b. Rosh Hashana 34a).

The reason for repeating each set three times, as well as the reason for repeating *tekia* after *tĕrua* is given in b. Rosh Hashana 34a. The word *tĕrua* is mentioned three times in three Biblical passages; then the expression *wehaavarta*—"And thou shalt cause to pass a sound of the Shofar"—which indicates a straight note—*tekia*.

Tekioth mĕumad are blown in a similar order in three sections of the Musaf service: After Malchuyoth: tekia—shevarim—tĕrua—tekia; after Zichronoth: tekia—shevarim—tekia; and after Shoferoth: tekia—tĕrua—tekia. The last tekia is prolonged and called "Tekia Gedola."

Originally, the blowing of the Shofar was set after the Scriptural reading, when the whole congregation is present. But once, probably during the time of rebellion against Roman tyranny, the government authorities were alarmed at the sound of the Shofar at the early hours of the morning and believed that the blasts of the horn were a sign of rebellion. They ordered the armed soldiers to attack the Jewish population (Jer. Rosh Hashana IV, 8; b. Rosh Hashana 32b). In consequence of this event, it was prohibited to blow the Shofar on New Year morning and was inserted in the Musaf service which used to take place later in the day (M. Rosh Hashana IV, 7). Since then, though the prohibition was annulled, the custom of blowing during the Musaf service was retained (see M.V., p. 385).

Later on, a mystic reason was given for the two sets of blowing: namely, to confuse Satan in his accusations (b. Rosh Hashana 16b).

Before the blowing, the Kabbalists introduced six verses from the Psalms the acrostic of which is *Kĕra satan*—tear the Satan. These verses are: Lamentations 3:56; Psalms 119:160; 122; 162; 66; 108 with an introductory verse from Psalm 118:5. They are recited in congregations which follow Kabbalistic customs (see Chapter VI).

The person who blows the Shofar recites two benedictions:

1. "Blessed . . . to hear the sound of the Shofar."

2. "Blessed . . . and hast enabled us to reach this season."

After the blowing four verses are recited: Psalms 89:16, 17, 18 and 84:5. The Sephardic, Italian, and Yemenite rituals have Psalm 89:19 instead of 84:5.

In the Sephardic-Oriental ritual and those who follow its customs — as the Hasidim — the Shofar is blown also during the silent Amida.

d. *Musaf* — The Additional Service. This Amida consists of nine benedictions instead of seven as is customary in the other Amidas of this and all Festivals and Sabbaths.

Of these, the first and last three including the insertions are identical to those described in the evening service.

Of the three intermediate benedictions, the first includes the Sanctification of the Day — *Kedushath hayyom* (M. Rosh Hashana IV, 5), and is called *malchuyoth* — the proclamation of the kingdom of God. The second is called *zichronoth* — Memorial, i.e., the proclamation of God's providence, reward and punishment according to the deeds of man. The third is called *shofĕroth* — the proclamation of God's revelation on Mount Sinai to Israel and of His redemption through the Messiah.

These three benedictions were apparently known before the fall of the Temple (M. Rosh Hashana IV, 5–6). The *Talmud* gives homiletical reasons for the three benedictions (b. Rosh Hashana 32a). The underlying idea is that it is well to proclaim first the sovereignty of God, then to announce His omnipotence and omnipresence, and then to declare His divine revelation unto man.

Each of these benedictions consists of ten verses, three of which are taken from the Pentateuch, three from the Writings, three from the Prophets, and the closing verse from the Pentateuch. Each benediction has an introduction and a conclusion which were probably composed by Rav in Babylonia at the beginning of the third century, though the Talmudic sources ascribe to Rav the parts to Zichronoth only (Jer. Rosh Hashana I, 3; Avoda Zara I, 2).[15]

As mentioned above, the first of the three benedictions include the *Kedushath hayyom*. This is expressed by the same paragraphs as in the intermediate benediction for the Musaf of the Festivals, with the reference to the New Year's Day and the Scriptural quotations concerning the day.

1. The *Malchuyoth* proper starts with the "Adoration" — *alenu* — which is the introduction to this section.

The verses for Malchuyoth are taken from:

a. Pentateuch: 1. Exodus 15:18; 2. Numbers 23:21; 3. Deuteronomy 33:5.

b. Writings: 4. Psalms 22:29; 5. 93:1; 6. 24:7.

c. Prophets: 7. Isaiah 44:6; 8. Obadiah 1:21; 9. Zechariah 14:9.

d. Pentateuch: 10. Deuteronomy 6:4.

The concluding paragraph is the same as in the evening and morning Amida.

II. *Zichronoth — atta zocher* — is ushered in with an introduction in which God's justice is recounted. Then the ten verses follow as proof of what has been said. In b. Rosh Hashana 27 it is explained that the passage: "This day on which was the beginning of Thy work" is said according to Rabbi Eliezer who holds that the world was created on Rosh Hashana (see above).

The verses for Zichronoth are taken from:

a. Pentateuch: 1. Genesis 8:1; 2. Exodus 2:24; 3. Leviticus 26:42.

b. Writings: 4. Psalms 111:4; 5. 111:5; 6. 106:45.

c. Prophets: 7. Jeremiah 2:2; 8. Ezekiel 16:60; 9. Jeremiah 31:19.

d. Pentateuch. 10. Leviticus 26:45.

A concluding paragraph is then recited which relates Abraham's trust in God in being ready to sacrifice his son; this paragraph closes the benediction.

III. *Shoferoth — atta nigletha* — is introduced with this passage which describes the revelation of God on Mount Sinai.

The ten verses are from:

a. Pentateuch: 1. Exodus 19:16; 2. 19:19; 3. 20:18.

b. Writings: 4. Psalms 47:6; 5. 98:6; 6. 81:4. Here Psalm 150 is inserted because it has ten times "Halleluya."

c. Prophets: 7. Isaiah 18:3; 8. 27:13; 9. Zechariah 9:14.

d. Pentateuch: 10. Numbers 10:10.

The last verse is included in the concluding paragraph which is a prayer for redemption and for the restoration of the sanctuary.

In their essence, the three sections are but an elaborate presentation of the ideas expressed in brief in the first three passages beginning with *uv'chen* which are inserted in the third introductory benediction explained in the evening service.[16]

On the second day the same order of the service is repeated.

At Minha, *ashre* and *uva letziyon* are recited; then follows the Amida as outlined in the evening service. "Alenu" closes the service.

At the repetition, the Cohanim recite the Priestly Benediction, as on the Three Festivals.

The service closes with "En Kelohenu," "Alenu," and the "Song of the Day" to which Psalm 27 is added. This psalm is recited from the beginning of Ellul up till after the Day of Atonement.

After the precentor finishes the repetition of the Amida, other sets of sounds are blown, and before or after the "Alenu" ten more blasts are sounded. According to the Kabbalists, there ought to be one hundred blasts. The *tĕkioth mĕyushav* constitute thirty (for each of the tekia, shevarim, and tĕrua count for one sound); the *tĕkioth mĕumad* likewise constitutes thirty sounds (three times ten).[17] After "Alenu" a "Tĕrua Gedola" is sounded in the Sephardic ritual.

In the Yemenite ritual, thirty blasts are sounded after the morning benedictions — *birchoth hashahar*, an effort being made to sound these blasts at sunrise. Whereupon the poem *shofet col haaretz* is chanted.

II. Poetical and Petitional Insertions. For the evening service there are no insertions in the Ashkenazic and Italian rituals, with the exception of Worms where "Maarivim" used to be recited (Maharil).[18] Before the service, the Sephardic and Yemenite rituals have a poem *ahoth ketanna* by Abraham Hazzan of the sixteenth century which is chanted in a traditional tune,[19] and then Psalm 81 is recited; the poem has a refrain: "May the year and its misfortunes now cease." In the Sephardic-Oriental ritual there is another poem for the second evening *hon tahon* which is a part of *bath ahuvath el* by Benjamin (see Appendix II).

The Sephardic Ritual. True to their tradition that additional prayers or poetry should not be inserted into the section of "Shema" and "Amida," the Sephardim have some "piyyutim" at the end of "Verses of Song." After the "Song of the Sea" there is a poem by Jehuda Halevi: *elohay al tedineni* — an alphabetical acrostic with a rhyme running through the lines. It is a petition for the forgiveness of our sins and a fervent confession of sins.

Following this, the Sephardic-Oriental ritual has *rĕe beshivtecha* by Moses b. Ezra and another poem *shoĕf kemo eved* by Solomon b. Gabirol. The content of both is similar to the first poem.

Then in all Sephardic rituals there follows the poem by Solomon *shofet col haaretz*. Each strophe of this poem consists of four rhymed lines, the fourth line being the refrain for all strophes. Its content is likewise a pleading for atonement and for the restoration of Zion. Here the Sephardic-Oriental ritual inserts a petition by Isaac Ashkenazi of the eighteenth century: *yom ze dar bameromim* — a petition to receive Israel's prayer on this day.

Then a petition by Jehuda Halevi *adonai yom lecha* follows in all Sephardic rituals. This poem is divided into four parts, each having as an acrostic one of the letters of the Tetragrammaton. In addition, each line starts and ends with the word *yhwa*.

Whereupon *Nishmath* is recited till after the closing paragraph of the "Verses of Song." Then, on the first day *yĕde rashim* by Jehuda Halevi is chanted, and on the second day *ya shimcha* by the same poet.

Both poems belong to the best poetic productions of that great poet; they have a traditional tune [20] which is sung by the precentor and the congregation.

Before the repetition of the Amida, the precentor chants *Reshuth* according to the Sephardic-Oriental ritual with the poem *adonai shamati shimacha* — in which the Tetragrammaton constitutes the beginning and the end of each line. Whereupon the congregation responds in unison with the chanting of the two strophes: *athanu lehalloth ponecha* — "We came to petition Thee, because mercy and truth prevail before Thee."

In the last benediction of the Amida *hayyom tĕam'tzenu* is inserted. It was originally an alphabetical acrostic found in full in the Italian ritual; here only one third of it is given, and in the Ashkenazic ritual still less.

In the Kaddish which follows the Amida a prayer is recited: *têanu wĕthêath'ru* — "May ye be answered and your request be granted from heaven. . . . And may God open unto us, and unto all Israel, the gates of lights. . . . (Here an alphabetical acrostic follows.) "And may He write you in the book of Life."

After the Kaddish, the Sephardic-European ritual has for the first day *lemancha elohay* by David b. Bekoda; it is a rhymed prayer for the acceptance of our supplication. For the second day, it has *yaane bevor avoth* — a plea that the merits of Abraham be remembered.

After the Scriptural reading, *eth shaare ratzon* by Jehuda Samuel Abbas (about 1200) is chanted according to the traditional tune.[21] In this poem, the Midrashic rendition of the sacrifice of Isaac is recounted.

In the Sephardic-Oriental ritual, *hammelech adonai* is chanted. Each stanza of this poem starts with *hammelech adonai* and ends with a refrain.

Then all the Sephardic rituals have *adonai bekol shofar*, each strophe of which begins and concludes with that phrase. The poet (Jacob) pleads for the sound of the Shofar of redemption. There is a traditional tune according to which precentor and congregation sing this poem responsively.[22]

Before Musaf there is in the Sephardic-Oriental ritual a poetical inauguration by Hayyim Modai similar in style to that before the Shaharith-Amida.

In the last benediction *hayyom tĕam'tzenu* is inserted in the Shaharith-Amida. Then *têanu wethêath'ru* is repeated.

The YEMENITE RITUAL does not permit such poetical insertions as are contained in the Sephardic ritual because they are considered an interruption of the service.[23]

Têanu wethêath'ru is recited after the conclusion of the service.

Before the *tekioth meyushav*, the poems *eth shaare ratzon* and *hammelech adonai* are recited.

Then the precentor utters a meditation in which he confesses his unworthiness and calls upon the merits of the patriarchs. He also blows the Shofar.

In the section "Offerings," the ITALIAN RITUAL has the confession *Ashamnu* and the meditation on bad dreams quoted in the *Talmud* (b. Ber. 55b) which the Ashkenazic ritual gives in the service of the Priestly Benediction. This is followed by several psalms and a selection of seventy-two verses from the Bible arranged by Moses Nachmanides [24] of the thirteenth century, even as on weekdays and Sabbaths.

After the Song of the Sea, *yĕidun yaggidun* by Solomon is chanted.

Before *Nishmath*, the "Reshuth" *echra ekkod* by Joab is recited.

Before the half-Kaddish to "Barechu," *ya shimcha* by Jehuda Halevi is chanted, and after the Kaddish *melech azur* by Eleazar Kallir is sung. It is the same Yotzer as in the Ashkenazic ritual, but the Italian ritual has also the *Zulath*, *melech ammitz* which is missing in the Ashkenazic ritual. This is followed by *yĕidun col avadecha* as on the Festivals.

Before the blowing of the Shofar, *adonai becol shofar* is chanted, and afterwards two strophes of *zechor berith* are recited.

At the repetition of Musaf, *un'thanne tokef* is read after the second benediction (see below).

After the second intermediate benediction, three piyyutim: *av lo hamal*, *av lo has*, and *asufim asufay* are recited by the congregation. They are all alphabetical acrostics. They are petitions for the acceptance of the prayers and the sounds of the Shofar.

After the Amida, an alphabetical acrostic *eth pĕne adonai* by Benjamin is recited before the Kaddish *ose shalom.*

The Italian ritual has the poetical insertions partly of the Sephardic and partly of the Ashkenazic ritual, as we have noticed on other occasions.

For the second day, only one other "piyyut" is given for Yotzer. This is *melech addir wenora* — an alphabetical acrostic, each strophe beginning with *melech* and closing alternately with the same word or with *yeshua.* This poem is a glorification of God and His hosts. In the last benediction, the whole *hayyom tĕam'tzenu* is inserted.

Just as the services for the Three Festivals, so also those for the High Holydays are furnished with many poetical and supplicational insertions in the ASHKENAZIC RITUAL.

For the first day the "piyyut" begins with:

1. *Yotzer.* In the first benediction of the section "Shema" the same poetry by Eleazar Kallir is used as in the Italian ritual. The content of this poetry is a glorification of God and His heavenly hosts. The closing part asserts that He Who searches and knows the heart of man will have mercy on Israel for the sake of the merits of the patriarchs. In the Shaharith-Amida, the *Kerova* is ushered in with a "Reshuth" *yarethi biftzothi* by Yekuthiel b. Moshe of the eleventh century in Speyer; this poem has a running rhyme. It is chanted in the traditional Mode which is used for the other "Reshuyoth" for the second and for that of the Day of Atonement, as well as for other prayers.[25] The precentor sings this poem solo. It is a petition for his successful intercession.

Then there follows *ath hil yom pekuda* by E. Kallir in which the significance of the Day is described. The previous poem finishes with the word with which this one starts *ath hil.*

Taalath zu kĕhafetz is the insertion in the second benediction; it is by the same author. In it allusions to Biblical stories are made.

After the second benediction there follows *even hug metzok.* The first lines of this poem have a straight alphabetical acrostic; the second lines have a reversed alphabetical acrostic. The sentences *yimloch* and *wĕatta kadosh* are used in almost all the Kerovas of the Festivals. The response: *atta hu adonai*, one of the oldest elements in the Ashkenazic synagogal poetry, is recited. It has an alphabetical acrostic but no rhyme, and is a hymn in both form and content. After this poem, there follows the phrase *hay wekayyom* — "Living and enduring, terrible and exalted and holy."

Tair wetharia is recited both by reader and congregation; then *addereth mamlacha* by E. Kallir follows. In case the first day falls on a Sabbath, *uv'chen wadonai pakad eth sara* and *om asher bĕtzedek* by E. Kallir are read. They recount Isaac's conception which, according to Talmudic literature, occurred on this day (see above).

Here Simon b. Abun's Kerova is chanted by the precentor in accordance with a traditional tune.[26] It is an alphabetical acrostic. After each two lines, the congregation responds with a Biblical phrase, and after each six lines one of the five refrains are recited.

After that *ettên lefoali* is recited; it is a poem by the same author.

On weekdays, two responses: *melech mĕmallet* and *melech zechor* follow; whereupon *aapid nezer* by E. Kallir is chanted in a traditional air.[27]

Addire ayuma by E. Kallir is a threefold alphabetical acrostic with the refrain: "The Lord is King, the Lord was King, the Lord shall be King for ever and ever." In this poem, the heavenly hosts and Israel are described in their devotional activities to praise God.

Lèel orech din follows. This hymn belongs to the old elements of the Synagogal poetry. In an alphabetical acrostic with the ending of *din*. God's ways in judging the people are specified. It is one of the most devotional parts of the service.

Silluk. This part usually starts with "And thus may the sanctification ascend unto Thee." For the first day, the poem *melech hammishpat* is recited. This poem is interwoven with Midrashic and mystic elements.

In the Kedusha, there are poetical insertions after each passage based upon mystic teachings concerning angelic spheres and their service as mediators between God and man.

Wehayyoth boaroth with the ending of *êsh* by Benjamin b. Samuel Imenu of Contances, Normandy [28] (beginning of the eleventh century), and *ehad kadosh* by the same author are recited.

Before Musaf, there are two meditations for the precentor: one *Hin'ni heani* and the other *el melech neèman*. Both embody the petition that "though I am an unworthy sinner, nevertheless, may my prayer be acceptable for the benefit of the holy congregation, and may God prevent Satan from causing evil, and may the good angels submit my prayers before the throne of God's glory, and may my voice be resonant and sweet."

The Kerova in the Musaf is by E. Kallir. It consists of six numbers:

Uppad mêaz in the first benediction; it is an alphabetical acrostic.

Têfen bemachon in the second benediction; it is a reversed alphabetical acrostic.

Af orah — a poem one line of which has the straight alphabetical acrostic and the other line the reversed alphabetical acrostic. After this poem, *yimloch* and *weatta kadosh* follow.

Then two responses follow: *el emuna* and *im lo lemaano*.

Ometz addirê. In this Kerova the author points out that all the righteous ones were found guilty upon Judgment — from Adam to Josiah. How then can we expect to be privileged?

El dar bammarom recounts God's deeds in contradistinction to man's deeds.

Silluk. For this section, the meditation *un'thanne tokef* is recited on both days and on the Day of Atonement. It describes the procedure of Judgment and the stir it occasions among the hosts on high. It gives a detailed account of the various decrees, concerning all men, and ends with the declaration: "But penitence, prayer, and charity avert the severity of the decree."

The paragraph before the last speaks of the benevolent attitude of God to man and of His consideration of man's weakness; it closes with the glorification of God.

This meditation was apparently composed by Kalonymos b. Meshullam b. Kalonymos (eleventh century in Mayence). There is a legend concerning its origin.[29] This legend recounts that once an Archbishop continually urged Rabbi Amnon of Mayence to change his faith. After several urgent requests, the Rabbi said that he wanted three days' time during which to think the matter over. When the time passed, he did not appear before the Archbishop; whereupon the latter sent his servants to bring the Rabbi by force. To the question why he had not come before, the Rabbi answered: "I have made my decree. My tongue which promised should be cut out, and my feet which refused to carry me should be mutilated. But let this be a punishment for my hesitancy in not having given you a definite refusal." The Archbishop ordered that the decree be executed. New Year's Day came, and the Rabbi, dying from the effects of his wounds, was at his own request carried into the synagogue. When the precentor was about to recite the Kedusha, Rabbi Amnon stopped him, saying: "Pause that I may sanctify His holy Name." He then recited this meditation and expired as soon as he finished it. After his death, he appeared to Kalonymos in a dream and taught him his composition.[30]

The style of this poem is sublime in its simplicity. The language is similar to that of the "prayers," with but an occasional rhyme. Both language and style are different from the other poems of the author.

In the Ashkenazic ritual, this selection is one of the most important prayers and is recited with deep religious emotions while standing. The Hazzanim ornamented this text with their best musical settings.

The poetical insertions in the Kedusha are by E. Kallir.
Wehahayyoth — based upon Ezekiel 1; the ending word is *kisse*.
Wĕam'cha theluim — the ending word is *ehad*.
Wĕatta ezon kol.
Tĕhilloth kĕvodecha.
These poems are a compilation of various Talmudic laws and rules pertaining to different parts of Jewish lore; they are but loosely connected.

Hamol al maasecha is a short prayer leading over to the response *haohez beyad;* it is an alphabetical acrostic without rhyme. This Kerova too seems to be of the old poetical elements.

Wĕyeĕthayu — is a hymn of probably the seventh century. It is an alphabetical acrostic and has occasional rhyme. Here the idea of the ultimate general recognition of the one living God is expressed. It has been rendered into English verse by Israel Zangwill.[31] The poem is quoted in M.V., p. 386.

The section of Malchuyoth begins with "Alenu." At the repetition of the Amida, the precentor and congregation kneel and prostrate themselves while chanting this paragraph. The Hasidim prostrate themselves also when reading this text in the silent Amida. The traditional tune has the most solemn character and seems to be of the twelfth century.[32]

Then the precentor recites the prayer *Hĕye im pifiyyoth*. This prayer was in use already at the time of Maharil and is printed in the oldest Ashkenazic Mahzorim. After this the precentor recites another prayer *ohila laêl*. Amram gives this prayer, and it is also found in the Italian ritual.

Then a poetical selection *ansicha malki* by E. Kallir is read; it is called "Tekiata." Each line closes with *yimloch;* it relates the mighty deeds of God.

If the first day falls on Sabbath, then *ahalela elohay* is recited instead.

This poetical selection is one of the few extant creations of Yose b. Yose (see Chapter V). His language and style is more similar to the prose of the prayers. He does not as yet employ rhyme, with the exception that every line closes with *melucha*. In this selection, the events in Israel's history are surveyed, and God's providential care is revealed to manifest itself to prove that He is the sovereign King. The poem has an alphabetical acrostic.

Both poems are inserted in the section Zichronoth. Kallir's *zecher tehillath* with *yizcor* as a closing word and *zecher* as an opening word of each strophe, while Yose b. Yose uses the word *leziccaron*. Both poems point out that God remembers the deeds of man throughout the ages.

In the section for "Shoferoth," Kallir's poem *essa dêi* has *shofar* as a key-word for the ending lines, while Yose b. Yose employs *kol*. Both have the alphabetical acrostic. The latter poem distinguishes itself by a noble poetical presentation of Israel's struggle throughout the ages and the hope it voices for the future; it may well be taken as one of the best productions of Synagogal poetry.

From the hymn *hayyom team'tzênu* only seven lines have been retained. Some Mahzorim, as Sabionneta, 1577, have nine lines.

In the *Tashlich* service [33] a selection of Biblical verses are recited: Micah 7:18–20; Psalm 118:5–9; and a long meditation.

For the second day, the Ashkenazic ritual has the following insertions:

Yotzer. *Melech amon* by Simon b. Abun in which the ideas of Malchuyoth, Zichronoth, and Shoferoth are utilized. The poem has an alphabetical acrostic and rhyme and consists of seven paragraphs after each of which there is a closing strophe. These strophes are chanted according to a traditional mode.[34]

Kevodo ihel is repeated from the Yotzer of the first day.

Kerova. The *Reshuth* for the precentor *athithi lehan'nach* is followed by *imrath'cha tzerufa*, *tamim poolach*, and a short prayer for the precentor *shullahti*, *medabber bitzdaka*. They are all by Simon b. Abun. There are also *shavti werao* based upon Midrashic material and the hymn *ammitz hamenussa*, an alphabetical acrostic with rhyme, in which there is an exaltation of God's attributes and in which the shortcomings of man are pointed out. The last hymn has *melech elyon* as a starting and *laade ad yimloch* as a concluding refrain. Then another hymn follows: *col shinane shahak*. Here the heavenly hosts and Israel are described in their effort to glorify God. Each stanza has three lines with the refrain: "God rules" etc. Two lines begin with *col*, and the third line has *elu wëelu*. All these poems are by Simon b. Abun.

Atta hu and *lëel orech* are repeated from the service of the first day.

Silluk. *Asher mi yaase* recounts the merits and trials of Abraham. The poetical selections of the first day are repeated in the Kedusha.

Kerova for Musaf has but the *Silluk un'thanne tokef* of the first day. The insertions in the Kedusha and the "Tekiata" are repeated.

The Minha service consists of *ashre* and *uva letziyon*, and the Amida as outlined in the evening service. At the repetition, the weekday Kedusha is recited. The service closes with "Alenu" and *avinu malkenu*.

Kapparoth. On the eve of the Day of Atonement there prevails a custom from old times to take a rooster (for men) and a chicken (for women) and to recite a prayer, saying that one's guilt be transferred to the fowl. In Talmudic times this custom was observed on the eve of New Year, using legume raised for that purpose (Rashi to b. Shabbath, 81b). But in Gaonic times it became customary to use chickens instead (O.H., p. 1089). Mahzor Vitry, p. 373, quotes the *Pesikta* for this custom and adds that the chickens are considered as a substitute for the "scape-goat" (azazel), which was used to expiate the sins of Israel.

M.V., *l.c.*, gives five verses from Psalm 107:17–21 to be recited three times, to which the Ashkenazic ritual added verses 10 and 14, Job 33:23–24. Preceding verse 10, the two words *bĕne adam* — O children of man — were inserted.

While circling the fowl around the head the following formula is repeated three times: "This is my substitute and my ransom, this rooster shall be killed that I may survive for a long and peaceful life."

The custom may also be performed with money. The formula of the recitation is then changed thus: "The coin is my substitute . . . and shall be given for charity that I may survive. . . ."

From the other rituals only the Sephardic-Oriental has the custom to which only the formula while circling the fowl around the head is used.

B. The Day of Atonement — *Yom Hakippurim*

This is the most important day in the Jewish religious calendar. It has been established, as Dr. M. Gaster so well puts it, "for the purpose of bringing home to us the consciousness of human weakness and frailty, of sins and transgression, and by means of self-imposed affliction and repentance to turn us from the evil ways which we have pursued in the course of the year, and to lead us, through prayers and confession, to the gates of Heaven, there to obtain mercy and forgiveness. It is thus a day which begins with physical mortification and ends with spiritual exaltation. It is a day of affliction and at the same time a day of solemn rest, a Sabbath of Sabbaths. For can there be a greater spiritual joy than to have passed through the valley of death, and to have approached the realm of bliss, to have left behind . . . the pangs and remorse of sin, and to have reached the haven of rest, the calm of purification and of spiritual contentment? The prayers for this day are adapted to this purpose, and are so arranged as to form a gradual ascent from the misery of grief, from the shame and trepidation of guilt to the joy of divine mercy and to the confident reliance on God's grace and love." [35]

Concerning the inner value of the liturgy for this day, M. Gaster says:

"Gradually the whole range of human activity is unrolled, and the tangled web of our complicated life with its weakness is unfolded. . . . We proceed to the description of man, with his failings and weakness, and the puny creature is contrasted with the greatness of the universe and the wisdom by which it is ruled. . . . We are thus slowly humbled from the proud position which we have taken up, and humility is the first step towards the recognition of the possibility of sinfulness. In the 'Widdui,' of which each 'Amida' contains one, we are taught to examine ourselves in the spirit of humility which has now been born within us, to see whether, with all the desire we may have to avoid failings and backslidings, we have succeeded in our endeavors. We then recognize, to our dismay, that there is no man who is absolutely free from sin. And as a natural sequence follows the Confession, the desire of repentance, the wish never to be found guilty again. By fasting and praying we fortify ourselves on this day against the temptation of the world, we conquer the demands of our physical life, we rise to greater heights of introspection and self-examination, and then we are more able to render account of our actions, and to judge ourselves in the light of these Confessions. The more we pray, the more heavy the burden of guilt grows; the consciousness dawns upon us that it is utterly impossible adequately to atone for all those sins which we now see in their fulness. But instead of despair at our futile efforts . . . hope springs up in our heart, for by the supplications we are directed to throw ourselves on the love and mercy of God. . . . We are taught and encouraged to approach Him as the repentant son who, with tears in his eyes, draws near to his father. . . . We are assured beforehand of His forgiveness, for He doth not love the death of the sinner, but that he return from his evil way and live. We throw ourselves confidently on His mercy, and the grand day closes with the sound of the Shofar, which in ancient times proclaimed the freedom of the people, and is now proclaiming to us the spiritual freedom gained by spiritual exertions and physical self-chastisement. We have in some measure expiated our sins, but He Who is the God of forgiveness cleanses us from all our transgressions."[36]

Accordingly, liturgical material has been provided to require the hours of the whole day. In orthodox congregations, no intermissions are granted between the services. Each service has been extended by additional prayers and poetry pertaining to the Day. In addition to the regular services which are used on weekdays and holidays, a closing service—"Ne'ila"—has been inserted.

Even the Minha service on the eve preceding that Day receives a solemn character by inserting the Confession into the Amida. The reason for its insertion is given in b. Yoma 87b. The putting on of prayer-shawls for the evening service adds sanctity to the service. Likewise, several ceremonies, as the putting on of white shrouds (*Kittel*) among the Ashkenazim, and taking off the shoes, increase the impressiveness of the Day.

1. The Evening Service. Since the times of Rabbi Amram, the evening service starts with the annulment of vows, called *Col Nidré*.

The custom of pledging donations and to vow to do or not to do certain things is very old among all ancient peoples, as well as in Israel. The Scriptures deal with this problem on several occasions (Num. 30; Lev. 22:18–21; 27:2; Num. 6:2–21; 15:3). "When a man voweth a vow unto the Lord, or sweareth an oath to bind his soul with a bond, he shall not break his word; he shall do according to all that proceedeth out of his mouth" (Num. 30:3). "The Bible endows the vow with great sanctity, and affords striking testimony to the caution taken to avoid profaning it. An absolving clause was sometimes included in the obligation, in view of an event arising which would render its fulfillment impossible." Therefore Ecclesiastes writes (5:4–5), "Better is it that thou shouldest not vow, than that thou shouldest vow and not pay. Suffer not thy mouth to bring thy flesh into guilt. . . ." [37]

The *Talmud* (b. Nedarim 23b) similarly warns everyone who vowed to fulfil his vows during the coming year, and on New Year to renounce them publicly. This is applicable to those vows only which concern themselves with man's relation to God, and in no sense do they apply to obligations between man and man. According to *Mishna* Yoma (VIII, 9), "The Day of Atonement atones for transgressions of man in his relation to God, but for transgressions between man and man there is no expiation on the Day of Atonement until the wrongful act has been rectified."

The annulment of vows was shifted from New Year to the Eve of Atonement on which we seek to be cleansed from our sins.

The custom was for a long time opposed by such outstanding rabbis as Rabbi Natronai and Hai Gaon, Amram Gaon states that it was not customary in the Babylonian academies to recite Col Nidré and that it was a foolish habit [38] (S.R.A. 47a).

In spite of the opposition, however, the custom spread among the Jewish communities and took deep root. The formula was handed down to us in Hebrew (S.R.A. and Roman and Italian rituals) and in Aramaic-Hebrew.

Before Col Nidré the ark is opened and two Scrolls, as in the Ashkenazic ritual, or seven, as in the Sephardic ritual, are taken out and the following passage is read by the rabbi three times: "With the consent of the heavenly tribunal and with the consent of the earthly tribunal: with the approval of our blessed God, and with the permission of this holy congregation, we decide it to be lawful to pray with those who have transgressed."

This passage was introduced by M. Rothenburg (Tashbetz § 131) and enforced by Maharil (Yom Kippur). The reason for introducing this passage may have been to exonerate those who have been compelled to renounce Judaism and to embrace another religion, as happened to be daily occurrences in the Middle Ages.

Then the precentor recites Col Nidré three times (*Hamanhig*, Kippur 521).[39]

The text of Col Nidré was originally intended for the past, its translation having been: "All forms of vows, bonds, oaths . . . excommunications . . . which we have uttered a vow, taken an oath, excommunicated, or bound ourselves from the last Day of Atonement unto this present Day of Atonement, which is now come unto us for peace. May these our vows be no longer deemed as vows, our oaths as oaths; and our bonds (be no longer considered) as binding. Be they all null and void; they shall not bind, nor shall they stand. Instead may we be granted forgiveness and pardon" (Gaster, *Mahzor*, Vol. III, p. 13).

However, Rabbi Jacob Tam, the grandson of Rashi revised the text and changed it to refer to vows that will be in the future: "From this Day of Atonement unto the next Day of Atonement." He claimed that there can be no nullification of vows for the past, and that the *Talmud* (Nedarim, *l.c.*) speaks of vows made in the future. Several communities adopted his correction; while the Ashkenazic ritual contains the revised text, the Sephardic and Italian rituals retained the old version. The Sephardic-Oriental and Yemenite rituals compromised by adding the new formula to the old and thus retain both sentences. The Aleppo ritual presents Col Nidré twice: once according to the old version, and the second time according to the corrected text.[40]

The Col Nidré gained in significance during the horrible times which the Marranos experienced in Spain as a result of the Inquisition. These "New Christians," who in their heart still clung to Judaism, would assemble on Yom Kippur even in secret cellars to renounce their newly adopted faith which in most cases was forced upon them. Col Nidré was the form of renunciation they used. These assemblies would frequently prove fatal to them, for the spies of the Church would discover those unfortunate people and hand them over to the Inquisition. For this reason, the text received religious significance.

About 1500, an Ashkenazic Hazzan in Southwestern Germany voiced the sentiments of the terror-stricken Marranos as they recited Col Nidré, in a touching tune which expresses the fear, horror, fervent pleading, and stern hope for ultimate salvation. This tune became very popular among the Ashkenazim throughout the world, whereas the Sephardim and Oriental Jews know nothing about the tune. They recite Col Nidré in the Seliha or Tefilla Mode.[41]

The text of Col Nidré has been in use among all Jewish communities with the exception of the Southern French congregations in the Carpentras and Avignon ritual, in which the text is recited as a silent devotion by each individual before the service. They start the service with *wenislah* — a passage from Numbers 15:26 which is said in all rituals. The Palestinian ritual has in addition another passage from Numbers 14:19–20.

Then the benediction *sheheheyanu* is said (S.R.A.), whereupon the Shema and its benedictions are recited as on Sabbaths and festivals. Before the Amida, Leviticus 16:30 is said.[42]

The Amida for the evening, morning, and Minha services consists of the three introductory and three concluding benedictions, including the insertions as outlined in the New Year's service.

The intermediate benediction differs in the various rituals. The Sephardic and Yemenite rituals have *atta vehartanu*, *mehal laawonothenu*, *yaale weyavo*, and *meloch* as in the New Year's Amida; while the Ashkenazic and Italian rituals do not have the last passage (so also is the version in S.R.A. and M.V., p. 390). In the first and the third paragraph the Day of Atonement is mentioned.

According to Rashi, the paragraph *mehal laawonothenu* was one of the benedictions which the High Priest used to recite on that Day (b. Yoma 68b). It is a prayer for forgiveness, and quotes Isaiah 43:25; 44:22, and Leviticus 16:30.

After the concluding benediction, the "Widdui" is recited. This starts with *tavo lĕfanecha*. The passage was already known in the third century (b. Yoma 87b). Then there follows *ashamnu* in an alphabetical acrostic which is first given in S.R.A. (ed. Frumkin, pp. 339–340).

Atta yodea — "Thou knowest the secrets of the world, and the most hidden mysteries of all living: Thou searchest all the inward parts and triest the reins and the heart. . . ." This passage is mentioned in b. Yoma (*l.c.*) in the name of Rav.

An alphabetical acrostic, each line beginning with: *al het*, developed gradually in post-Talmudic times. The oldest source goes back to the beginning of the seventh century;[43] it mentions but six. S.R.A. (ed. Koronell) has eight. Frumkin's edition, however, gives the complete alphabetical acrostic. The Italian and Sephardic-Oriental rituals too have the entire alphabetical acrostic. In the Ashkenazic ritual this was extended to a double alphabetical acrostic. Only the Sephardic and Yemenite rituals retained the original six lines mentioned above.

In the Ashkenazic ritual, the passage *wĕal cullam* serves as a refrain; it reoccurs four times.

Then eight lines, each beginning with *wĕal hataim* follow. These lines are quoted in S.R.A., and enumerate all kinds of offerings the people had sacrificed to atone for their sins. This passage finishes with: "For Thou art the Forgiver of Israel and the Pardoner of the tribes of Jeshurun in all generations, and besides Thee we have no king to pardon and forgive our sins. We have but Thee alone." Whereupon the prayer by Rav Hamnuna (b. Yoma, *l.c.*) is recited; it is *elohay ad shello notzarti* — a prayer ascribed in b. Ber. 17a to Rava as his daily meditation.

If Yom Kippur falls on a Sabbath, the additional paragraphs for Sabbath are inserted as on the Festivals and New Year.

In the repetition, the precentor recites parts of the intermediate benediction of the Amida and the "Widdui." In the main part, the repetition consists of poetical and supplicatory additions.

After the repetition, "Alenu" and Kaddish are said.

2. In the morning service — *shaharith* — the Amida is the same as on New Year. The Amida is repeated as outlined in the evening service.

In the Sephardic ritual, the Cohanim bless the congregation in the morning, Musaf, and Ne'ila services.

3. The same ritual as on New Year is used for taking out the Scroll.

4. The reading from the Pentateuch is taken from Leviticus 16:1–34 [44] (b. Megilla 31a); to this portion six persons are called upon. From the second Scroll Numbers 29:7–11 is read. The first portion is an account of the service of the High Priest on that day; the second passage gives details concerning the sacrifices.

Isaiah 57:14 to 58:14 is the Haftara, because the prophet speaks of fast and repentance.[45]

5. *Hazcarath neshamoth* — The Memorial Service — is in the Ashkenazic, Sephardic, and Italian rituals only. Although sacrificing for the dead in order to atone their sins was a well-known custom during the Maccabean period (II Macc. 12:44) and is referred to in the Midrashic literature in the form of prayer and charity, yet only of comparatively late date did this custom take root in the liturgy as a fixed service on certain days.

The idea of praying and giving charity for the dead is given in the *Sifré* to Deuteronomy 21:1–9 and *Tanhuma*, Haazinu beginning. From the phrase "Forgive Thy people Israel whom Thou hast redeemed" (Deut. 21:8), the *Midrash* derives that the dead need redemption, and that the living have to redeem them. For this reason, the *Tanhuma* says, do we remember the dead on the Day of Atonement and give charity for them in order to save them from Gehenna and cleanse them from their sins. It is also customary to have a Memorial Service on Sabbath to keep the dead out of Gehenna on the day of rest.

On the other hand, the dead help the living. According to b. Sota 34b, Kaleb prostrated himself on the graves of the patriarchs and petitioned them to intercede for him. In the same manner, b. Taanith 16a explains the reason why the people prostrate themselves on the graves of their relatives on a public Fast-day, as on the Ninth of Av (Tosafoth, ad loc.).[46]

M.V., pp. 173, 392, and *Sefer Hasidim* § 1171–1172 speak of the custom of Memorial Service as based upon *Pesikta Rabbathi* § 20. M. Vitry (*l.c.*) as well as *Siddur Rashi* § 214 order Yom Kippur as the proper time for that service. A later source [47] explains that the form Yom Kippurim in plural refers to the atonement of both the living and the dead. *Col-Bo* § 70 says that the memory of the dead breaks the heart, and for this reason, this custom has been instituted. This idea is expressed in b. Taanith 16a: "Why do the people prostrate themselves on the graves?" says Levi b. Hama, "to indicate that we are considered as the dead before God."

It first became customary in Germany to remember the dead on the Day of Atonement. Later, since the eighteenth century, Memorial Services were held also on the Three Festivals and on plain Sabbaths with no special distinction (see Chapter X). Finally, it was restricted to but two Sabbaths: before Shavuoth and the Ninth of Av.

In the Polish ritual, *Hazcara* may be held on each plain Sabbath. It seems that with the increase of persecutions during the Crusades the custom gained popularity. Lists of at least distinguished men and women massacred during persecutions were read at the public service, usually, at the Col Nidré service. These lists were called "Memor-books" — from the Latin "Memoria." "The earliest Memor-book extant is that of the community of Nuremberg. It was begun in 1296, and is so complete that it must have had predecessors which served as models for it. At all events, notwithstanding their names, the Memor-books are not borrowed from the Christian Church, but are a product of Jewish piety. . . . Indeed, the Christian Church adopted this custom, which developed into the ritual observance of All Soul's Day, from Judaism. . . . Many passages in the Church Fathers indicate that the prayers for the dead are Jewish in origin, and from the time of the Apostles who were Jews." [48]

The Memor-books begin with the prayer: "May God remember the soul of. . . ." This prayer, given below under (a), was transferred into the ritual.

The Ashkenazic Memorial Service consists of the following numbers:

a. A silent prayer in memory of a departed father or mother: *Yizcor* — "May God remember the soul of my honored . . . who has gone to his (her) eternal home. Because I pledge charity for him (her), may his (her) soul be bound up in the bond of life with the souls of Abraham, Isaac, and Jacob, Sarah, Rebekah, Rachel, and Leah, and with the souls of all other righteous who are in the paradise."

b. The reader then recites a prayer for those who donated to charity, and utters a petition for the dead.

c. *El male rahamim* — apparently since the seventeenth century in the East European countries.[49] "O God, Who art full of compassion, Who dwellest on high, grant perfect rest beneath the shelter of Thy divine Presence, in the exalted places among the holy and pure, who shine as the brightness of the firmament, to . . . who has gone to his (her) eternal home. Because his (her) son (daughter) donated to charity for the remembrance of his (her) soul, may he (she) rest in the paradise. Therefore, Lord of compassion, shelter him (her) evermore under the cover of Thy wings and let his (her) soul be bound up in the bond of life, and may he (she) rest in peace upon his (her) couch."

d. *Av harahamim* — as on Sabbaths — is then recited (see Chapter X, III).

Mahzor Adler (*Day of Atonement*, pp. 118–119) has newly composed petitions. It is interesting to note that some scholars, as Abraham b. Hiyya Hannasi (died 1136 in Barcelona), did not consider the prayer for the dead of any value (see Chapter VIII, Kaddish).[50]

6. The Musaf service has the same three introductory benedictions including the insertions. For the intermediate benediction, the Sephardic and Yemenite rituals follow S.R.A.: *atta vehartanu*, *mipěne hataenu*, *alenu*, *mehal laawonothenu*, *yaale weyavo*, *meloch*. In the Ashkenazic and Italian rituals (as M.V.) the last two items are missing, and *alenu* is recited in the repetition only. All rituals have the same three concluding benedictions and the "Widdui."

In the repetition of the Amida, aside from the poetical and supplicatory insertions, the main feature is the *Avoda*, i.e., "Service" — which describes the service which used to be rendered by the High Priest in the Temple of Jerusalem during the day. Because on the Day of Atonement the important duties, such as sacrificing, praying, confessing, and reading from the Scriptures were executed by the High Priest, the "Avoda" became an obligatory part of the service in the re-repetition of the Amida [51] beginning with Talmudic times. As basis for the Avoda-text, *Mishna* Yoma was used, omitting parts which have no direct bearing upon the service. Gradually, the precentors would compose their own texts, utilizing several Mishnaic passages and following the Mishnaic presentation of the service. The passages taken from the *Mishna* and still retained in all Avodas are: Yoma III, 8 and the first sentence of 9; IV, 1–2; V, 1, 3–4; VI, 2 and a summary of 3–7; VII, 1 and part of 3.

The oldest text discovered up to the present is *shiv'ath yomim* — two passages of which are quoted in Yoma 56b.[52] There it is recorded that a precentor recited this Avoda for Rava (280–352). Several texts were composed along the lines of that "Avoda," but they all have poetical forms and expressions and shall be discussed among the poetical insertions.

7. The Minha service is ushered in by taking out the Scroll and reading from Leviticus 18 : 1–30 to which portion three persons are called upon. The Haftara consists of the Book of Jonah (b. Megilla 31a).

The reason for the reading of the Pentateuchal section is, according to b. Yoma 19b–20a, to remind the people of these ethical principles in sexual life (Abudraham, p. 155). The Book of Jonah teaches that there is no escape from God's judgment, which, however, may be influenced by repentance.

The Amida is repeated as at the morning service.

8. Ne'ila, i.e., The Concluding Service. The service begins with *ashre* and *uva letziyon*. The Amida is the same as in the Minha and morning services.

In the insertion *zochrenu* the word *cothvenu* — inscribe us — is changed to *hothmenu* — seal us. The same change is made in the insertion *uch'thov* to *wahathom*, and in *uv'sefer hayim* from *wĕniccothev* to *wĕnehathem* (b. Rosh Hashana 16b).

After the concluding benediction, a short "Widdui" is recited, consisting of *ashamnu-tavo*. Then *atta nothen yad* follows. This paragraph is given in S.R.A. 49a. Maimonides, however, leaves out the first passage and starts with *ma anu*, following b. Yoma 87b. This version was adopted by the Sephardic and Yemenite rituals, while the Ashkenazic and Italian rituals retained Amram's version.

The paragraph speaks of God as being ready to receive the sinners who atone and to pardon them.

The next paragraph *atta hivdalta* is also given in S.R.A. and appears in all rituals. After a short introduction, several Biblical verses are quoted which tell of God welcoming the contrite spirits of transgressors. *Elohay ad shello notzarti* closes the Amida.

At the end of the repetition *avinu malkenu* is recited. Then "Shema" is repeated once, *Baruch shem* thrice, and "The Lord He is our God" — *adonai hu haĕlohim* — seven times; they are mentioned in M.V., p. 395. Whereupon the Shofar is sounded; in the Ashkenazic congregations only "Tekia" is sounded, while in the Sephardic, Italian, and Yemenite rituals: tekia, shevarim, tĕrua and tekia are sounded,[53] according to S.R.A. 49b.

Then the weekday evening service follows as on the outgoing Sabbath: and then "Havdala" is recited.

Poetical and Supplicatory Insertions. The insertions in the services of the Day of Atonement are very numerous. Every ritual presents its best, giving full expression to the ideas and motives which stirred the heart of the Jew on that day. There was also a practical purpose involved: namely, to fill out the whole day with prayer, praise, and supplication.

Before Col Nidré, the Sephardic, Italian, and Yemenite rituals have *shema koli* by Hai Gaon (died 1038). Prior to that poem Sephardic-Oriental and Yemenite rituals have *lecha êli* which some attribute to Abraham b. Ezra and others to Jehuda Halevi.

The first-named poem is one of the oldest examples of rhyme in Hebrew. It pleads that He Who heard the prayers of the heroes of Israel (here all the heroes from Abraham to Honi Hameaggel are mentioned) may also receive our petitions.

The other poem pleads that God Who owns everything, the whole universe as well as our innermost beings, may accept our meditations and receive us under the shield.

Both poems have the Hazağ meter.[54]

After the Amida, selections of Biblical verses are recited responsively, and then there follow *anna adonai*, *rahamecha yerau* with the refrain *shomea tefilla*, *ashru darkechem* with the refrain *haneshama lach* by Abraham b. Ezra and *mishtahawim lehadrath*. All Sephardic rituals chant *anna bêkorenu* by David b. Bekoda responsively in a traditional tune.[55]

El melech yoshev is one of the important supplications which is repeated over and over again during the services of the day and during the services of all Fast-days. It belongs to the oldest Selihoth.[56] Its content is as follows: "O omnipotent King Who sittest on the throne of mercy . . . pardoning the iniquities of Thy people. . . . Thou hast taught us to repeat the Thirteen Attributes of Thy mercy. Remember unto us, this day, the covenant of the Thirteen Attributes, as Thou didst reveal them of old to the meek (Moses). . . ." Here the attributes are recited.[57]

A collection of supplications in simple responsive form then follow. They are: *rahamana idcar* in Aramaic in which the merits of Israel's heroes are enumerated; the refrain is *bedil wayyaavor* — for the sake of the attributes of mercy proclaimed when Thou didst pass (before Moses — Exod. 34:5–9); *anshe emuna* is an alphabetical acrostic without rhyme; *tamahnu meraoth* — an inverted alphabetical acrostic; *bĕterem shehakim* — a poem with rhyme and refrain; *anenu avinu anenu* patterned after I Kings 18:37: "Answer me O Lord, answer me"; *adon haselihoth* — an alphabetical acrostic which has a traditional tune;[58] the response *adonai hanenu* with rhyme; *asê lemaan shĕmecha; elohenu shebbashamayim* — both alphabetical acrostics; *al taas immanu cala* — an interchanged alphabetical acrostic; *ashamnu miccol am* — an alphabetical acrostic; *ribbono shel olam ethwadda* — a confession with rhyme, each strophe finishing with a Biblical phrase. Then the confession *Ashamnu* is repeated. After that there follows *lĕenenu ashku amalenu* with the acrostic from *lamed* to *taw*. In this poem the Jew complains of his sufferings from his many enemies. These sufferings came upon him for his sins. After parts of the "Widdui" are repeated, the hymn *addir wenaor* with the refrain *mi el camocha* is chanted. In the Kaddish *têanu wethêath'ru* is recited, as in the Italian ritual for the New Year.

All the Selihas mentioned belong to the old Seliha literature created in Babylonia and probably also in Palestine long before the "Payetanic" time. They have a simple folk-style and were taken over into all the rituals.[59]

In the ASHKENAZIC ritual the poetical insertions start with *yaale tahanunenu* which is also found in the Italian ritual in an inverted alphabetical acrostic. This poem has been rendered into an English version by N. Salaman:[60] "O let our prayer ascend from eventide, And may our cry come in to Thee from dawn, And let our song be clear till eventime."

A selection of Biblical verses in responsive reading then follow *shomea tefilla.*

Adonai elohê hatzevaoth, *el erech appayim* are recited in responsive form; they are alphabetical acrostics. In the latter Seliha the Thirteen Attributes are inserted. Both belong to the oldest Selihoth.[61] The Polish ritual has instead *darkecha elohenu* attributed to Yose b. Yose and *el melech yoshev*, while the Ashkenazic ritual has it later.

Then there follows *selah na ashamoth* by M. Rothenburg; it is an alphabetical acrostic and is recited in responsive form; after this, "El Melech Yoshev" and the Thirteen Attributes are recited.

Then the "Akeda" *tummath tzurim* by Benjamin b. Zerah[62] follows; it is an inverted alphabetical acrostic and is recited in responsive form. It relates the story of Isaac's sacrifice, and is chanted in the Akeda tune.[63] After the Seliha "El Melech Yoshev," etc., is repeated.

The Polish ritual has here *omnam ken* by Yom Tov of York (killed in the York massacre of 1189). This poem has been rendered into English by I. Zangwill:[64]

> Ay, 'tis thus Evil us hath in bond;
> By Thy grace guilt efface and respond
> "Forgiven."

It has also an alphabetical acrostic; each strophe ends with *salahti*. Then *ki hinne cachomer* follows. This remarkable poem in alphabetical acrostic (in the Polish ritual only up to *caf;* in the Ashkenazic Selihoth for fifth day of the *asereth yemê teshuva* there are two more stanzas) gives a description of the various handicrafts and manual arts and compares them with man's nature as the creation of God. The poem is probably of French origin, about the twelfth century.[65] The English rendition of this poem by Elsie Davis is printed in Adler's *Mahzor*, p. 35.

Oth'cha edrosh by Simon b. Isaac b. Abun is an alphabetical acrostic recited in responsive form. This poem has a traditional tune.[66] Each stanza has eight lines; each four have a separate rhyme; and the first and fifth lines start with the last word of the preceding line.

Then a section of Biblical verses is recited, beginning with *zechor lanu berith*, after which, in the Polish ritual, *shema kolenu* is chanted which is followed by *al taazvenu*, a short responsive hymn *ki anu ammecha*, and by *hirshanu ufashanu*. The confession "Ashamnu," and the alphabetical Widdui *al het* are repeated. Then the selection of Biblical verses; *wedawid avdecha*, *adonai menath helki* based upon the Thirteen Principles of Maimonides follow. Then *el rahum* an alphabetical acrostic; *anenu adonai anenu* as in the Sephardic ritual, *mi sheana*,[67] which relates the petitions of the heroes follow, and they close with the Aramaic *rahamana dêanê*. The whole section may be considered as part of the old pre-"Payetanic" Seliha literature.

Then *avinu malkenu* is recited, and is followed by "Alenu" and Kaddish.

After the service, the rhymed Song of Unity — *shir hayyihud* — by Samuel the Pious of the twelfth century, and the "Song of Glory" — *shir haccavod* — by his son Juda are chanted responsively, and then "The Royal Crown" — *kether malchuth* — by Solomon b. Gabirol is read in all rituals.

In the latter poem, the author first leads the human mind to the admiration of the universe, then to reflection, and finally to devotion and moral improvement, "for by means of the contemplation of the heavenly host, man is not only taught to 'look through nature up to nature's God,' but he also becomes penetrated with a spirit of humility; and presumptuous notions of pride and selfishness are repressed in his bosom, when he reflects what an insignificant atom he is in the immensity of Creation." [68]

In his opening the poet says: "Through my prayer will man benefit: for he will learn by it how to plead. . . . Therein have I related the wonders of the Ever-living. . . . I have placed it at the head of all my hymns of praise, and called it 'The Royal Crown.'" The poem is in rhymed prose.

In the morning service, after the Song of the Sea, the SEPHARDIC-ORIENTAL ritual has *shofet col haaretz* by Solomon b. Gabirol;[69] in the Yemenite ritual this poem is said before *baruch sheamar*. We meet the same in the Ashkenazic ritual in the supplications for the days of penitence.

The insertions in the Sephardic rituals start with *adonai negdecha col taawathi* by Jehuda Halevi — a poem in the Hazağ meter. This is followed by *elohim eli atta* by Solomon b. Gabirol.

After the conclusion of the closing benediction of "Verses of Song," *shinanim shaananim* by the same poet is chanted. In this poem the procedure of the angels singing praise to God is described.

Before the repetition of the Amida, the "Reshuth" *adonai shamati shimacha* is chanted by the precentor according to the Sephardic-Oriental ritual.

Before the Kedusha, the poem *afude shesh* by Jehuda Halevi is chanted. It is a description of the angels while singing hymns to God. This is followed by *elohim el mi* by the same poet; it is an alphabetical acrostic. The poet exults in the greatness of God: "Unto whom shall I liken Thee, since there is none to be compared to Thee?" Then follows *adonai tzevaoth* by the same poet. It has four sections and describes the heavenly hosts and the creatures of the earth; it utilizes Psalm 104. The closing paragraph of Jehuda Halevi's "Seder Kedusha" is *barechu adonai bechol mekomoth* with the acrostic *beyom hakkippurim*. It relates God's providence in granting the prophetic spirit to Moses and in bestowing the divine spirit upon His chosen ones.

In the "Widdui," the confession *ribbono shel olam kodem* . . by Nissim "head of the academy in Babylonia in the eighth century" or of Kairwan in Northern Africa in the eleventh century,[70] is included. This consists of seven paragraphs in prose. Here the *Ashamnu* is repeated; then follows *lĕenenu ashku amalenu* and the *al het*, *addir wenaor* (see above). In the repetition, the Seliha and "Widdui" are recited in the intermediate benediction after the phrase *lifne adonai titharu.*[71]

The supplicatory part is concluded by repeating the responsive section mentioned in the evening service.

The Sephardic-European ritual has *avinu malkenu* and the poem *lĕmaancha elohay* by David b. Bekoda of the twelfth century. The latter is a petition to be chanted by the precentor, and is used also in the New Year's service.

For the morning service, the ASHKENAZIC ritual has a great number of piyyutim, Selihoth, and Widduim in common with the Italian ritual. These are Yotzer and Ofan piyyutim. A great part of the Italian Kerova for Shaharith is inserted in the Ashkenazic Musaf Kerova.

Yotzer. Az beyom kippur — an alphabetical acrostic.

Ofan. Kadosh addir baliyatho — with the refrain *baruch shem kevod,* each line beginning with *kadosh;* it is an alphabetical acrostic.

Kerova. The "Reshuth" *emecha nasathi* by Meshullam b. Kalonymos. *Immatzta* is by the same author; it starts with the last word of the preceding poem.

In the second benediction there are:

Taawath nefesh in inverted alphabetical acrostics. These poems have four words to the line in strict meter, with the exception of the last two strophes in *immatzta* which have three words to the line.

Enosh ma yizke is an alphabetical acrostic without rhyme; it is also found in the Italian ritual. It has the refrain *ad yom motho* — "Until the day of man's death Thou dost wait for him to repent, that he may incline toward immortal life." The poem is a reflection of man's efforts and deeds, and comes to the conclusion that "If he perform righteous deeds, they will follow him to his eternal home." This is followed again by Meshullam's poem *ihadta yom ze;* whereupon *atta hu* as in the New Year's service is chanted.

More hataim is a double acrostic, with the name of the poet Meshullam b. Kalonymos given. The poem has three lines to the strophe, the third line being taken from Psalm 145. After three strophes, one of the refrains is recited. The poem has a traditional tune.[72]

Eder yekar eli, by the same poet, has three words to the line, and is sung according to the tune of "Aapid." [73] In the same meter is the poem *anna elohim hayim* which utilizes several Biblical phrases.

Hayyom yiccathev, by Joseph b. Isaac b. Stan Abitur of the tenth century, is a prayer chanted by the precentor: "Upon this day shall be written in the book of memorial life and death. Thou branch (Israel) awake, I beseech Thee! Rouse thyself, stand, stand up! Arise,

I beseech thee, and supplicate; entreat now for the soul before the face of Him Who dwelleth on high."

This is followed by *ayuma bahar* which is by the same author.

Then the response *ach athim* follows. Each line starts with *ach* and ends with the refrain "for Thou art compassionate for every creature." It is by Meshullam b. Kalonymos.

A hymn by the same poet follows. It is composed of Biblical phrases in an alphabetical acrostic; each stanza starts with *imru lelohim* and has in the closing line *lachen yithgae.* This is followed by *maase elohenu;* it is in the same structure and by the same poet.

Asher tĕhillathecha. In this hymn the same poet develops the idea that though God "is the mighty Whose praise is with the angelic hosts, yet He graciously accepts the praise of those whose days are few."

Here a collection of responses by the same poet is chanted.

Then follows *haadereth wĕhaĕmuna*, found in *Hechaloth*, probably of the sixth century, preceded by six other responses by Meshullam b. Kalonymos.

Ze el ze shoalim is the refrain for an alphabetical acrostic, in which a glorification of God through the angelic hosts is rendered. Then *lĕel orech din* is chanted.

Silluk. Mi yĕthanne tokef, by Meshullam b. Kalonymos. It has four words to the line, but only two or three words in the conclusion for the Kerova.

In the Kedusha *el berov etzoth* by Meshullam b. Kalonymos is also found in the Italian ritual. It describes the powers of the spirit. The second part *tamid tithlonan* recounts the qualities and the fate of the soul. The third part *elecha wĕadecha* relates the nature of flesh; and the fourth part *elecha teluyoth* is a prayer to help man for the sake of His Name.

After the Kedusha *ki makdishecha* is recited as on New Year. Then follow seventeen responses in alphabetical acrostics, beginning with *haaddir*. They seem to be compositions of Meshullam b. Kalonymos.[74] They are in the nature of laudations based upon Biblical phrases, the last of which *haazurim bĕahav* has *adonai ĕlohenu* and *adonai ehad* as alternating refrains.

Here the third benediction with its insertions is repeated, followed by the first three paragraphs of the intermediate benediction. Whereupon the Selihoth begin with *zechor rahamecha*, according to the Polish ritual. The Ashkenazic ritual starts with *el erech appayim*, and the Thirteen Attributes and a few responses. Then follows *adon din* by Zevadya. The form of this poem is called *shelishiya* — "Triplet" — because each strophe has three lines. The first line is chanted by the precentor, and the third by the congregation. There are four words to the line. This poem is followed by *adon bĕshoftecha* by Elijah b. Shemaya; it is a *sheniya* — a two-liner. This poem, too, has four words to the line, and is chanted responsively.

Taale tĕfillathenu, by Moses b. Meshullam of the tenth century, is followed by *eshpoch sihi* by Gershom b. Juda, called the "Light of the Exile" (died in 1040 in Mayence); it has the triplet form.

Tigrath yad has five words to the line and several Talmudic expressions; it is recited in responsive form.

Then two more two-liners follow: *ach bĕmetheh din* and *al na tĕyasser;* the latter is by Benjamin b. Zerah. Then follows an "Akeda" by Mordechai, *mefal'ti eli* and *adonai rabbath tzeraruni* by David b. Shemuel of the eleventh century — a contemporary of Rashi.[75] Another "Akeda" by Benjamin follows; it is *emunim bĕne maaminim.* After that *shofet col haaretz* by Solomon b. Gabirol or Abun follows.

Adabĕra thahanunim by Kalonymos b. Juda [76] has the same structure and tune as *oth'cha edrosh* in the evening service.

The whole section up to the last Seliha is missing in the Polish ritual. From *zechor lanu*, both Ashkenazic and Polish rituals are identical.

The Widdui part is repeated as in the evening service up to *wedawid avdecha*, after which responses are included, and the intermediate benediction as well as the concluding benediction is at an end. *Avinu malkenu* then closes the service.

The Musaf insertions in the Sephardic ritual are comparatively few in number. Before the Amida, the Sephardic-Oriental ritual has *yanuv pi* by Israel Najara and *adonai elohê yeshuathi* by Hayyim Modai.

The latter "Reshuth" is an imitation of the style of those for Shaharith and for New Year. The Sephardic-European ritual starts with *athanu lehalloth.*

The Kerova consists of *bimrome eretz* and *eretz hithmoteta* by Jehuda Halevi. The first describes the Kedusha service by the heavenly hosts; the second gives a poetical description of the earth trembling before God.

In the intermediate benediction, the meditation *heyê im pifiyyoth* is recited by the precentor after the "Alenu"; then follows the "Reshuth" to the "Avoda": *aromim'cha hizki* by Solomon b. Gabirol. The fourth line of each stanza of this poem is taken from the Bible. Whereupon the "Avoda" *atta conanta* attributed to Yose b. Yose follows.[77] The text follows the *Mishna* Yoma; the language is simple without rhyme, and proceeds in an alphabetical acrostic. First a survey of Biblical history up to Aaron the priest is given; then a detailed description of the service of the High Priest on the Day of Atonement is rendered, in which parts of *Mishna* Yoma are included, as pointed out above in the description of the first "Avoda" (see Chapter V). At the end, a short prayer which the High Priest used to utter after he completed the service is recited. The prayer is mentioned in *Mishna* Yoma V, 1, and is given in b. Yoma 53b.

Another prayer in an alphabetical acrostic follows; it petitions God for the prosperity of the people. The "Avoda" closes with a glorification of the High Priest. He was, when he came out of the Sanctuary "like an amethyst set in a crown; like a ruby fixed in a mitre . . . like an angel of God. . . ."

Then lamentations beginning with *ashre ayin* follow. The first of this section is by Solomon b. Gabirol; the second by Jehuda Halevi; the third by Abraham b. Ezra. They express their grief that all that glory of the Temple service has been lost to us and that we suffer in the bitter exile.

But God in His great mercy has given us this Day of Atonement on which we may offer, instead of bulls, the prayers of our lips (Hos. 14:3).

A plaintive poem is then chanted *shamem har tziyon* "Through the iniquities of our fathers, Mount Zion has become desolate . . ." and three petitions, each beginning with "Our God and God of our fathers" follow. Whereupon the "Widdui" is repeated, and a long confession by Shem Tov b. Ardutiel (beginning of the fourteenth century) [78] is read. In this confession, the old *ashamnu*, *al het*, and other parts of the "Widdui" are used.

Then the rest of the "Widdui" and the "Amida" is repeated. The priests bless the people, and the Musaf insertions close with *hayyom tĕam'tzenu* (only from *alef* to *yod*). Whereupon responsive Selihoth are repeated as in the morning service.

The Yemenite ritual has the same "Avoda" as the Sephardic ritual, after which "The Royal Crown" by Solomon b. Gabirol is recited.

Selihoth and piyyutim have no fixed limit. They may be chosen and recited ad libidum. For this purpose, a selection is given at the end of the Mahzor.

In the Ashkenazic ritual, the repetition of the Amida has the following:

Kerova — shoshan emek ayuma.[79] It has four lines to the strophe, each line consisting of three words. *Shabbath shabbathon* and *yom miyyamim* have the same meter with the acrostic *yom kippurim; tzefê bevath temutha* has the same meter likewise with the acrostic *tzom haasor*. These poems are probably by E. Kallir,[80] and are found in the Italian and Roumanian rituals for Shaharith.

The Polish ritual has another number: *enosh ech yitzdak;* it has five words to the line.

Essa dei by E. Kallir is also found in the Italian and Roumanian rituals. Its form is identical to the Kerova *more hataim* of the Shaharith service, and is chanted according to the same tune.

Here two responsive passages follow: *eth lahshi* and *adon lekol.* Both have Eleazar as an acrostic. Then there follows *en aroch elecha* by the same poet, and is also found in the Italian and Roumanian rituals. This poem is sung according to the tune of "Aapid."

Here two responses follow, and then the hymn *asher emathecha* in an alphabetical acrostic. This hymn recounts God's greatness over all worlds and yet He desires the praise from man who, formed of dust, strives and fails. This antithesis is worked out in double stanzas, one half beginning with *asher emathecha* and finishing with *umôraacha alêhem*, and the other half beginning with *wĕavitha thehilla* and closing with *wĕhi thĕhillathcha*. It has four short lines to the stanza, each line having two words. The same hymn is found in the Italian and Roumanian rituals.

In addition to these, the Polish ritual has the hymn *imru lelohim* with endings from I Chronicles 16. It has four lines to the stanza, each line having three words. Only the first ten stanzas are in an alphabetical acrostic (from *alef* to *yod*), and finishes with the last stanza *taw*. The same in complete form is found in the Italian ritual, save that the ninth and the last stanzas are different.

Maasê elohênu has the same content and form as *asher emathecha.* This poem too is found in the Italian and Roumanian rituals in complete form, giving the antithesis in each double stanza, one half beginning with *maasê elohênu* and finishing with *lachen yithgaê*, and the other half beginning with *maase enosh* and finishing with *wĕech yithgaê*. In the Polish ritual, the second half of each stanza was omitted, and only one, which is not found in the other rituals, was retained.

All three hymns are ascribed to Meshullam b. Kalonymos.

Then there follows the hymn *ammitze shehakim* in which the heavenly hosts and Israel are praising God alternately, the one singing *kadosh* and the other *baruch.* This response is also found in the Italian ritual.

Êlê marom is a similar hymn; it utilizes phrases from the Kedusha. In the Italian ritual this has several variations.

Silluk. The Polish and Italian rituals have *unethanne tokef* while the Ashkenazic ritual has *mi yaaroch êlecha.*

In the Kedusha, the Ashkenazic ritual has *êlecha tĕluyoth enenu* by Meshullam b. Kalonymos, while the Polish ritual has *az millifne.*

Bĕreshith by E. Kallir; this poem has four paragraphs, each beginning with the same phrase. Though based upon a meter of three words to the line, the poet makes several diversions.

Haohez beyad follows after the Kedusha in the Ashkenazic and Italian rituals.

Here follow four responses in the Ashkenazic ritual, the last being also in the Italian ritual. This is based upon *adonai ĕlohenu adonai*.

The Polish ritual does not have these selections.

In the Ashkenazic ritual, even as in the Sephardic ritual, the third benediction and its insertions and the first part of the intermediate benediction are repeated. After the meditation *heyê im pifiyoth* and *ohila* the "Avoda" is recited. The Ashkenazic ritual has the composition *ammitz coah* by Meshullam b. Kalonymos. It is an alphabetical acrostic, without rhyme, and with five words to the line. The poet starts to describe the story as told in Genesis, continues until Aaron the priest, and then, basing himself on *Mishna* Yoma, he recounts the procedure of the service. He too takes the well-known passages from the *Mishna*, as *anna hashem* and *wĕhaccohanim;* the last one has a fine traditional tune.[81] There is also *wechach haya mone*. These passages are repeated as in the other "Avodas" three times. During the singing of *wĕhaccohanim*, the precentor and congregation prostrate themselves. The "Avoda" closes with an alphabetical prayer, after which the hymn *kĕohel hannimtah* with the response *marê cohen* is chanted. The style and language of this Avoda are more intricate than the Sephardic Avoda. Then the lamentations follow; they are similar in style to those of the Sephardic ritual. Then a selection of alphabetical numbers follows, preceded by *ashrê ayin*. This selection has three words to the line but no rhyme. It expresses the deep-felt sorrow over the loss of the Temple and the exile. The last piece finishes with the hope of the restoration of the Temple and the return to Zion. The Polish ritual has some other selections which express the idea that our fate is the consequence of our sins.

The Italian ritual has the "Avoda" *ezcor sella* and the "Reshuth" *bêur divre nechohoth* attributed to Johanan Cohen b. Joshua[82] of the tenth century. Its content is about the same as in the other Avodas. It too starts out with Genesis and relates the Biblical story up to

Aaron, then, following *Mishna* Yoma, it gives the contents of the paragraphs mentioned above. The prayer is the same as in the Ashkenazic Avoda. No plaintive selections follow.

In the Ashkenazic ritual, after the Avoda section, the Selihoth start. Of these the generally used numbers are: *ech essa rosh* by Simon b. Abun, *achap'ra panay* by Eliezer b. Nathan (Rabban) which describes the Avoda, *afes meziah* by Simon b. Abun which is a complaint over the loss of the Temple, having four words to the line, *omnam anahnu* by Gershon b. Juda, *ani hu hashoêl* by Baruch b. Shemuel who died in 1221. This latter poem has the iambic meter with three feet to the line [83] and four lines to the stanza, and with an alphabetical acrostic and rhyme. The name of the poet is in an acrostic. The poem is in the first person singular and relates about the Avoda, the loss of the Temple cult as a result of sins, and pleads for mercy. The poem has also a traditional tune.

Ahavath izzuz, by Benjamin b. Zerah, has four words to the line and is an "Akeda." *Im avarnu* is called Pizmon.[84] *Im yos'fim* by Ephraim b. Isaac of the twelth century and *eth haběrith*, by Meyir b. Isaac, have five words to the line. Here the Thirteen Attributes with *êl melech* is recited; then *zechor rahamecha* follows.

The Seliha *gadol awoni* by Gershom b. Juda has an interesting structure, for in it each line starts with the last word of the preceding one. It has eight lines to the stanza; the precentor chants six, and the congregation joins in with the last two lines.

The Polish ritual has instead *êle ezkěra*, which describes the persecutions of the Ten Martyrs, according to Talmudic stories, by Juda. The language is hard and often obscure, having many Talmudic expressions. It has an alphabetical acrostic with rhyme.

The rest of the confession and the Amida is now repeated with the insertions mentioned in the morning service and with the Priestly Benediction. *Hayyom těam'tzenu* closes the service.

The Carpentras ritual has the Avoda of Abraham b. Ezra: *ěmune levav hevinu* with the "Reshuth" *azkir seder*. The closing hymn *ma neh'dar* and the lamentation *ashrê ayin* are by Moses b. Ezra. In this ritual a "Rehuta" is attributed to Rashi: *êl nigla bemiddoth*. It is repeated in all the services of the Day of Atonement. In it the Thirteen Attributes (Exod. 34:6–7) are interwoven, one word in each strophe. The name of the author is in an acrostic.[85]

Mention should be made of the wonderful "Bakasha" *bor'chi nafshi* by Bahya b. Pakuda which is recited in many Sephardic congregations after Musaf. It was found in his work *Hovoth Halevavoth*.

4. In the Sephardic-Oriental ritual, *athanu lehalloth* is chanted for the Minha service before the repetition. In the Sephardic-European ritual, *běne elyon begovhi* is said for Kerova. It speaks of the loftiness of the angels and of the purity and devotion of Israel on the Day of Atonement.

Anshe hesed is by Moses b. Ezra (in acrostic); each line ends with *cavod*.

In the Widdui, the confession *ribbono shel olam*, *way'hi baaloth hamminha* by Isaac b. Israel of the thirteenth century [86] is recited; the last line of each stanza is chanted by the congregation. It is a usual confession, having the same original turns. For example, "I made application to my head, forehead, and face, to intercede for me before the Lord. . . . But my head answered me: How dare that head lift itself up which hath behaved with so much levity? My forehead replied: How can a man, born of woman, justify himself when the sin is engraven on the tablet of his heart, and the forehead is so brazen? . . ."

Then the Seliha and the Widdui with all the responses of the morning service are repeated, including *avinu malkenu*. The Sephardic-Oriental ritual has the complete *Hayyom tĕamtzenu* as in the morning service.

In the Ashkenazic ritual there is a Kerova *ethan hikkir* by Elijah b. Mordechai of the eleventh century consisting of three paragraphs. This is followed by *erelê hod* with a refrain *michaêl miyyamin*. The poem is by E. Kallir [87] and is based upon Isaiah 6, phrases of which are used as fourth lines of each strophe.

A short Silluk *ki rechuvo baaravoth* by Elijah b. Mordechai is given. In it the seven heavens are described (taken from b. Hagiga 12b).

In the Kedusha *êlecha teluyoth* by Meshullam b. Kalonymos is repeated from the Shaharith service.

For Selihoth there are *ezon tahan* an alphabetical acrostic with four words to the line, *masath cappay* by Mordechai b. Shabatai of the thirteenth century with his name in an acrostic, *eth haberith* by Meyir b. Isaac, *echacha eftze pe* by E. b. Shemaya with six words to the line, *eth hakkol* by Kalonymos b. Juda which is a heart-rending outcry of Israel's suffering, *elohim al domi* — "O God, do not keep silent at the bloodshed of mine" — by David b. Meshullam. Here a nerve-wrecking description of the martyrdom during the first Crusades is given: "The congregations did not follow the call to abandon their faith and to embrace the Cross; therefore, they were all willingly slaughtered, and the blood of the parents were mingled with those of the children." "Where was a similar thing heard that parents would lead their children to be killed like in a wedding procession, and while slaughtered 'Shema' was shouted."

Ezkĕra elohim, by Amittai b. Shefatya of the eighth or ninth centuries, is chanted in the Polish ritual in the Ne'ila service. The Seliha relating the story of the ten martyrs is recited here according to the Ashkenazic ritual.

Instead of the Selihoth given above, the Polish ritual has here *êl na rĕfa na* — a petition of the thirteenth century (of France) "to hear our supplications even as the prayers of the national heroes were accepted." It is an alphabetical acrostic and has rhyme. In it Abraham, the ancestors at the Red Sea, Joshua, Samuel, Elijah, Jonah, David, and Solomon are mentioned.

Then Selihoth and Amida are repeated as in the morning service. There is the insertion *yom asher huhak* — an alphabetical acrostic with Biblical verses. The type of poems beginning with *yom* is to be found at the end of the morning and Musaf services in the Ashkenazic and Italian rituals.

5. In the Sephardic ritual, the Ne'ila service is ushered in with *êl nora alila* — a petition by Moses b. Ezra which is sung both by precentor and congregation according to a traditional tune.[88] The poem has an abridged Hazağ meter and three words to the line, the fourth line being a refrain *bĕshaath han'ila*. The poet pleads for the acceptance of the prayers and for forgiveness at the time of the closing of the day.

Before the repetition of the Amida, *athanu lehalloth* is chanted. In the Kedusha there are *erêlim wehashmalim* by Moses b. Ezra and *emeth bĕsofrĕcha* by Abraham b. Ezra.[89] There is a short confession *ribbon haolamim* by Israel Najara mentioned above. There is also *shevet yehuda* by Shemaya of the thirteenth century. This Seliha is often used in the Sephardic and Oriental rituals. It has short two-line strophes with Biblical phrases used for the second lines; the author pleads for salvation and redemption. The Sephardic-Oriental ritual has also the whole *Hayyom tĕam'tzenu*.

The Polish ritual has *bor'chi atzula* by Jehuda Halevi which the Sephardic-Oriental ritual has after Minha. This fine hymn has an alphabetical acrostic. Each strophe begins with "Bless ye (my soul)" and ends with "The Lord." The poet calls the soul which is well known to the heart but hidden from the eye, which dwelleth in an abode of clay but its source is in the heavens, to praise its Creator and Protector. After that, the Aramaic response *rahamana idcar lan* is recited.

The Ashkenazic and Polish rituals have the Kerova *av yedoacha minnoar*, by Simon b. Abun, which is also found in the Italian ritual. *Shaare armon* is an alphabetical acrostic of which only up to *lamed* is given.

In the Kedusha the same insertions are recited as at Minha.

Here follow *pethah lanu shaar* — "Open the gates for us, yea, even at the closing of the gates"; and *hayyom yifne* — "The day is passing . . . O let us come into Thy gates at last"; *anna el na* and *el malê* with the Thirteen Attributes are repeated.

The Ashkenazic ritual has here the first stanzas of twelve Selihoth from other services.[90]

Then follow four stanzas of *zechor berith* by Gershom b. Juda.

The Polish ritual has instead *umi yaamod het*, consisting of eleven stanzas; it seems to be a compilation of various Selihoth. Stanzas four to five have in an acrostic the name Solomon Hakatan, and stanzas six to eleven (*merubbim tzorchê amcha*) have in an acrostic the second part of the alphabet from *mem* to *taw*. However, all the lines have as bases a meter of five words.

This is followed by *yadecha peshot* — one strophe, and by two strophes of *zechor berith* mentioned above.

Of the Selihoth of which only the first stanzas are given in the Ashkenazic ritual, only two are retained and two more are added: *yahbiênu tzel yado* and *yashmiênu;* while four strophes and the refrain are given of the Seliha *ezkĕra elohim* by Amittai (see above).

Then *rahem na* and *shaare shamayim* are chanted; they are also used on "Hoshana Rabba" (see Chapter XV). The two responses: *ĕlohenu shebbashamayim* and *anenu elohay* are recited, and at the end the Polish ritual has *leshana habbaa birushalayim:* — "Next year in Jerusalem!"

CHAPTER XVII

THE SERVICES FOR FAST-DAYS AND PENITENTIAL DAYS

The custom of proclaiming a Fast-day with special services on occasions of calamities is old in Israel as well as among the ancient peoples. The Bible records several such Fast-days, as in Judges 20:26; I Samuel 7:6; 14:24; 31:13; Esther 4:3, 16; Ezra 9:4–5; and Joel 1:14; 2:15 urges the people to announce a Fast-day.

The cause for Fast-days was not only that of national character, but also of personal grief, as given in II Samuel 3:35; 12:16.

We hear that the Maccabees called for Fast-days (I Macc. 3:47–53), that at calamities as told in Judith the people fasted (4:12).

In the course of time several days were set aside as Fast-days in commemoration of historical disastrous events. Zechariah 8:19 names the fast of the fourth month (Seventeenth of Tammuz), that of the fifth month (Ninth of Av), and that of the seventh month (Third of Tishrê — the fast of Gedaliah) and that of the tenth month (Tenth of Teveth). Three of these commemorate the siege of Jerusalem and the destruction of the Temple, while the fast in the seventh month (Third of Tishrê) is in commemoration of Gedaliah, the governor of Palestine who was killed (II Kings 25:22–25) and with whose death the independence of the Jewish people was lost. Later, the fast of Esther on the thirteenth of the month of Adar was added (Esth. 9:31).

The Day of Atonement was an exception; it was instituted for the sake of seeking forgiveness of sins.

Besides these national Fast-days, spiritual leaders would call for a Fast- and penitential day whenever there was a drought and want of rain. This used to occur and still continues to take place in Palestine quite often. The greatest part of the *Mishna*

Taanith is dedicated to such extra Fast-days; it also describes the services for such occasions.

According to the prophetic and Talmudic conception, all disasters came as a result of sins. In order to revoke the trouble, a Fast-day was instituted on which sacrifices and petitions and confessions were offered. Thus I Samuel 7:6 relates that the people "fasted on that day and said: We have sinned against the Lord." The same reason is given for a Fast-day for rain, since "rain is withheld only because of the sins of Israel" (b. Taanith 7b).

Besides these Fast-days, several others were instituted, some commemorating national sad events and some in memory of great personalities. In S.R.A. and in the appendix to Megillath Taanith a long list of these Fast-days is given.

The custom to fast on Monday,[1] Thursday, and the following Monday in the month of Mar-heshwan is mentioned in b. Taanith 10b to 12a and Megillath Taanith §12; it was instituted for rain. Later, probably in the thirteenth century, the custom was enforced by reading into it another idea: to atone for the sins which caused the persecutions (Crusades, etc.). In Megillath Taanith, end, and in S.R.A. 34b three reasons for these Fast-days are given: The destruction of the Temple, the burning of the Tora, and the desecration of the Name. The custom was extended to twice a year: to the month of Mar-heshwan and the month of Iyyar.

The latest public Fast-day was instituted toward the end of the sixteenth century, and became generally observed since the seventeenth century. This is the "Minor Yom Kippur" on every eve of the New Moon, with the exception of Tishrê. This Fast-day was instituted by Moses Cordovero, one of the leaders of the Kabbalistic school in Safed (1522–70) (see Chapter VI). Since the New Month was considered something in the nature of New Year, a day of atonement (b. Shevuoth 9b), so it was thought most advisable to fast and confess on the previous day, in order to appear cleansed on the first day of the New Month. At about the same time came the custom to fast every Thursday during eight successive weeks, beginning with the week on which Sabbath the portion Shemoth (Exod. 1–6:1) is read through the week of "Tetzawe" (to Exod. 30:10)—*Shovĕvim tat.* This custom is based on mystic notions.

Aside from these public fasts, local Fast-days used to be instituted in commemoration of a certain sad event which local communities experienced. The number of such Fast-days is great; they have been neglected to a large extent — and partly forgotten.[2]

There are also family Fast-days, commemorating some serious happenings to the family or to the head of the family.

Of all the Fast-days, only the five Biblical days are generally observed and are called "Public Fasts" — *taaniyoth tzibbur.*[3]

There are only Ten Days of Penitence — *asereth yemê teshuva* — extending from New Year to the Day of Atonement; but usually the whole month of Ellul is considered as such, and in the Oriental communities "Selihoth" are recited every morning during the whole month before sunrise. In the European communities, however, it has been limited to the week in which New Year occurs, and during the whole month the Shofar is sounded every morning after services.

The services on the public Fast-days are marked with Selihoth insertions in the repetition of the Amida and with a special Scriptural reading in the morning and Minha services. This reading is taken from Exodus 32:11–14; 34:1–10, because it deals with the plea of Moses for Israel and with God's forgiveness (M.V., p. 234).

The verses of Exodus 32:13 second part, 34:6 second part, 7 first part and 9 second part are chanted by the whole congregation and repeated by the reader according to the Pentateuchal Mode for the High Holydays.[4] This custom of the congregation reciting the verses was well known in the twelfth century.

At the Minha service, the Haftara from Isaiah 55:6–13 and 56:1–8 is read. From the benedictions of the Haftara the two before and the three after the Haftara are recited (see Chapter X). In the Amida, the petition *anenu* — "Answer us, O Lord, answer us on this day of the fast of our humiliation" is inserted in the thirteenth benediction, while at the repetition the precentor recites it between the seventh and eighth benediction, as mentioned in b. Taanith 11b and 13b. The text of that insertion is found in Jer. Taanith II, 2.

According to the Italian, Roman, and Ashkenazic rituals, the Selihoth are inserted in the sixth benediction at the repetition of the Amida. The first two rituals have also "Kerova." In the Sephardic, Yemenite, and Polish rituals, the Selihoth are recited after the repetition.

In the Italian and Ashkenazic rituals, the passage at the end of the Selihoth *wĕal yĕakev het wĕawon eth tĕfillathenu* is a link to the Amida.

The common elements in all the rituals are:

The Thirteen Attributes and the Widdui. The closing responsive Selihoth are found in the Sephardic and Ashkenazic rituals. The poetical numbers, however, are different in the various rituals. We may deduce from this that the common elements are older ones which are also signified by their simple style, while the more intricate pieces are later creations of various localities (*cf.* Appendix VI, a).

For the Twentieth of Siwan, the Selihoth have been taken from the treasury of the liturgy. In addition, Shabbathi Cohen (1621–62) composed Selihoth which relate the gruesome story of the Chmelnitzky pogroms in 1648–9. They were printed in Amsterdam in 1651. All in all there are six numbers. In style and form they follow the Selihoth treated.

The Ashkenazic ritual follows a certain system with regard to the number and order of the poetical insertions into the Selihoth. There are two orders: a short one and a longer one.

The short order consists of three Selihoth, a Pizmon, and a responsive reading, totaling all in all five numbers.[5] This order is found in the service of the Tenth of Teveth, the Fast of Esther, the Seventeenth of Tammuz, *Ba Ha B*, and in the Selihoth before New Year. The Polish ritual has only two Selihoth and a Pizmon, totaling three numbers.

The longer order consists of an opening, three Selihoth, one Shalmonith, one Sh'lishiya, one Akeda, one Pizmon, and two or three concluding Selihoth, making a total of ten or eleven numbers. This order is used for the Selihoth of the Ten Days of Penitence. The Polish ritual has two numbers less.

The Selihoth for the eve of New Year and the Day of Atonement constitute an exception to this order.

For the eve of New Year, the Ashkenazic ritual has one opening, three Selihoth, six Sh'niyoth, four Sh'lishiyoth, three Akedoth, three Pizmonim, and three Tehinoth, totaling all in all twenty-three numbers.

For the Day of Atonement, it has one opening; three Selihoth, six Sh'niyoth, four Sh'lishiyoht, three Akedoth, three Pizmonim, and one Tehina, the total being twenty-one numbers.[6]

In the Polish ritual, the Selihoth for the eve of the Day of Atonement are reduced to three, because the day is considered a holiday on which one ought not to indulge in too many supplications.

The literature of supplications, generally called "Selihoth," is enormous. For about fifteen hundred years Israel continued to create poetry expressing inner contrition and distress, and disasters and persecutions which came from without. Communities which were left more at ease, as the European Sephardic group, have a scanty Seliha-literature, while others, and these constitute the great majority of groups, which went through the turmoil of the dark ages, gave vent to their wounded souls, writing Selihoth with the blood of their hearts.

The Ninth of Av — *tisha bĕav.* The most important Fast-day next to the Day of Atonement is the Ninth of Av which commemorates the destruction of the First and Second Temple (M. Taanith IV, 6), and the fall of Jerusalem. For this reason, it became customary to mourn not only on that day, but to start the season of mourning three weeks before, from the Seventeenth of Tammuz; for "Whoever mourns over Jerusalem will merit to behold its joy" (b. Taanith 30b).[7]

The fast starts with sunset of the previous day and lasts, like that of Yom Kippur, for twenty-four hours; while the other fasts last only from dawn to sunset of the same day.

During the three weeks prior to the Ninth of Av, mourning is expressed in the services by taking the Haftaras on the three Sabbaths from prophetic portions which contain sinister prophecies. For the first Sabbath: Jeremiah 1; for the second Sabbath: Jeremiah 2:4–28 and 4:1–2; for the third Sabbath: Isaiah 1:1–27.[8]

In some rituals, as in the Ashkenazic, Italian, and Roumanian, insertions of a plaintive character are recited on these Sabbaths. Of these insertions, that for the third Sabbath by Eleazar b. Nathan — *elohim bĕoznenu* — describes the horror of the first crusades.

The mourning is signified by walking without shoes, by sitting on the floor, by taking off the curtain from the ark (Parocheth), by removing the ornaments from the Scrolls, by refraining from putting on the prayer-shawl and the Tefillin during the morning service, and by chanting the prayers in a sad, sorrowful mode.

In some congregations, Psalm 137 is chanted in the evening.[9]

The *Talmud* emphasizes the great significance of the day and orders that only sad literature be read, especially the Book of Lamentations and Job (b. Taanith 30a). The custom to read the Book of Lamentations is first mentioned in Soferim XVIII, 4: "Some read the Book of Lamentations in the evening; others postpone it to the next morning." Furthermore, Jeremiah 14:19–22 and Psalms 79 and 137 are recited. S.R.A. 43b adds the insertion *nahem* or *rahem* given in Jer. Taanith II, 2 in approximately the same form, and according to the *Talmud* it is inserted in the fourteenth benedictions (*l.c.;* see Chapter VIII). In this insertion the compassion of God is asked for mourners of Zion and for the despised and desolate city which has been devoured by legions who have killed the pious.[10]

Another change became customary in Palestine, Rome, and Spain, and that is not to recite the Song of the Sea at the morning service (M.V., p. 226; *Hamanhig* adds France and Provence). Instead, Deuteronomy 32 is read in the Sephardic and Yemenite rituals. This change was not accepted in the Ashkenazic ritual.

The Scriptural reading is taken from Deuteronomy 4:25–40. The Haftara is from Jeremiah 8:13–23; 9:1–23. The readings are mentioned in b. Megilla 31b. The same readings are used for Minha as on the Fast-days.

In the *Talmud*, the Lamentations are called *Kinoth*. This name was later adopted for the poetical productions recited on the Ninth of Av, which compositions started in Gaonic times and continued for centuries. These elegiac poems were first interwoven with verses from the Book of Lamentations.

But before that time, Selihoth used to be inserted in the Amida as on the other Fast-days (S.R.A. 43b). For that purpose, Kerovoth were composed, as the ones in the Italian and Ashkenazic rituals by E. Kallir.[11] Both these Kerovoth have insertions in the three introductory benedictions and in the eleven of the intermediate benedictions closing with *bonê yerushalayim.*

The Italian ritual starts with *Zĕchor echa.* The paragraphs are short; but in the last insertion there are twenty-one elegies by E. Kallir. In many congregations, however, these are recited after the Amida is completed, in order not to divert from its contents. This is done in the Sephardic and Ashkenazic rituals. For this reason, the Ashkenazic Kerova, *aavich beyom mevech*, does not have the Kinoth inserted as has the Italian ritual.

In the Ashkenazic and Sephardic rituals the number of Kinoth grew to about sixty, and it was therefore considered wise to recite them after the Amida.

The Kinoth have their origin in the Seliha, having the idea that trouble and distress grow out of sins for which the people are punished, that only penitence can revoke the severe decrees, and that salvation can come only after the sins are forgiven. The same idea was applied to the greatest blow the Jewish people suffered: the destruction of the Temple and the fall of Jerusalem which resulted in the dispersion of the people in exile. The people believed that only through repentance and wholehearted return to God can redemption come. But the pain of that national calamity was so intensely felt by the spiritual leaders that instinctively they would break forth in lamentations, lamenting the lost glory, the brutality of the Babylonians and the Romans, the devastation of the holy city, the massacre of hundreds of thousands of men, women, and children, the desecration of all sacred things, the burning of the holy Scriptures, and the torture of the sages. Into the scope of this theme they cast not only the destruction of the First and Second Temple, but also the fall of Bettar and the last attempt by Bar Cochba to regain independence. Thus the content of the Kinoth became the outcry of the Jew concerning the loss of his home and his spiritual center. All suppressed pain which accumulated in his heart, due to his peculiar situation among the nations of the world, found expression in the Kinoth. All his troubles, he traced back to one source: to the loss of his homeland and the ruin of the Sanctuary.

Material for the Kinoth was drawn from Lamentations, from the Prophets and Psalms, and from the Midrashic interpretations and Agadic stories concerning the Destruction and the Bar Cochba revolt. Very few of the Kinoth allude to later events, such as the Crusades, the burning of the *Talmud*, and the expulsion from Spain (*cf.* Appendix VI, b).

S. Baer edited a corrected text of the Ashkenazic and Polish "Selihoth" and "Kinoth" (Roedelheim). A German translation was added by Mendel Hirsch.

The Sephardic Selihoth are partly inserted in the Mahzor for the High Holydays. The Selihoth for the Four Fast-days together with the Kinoth are printed in a separate volume, called "Hamêsh taaniyoth." Popular are the Leghorn and Vienna editions. In the Italian and Yemenite rituals Selihoth and Kinoth are incorporated in the Mahzor.

CHAPTER XVIII

PRIVATE DEVOTION

Private devotion has been the source out of which fixed public and private worship sprang forth. They not only received the inspiration and expression, but were also molded into set forms through the devotions of individuals in moments of spiritual awakening and aroused emotion on certain occasions. These devotional utterances were adopted by the people as their standard prayers.

Human nature, however, always craving for spontaneous expression, sought for new and fresh outpourings of the soul, as soon as those adopted and fixed prayers became routine. "Do not make your prayer routine, but free supplications and petitions before God" was the constant demand of the sages (b. Ber. 28b). For this reason, people were urged to insert in the last of the intermediate benedictions their own personal petitions (b. Avoda Zara 8a); but if one is afflicted with some trouble, he may then add his own prayer in any of the intermediate benedictions (*l.c.;* b. Ber. 34).

In accordance with this idea, an extensive literature of private devotions, called *tehinoth*, was created through the ages. Many men of piety in Israel would compose their private devotions which, in turn, would be accepted into the regular service or would be included as private devotions to be recited in the service. In the course of our study, we have met several of these silent and private devotions in the public services.

But the rivulet of that warm and soulful outpouring never ran dry in Israel. In every generation "devotions" were created, giving expression to troubles, desires, and yearnings which moved the heart. They were not always incorporated into the liturgy, but were collected separately and preserved for the use of the pious.

The devotions are in Hebrew. But since the sixteenth century, devotions have been written in Judeo-German, Judeo-

Spanish, Judeo-Italian, and in Judeo-Greek, aside from those written in much earlier times which were in the Oriental languages, such as Arabic, Persian, etc.

The devotions are (a) for certain seasons and occasions, and (b) general meditations suitable for any time.

The most important meditations of the first type are as follows:

(a) 1. *Maamadoth* to be recited every day after the morning service.[1] There are separate sections for each of the seven days of the week. The idea was taken from the custom cited in M. Taanith IV that during the latter period of the Second Temple representatives of the people would be delegated to Jerusalem to stand by at the sacrifices in the Temple, while the people at home would assemble at the times of the sacrifices and recite on each day of the week a section from Genesis 1. This custom was retained even after the fall of the Temple and the cessation of sacrifices.

According to b. Taanith 27b, this institution upholds the world. The main idea of reading a passage from Genesis 1 was extended to the reading of portions also from the *Mishna* and the *Talmud* dealing with the sacrifices, the reading of which was considered as actual sacrifices (*l.c.*). This idea is derived also from a Talmudic statement in b. Kiddushin 30 that everybody should divide his time of study into three: for the Scriptures, for *Mishna*, and for *Gemara*. Later on Agadic selections and meditations were added. S.R.A. 16–17 was the first to give us a complete text for the Maamadoth.

In the course of time, several more selections were added through Kabbalistic influence, and the Maamadoth came to close with two petitions.[2] Taking this idea as basis, the *Hok Leyisrael* was compiled which has in addition an abundant collection of mystic and Kabbalistic passages.

2. It was advised to read every day the portion of Genesis 22:1–19 which deals with the sacrifice of Isaac; the story of the Manna, *parashath hamman* — Exodus 16:4–36 — and the Ten Commandments; the Thirteen Principles — *shelosha asar ikkarim* — of Faith based upon Maimonides. These readings are to strengthen faith in God and obedience to His will (Akeda) and His providence (Manna).

The same order is followed by M. Cordovero in his compilation of the readings for the night of Pentecost and Hoshana Rabba, called *tikkun*. In this compilation there are the first and the last passages of each of the Scriptural books and Talmudic tractates, including passages of the Midrashic and mystic literature.

3. Prayer at midnight—*Tikkun Hatzoth*. Based upon the verse in Psalm 119:62: "At midnight I will rise to give thanks unto Thee," it became customary to rise at that hour for prayer and meditation. The *Talmud* has several references to this custom. Since the tenth century the supplications for this occasion have dealt with the destruction of the Temple.[3]

With the growth of mysticism, this custom too received greater and greater importance, until a ritual was finally compiled for that purpose. This was first published in *Shaare Tzion* in 1662 by Nathan Hanover. This ritual has two parts: one part, called *Tikun Rahêl*, consists of sections of the Tahanun, Widdui, and Kinoth; part two contains several Psalms, a poem — *dodi yarad leganno* — used also for Shavuoth, the closing paragraph of the intermediary benediction of the Musaf service for the Three Festivals, and the first chapter of *Mishna* Tamid. This service appeared in a more elaborate form in *Likkute Tzevi* (Sulzbach, 1796).

For the last one hundred and twenty years the meditation "Pure Prayer" became popular with the East European Jews to be recited before "Col Nidré." The meditation was first printed in *Hayye Adam*, Chap. 144, 20, by Abraham Danzig in 1810. According to Danzig's statement, he copied it from old works without giving the source. In a simple style the meditation recounts the manifold human weaknesses and pleads for forgiveness. The prayer resembles in its style and content the confession by R. Nissim, treated in the service for the Day of Atonement.

Last, but not least, the book of meditations *par excellence*, the Book of Psalms, should be mentioned. This book always has been the true source for devotion to the Jew in all walks of life. In it he used to find real consolation and strength. The Psalms were recited in private devotion and by special societies called "Hevra Tehillim." Whoever witnessed a chanting of

Psalms in the synagogue on Sabbath at sunset, or on other occasions, will remember the high devotional spirit which animated the participants.

The Psalms were divided for the seven days of the week: For Sunday 1–29; for Monday 30–50; for Tuesday 51–72; for Wednesday 73–89; for Thursday 90–106; for Friday 107–119; and for Sabbath 120–150. The Psalms are printed in this division in all larger prayer-books. Before the recitation of the Psalms the verses from Psalm 95:1–3 were read, and the recitation was concluded with the reading of Psalms 14:7, 37:39–40. Likewise, meditations of Kabbalistic source were added before and after the citation.

Beth rahêl, by Naphtali Cohen (1649–1719) contains confessions and petitions for every day of the week, hymns for some holidays, and supplications for the Ten Days of Repentance, and concludes with the Kabbalistic prayer: " . . . On the Day of Atonement may all the celestial lights be revealed throughout the world . . . so that we may be influenced by the supernal blessing."

The Italian and Levantine Jews developed the custom of rising before dawn to recite songs and prayers. For that purpose, several collections of supplications in prose and poetry were published, such as *Seder Ashmurath Habboker*, *mĕirê shahar* (Mantua, 1624) by Aaron Berachia Modena, which is similar in content to the *Tikkun Hatzoth* and contains prayers for every day as well as for the holidays. *Kenaf Renanim* (Venice, 1626) by Joseph Yedidia Carmi is in the same form.

(b) For general use there are innumerable meditations. Beginning with the sages of the *Talmud*, the Gaonim and Rabbis have composed prayers to be recited on any occasion.[4] Every spiritual movement would inspire devotional souls. Many beautiful meditations were created by Kabbalists, moralists, and Hasidic Tzadikim. Among the last named Rabbi Nahman of Bratzlaw (1772–1810) ranks foremost as composer of meditations. These devotions have been collected and published in separate books.[5]

Exponents of Hasidism call such private devotions by the name of "Sihoth" — which means heart to heart conversation. They repeatedly urge people to approach the Holy One and to bare their souls before Him in words which embody their own individual yearnings and desires, their own hopes and griefs and joys.

Rabbi Elimelech of Ližansk, and particularly Rabbi Nahman of Bratzlaw, never lost sight of the value of "Siha" to a complete spiritual life. Every man, Rabbi Nahman of Bratzlaw wrote, ought to retire to a place of solitude each day for an hour or two, and pour out his heart before God and implore Him for strength and vision to draw nigh unto Him and to serve Him in truth and sincerity. It makes no difference where one stands in such moments, be it in fields, in a room, in woods, or on mountains, as long as he is alone and undisturbed.[6]

The function of these devotional prayers is one and only one, namely, to draw nigh unto God and to be conscious of His presence. They are to cause man to speak to God even as he would speak to his most intimate friend, and they are to bring about a union of his soul with the soul of the Holy One.

Since devotional prayers are thus spontaneous outpourings of the human heart, it necessarily follows that they must be simple in style and language, so that even the most humble be capable of expressing his thoughts and emotions in such prayers. Rabbi Nahman of Bratzlaw, in fact, was himself a lover of simplicity in devotional prayers, and he urged people to pour out their hearts in prayers of simple style and language.[7] In general, he writes, one ought to make the content of his devotional prayer the thought: "O God, when will I too merit to rise to so high a state and hold communion with Thee. . . ." The language of such prayers, he maintains, ought to be such as one understands best and in which one is most fluent.[8] While he realizes the value of Hebrew and ascribes to it a most important position in Jewish life, he nevertheless maintains that it is not only permissible to pray in "Ashkenaz" — Yiddish — but that it is far better, for it makes it more possible to cleave unto God — since one understands the words of his mouth. He even declares that the only reason for using Hebrew in the official liturgy is that it is the established language; otherwise, it would have been far better to pray in Yiddish — or in any other language which one understands best.[9] He himself uttered devotional prayers in Yiddish, and he wrote them down in the same tongue.[10] Other exponents of Hasidism improvised similar prayers, using both Hebrew and Yiddish in the same prayer,[11] and uttered them in synagogues, as well as in homes and fields and woods and other places of solitude.[12]

"Siha" as distinguished from the regular prayers of the liturgy plays so important a rôle in Hasidic life that it eclipses at times the importance of the regular services. As a whole, however, Hasidism never attempted to abandon the official liturgy; it merely stressed the value of improvising devotional prayers which are to be used before and after the services or any other time during the day. With this view in mind, exponents of Hasidism actually wrote such prayers; some are even ascribed to the Besht.[13] Of Rabbi Shneur Zalman of Liadi it is told that in moments of spiritual awakening he was wont to cry out: "Master of the universe, I desire neither Thy paradise nor Thy bliss in the world to come; I desire Thee and Thee alone![14]" This short prayer epitomizes the noblest and highest thought which runs through Hasidic devotional prayers at large, and especially through those prayers which leading exponents of Hasidism composed for their own daily use.

The prayers of Rabbi Levi-Yitzhak of Berdytschev are unique in Hasidic life. They are really conversations with God. They usually contain no element of petition; they are a defense of the name of the Israel and a justification of Jewish life. Thus, once on New Year's Day, Rabbi Levi-Yitzhok approached the holy ark and said:[15]

"Good morning, Master of the universe!
I, Levi-Yitzhok of Berdytschev, have come to hold
Judgment with You concerning Your people Israel.
What have You against Israel?
Why have You imposed Yourself upon Your people Israel?
Everywhere You say 'Command the children of Israel.'
Everywhere — 'Speak to the children of Israel.'
Father of mercy, how many nations are there in the world?
Persians, Babylonians, Romans.
The Russians — what do they say?
That their emperor is master.
The Germans — what do they say?
That their Kaiser is ruler.
The English — what do they say?
That their king is ruler.

But I Levi-Yitzhok of Berdytschev say
'Magnified and sanctified be the Great Name.'
And I Levi-Yitzhok of Berdytschev say:
'I will not move from this place, from this very spot,
Until there will be an end,
Until there will be an end to this exile.
Magnified and sanctified be the Great Name. . . .'" [16]

Rabbi Elimelech of Ližansk composed a number of devotional prayers. One of them is now printed at the beginning of Hasidic prayer-books. The following is an excerpt from that prayer:[17]

"My Father in heaven! Cause me to merit that Thy faith be ever rooted in my heart, and remove all partitions which stand between me and Thee. Cause me to merit that in the hour when I engage in the study of Tora and in Thy service my thoughts be pure and clear, so that I be able to worship Thee with truth and a perfect heart, and save me from all errors and impediments. Cause me to merit that I unite my heart, my words, my actions, and all my movements and emotions, both revealed and hidden, to Thy service with truth and sincerity. Sanctify me and purify me, and plant in my heart love and fear of Thee. Guard me against all strange thoughts, against haughtiness, anger, and ill-temper, and against all evil things which undermine Thy worship — so holy, so pure, so beloved of Thee. Imbue me with Thy sacred spirit, that I may cleave unto Thee and yearn after Thee. Save me from all envy and jealousy, so that no thought of hatred ever enter my heart. Give me the vision to see in everyone his good qualities, and close my eyes from beholding his defects. Lead me in the path of truth, so that I speak with my friends truthfully and righteously. Amen."

Rabbi Nahman of Bratzlaw used to teach by means of stories and parables. The following is an excerpt from his prayer for good stories: [18]

"Lord of all worlds! Thou art the God who doest wonders through the true righteous men in every generation. Even in our generation there are righteous men who perform real miracles. In Thy great mercy endow me with merit and help me to be able to recount the stories of those true righteous men, all the wonders they have done in public and in secret. For their praise is Thy praise and their glory is Thy glory. And through that may my thoughts be purified from all confused and dangerous ideas which spring forth from petty minds. And may this save me from all tribulations produced by those petty minds. O help me to occupy myself with the lore of the true "tzadikim," the great minds. Thou hast made known unto us that corresponding to each story of the true righteous there is a story of the wicked. Teach me, therefore, whose story I shall recount. There are, too, stories of those who mix up the good with the evil, and wrap themselves in the garment of others; so that the difference between them and the true righteous is as great as the difference between light and darkness. O, may I merit to recount the lore of the true righteous men, so that my thoughts be purified. . . ."

Meditations in the spoken language, in Judeo-German and in Italian started already in the sixteenth century. They were of two types: a. Translations of Hebrew; b. Original compositions, but in the style of the Hebrew prayers, utilizing Midrashic and Kabbalistic elements.[19]

The oldest collection of original "Tehinoth" is that of Abraham Apoteker (Prague, 1590), and there is that of Hayyim Ashkenazi Levi (Basel, 1609). It was primarily the occupation of pious women to compile meditations.[20] It was through their initiative that men decided to take over the task. The title page of the Tehinoth published in Sulzbach, 1798, announces that the book was composed "Because many pious women and especialy my wife approached me to write this collection."

The "Tehinoth" are recited either during the public service at certain points or on certain days or occasions.

The "Tehinoth" in Judeo-German were intended primarily for women and for those unfamiliar with Hebrew. Some of the compilers of translations of Hebrew prayers went so far as to recommend their translations as a substitute for the original prayers. Thus in the introduction to the Siddur by Joseph b. Yakar (Ichenhausen, 1544) the translator says:[21] "I consider those people foolish who wish to recite their prayers in Hebrew although they do not understand a word of it. I wonder how they can have any spirit of devotion in their prayers." Another translator (*Mahzor*, Amsterdam, 1709) says: "Prayer without devotion is like the body without a soul. This means that whoever utters his prayers to God, but does not speak with an earnest heart, he is like a human body which has no life in it. Therefore, any man or woman who cannot read Hebrew must admit that such a *Mahzor* as this will be more useful to him. . . . When everyone will be able to utter his prayers with devotion and will understand what he says, we will merit the coming of the Messiah." [22]

There is another translation called "Liebliche Tefilla und Kräftig Arzhei für guf un' Neshomoh"—"Pleasant prayer and invigorating medicine for body and soul"—by Aaron b. Samuel of Hergerschlitt (Fürth, 1709). In his introduction, the translator says: "It is customary with us that a child must study Hebrew from his early youth which his young mind does not grasp; neither does the teacher know more about it than he learned. As a result, nobody can acquire a religious spirit by such instruction (or by reading religious literature in that language). Therefore religiosity cannot be planted within the spirit of our youth. . . . In order to remedy this deplorable condition, we have decided to translate selected prayers and meditations into the spoken German. Thus, these prayers will penetrate the heart of man and will also reach before God. . . . This translation will do away with the accusation of the Gentiles that we have prayers full of deception toward them. . . ." The translator also tries to justify his action by quoting Sefer Hasidim: "If people who do not know Hebrew come to you, tell them to study the prayer-book in the language which they can understand." [23] This view goes back to the *Talmud* (b. Sota 33a): "Prayer is petition which should be uttered in the language one knows." This in turn is based upon the *Mishna* Sota VII: "Shema, Prayer, and Grace may be said in any tongue."

His Tehinoth, the author writes, are "for a peasant who is not a learned man, for husband and wife that they live in love, and for a maid or a servant." But as soon as the book came off the press the rabbis issued a prohibition against its use because of the author's advice to abandon Hebrew and substitute Yiddish for the prayers. The author was seemingly excommunicated; and after having lost his livelihood, he became a trader and fell into poverty according to his own testimony in his preface. "My parents abandoned me, and without a single friend in the whole world I put my trust in God and in His dear books." [24]

The "Tehinoth" deal not only with religious matters, such as mercy, forgiveness, etc., but also with the daily life of the medieval Jew in his insecure trade and occupation. The wife prays for his well-being during his travels on business through districts which had no protecting laws for the Jew. The following meditation reflects the conditions of the Jew at that time: ". . . Lord of the world, prosper my husband in all his ways. Lead him, dear God, upon the right way that he may have good fortune and blessing in all his work. O deliver him upon his way from all troubles and all evil misfortunes which frequently come to man. I beg of Thee, dear God, protect my husband against false accusations that he may be guarded from terror.

"Grant him knowledge and increase his understanding that he may complete his business successfully and be able to sustain his wife and his children. Guard him against envy (the evil eye) so that no harm may come to him and no disgrace and that none may say that he has defrauded any man.

"Lord of the world, let my husband gain his livelihood without desecrating Thy holy name. Grant him blessing and prosperity that my children may never know poverty and never need the charity of men. Protect my husband upon his way from all pain, that he may come home in joy and in peace, and in prosperity, and in honor. . . ." [25]

"The 'Tehinoth' are folk literature. They represent primarily neither the keen realization of the philosophically minded, nor the precise legal instinct of the codifiers, nor the far-flung fancy of the Kabbalist. They are the prayers of the people, reflecting the uncritical sincerity of humble men and women." [26]

With the progress of enlightenment among the Jews in Western and Central Europe, the language of the countries became their vernacular, replacing the idioms they have developed in the Ghetto. The "Tehinoth" too were rewritten in the modern tongues. In Germany M. Letteris compiled a *Book of Meditations for Israelitish Women* which passed its fifth edition in 1852. The book contains prayers and meditations for week- and holidays, original and translated prayers, meditations for the girl, the bride, the married woman, the mother, the stepmother, the widow, the maid, prayers on the grave of a mother, a daughter, etc.

The Voice of the Daughters of Zion (Roedelheim, 1856) is of a similar type. Of a like character are some collections published in English, as *Book of Life* (London, 1861) by Ascher or *Devotions for the Daughters of Zion* by Bresslau (London, 1861).

Recognizing the great value of meditations, the Reform Movement made extensive use of this form of worship. The meditations incorporated into the *Union Prayer-Book* are numerous. They accompany public services as well as private devotions in the home and on various occasions in the life of the Jew and Jewess.

Furthermore, *Prayer and Praise* published by the C.C.A.R. under the chairmanship of S. Freehof, follows the style of Maamadoth, and has, in addition, a large collection of private devotions.

CHAPTER XIX

THE LITURGY OF REFORM JUDAISM

The first attempt to reform the prayer-book was made in 1795 by the society founded in Amsterdam by "Felix Libertatum." The society was called "Adath Jeshurun."

In Westphalia the Jews received all official rights from Napoleon. There was a Board to take care of all Jewish affairs. Israel Jacobson, a layman of deep consecration to Judaism, was the head of this Board, and he tried to carry into effect the laws made with regard to Synagogue services. He built a temple in Seesen at his own expense in 1810. It was the first time that a Jewish house of worship was called "Temple." He himself made the following corrections in the prayer-book.

1. He abolished piyyutim.
2. He shortened the prayers.
3. He introduced German chorals, the organ, and the sermon in German.

He justified his procedure by saying that the prayers must be in German because the people do not understand Hebrew. The party which opposed him claimed that the more Hebrew used in the prayers the more Hebrew would the people come to know.

As soon as Jacobson established his Reform Temple, the same type of service was established in Frankfurt on the Main, in Cassel, and some other places. The sermon was introduced as obligatory in these services.

The sermon in the public service on Sabbaths and the Festivals was discontinued for several centuries. Only twice a year, before Passover and before the High Holydays, the rabbi used to give a discourse on Sabbath afternoons on religious regulations pertaining to these holidays. Then, there was the "Maggid," the folk-preacher, who would deliver religio-ethical sermons on Sabbaths and also on weekdays in the afternoon, but not during services. Only the large communities had a permanent "Maggid," whereas the smaller places were visited by wandering "Maggidim." [1]

In the school which Jacobson established he introduced the first children's service, and published the first *Jewish Songster* in Cassel, in 1810.[2] He was also the first to introduce the idea of confirmation on Shavuoth, and he himself confirmed his own son. His innovations have remained part of Jewish Reform practice and have exerted an influence upon Conservative Judaism.

After the fall of Napoleon, Israel Jacobson organized a Reform service in 1815 in his own home in Berlin. He himself officiated and preached in German, and he influenced a number of young Jewish students to preach in German, among them being Zunz and Kley. He omitted all piyyutim, the "Tefilla Belahash"—silent prayer—(see Introductory Notes) and the entire Musaf. He was also the first to do away with the chanting of the Tora.

The opponents of Reform, invoking an existing law in Berlin which forbade the conducting of religious services in any place other than the synagogue, closed the service in Jacobson's home. However, as the synagogue had to be temporarily closed for repairs, Hertz Meyer Beer opened his home for services of a Reform character. With the reopening of the synagogue Beer's services were discontinued. Beer then suggested that either two services be held in the synagogue or that the synagogue be divided into two sections.

The Reformers were defeated, and the government decreed that the Jewish worship may not be changed from its old form. Hence, the work of Jacobson could have no effect in Prussia. But in Hamburg which was a free state he met with some success. There a group of people founded a society called "Der Israelitische Tempel Verein" in 1818, and opened a Temple. The Board included men of fine scholarship and prominence. Isaac Frankel, the translator of the Apocrypha from the Greek (or German) into Hebrew, and Meyer Bresselau worked out a prayer-book in 1819, called *Seder Haavoda Keminhag Beth Hadash Asher Be' Hamburg*. They dedicated the prayer-book to Jacobson as a token of deep appreciation to the founder of Reform Judaism. All succeeding prayer-books of the Reform Movement are based on this first attempt.

The innovations in this prayer-book were as follows:

1. German translation of all prayers.

2. Some prayers were in Hebrew and in German, while some were in German only.

3. All references to national restoration in Palestine were eliminated. Such prayers were rephrased to mean the general restoration of mankind. The idea of a personal Messiah was changed to a Messianic Era for all humanity.

4. All references to sacrifices were either omitted or were changed to describe merely conditions of the past without implying any hope to restore the sacrificial cult in the future.

5. The greatest part of medieval poetry was omitted.

This prayer-book was condemned by almost all the prominent rabbis in Central Europe.[3] The Hamburg Rabbinate issued a prohibition against its use.[4]

The editors of the second edition of this prayer-book laid down the following principles in 1841:

1. The prayer-book was to preserve the positive foundation of the religion according to its history and peculiarities.

2. The spirit of it should be in agreement with the current views of European culture and life.

3. The traditional elements should be retained as long as they do not contradict the above mentioned principles.

4. The general contents of the prayer-book and that of divine worship should be permeated with the *pure doctrines* of the ancestral religion. Contradictory elements should be omitted.

"The editors considered the unity of language of no importance, since in olden times, alongside the sacred Hebrew tongue, the Aramaic idiom was permitted into the service, because this was the vernacular of the people. The goal was always dignity, truth, and effectiveness."[5]

The appearance of the second edition brought another prohibition against its use by the Hamburg Rabbinate; this caused a heated fight. The Reform congregation in Hamburg turned to a number of liberal-minded rabbis for their opinion. This time, twelve rabbis answered in favor of the policy of the new prayer-book.[6] For, during the period between 1818 and 1841, a generation of modern trained rabbis grew up in Germany with Reform tendencies.

The prayer-book prepared for the Reform congregation in Berlin (organized in 1845) — *Gebetbuch fuer jüdische Reformgemeinden*[7] consists of two volumes. Volume I is for weekdays, since "the congregation for which this prayer-book was prepared abolished the Sabbath service, and since 1849 has conducted services on Sundays only."[8] This volume contains fifty-four hymns to be sung at the beginning and at the end of the service. Then there follow nine services, or cycles, as they are called, in order to change off from time to time. These cycles are alike in structure. They start with a prayer by the reader followed by a digest of "Adon Olam," "Baruch Sheomar," and "Yotzer." Whereupon choir and congregation recite the first verse of "Shema" and "Gevuroth" in German. The idea of resurrection is retained in "Gevuroth," but the idea of a Redeemer was taken away. A silent prayer for mourners follows. Of the "Kedusha," "Kadosh," "Baruch," and "Yimloch" are retained in Hebrew, while "Hodaa" and "Shalom" are paraphrased in German. There is an insertion for Hanucca and the Ninth of Av. The latter insertion states "We remember today the day on which Jerusalem fell by the mighty hand of the enemy, on which day Judea ceased to be a people of the Lord and its sons and daughters were dispersed in all the parts of the world. . . . Lamenting did they go into captivity, saying that we are doomed to be extinguished among the nations of the world. . . . In days of severe oppression they hoped that Thou wilt cause them to return to the land of promise and that Thou wilt reëstablish the empire of Juda and rebuild the Temple in Jerusalem. . . . Thou didst hear their petitions, but didst not fulfill their prayer, not because Thou wast angry with them, but because Thou hast chosen them to Thy service. Thou didst send them among the peoples of the world. . . . Not because Thou wantest to punish them did they endure persecutions and oppressions, but because Thou wantest them to be able to testify to the invincible power of Thy truth. Therefore, they ought to declare Thy Name in the presence of their abusers, even under severe sufferings. . . . A great and holy work didst Thou entrust into our hands, O God. Thou hast desired that we shall carry the light of Thy Wisdom silently through the world, until the time will come when the eyes of the nations will open to Thy light. Thou hast willed that we shall not ask "What have I transgressed that such a heavy burden shall weigh down upon me and bend me to the ground,' but that we carry it with humility . . . until the hatred of the people shall disappear before the radiance of love which we proclaim in Thy name."

A number of meditations is given dealing with grace, love, harvest, peace, Israel's destiny, etc.

The second volume contains prayers for the High Holydays and the Three Festivals. In the New Year's Day service, which has the same structure as the weekday services, there is included a prayer regarding the revelation on Mount Sinai (p. 26), the Priestly Benediction in Hebrew, and "Alenu" paraphrased in German. It contains also a service for the second day of the New Year. In the service of the evening of the Day of Atonement, "Wenislah" and "Wayyomer" are in Hebrew. The insertions in the third benediction of the Amida are paraphrased in German; likewise are "Atta Behartanu" and the "Widdui." In the morning service, "Nishmath," "Elohai Neshama," "Pethah Lanu Shaar" and other passages are paraphrased in German. It also contains the hymn "Seele, was betruebst du dich" which was rendered into English into "Why art Thou cast down, my soul?" and which was taken over into the *Union Prayer-Book*, Volume II, p. 327.

With the exception of the few Hebrew phrases already mentioned, this prayer-book is entirely in German. Its underlying ideas are universalism, theism, and the mission of Israel. When S. Holdheim became the preacher of the Berlin congregation, he was not in agreement with the tendencies of this ritual. "He found that it was lacking the historical moments, the lack of which gave the ritual a 'semi-Jewish' character." He demanded a revision of the prayer-book.[9] Nevertheless, in his introduction to the revised ritual he established the following principles:

"Everywhere the national and dogmatically narrowing point of view had to yield to the living flow of the purely human and truly religious thought; for a noble, truly pious nature, belief in the universal Father of mankind has more attractive force than the belief in the God of Israel; the doctrine that all men are created in the image of God is of higher poetic worth than the election of Israel. The teaching of a universal law of human brotherhood and love for the neighbor has a greater potency than a particularistic ceremonial legislation. . . . We call particular attention to such prayers as have for their themes the holiness of God and of man, the priestly mission of Israel, the purified Messianic idea. . . . "[10]

"Holdheim carried out his theories to their logical end no matter what the cost. He had not the historical sense nor the consciousness of the solidarity of Israel that Geiger had. Geiger felt that reform must move slowly, not by leaps and bounds; hence frequently his practice lagged far behind his theory; he desired constructive reform, which should permeate all Jewry; his aim was to retain as far as possible the connection with the whole house of Israel and therefore he was content to sacrifice theory for the time, assured that in the progress of the years his theory would be translated into practice."[11]

The negligence of the daily services in the Reform Movement Dr. Philipson holds was due to environmental conditions. "Church-going among the Christian population is confined largely to the weekly day set apart as the religious day; what more natural than that Jews in this environment should stress the Sabbath and holiday service to the neglect of the daily service?"[12] This, however, holds true only of the Protestant denominations.

During the following years, the ritual of the Berlin Reform Congregation was reduced considerably, until it reached at present the minimum size of sixty-three pages for the whole year. The latest edition contains one service for Sunday, with the nucleus of "Yotzer," "Kedusha," "Kaddish," "Shema," "Alenu," and "Adon Olam." Together with the Scriptural reading this service fills all in all eight pages. For the Three Festivals, a hymn and a short meditation are inserted for each holiday, comprising also eight pages. For New Year's Day, a few meditations and hymns are given which contain the idea of repentance and the idea of God as the source of love. "Un'-thanne Tokef" is rendered in the main in German, and the sentence "Utheshuva" is given in Hebrew. Then Psalm 47 follows, and the proclamation of God as the sovereign, "Adonai, Adonai," and the Priestly Benediction are recited in Hebrew. For the second day, "Alenu" is rendered in German and is recited in the place of "Un'thanne Tokef." The whole New Year's service comprises nineteen pages. The evening service for the Day of Atonement opens with Psalm 130, followed by a paraphrase of Psalms 51 and 42 for solo. "Ki Vayyom Hazze" and "Adonai, Adonai" are given in Hebrew. "O Tag des Herrn" (by L. Stein, rabbi in Frankfort o/M) constitutes the main feature of the service. The morning service is ushered in with a hymn, followed by Psalm 103. Then the Kedusha, again "Ki Vayyom Hazze," and a reminiscence of the Avoda are recited. The main service is the same as on other days. Then there follows the Memorial Service and "Kaddish" of which the first four words and the response "Yehê Shemê" are given in Hebrew. The Ne'ila service, here called "Evening Service" has in addition a paraphrase of "Adonai, Ma Adam." Of "Avinu Malkenu" only the idea has been retained in German. Of the five passages only the first two were taken from the traditional text; the others are:

1. A petition to be saved from temptation.
2. A petition for love and brotherhood.
3. A petition for eternal peace and justice.
4. A petition for the Day of the Lord.

At the end the response *adonai hu haĕlohim* is printed in Hebrew seven times. The whole ritual for the Day of Atonement is covered in twenty pages.

There is a special service for Hanucca in which the brave heroism of the Hasmoneans to save the Jewish religion is emphasized. Instead of "Maoz Tzur" a German stanza in the meter of that Hebrew hymn is given. A Confirmation Service closes the prayer-book; it consists of the regular ritual, plus Isaiah 59:21; Psalm 115:12–15, and an introductory hymn.

From its very beginning the congregation introduced the following reforms:

Men and women shall sit together. The men shall be without hats and without Tallith. Besides "Shema," "Kedusha," and the Priestly Benediction, the whole service shall be conducted in German. The prayers shall be accompanied by choir singing and instrumental music. The prerogative of the Aaronites shall be abolished. The blowing of the Shofar shall be omitted.

At its beginning the Reform congregation found enthusiastic response from Berlin Jewry. But gradually it deteriorated to an insignificant body. And this in spite of the efforts made in the eighties by the preacher M. Levin to lead the congregation back to traditional Judaism.

However, its reforms exerted a strong influence upon the Reform congregations in America.

The prayer-book compiled by Leopold Stein in Frankfort o/M *Seder Haavoda* (Vol. I, 1882, Vol. II, 1878) is of an entirely different tendency. In this ritual almost all the standard prayers were retained. The changes are in conformity with the ideas of the compiler, i.e., abolition of sacrificial elements, the Davidic dynasty, and of the return of Israel to Palestine. He upholds, however, the hope of the rebuilding of Zion and of a Messiah who will spread the word of God from Jerusalem. In his introduction the compiler states: "We left the Messiah, the bearer of our lofty ideals, his sacred place (Zion). Where else? Not in Berlin, the metropolis of Protestantism; not in Rome, the center of paganism of old and now of the Catholic world; but in Jerusalem, the holy city, from there the light will shine again for all mankind." This idea is somewhat similar to the *spiritual* or *cultural Zionism* of the present day.

The compiler gave a selection of Table-songs (Zemiroth) in a German poetical rendition; the Haggada in a fine translation; and the Book of Esther in German. His emendations in the Hebrew are most successful from a linguistic standpoint, and his notes and explanations are better than those in other Reform rituals.

Since 1819 many attempts were made in Germany along this direction. Almost every rabbi with Reform tendencies edited a prayer-book in accordance with his views. However, the one which gained most popularity was the prayer-book edited by A. Geiger in 1854 and revised in 1870. In his preface the editor laid down the following principles:

1. The prayer-book shall retain in general its historical character in conformity with the history of Judaism. There-

fore, Hebrew remains the main medium of prayer, though here and there not free from Orientalism in expression.

2. Short German prayers, however, shall be included, especially in the services for the festivals. Furthermore, the Hebrew text must be paraphrased in a German rendition, closer to our train of thought.

3. The services must be shortened to such an extent that all repetitions and parts without important content should be omitted, that the spirit of devotion shall not be disturbed.

4. The historic moments in Judaism must be presented in the light of the pure progressive conception. Particularism and one-sidedness must be omitted.

5. All materialistic descriptions of God, angelology, and the belief in bodily resurrection must be eliminated. The latter must be expressed in such a way as to include the concept of spiritual immortality.

6. The historical position of Israel must be interpreted in a way whereby Judaism is the bearer of the religion of truth and light. Israel's mission is to proclaim this message to the world, until it will be accepted by all men, and Israel will ultimately broaden to embrace the human race.

7. The division between Israel and the peoples has no right to be placed in a prayer-book. On the contrary, expression should be given to the joy that such partitions are disappearing. Our hope for the future shall be the unity of all nations into one family of truth, justice, and peace. The hopes of the restoration of a Jewish state in Palestine and the rebuilding of the Temple as a center for Israel as well as the gathering of the exiled, are extinct in our consciousness. The expression of these hopes in prayer would be an untruth.

8. All references to the sacrificial cult must be omitted.

With all these principles, Geiger's prayer-book still gives the appearance of a Hebraic book of worship when compared with Holdheim's prayer-book.

In addition, Geiger's prayer-book has a service for Purim, for the Ninth of Av with some Kinoth, and for "Hoshana Rabba" with several "Hoshanoth." The Musaf and the most important piyyutim are retained. With the exception of very few, as the prayers for the Government and congregation, some meditations, and the interpretation of the "Avoda," the prayers are conducted in Hebrew.

The first Reform prayer-book in America was published by the Charleston congregation in 1830 — the first Reform congregation in the United States of America; this prayer is called: "The Sabbath Service and Miscellaneous Prayers, adopted by the Reformed Society of Israelites, founded in Charleston, South Carolina." Though patterned after the Hamburg Prayer-book, it went considerably further in its striving to go back to Moses and the prophets. "The stress laid in the Charleston Prayerbook on the immortality of the soul and on the ethical and universal character of Judaism appears as a distinctive feature in all subsequent Reform rituals."[13]

The ritual mostly used by the Reform congregations in America for almost forty years was that edited by Isaac M. Wise — "Divine Service for the American Israelites" — *Minhag America* — published in 1859 and withdrawn by the editor in 1894. Though based upon the principles outlined at the beginning of this chapter, this ritual retained Hebrew as the language of prayer and gave an English (with some German) translation of the texts. A great part of the traditional texts and poetry was retained; the Musaf service was also kept.

Mention ought to be made of another prayer-book with Reform tendencies which was arranged by Benjamin Szold and Marcus Jastrow, called *Abodath Israel*. It was published with a German and English translation in 1873. Following A. Geiger's emendations in the Hebrew texts, it differs from the ritual of Isaac M. Wise in being more radical with regard to the selection and retention of the texts. It gives but a minor part to English prayers. It is still used in a few congregations.

After a century of experimentation and attempts to reform the traditional ways of worship and the material of the liturgy, the Reform Movement in the United States of America finally based itself upon principles common to all Reform congregations and adopted a ritual now in general use.

These principles are:

1. Omission of all references to the sacrificial cult.

2. Omission of all references to bodily resurrection, being replaced by the idea of the immortality of the soul.

3. Omission of all references to the restoration of the Jewish State and the return of the Jews to Palestine (although a number of Reform rabbis are Zionists).

4. Omission of almost all poetical insertions (piyyutim), in order to make the services more comprehensible, simpler, and shorter.

5. Omission of repetitions. For that purpose, the repetition of the Amida was eliminated, and the Additional Service (Musaf) was either omitted entirely or shortened.

6. The prayers should be understood by the people. Hence, the greatest part of the Hebrew text was dropped, and prayers in the vernacular were introduced.

7. The Scriptural reading from the Pentateuch was shortened and read without cantillation. The reading for the Haftara may also be taken from the Hagiographs, and is to be given in the vernacular only.

8. The sermon was made obligatory in almost every service.

9. Prayers and meditations were inserted which reflect the modern train of thought.

10. Omission of angelology and mystic elements, as well as prayers expressing antiquated and obsolete beliefs and ideas.

11. Omission of a personal Messiah, being replaced by the concept of a Messianic Age.

12. The mission of Israel among the nations of the world is emphasized.

13. The idea of universalism is stressed. Rabbi David Philipson states: "The chief and underlying principle of the reform movement is the universalistic interpretation of Judaism as over against the nationalistic. If the reform does not signify this, it signifies nothing. This is the burden of its thought." [14]

The ritual now in use is: the "Union Prayer-Book" — *seder tefilloth yisrael* — edited and published by the Central Conference of American Rabbis, under the chairmanship of K. Kohler, introduced since 1892–4, third revised edition 1922–4, 1925–7 under the chairmanship of D. Philipson.

This ritual is used by almost all Reform congregations in the United States, approximately two hundred and eighty.

In its structure and choice of Hebrew texts this prayer-book is based mostly upon that edited by D. Einhorn — *olath hatta-*

mid — published in German in Baltimore in 1856–8. It was twice translated into English, once in 1896, and again in 1897 (by Emil G. Hirsch).

K. Kohler characterizes Einhorn's *Prayer-Book* and its influence upon the *Union Prayer-Book*, as well as Einhorn's ideas of modern Jewish liturgy, as follows: "Isaac M. Wise . . . wanted to make haste slowly in his Reform work." But "David Einhorn . . . would not give up one iota of his Reform principles, be the number rallying around his banner ever so small. Hence, the former worked and agitated for his *Minhag America*, that is, a revised form of the old prayerbook in which, exactly as was done by the Hamburg Temple, by Meyer of Stuttgart, Stein, Geiger, Merzbacher and others. . . . Einhorn, however, stepped forth with a prayerbook, all made of one piece, all conceived and written in the spirit of reform, the work of a religious genius, a veritable treasure-house of inspiring thought, a production embodying the best elements of the ancient ritual and at the same time voicing the deepest yearnings and longings of the modern Jew. . . .

"As Einhorn stated in his preface, all the other Reform prayerbooks removed the old familiar formulas and features without replacing them by corresponding new ones expressive of the views and feelings of the modern Jew; whereas the precious thoughts handed down in the old ritual are preserved here in spiritualized form. No ambiguity as to words here, no halting between two opinions. Every lie uttered in prayer is blasphemy before God's throne, be it the antiquated belief in resurrection or the hope for the return to Jerusalem. A Reform prayerbook must, in clear, unmistakable accents, give utterance to what the Jew in our advanced state of thought really believes and fervently feels. The only Reform ritual which previously attempted to do this was that of the Berlin Reform Congregation . . . yet it, too, had its great deficiencies. It lacks the pulsations of the Jewish heart. It appeals to reason, rather than to the soul. It fails to echo forth the pangs and longings of the Jew in the past, remorse-stricken at his sins in view of the unequalled sufferings he was undergoing, while torn away from his ancestral home. And herein lies the great merit of Einhorn's ritual. It voices the spirit of ancient Israel as it lives in the new age and in the religious consciousness of the modern Jew. The glow of love is there, and reverence and loyalty to the past permeates the whole, while the new demands are fully recognized. Weeping over the glory of days gone by is transformed into outbursts of thanksgiving and joy over the dawn of the new day of promise and of hope for both Israel and humanity . . . Meanwhile the C.C.A.R. decided to give the Union of American Hebrew Congregations a uniform prayerbook. . . . I for my part can not help saying that it was an adoption by organized American Reform Judaism of Einhorn's views when in 1894 the second volume of the Union Prayerbook, based upon Einhorn's ritual as submitted by the writer, was adopted by the Conference in Atlantic City under the presidency of Isaac M. Wise, who solemnly declared that in the interest of the union and consolidation of American Reform Judaism he was ready to part with his long cherished *Minhag America* and adopt the new prayerbook instead. . . . Whatever shortcomings the Union Prayerbook . . . may have, owing to the fact that it lacks the fire of genius and the uniqueness of style of its model, Einhorn's spirit will ever live in it and ever quicken anew the religious consciousness and devotion of the worshippers who use it, as no other ritual." [15]

The book is divided into two volumes. Volume I contains services for Sabbath, the Three Festivals, Weekdays, and Prayers for Private Devotion. A table of Bible readings is given at the end.

I. The Evening Service for Sabbath starts with a meditation concerning the value of Sabbath as a day of spiritual rest and communion with God. The service begins with Psalm 92 which the choir is supposed to sing either in Hebrew or in English. The next paragraph is read responsively; it consists of a selection of Psalm verses in which some of the verses from Psalms 95–99 — *lechu neranena* — are included. The poem *Lecha Dodi* is omitted.

Then follow the "Barechu" and the two first benedictions of "Shema," the wording of the benediction being abbreviated. Of the Shema only the first paragraph and one sentence of the third paragraph (Num. 15:40 and the first three words of 41) are given. The next paragraph is again a responsive reading of *emeth weĕmuna* of which these sentences speaking of revenge and the miraculous passing through the Red Sea are left out. The same is true of the next passage: "Mi Chamocha" which is sung by the choir and which concludes with the third benediction. The fourth benediction *hashkivenu* is eliminated. From *wesham'ru* (Exod. 31 : 16–17) the last verse "that in six days the Lord made the heavens and the earth, and on the seventh day He rested and ceased from work" has been omitted because "doubt had been thrown on the verification of the six day creation."[16]

In the Amida, which is mostly recited by the Minister, the first two and the intermediate benediction are retained. In the first benediction, the word *goêl* (personal redeemer) is changed to *gĕula* (redemption). In the second benediction, the reference to bodily resurrection has been omitted. The benediction concludes with "Who hast implanted within us immortal life." From the intermediate benediction only the closing paragraph has been retained. This is read in unison.

A silent devotion closes with "May the words of my mouth . . . be acceptable in Thy sight. . . ." (Psalm 19 : 15) which is sung by the choir.

Here follow a selection of recitations for the minister and responsive readings for four or five Sabbaths of the month, for the Sabbath during Passover and Tabernacles, for the Sabbath of Repentance, for the Sabbath during Hanucca (which contains an abstract of the II Maccabees, including the benediction over the lights and the hymn "Maoz Tzur" in English paraphrase), and for the Sabbath preceding Purim. The material for responses is culled chiefly from the Psalms, while the prayers for the Minister are free compositions.

After these readings an "Anthem" [17] or hymn is sung, whereupon the "Adoration" — a free English rendition of *alenu* — is read; this is deleted of all particularistic references. Of the Hebrew text only one sentence — *waanahnu corĕim* — was retained. The Mourner's Kaddish with the insertion composed for the first Reform prayerbook in Hamburg, 1819, is recited by Minister and mourners. This passage reads *al yisrael wĕal tzaddikaya* — "On Israel and on the righteous ones and on all those who departed from this world . . ." (see Chapter VIII).

The service is concluded with the singing of "Adon Olam" either in Hebrew or English.

Every Hebrew text is rendered in a free translation or paraphrase in English. The paragraphs for unison and responsive reading, though some of them are given in both languages, are usually recited in English. This is true of all the services, with the exception of very few sentences like "Barechu" and "Shema" which are recited in both Hebrew and English and the three responsive sentences in the "Kedusha" (Kadosh, Baruch, Yimloch) which are usually sung in Hebrew only.

II. The Sabbath morning service likewise begins with a meditation. The choir then sings "Ma Tovu" either in Hebrew or English. Then three paragraphs are read in English. They are free translations of the "Morning Benedictions"—(*elohay neshama*, *ribbon col haolamim*, and *yehi ratzon*)—(see Chapter VIII).

Nothing has been retained from the "Verses of Song." The Minister proceeds with the "Barechu." The first two benedictions and the third benediction of the "Shema" are given in a very short form in Hebrew and in English, omitting all references to angelology and revenge and all special insertions for Sabbaths (see Chapter X). The "Shema" appears in the same form as described in the evening service.

The Amida has the first two benedictions as in the evening service. The "Kedusha" consists of parts of the "Shaharith" and "Musaf" Kedushas as follows:

a. *nekaddesh* — Shaharith.
b. *kadosh.*
c. *addir* — Musaf for holidays.
d. *baruch.*
e. *ehad hu* — Musaf, *shenith* omitted.
f. *yimloch.*

Then there follows the third benediction, omitting the sentence "for Thou art a great and holy God and King."

From the intermediate benediction only "Our God . . ." was retained, as in the evening service.

A similar collection of readings, as in the evening service, for the four or five Sabbaths of the month, and so forth, follow. In the three concluding benedictions, the references to the restoration of the Temple and the sacrificial cult, the return of the

Shechina to Zion, the prayer *yaale weyavo*, the passage for Hanucca, the second part of the benediction of "Hoda'a" including the seal, and the Priestly Benediction are omitted. In the last benediction, the wording was changed to include all peoples; it concludes with the old formula —*Ose hashalom*. Its English is really a new prayer for peace.

A short silent devotion based on *elohay netzor* with the singing of "May the words" by the choir closes the Amida.

On semi-holidays, Hanucca, and the New Moon a much abbreviated "Hallel" is read. It consists of Psalm 118:1–4 in Hebrew and English; verses 5–8 and 14–19 are read responsively in English; and the last verses are repeated in Hebrew.

Before taking out the Scroll Psalm 24:3–6 is read in English, while verses 7 and 8 are sung by the choir either in Hebrew or English. Then the Minister recites usually in Hebrew and English—*beth yaakov, tora* (Isaiah 2:5; Deut. 33:4) and the "Shema." An abbreviated *lecha adonai* is sung by the choir.

The Minister says the benediction over the Scriptures in Hebrew (see Chapter VIII), and reads a few verses from the weekly portion, after which he recites the concluding benediction over the Tora. The first benediction over the Haftara and the Haftara itself he reads in English.

For the announcement of the New Moon an abbreviation of Rav's prayer—*yehi ratzon*—is given in English. The prayer for the congregation and the Government is in English.

When returning the Scroll to the ark "Gadlu" is recited and "Hodo" is sung by the choir. The Minister recites either in Hebrew or in English a few Biblical sentences beginning with *torath adonai* and ending with "Behold, a good doctrine has been given unto you; forsake it not" (Prov. 4:2). Whereupon the choir sings in Hebrew or in English *Etz hayyim* (Prov. 3:18, 17), while the verse of Lamentations 5:21 which concludes this paragraph is omitted.

Here a hymn is to be sung; then there follows the sermon, and after that another hymn. Psalm 145 is given as a responsive reading. The service concludes with the "Adoration" and the "Mourner's Kaddish." The closing hymn is "En Kelohenu" in Hebrew. The Minister dismisses the congregation with an improvised benediction.

The Musaf service is omitted.

III. The Sabbath Afternoon Service consists of a few verses from *uva letziyon* (see Chapter VIII), of "Ashre," Psalm 145 in the form of a responsive reading in Hebrew and English, of the three introductory benedictions of the Amida, and of the Kedusha as outlined in the evening service. An abbreviated form of the first paragraph of the intermediate benediction is given. After that, the Scroll is taken out for which the same service is repeated as in the morning. This is followed by a responsive reading from Psalm 104, and the service closes with the Adoration and Kaddish. Selections from Tractate Avoth in English translations follow this service for the Sabbaths between Passover and the Feast of Weeks. Since no service is held on Sabbath afternoon in any temple, the afternoon service is consequently seldom used.

IV. The services for the Three Festivals consist of the same elements treated in the Sabbath services, with but the few following changes:

The evening service begins with psalm-verses in Hebrew and English (p. 171), followed by the Minister's reading in which the remembrance of Israel's past "when Israel dwelt in his own land as a nation" and God's protection of His people are related. But "now that the whole earth has become their habitation, the children of Israel still assemble on this day of sacred memories to offer unto Thee the more acceptable sacrifices of prayer . . . charity, and benevolence." The responsive reading then follows. Before the Amida the verse of Leviticus 23:44 is read.

The intermediate benediction is a digest of that text in the Orthodox ritual (see Chapter XV), omitting all references to the restoration of the Temple, the sacrificial cult, and the gathering of Israel in Palestine. The mission of Israel is pronounced in the revised sentence, "Thou hast chosen us from among all nations to be Thy precious people" (the last expression is taken from Exod. 19:5).[18] Responsive readings from Psalm 107 then follow for the first and seventh day of Passover with a concluding prayer by the Minister in which it is stated that "not only didst Thou bring our fathers out of the slavery of Egypt, but in every land and in every age hast Thou guided and protected us." In the Minister's prayer for Shavuoth, the statement is made that "Thy law has become a light unto the nations; the promises, spoken through Thy prophets, are the hope of the world; Israel still yearns to be the messenger of Thy word."

In the prayer for Succoth we read: "As from the tiny seed Thou bringest forth the blossom and the fruit, so didst Thou cause Israel, the seed of Thy planting, to grow into a sturdy tree, bearing fruit for the nations of the earth. . . . Animated by faith in Thee may we never cease to hope and to labor for that spiritual harvest, when all Thy children, shall be gathered together under the banner of Thy truth."

In the prayer for Shemini Atzareth thanks are given for the bountiful harvest, and the desire expressed not to forget the poor and the needy.

The "Adoration," "Kaddish," and the hymn "Yigdal" in Hebrew and English close the service.

The Morning Service is ushered in with Psalm 100 in Hebrew and English. From the "Verses of Song" an abbreviated form of "Nishmath" (see Chapter X) is given in both languages. The "Shema" and its benediction and the Amida are the same as on Sabbath, save the intermediate benediction which is the same as in the evening service. Then responsive readings and prayers for each holiday are given expressing the same ideas as those for the evening service mentioned above.

In the concluding benediction, the Priestly Benediction is included. The "Hallel" consists of Psalms 113, 117, and 118 in both languages.

When taking out the Scroll, Isaiah 2:1–4 is read in English and *en camocha* till *bashalom* is recited (see Chapter VIII). Then "Adonai, Adonai . . ." — the Thirteen Attributes — is recited by the Minister and sung by the choir, omitting the last word *wenakkê*. The rest of the service is the same as on Sabbath morning.

Only one Scroll is taken out. The readings from the second Scroll which deal with the sacrifices are omitted.

The readings are abbreviated and changed to a large extent.

For the first day of Passover: Exodus 12:37–42; 13:3–10, and for the seventh day: Exodus 14:30–31; 15:1–18. For Shavuoth: Exodus 19:1–8, 20:1–18. For the first day of Succoth: Leviticus 23:33–44, and for Shemini Atzereth: Deuteronomy 34. The portions for the Haftara readings are entirely different selections from those in the Orthodox ritual.

Since the second days of the holidays were omitted, the Feast of the Rejoicing in the Law was also dropped.

On Shemini Atzereth, a short prayer in English substitutes the Prayer for Rain and Dew of which only three Hebrew sentences were retained.

Psalm 150 is the closing hymn. It is usually sung by the choir in an intricate musical setting, and cannot, therefore, be called a hymn.

V. The Evening Service for Weekdays starts with a few psalm-verses in both languages; the first two are also employed in the Orthodox service (Psalm 134:1–3). Then there follow six responsive readings for each day of the weekdays. The text of the Shema and its benediction is the same as on Friday evening. The Amida consists of the first two benedictions already explained and of 4, 5, 6, 8, and 13 of the intermediate benedictions. Only the last benediction has the eulogy.

VI. The Evening Service at the House of Mourning is ushered in with a prayer and a responsive reading. Then there follows the "Shema" and its first two benedictions, and then Micah 6:8 and a recitation for Minister and congregation, based upon the second and the eighth benedictions of the Amida, are read. The "Adoration" and "Kaddish" close the service.

VII. The Morning Service for Weekdays consists of an English prayer by the Minister, the "Shema" and its first two benedictions in both languages, of six responsive readings for as many days of the week, and of "Mi Chamocha" and the seal of the third benediction in English only. The first two benedictions of the Amida are also in English only, the three Kedusha responses are in Hebrew, while the rest of the service is in English, the concluding benedictions being in that language. The "Adoration" and "Kaddish" close the service.

VIII. There is a selection of Daily Prayers for individuals, for adults and children, for morning and night. They consist of a short introduction, the first two verses of "Shema," and in the night prayer the Hebrew sentence: "Into His hand I commend my spirit when I am asleep and awake. For Thy salvation I hope, O Lord."

There is a short rendition of Grace in English with the Hebrew ending to be recited before and after the meal.

There is also the "Kiddush" for the Friday evening meal and for the Festivals. Parts of Proverbs 31 are given for Friday evening. Then there follows a thanksgiving for the blessings of God during the week. The benedictions over wine and bread are given in both Hebrew and English. In the Kiddush for the Festivals there is a special insertion for each holiday.

In this section there is also a very short home service for the celebration of Hanucca.

IX. The "Miscellaneous Prayers" contain meditations for bride and bridegroom, for the consecration of a home, for family celebrations, for a journey, a prayer before passing through danger, a prayer in time of trouble, a prayer on the birth of a child and one on naming a child, prayers on sickness, prayers said by one in dying condition which concludes with "Shema," a prayer when in bereavement, and a prayer on the anniversary of a death.

It also contains prayers in the cemetery on dedicating tombstones, at the grave of a husband, wife, brother, sister, child, relative or friend, teacher or a great person. They are all in English but follow along the same lines of the traditional texts treated in Chapters IX and XVIII.

The second volume is dedicated to the services for the High Holydays.

A. Services for New Year's Day:

I. The Evening Service for the New Year is introduced by an impressive meditation in which the actions of man in the past year are surveyed. "Let no self-deception hide from me the record of sin and short-coming, of opportunities neglected, of time misspent, of abilities and powers perverted to lower purposes against my own better impulse and knowledge."

The choir then sings Psalm 121 in Hebrew or English. A prayer by the Minister and a responsive reading (Psalm 90) follow. The "Shema" and its benedictions are repeated as on Sabbath and the Festivals. Before the Amida, Psalm 81:2, 4–5 is inserted. In the Orthodox ritual, verse 2 is not mentioned. The Amida consists of the first two benedictions including the insertions "Zochrenu" and "Mi Chamocha." Of the five paragraphs inserted in the third benediction only the last one has been retained. A responsive reading (Psalm 103) and a prayer by the Minister follow; in this prayer the hope is voiced that "God's truth become manifest to all men, so that, united in fellowship, they may strive to do Thy will with perfect hearts." This idea was taken over from the traditional Amida. The universalistic ideas of the four inserted paragraphs in the third benediction, mentioned above, are embodied in one paragraph (pp. 26–27). The rest of the Amida is merely a repetition of the Amida for the Festivals. Then five verses of the "Avinu Malkenu" are read in Hebrew or English. The sermon, "Adoration," and "Kaddish" follow; and "Adon Olam" closes the service.

II. The Morning Service too is ushered in with a meditation in which God is asked to "strengthen and guide us in the coming year." It is the viewpoint of Reform as of traditional Judaism that man is too weak to change his conduct by his own powers; and, therefore, needs divine help; at the same time, it upholds man's freedom to choose between good and evil.

As on the Festivals, the service begins with Psalm 100, and the paragraph "Nishmath" is also repeated. The "Shema" and its benedictions follow in the same wording as on Sabbaths and the Festivals. The Amida is the same as in the evening service, plus the Kedusha and a digest of the concluding paragraph of the intermediate benediction in both languages. The concluding benedictions are the same as on the Festivals.

For taking out the Scroll the Sabbath service is used plus "Adonai, Adonai." Four of the five verses of the "Avinu Malkenu" recited in the evening service are used plus four additional verses taken from the traditional text.

The reading from the Pentateuch is from Genesis 22 (i.e., the reading for the second day in the Orthodox ritual). The Haftara is taken either from I Samuel 2:1–11 or from Isaiah 55.

After the reading, the "Shofar Service" follows. The names and ideas of Malchuyoth, Zichronoth, and Shoferoth, as presented in the Musaf service of the Orthodox ritual, are retained in their universalistic aspects only. After each part, the Shofar is sounded: tĕkia, shĕvarim, and tĕrua. The parts are composed of responsive readings and of prayers read by the Minister.

The sermon, the "Adoration," and the "Kaddish" conclude the service which, as on the Festivals, closes with Psalm 150 as a hymn.

B. Services for the Day of Atonement:

III. The Evening Service is preceded by a meditation which speaks of confession and pleads for the welfare of the family. This is followed by a hymn "O come, day of God," based on Leopold Stein's "Tag d. Herrn," and then Psalm 130 is read by the Minister with responses by the choir.

The text of Col Nidré is omitted, and the traditional text "Wenislah" is recited. The Shema and its benedictions and the Amida are repeated as in the evening service for the New Year. Before the Amida Leviticus 16:30 is recited. Of the poetical insertions only "Yaale" is retained; it is paraphrased in English: "Unto Thee." A responsive reading follows, and short excerpts from the "Seliha" and "Widdui" service are given. The alphabetical confession "Ashamnu" is reduced to three words, "Al Het" only to nine verses, and the hymn "Ki Anu Amecha" is abbreviated. The seal of the intermediate benediction closes the main section of the service.

Then there follow a responsive reading from Psalm 139 and the five verses from "Avinu Malkenu" as in the Evening Service of the New Year. The sermon, "Adoration," and "Kaddish" follow, and the service closes with "Yigdal."

IV. The Morning Service also begins with a meditation, followed by an English rendition of "Adon Olam." A selection of the "Verses of Song" from the Sabbath and Festival services is given in both languages. This selection consists of: I Chronicles 16; Psalms 145–148, 34, 33, and 19. Then the same text as on New Year follows with the concluding benediction as in the Evening Service. The four insertions in the third benediction are given in both languages. In the second paragraph, the passage: "Joy to Thy land, gladness to Thy city, a flourishing horn unto David Thy servant, and a clear shining light unto the son of Jesse, Thine anointed" is paraphrased and rendered in English "Hasten the day that will bring gladness to all the dwellers on earth and victory of the spirit to those who bear witness to Thy unity."[19]

The responsive reading is paraphrased from the "Selihoth." The "Kerova" — *enosh ma yizke* — is likewise a paraphrase from the "Shaharith" service of Yom Kippur.

A confession (Widdui) is given in the form of a silent meditation. Its spirit may be gathered from the following extracts: "Day after day I have sought my own pleasure and gain without a thought of the higher purpose of my life. Again and again I have turned a deaf ear to the promptings of my better nature and have permitted the evil inclination to swerve me from the path of purity and right." "Give me the strength in the coming days to withstand folly and temptation, evil and wickedness. In all my doings make me to recognize every day and every hour that I am shaping for weal or for woe the destiny of my immortal soul."

Then there follow prayers for the aged, for women, for young men, for children, for members of the congregation, and for the individual. Whereupon the same texts for the "Seliha" and for the "Widdui" follow as in the evening service. The service for taking out and returning the Scroll is the same as on New Year. The readings are from Deuteronomy 29:9–14; 30:11–20; and from Isaiah 57:14–21, 58.

V. The Afternoon Service is ushered in with the soulful poem "The Sinner's Tear" which is sung by the choir. The "Seliha" — *elêcha teshukathi* — by Meyir Rothenburg which is a "piyyut" for the Sabbath before Succoth is paraphrased in English with responsive readings from Psalms 143, 25, and 101. The Minister then reads selections from Job 8 and 11, and *elohim êli ata* by Solomon b. Gabirol which is the "Reshuth" for "Nishmath" on Yom Kippur in the Sephardic ritual, while both Minister and congregation read responsively from Isaiah 25–26, Psalms 86, 18, 65, and 40. Then *Uněthanne tokef* and *Alenu* are given in both languages in abbreviated forms.

The "Avoda" follows in a paraphrased form mostly in English; only a few sentences are retained in Hebrew. Preceding this section, a confession by the Minister is read: "We have by Thy grace taught the world the sanctity of a weekly day of rest, and that the Sabbath is the sign of the tie that binds us to

Thee. Yet, we have denied our teaching by refusing to allow the week of toil with hours of rest and worship. Thus we are discrediting ourselves as ministers of the Lord, as a kingdom of priests, planted by Thee, and as a holy people, called by Thee to give light to the world. . . ." "Also the world's injustice, and the persecution of Israel, have forced upon us the task of self-defense to such a degree as not to leave us strength to examine our own lives with impartial search for the truth. We have not made our sufferings a discipline for our souls. . . ." And concludes: "Praised be Thy Name, O Holy One of Israel, Who hast sanctified us for Thy service and hast consecrated us as a messenger of good tidings to mankind."

The content of the Avoda is not as in the Orthodox ritual — i.e., a description of the splendor of the service in the Temple of Jerusalem, with a plea for the restoration for which we are yearning as the culmination of our hopes for our future, but as a memory of the beginning of our worship of the living God. "When spiritual darkness covered the earth. . . . And today, wherever we dwell, we still look back with reverence to that sacred spot, remembering that from Zion went forth the Law and the word of God from Jerusalem." The High Priest "felt himself to be as human as others and as prone to sin, for there is no man so righteous that doeth good and sinneth not. Like unto the High Priest, may Israel's teachers today bear themselves humbly and be watchful of their responsibility. . . . Like unto the congregation of old, may all Israel be reunited with Thee this day. . . . May they who have grown cold and indifferent be filled with fervor, so that the house of Israel may again become one congregation, bound together in the worship of Thee and in devotion to Thy service. . . . The prophetic spirit lives in Israel as of yore; still is he Thy servant and Thy witness unto the peoples of the earth. Confidently we await the blessed day when Thou Who didst reveal Thyself to our fathers shalt be acknowledged as God by all mankind. . . . Let superstition, falsehood, malice vanish everywhere. Send forth Thy light and Thy truth to those who grope in darkness, and knowledge of Thee to those who follow after strange gods; and may Thy house be called a house of prayer for all peoples. . . . On this day our fathers everywhere recalled with deep sorrow the solemn rites of atonement in the Temple at Jerusalem and lamented the glory which had departed from Zion's hill. . . . But Thou, O Lord, dost not delight in sacrificial altars; and priestly pomp pleases Thee not. Thou hast taught us through Thy prophets what is good and what Thou dost require of us: to do justly, to love mercy, and to walk humbly with Thee . . . to break the bonds of wickedness and to free the oppressed. . . . And when Thou didst send us forth to all parts of the earth, it was but to bear witness to this, Thine eternal truth, and to glorify Thy holy Name throughout the world. . . . When Thy holy Temple was destroyed, and Israel was driven from his home to become a wanderer in foreign lands, little did Thy people in their mournful plight foresee that larger destiny which Thou hadst appointed for them. By Thy grace, O god, it has also been given us to see in our dispersion over the earth not a means of punishment but a sign of blessed privilege. Scattered among the nations of the world, Israel is to bear witness to Thy power and Thy truth and to endeavor to unite all peoples in a covenant of brotherhood and peace.

"And though we cherish and revere the place where stood the cradle of our people, the land where Israel grew up like a tender plant, and the knowledge of Thee rose like the morning-dawn, our longings and aspirations reach out toward a higher goal. The morning-dawn shall yet brighten into a radiant noon-day; the tender sprout shall yet become a heaven-aspiring tree beneath which all the families of the earth will find shelter. This is the gracious promise proclaimed by Thy prophets . . . all Thy children will unite in peace and love to serve Thee."

Here follows a selection of the "Selihoth" in both languages, concluding with "Hayyom Teamtzenu."

Readings "selections from the Bible and Jewish Literature" are appropriately provided, both, to familiarize the people with these wonderful creations, and to fill in the time. The selections are well chosen; they are from the Bible, from the Apocrypha, from the *Talmud*, and from medieval Jewish writers, like Maimonides, Bachya Ibn Pakuda, etc.

The Scriptural reading in the afternoon is taken from

Exodus 33:12 to 34:9. The Haftara is taken from Jonah 3–4. The service for taking and replacing the Scroll is the same as on the Three Festivals.

The injustices which prevail in the social-economic life is stressed in a long reading by the Minister. "Great plenty and abject poverty, limitless power and utter weakness exist side by side." This condition is certainly contrary to the ideal of Israel's prophets and lawgivers.

VI. The Memorial Service is in its form a new creation. Its place is before the Concluding Service. This fact introduces new content and interest into the worship of the day.

It begins with the singing of *adonai ma adam* by the choir either in Hebrew or English — "O Lord, what is man?" A responsive reading, chosen from parts of the Psalms dealing with the destiny of man and his inevitable end, follows. "Passions burn in the human breast and beguile to pleasure and to sinfulness." "Human life is a continual struggle against forces without and passions within." "Discontent abides in the palace and in the hut." "The grave levels all distinction and makes the whole world kin." But "only the dust returns to dust; the spirit which Thou hast breathed into us returns to Thee, its everliving source." Punishment after death is certain, and "he who toils but for vain things and boasts of his might, must dread the grave. . . ." "Suffer us not to pass away in our sins, O Judge of life and death."

Psalm 23 is read and the poem "Why art Thou cast down, my soul?" is sung by the choir.

In a prayer by the Minister (p. 329), the belief in the immortality of the soul, in reward and punishment, and in the supreme justice of God is expressed. Whereupon a meditation and "Shivithi" in Hebrew and English follow. Silent devotions in memory of parents, of a husband, a wife, of children and other relatives, close the service; these devotions embody the hope that God grant eternal bliss to those who passed away and have them in His keeping. The recitation of "Kaddish" brings the Memorial Service to an end.

VII. The Concluding Service (Ne'ila) is introduced by a hymn, "The sun goes down," and a responsive reading. The Minister then reads Job 22 and 20, 25 and 28, whereupon the first two benedictions of the Amida with *wĕhothmenu* instead of *wĕchothvenu*, and the Kedusha are recited. This is followed by two poems from the Sephardic ritual, *bĕterem shehakim* and *êl nora*, and several short Selihoth from the Ashkenazic ritual in both languages. Then *atta nothen yad* and *atta hivdalta* from the Ashkenazic ritual follow, and the same passage from the conclusion of the intermediate benediction as in the previous services of the day is recited. Of the last part of the Ne'ila service only *pethah lanu shaar* and "Shema" and "The Lord, He is God" with the Shofar blasts have been retained.

The Minister then prays before the open ark.

In surveying this ritual we see that in its main outlines and in its religious and human ideas it is based upon the traditional liturgy, inspired by the prophetic spirit, including additional insertions dealing with modern thoughts and problems according to the conception of Reform Judaism.

However, the tendency toward universalism and rationalism, stripped of all leanings toward nationalism and mysticism, robbed this ritual to a large extent of its Jewish coloring and warmth. The omission of many texts resulted in the omission of many traditional tunes endeared to the Jew of all the ages. The predominance of responsive readings did away with congregational singing which used to give much life to the services.

The C.C.A.R. published also a *Haggada* for the Seder Service on Passover night. (First edition under the chairmanship of H. Berkowitz, the second under that of S. S. Cohon.) The last edition is unique in several aspects. In an introduction the underlying ideas of the Feast are explained, and the high value of the Seder Ceremonies emphasized. The Haggada follows the traditional texts as closely as a modern mind permits, and in keeping with Reform principles. The text is given in Hebrew with an English translation. In the paragraph "Ho lahma," the closing phrase "This year we are here in exile, but next year we hope to be free men in the land of Israel," has been changed in the Aramaic and in the English to "May it be God's will to redeem us from all trouble and from all servitude. Next year at this season may the whole house of Israel be free." All midrashic and homiletical elements were omitted, and the Biblical story taken from Genesis 47, Exodus 1 : 8–12, and some other passages, in a concise form. The Mishnaic text was also retained (see Chapter XIV). The wording of the closing benediction was changed, instead of "rejoicing in the rebuilding of Thy city, and exulting in Thy service, that we may there, by Thy gracious will eat of the sacrifices and paschal lambs, whose blood shall be sprinkled upon Thine altar . . ." the Reform Haggada reads: "Grant deliverance to mankind through Israel Thy people . . . so that Thy name shall be sanctified in the midst of all the earth, and that all peoples be moved to worship Thee with one accord. . . ." The idea of the future Passover is expressed in the final benediction, p. 78. In the "Grace" all nationalistic allusions are omitted but the concluding songs are retained. The poem "Wayhi bahatzi hallayla" is beautifully rendered into English verse by H. Berkowitz.

The Haggada is furnished with musical settings for the Kiddush, and some songs, few tunes of which are traditional. The book is also artistically illustrated.

In an appendix the history of the Passover, some excerpts of prominent Jewish thinkers on that festival, a description of the preparations for the Passover, survivals of the ancient Passover, Passover and Christendom, Reform Judaism and Passover, and the growth of the Haggada, are adequately treated.

Another successful publication of the C.C.A.R. is the *Rabbi's Manual* (first edition, under the chairmanship of W. Rosenau, and second edition under that of S. S. Cohon). The last edition contains services for various occasions in the life of the individual, and for the important events in congregational activities. In an appendix historical and explanatory notes, treating various customs and laws, are given. The material is drawn mostly from traditional sources. The greatest part is in English; some Hebrew texts are skillfully recast (see p. 40), and some have no Hebrew translations (pp. 59–60, 75–76).

The *Union Hymnal*, another publication of the above-mentioned body, the third revised edition of which has now come off the press, has been discussed in my *Jewish Music*, pp. 331ff.

In 1841 a prayer-book was published in London by a group of twenty-four men, eighteen of whom were Sephardim and six Ashkenazim. This group established a Reform congregation, called "The West London Synagogue of British Jews." Their aim was to create a divine service which will "inspire feelings of devotion" and "to enable Jews generally to form a united congregation under the domination of British Jews." [20] This ritual is a combination of both Sephardic and Ashkenazic rituals, modified according to Reform principles. It retained, however, the restoration of the Temple in Jerusalem and the sacrificial cult, the return to Palestine and the reëstablishment of the Davidic dynasty. It made an innovation by giving the Kaddish in Hebrew (according to the fourth edition 1882), and by placing the Ten Commandments before taking out the Scrolls.

In 1931 a sixth edition appeared. The first volume contains daily, Sabbath, and occasional prayers. In this edition there are several new prayers in Hebrew and English. Though the Hebrew is rather faulty, yet the mere fact that a Reform Society considered post-Biblical Hebrew permissible and found it necessary to compose new prayers is quite unique in itself.

There are some other departures from the accepted Reform innovations, as for example "a personal redeemer," resurrection, while the orthodox version, *hammahazir shechinatho letziyon*, was only changed to *hammashre shechinatho al tziyon* — "Who causest Thy holy spirit to rest upon Zion." Of the intermediate benedictions of the weekday Amida only the personal petitions (Benedictions 4, 5, 6, 8, 9, and 16) were retained. In this new edition all references to the return to Palestine and the reëstablishment of the Davidic dynasty were omitted. Only the first, second, and last stanzas of the Hanucca hymn "Maoz Tzur" were retained. A selection of Psalms in Hebrew and English was added.

The services are conducted mainly in Hebrew.

The "Liberal Jewish Synagogue" in London published a "Liberal Jewish Prayer Book," compiled by its Minister, Rabbi I. Mattuck, in three volumes. Volume I, 1926, contains services for weekdays and Sabbaths. The main innovation in this book is the variety of services. There are fifteen of them which may be used for Sabbaths, and, omitting certain paragraphs pertaining to the day of rest, they may be used for any day. It has very few Hebrew texts: "Barechu," "Shema" and its first paragraph, and usually the second benediction of the Amida. The English is generally a paraphrase. "We have here and there read a new meaning into an old prayer, one, however, not unrelated to its original meaning," says the editor. In addition new prayers were composed which "often express more especially the distinctive ideas of Reform Judaism." Whereas of the traditional prayers only those "have been retained which in themselves or by reinterpretation express ideas which we believe or desires which we feel." "Some of the new prayers were drawn from non-Jewish sources. . . . Because they were felt to express inspiringly much of our thought and aspirations in a way acceptable to all theists. . . . The best poetry speaks the language of universal religion. . . . Divine inspiration is universal. . . . God inspired the great and good among all the families of the earth.

"Though there are also prayers which are just theistic, we believe that they add to the Jewish quality of the Services. . . . showing that Judaism stands for the teaching of a pure and universal theism.

"In our view, the language of prayer does not hold any intrinsic merit or power, but draws its value from its appeal to those who pray. This Prayerbook is primarily issued for Jews whose tongue is English, and who, therefore, wish to say their Jewish prayers in that language."

Liberal Judaism maintains the viewpoint expressed by I. Abrahams: "The formulation of the highest truth needs constant revision and even more surely do the forms in which that truth is clothed. When dogma takes the place of love, religion is dead. And a liturgy that cannot expand, that cannot absorb the best religious teachings of the age . . . such a liturgy is a printed page; it is not a prayer fresh from the suppliant's heart." [21]

In order to avoid monotony, the service is interspersed with hymns or psalms to be sung by congregation and choir.

The second volume for the High Holydays (London, 1923) is largely modeled after the *Union Prayer-Book*. However, more traditional Hebrew texts are retained in this ritual than in the American prayer-book. Here, too, hymns and Psalms break the monotony. For New Year the Scriptural reading is taken from Deuteronomy 30:8–24, and for the Afternoon Service of the Day of Atonement Leviticus 29:1–4 and 9–18 is read.

The third volume contains services for the Three Festivals (London, 1926). They are richer in color and content than those in the *Union Prayer-Book* and contain more traditional material and a greater variety of prayers for each individual Festival. For the last day of Succoth, a reminiscence of the "Hoshanoth" and the "Hakafoth" has been retained. The benediction "Hashkivenu" is likewise given, but the sentence *wĕhaser satan mil'fanenu umêaharênu* is changed to *wĕharhek mimmenu awon wafesha.* This benediction is inserted only for the last evening of Passover and for the Sabbath evening service. The Scriptural readings are changed. For the first day of Passover: Exodus 12 and 13; for the last day: Deuteronomy 4; for Pentecost: Deuteronomy 5; and for the last day of Tabernacles: Deuteronomy 31. The Pentateuchal paragraphs are printed in Hebrew with the English translation.

Since "in the Jewish view, public worship is not only an occasion for communal and individual prayer, but also for instruction," many Biblical passages have been inserted "to supply what might be called the didactic element in the service."

The German liberal synagogues had no uniform prayer-book. In 1929 an attempt was made to compile a book of worship acceptable to all liberal congregations.

This prayer-book, *tefilloth miccol hashana*, was published by the Liberal "Kultus-Ausschusses des Preussischen Landesverbandes jüdischer Gemeinden." The Hebrew text follows Geiger's prayer-book mostly. The German translation diverts from the adopted custom to paraphrase the Hebrew, but tries to follow a literal translation. At the same time, however, the attempt was made to construct the style of the German in a way that it may be used as an independent text for public worship.

In the choice of the texts the editors showed their efforts to satisfy all the various tendencies of the different congregations. Compromises were made in all directions, from the radicals to the conservative elements among the liberal group, and from the "German citizens of Jewish religion" to the Zionists. With regard to the linguistic problem, though almost every prayer is given in German and Hebrew, a large selection of German prayers, meditations, and hymns has been added at the end of the book for insertions or substitution for those congregations that prefer German. So that "the possibility is given to render the service in Hebrew exclusively, or to intersperse the Hebrew with German prayers and hymns" (Preface XVII).

The following innovations ought to be mentioned:

The prayer-book has a Hanucca evening service in which the "Hallel" is given; a Purim evening service with the Book of Esther and Psalm 22; an evening and morning service for the Ninth of Av with a few selected Kinoth and the Lamentations divided for both services.

The "Verses of Song" are divided for the seven days of the week. The Psalms for Friday evening, too, are divided for the Sabbaths of the month.

It has a Hebrew version which replaces the text of Col Nidré. This, however, was done already in one of the later editions of the Hamburg *Prayer-Book.*

With all the efforts of the editors to come close to the form of the old ritual, they tried to uphold the principles of Reform Judaism, as outlined above. Though the upbuilding of Palestine is mentioned, there are no references to the return to Zion. In their efforts to please every tendency, they introduced peculiar versions. For instance, one passage reads: "Sound the great horn for our freedom; lift up the ensign to gather those who fear Thee *in* all corners of the earth. . . . Blessed . . . Who gatherest His people Israel." This passage is peculiar because it does not state where they are to be gathered to. Instead of *berahamim tashuv* another passage reads *welirushalayim ircha rahamim tashiv*—"And to Thy city Jerusalem return mercy" instead of "return *in* mercy." The expression *rahamim tashiv*—"return mercy"—is artificial Hebrew.

In some places sacrifices are interpreted to imply prayers and meditations, with the exception of the readings from Leviticus 23:25 on New Year's Day and 27 on the Day of Atonement in which the sacrifice of "burnt-offering" is specifically mentioned.

Rabbi C. Seligmann in his *Israelitisches Gebetbuch fuer die Neue Synagoge in Frankfurt a/M* 1911, was much more successful in the unity of expressing his ideas in a unified form and in keeping with the spirit of traditional Judaism. He also succeeded in breathing into it vitality and a noble inspiration. But the compiler withdrew this book of worship in favor of the union ritual treated above of which he was a co-editor. The other editors were I. Elbogen, and H. Vogelstein.

APPENDIX I

JEWISH ELEMENTS IN THE EARLY CHRISTIAN LITURGY

"The influence of the Jewish Liturgy on the early Church and its forms of worship is nowhere so clearly to be discerned as in the prayers which have been preserved in early Christian literature and in the earliest forms of the Christian Liturgy. Nobody, in reading the pre-Christian forms of prayer in the Jewish Liturgy and the prayers of the early Church, can fail to notice the similarity of atmosphere of each, or to recognize that both proceed from the same mould. Even when one perceives, as often happens, variety in the latter form, the *genus* is unmistakable." [1]

The time for prayer, the three times daily was taken over from the Synagogue: the third hour for the morning service (Acts 2 : 15); sixth hour for the afternoon service (Acts 10 : 9); and the ninth hour for evening service (Acts 3 : 1).[2]

In the Christian liturgy emphasis is laid upon Praise and Thanksgiving, "for the power of God is seen in the creation, for His guardianship, for deliverance from evil, and for spiritual enlightenment, concluding with confession and prayer for forgiveness; the petitions are less prominent, as in the Jewish prayers . . . the historical reminiscences which occur in many of the Jewish prayers are often taken over by the Church and adapted in a Christian sense." [3]

In the following we present comparative tables of Jewish and Christian prayers. We utilize in part excerpts of studies by Kohler,[4] Oesterley,[5] and Finkelstein.[6]

ELEMENTS OF THE AMIDA

Amida	*I Clement*
Ben. 3. Thou art holy, and holy is Thy name; and holy ones praise Thee every day. Blessed art Thou, O Lord, the Holy God. Insertions for the High Holidays: And Thou, O Lord, shalt reign, Thou alone over all Thy works . . . that they may all form a single band to do Thy will with a perfect heart. . . .	LIX, 3. - (Grant us) to hope in Thy Name, the first source of all creation; open the eyes of our heart to know Thee that Thou alone art the Highest among the highest and remainest Holy among the Holy ones.
Ben. 2. Thou art mighty for ever, O Lord, O Thou that quickenest the lead, Thou art mighty to save. . . .	Thou dost humble the pride of the haughty, that destroyest the imaginings of the nations that settest

Thou sustainest the living with mercy, that dost support the fallen with great mercies, that healest the sick, that loosest the bound, that preservest alive with them that sleep in the dust. Who is like unto Thee, Master of mighty acts; and who resembleth Thee, O King, that killest and makest alive, that causest salvation to spring forth?

on high the humble, that abasest the lofty, that makest rich and makest poor, that killest and makest alive, the only finder of spirits and God of all flesh; that lookest on the abysses, the discerner of the works of men, the helper of those in danger, the Saviour of them that despair, the Creator and Guardian of every spirit.

LIX, 4. We beseech Thee, Master, to be our help and succour. Save those of us who are in affliction, have mercy on the lowly, raise the fallen, manifest Thyself to the needy, heal the sick, turn those that are gone astray of Thy people; feed the hungry, ransom those who are bound, raise up the weak, comfort the fainthearted. . . .

Ben. 4. Thou dost favourably grant knowledge unto men, and dost teach discernment unto men; grant us from Thee knowledge and understanding and discernment. Blessed art Thou who didst graciously grant knowledge.

Ahava. O our Father, our King, for our fathers' sake, who trusted in Thee, and whom Thou didst teach the statutes of life, be gracious unto us too, and teach us. Enlighten our eyes in Thy Law, and let our hearts cleave unto Thy commandments, and unite our hearts to love and fear Thy name; that we may never be put to confusion.

Liturgy of Sarapion

. . . Grant us knowledge and faith and piety and sanctification. Take away every passion, every lust, every sin from this people; make them all to be pure. . . . Give us holy understanding and perfect usefulness. Grant that we may seek Thee and love Thee. Grant that we may search Thy divine words and study them. Stretch out Thine hand unto us, O Master, and raise us up. Raise us up, O God of Mercies, that we may look upwards; open our eyes; grant us boldness. . . .

Ben. 10. Sound the great horn for our freedom; and lift up the ensign to gather our exiles from the four corners of the earth. Blessed art Thou, O Lord, that gatherest the outcasts of Israel.

Didache IX, 9

As this broken bread was scattered upon the mountains, but was brought together and became one, so let Thy church be gathered together from the ends of the earth in Thy Kingdom. . . .

Ben. 13. Upon the righteous and upon the pious, upon the elders of Thy people the house of Israel, upon the remnant of their scribes, and upon the proselytes of righteousness, let Thy mercies be stirred, O Lord our God; and grant a good reward unto all that trust in Thy Name in truth; and set out our portion with them for ever; let us not be ashamed, for in Thy name have we trusted, and we have relied upon Thy salvation. . . .

Sarapion's Liturgy

On Thee do we call, Saviour and Lord, the God of all flesh and Lord of all spirits, the Blessed One, the Giver of every blessing. Sanctify this bishop, keep him from every temptation, and grant him wisdom and understanding, yea grant that we may make good progress in Thy knowledge. We pray to Thee also for his fellow-elders ("presbyters"); sanctify them, give them wisdom, understanding, and the true doctrine; grant that they may teach Thy holy truths rightly and blamelessly. Sanctify also the deacons, that they may be pure in heart and body, and serve Thee with a pure conscience. . . .

Kedusha. We will sanctify Thy Name in the world even as they sanctify it in the highest heavens, as it is written by the hand of Thy prophet: And they cried one to the other and said, "Holy, holy, holy is the Lord of Hosts, the whole earth is full of His glory."

I Clem. XXXIV, 5ff.

Let our glorifying and confidence be in Him; let us be subject to His will; let us consider the whole multitude of His angels, how they stand ready and minister to His will. For the Scripture saith, "Ten thousand times ten thousand stood by Him, and thousand thousands ministered unto Him," and they cried "Holy, Holy, Holy is the Lord Sabaoth, the whole creation is full of His glory." Therefore, we too must be gathered together with one accord in our conscience, and cry earnestly unto Him, as it were, with one mouth, that we may be partakers of His great and glorious promises. . . .

The sanctification has been retained in the Mass of the Catholic liturgy, in the Sanctus. *Roman Missal 1924*, p. 17. We compare, furthermore, passages from other parts of the daily prayers, such as:

Gĕula. From Egypt didst Thou redeem us, O Lord our God, and from the house of bondage didst Thou deliver us. . . . Wherefore the beloved praised and extolled God, who liveth and endureth . . . who

I Clem. LIX

. . . and will pray with eager entreaty and supplication that the Creator of all things may guard unhurt the number of His chosen . . . through His beloved Servant Jesus Christ, through whom He bringeth low the haughty, and setteth on high the meek; who leadeth forth the bound, and redeemeth the lowly; who helpeth the poor, and answereth His people when they cry unto Him. . . .

called us, from darkness to light, from ignorance to the knowledge of His glorious name. . . . Open the eyes of our hearts to know Thee, the only highest in the highest. . . . Who humblest the pride of the haughty, who destroyest the imaginings of the nations, who dost set up the meek on high, who dost humble the lofty, who makest rich and makest poor, who alone art the Finder of spirits, and God of all flesh; who dost look into the abysses, and beholdest the work of man, who art the Helper of those in danger, the Saviour of those without hope . . . who multipliest the nations on earth, and hast chosen out from them all those that love Thee. . . .

Amidah, Day of Atonement. Thou knowest the secrets of eternity and the most hidden mysteries of all living. Thou searchest the innermost recesses. . . . Nought is concealed from Thee, or hidden from Thine eyes.

I Clem. LX

Ben. 6. Forgive us, our Father, for we have sinned; pardon us, Our King, for we have transgressed. For Thou art the God of goodness, Thou dost forgive. . . .

. . . O Merciful and compassionate, forgive us our iniquities and unrighteous acts and transgressions and shortcomings. Reckon not every sin of Thy servants and handmaidens, but cleanse us with the cleansing of Thy truth, and guide our steps to walk in holiness of heart, to do the things that are beautiful and well pleasing in Thy sight.

The institution of reading the Scriptures was also taken over from the Synagogue. "Up to the second half of the second century the Church understood by the Scriptures the books of the Old Testament."[7] Even "the place of instruction" customary among the early Christians was borrowed from the Jewish *Beth-Hammidrash.*[8] In the Egyptian Church Order we read: "And it shall be reckoned great loss to him who fears God if he goes not to where is the place of instruction, and especially for him who can read."[9]

Among others, the response of *Amen* at the conclusion of a prayer,[10] the reciting of psalms,[11] the confession,[12] and the Decalogue,[13] which was discarded from the Jewish Liturgy (see Chapter VIII) were taken over from the Synagogue.

Over the Cup[14]

"Blessed be Thou . . . who createst the fruit of the vine."

Didache

We give thanks to Thee, our Father, for the holy wine of David Thy servant which Thou hast made known to us through Jesus Thy servant.

The benedictions of Grace were taken over and Christianized.[15]

Ben. 1

Blessed art Thou, O Lord our God, King of the Universe, who feedest the whole world with goodness, with grace and with mercy. Blessed art Thou, O Lord, who feedest all.

2. Didache

Thou, Master Almighty, didst create all things for Thy name's sake; both food and drink Thou didst give to men for enjoyment in order that they might give thanks to Thee, but to us Thou hast graciously given spiritual food and eternal life through Thy servant. Before all things, we thank Thee that Thou art mighty; To Thee be the glory forever.

Ben. 2

We thank Thee, O Lord our God, that Thou hast caused us to inherit a goodly and pleasant land, the covenant, the Tora, life and food. For all these things we thank Thee and praise Thy name forever and ever. Blessed art Thou, O Lord, for the land and for the food.

1

We thank Thee, holy Father, for Thy holy name, which Thou hast caused to dwell in our hearts, and for the knowledge and faith and immortality which Thou hast made known to us through Jesus Thy servant; To Thee be glory forever.

Ben. 3

Have mercy, O Lord our God, on Thy people Israel, and on Thy city Jerusalem, and on Thy Temple and Thy dwelling-place and on Zion Thy resting-place, and on the great and holy sanctuary over which Thy name was called, and the Kingdom of the dynasty of David mayest Thou restore to its place in our days, and build Jerusalem soon. Blessed art Thou, O Lord, who buildest Jerusalem.

3

Remember, Lord, Thy church, to deliver it from every evil, and to make it perfect in Thy love and gather it from the four winds, it the sanctified, into Thy Kingdom which Thou hast prepared for it; For Thine is the power and the glory forever.

Let grace come and this world pass away. Hosanna to the son of David. Whoever is holy, let him come; whoever is not let him repent. . . .

K. Kohler proves [16] that in the Didascalia the seven benedictions of the *Amida* for Sabbaths and festivals are taken over. The Christian text is much longer and more elaborate. We give here excerpts of these prayers which prove their Jewish origin:

Ben. 1

"Our eternal Saviour, the King of the godly kings, who alone art almighty and Lord, God of all things, God of our holy and blameless forefathers, God of Abraham, Isaac, and Jacob, the merciful and compassionate, long-suffering and abundant in mercy, to whom every heart is seen in its nakedness, and every secret thought is revealed, to Thee the souls of the righteous cry aloud; upon Thee do the hopes of the saints put their trust. . . . Thou protector of the offspring of Abraham, blessed be Thou forever."

Ben. 2

"Blessed art Thou, O Lord, King of the worlds, who hast made by Thy word the universe and through him (it) in the beginning didst turn the chaos into order. . . . And besides all these things, O Lord God, who can worthily explain the motion of the rain-bringing clouds, the effulgence of the lightning, the noise of the thunder in order to supply the proper food. . . . But when man was disobedient, Thou didst deprive him of the life which should have been his reward, yet didst Thou not destroy him forever, but laidst him to sleep for a time, but then by an oath didst Thou call him to a resurrection and thus loose the bond of death. (Be blessed) Thou, who reviveth the dead through Jesus Christ our hope.

Compare the beginning of this prayer with the benediction for the appearance of the new moon: "Blessed art Thou . . . by whose word the heavens were created, and by the breath of whose mouth all their host. . . ." (Singer, p. 292.)

Ben. 3 and Kedusha

"Great art Thou, O Lord and great is Thy power, and of Thy understanding there is no counting. . . . And the shining host of angels . . . say to Palmoni (one to the other): There is but one holy and the holy Seraphim together with the six-winged Cherubim, who sing to Thee their triumphal song, cry out with never-ceasing voices: Holy, Holy, Holy is the Lord Zebaoth, etc. The powers cry aloud and say: Blessed be the glory of the Lord out of His place.

Benediction for Sabbath

"O Lord, Almighty! Thou hast created the world by Thy word and hast appointed the Sabbath as a memorial thereof, because on that day didst Thou rest from Thy work and madest us also rest in order that we may meditate upon Thy laws. Thou didst enjoin the observation of the Sabbath, not affording any pretext of idleness, but as an opportunity of worship. . . . In order that man might have no pretext to pretend ignorance, therefore He ordained the Sabbath for them to cease from work, so that no one might be willing to let go one word out of his mouth in anger on the Sabbath day, for the Sabbath is the ceasing of the work of creation, the completion of the world, for the study of the Laws, and the grateful praise of God for the blessings He gave to men.

For the Festivals

"Thou hast appointed festivals for the rejoicing of our souls in order that we may come into the remembrance of that wisdom which has been created by Thee for (Thy) peculiar people Israel, the God-beloved, 'The one who seeth God.' (For Passover) "For Thou, O Lord, broughtest our fathers out of Egypt and didst deliver them out of the iron furnace from clay and brick-making, and didst redeem them out of the hands of Pharaoh and of those under him and didst lead them through the sea as through dry land, and didst feed them in the wilderness on all sorts of good things. (For Pentecost) "Thou gavest them the Law pronounced in Ten Words by Thy voice and written with Thy hand."

Ben. 15–17

"Thou who didst fulfil Thy promises made by the prophets and hast had mercy on Zion and compassion on Jerusalem by exalting the throne of David, Thy servant, in the midst of her (by the birth of Christ who was born of his seed according to the flesh, of a virgin,) do Thou also now, O Lord, God, accept the prayers which proceed from the lips of Thy people, who call upon Thee in truth, as Thou didst accept the offerings of the righteous in their generations. . . . So do Thou receive also now the prayers of Thy people which are offered to Thee with acknowledgment of Thee in the spirit."

Ben. 18

"We thank Thee, O Lord Almighty, for all things that Thou hast not taken Thy mercies and Thy compassions from us, but that Thou dost in every generation after generation save, deliver, help, and protect us. . . . Thou sweetenest life to us. Thou providest us with food. Thou hast announced to us repentance. Glory and worship to Thee for all these things now and forever and through all ages."

Kohler holds that these prayers were first created by the Essenes and were later reworked by the first Christians.[17]

The Lord's Prayer [18]

9. "Our Father" occurs in the fifth and sixth benedictions of the *Amida* and in the second benediction of *Shema*. "Hallowed be Thy name" as well as verse:

10. Constitutes the beginning sentence of *Kaddish:* "Magnified and sanctified be His great name in the world which He hath created according to His will. May He establish His kingdom during your life. . . ." This is also the contents of the first sentence of the *Kedusha*. In the morning benedictions there are similar sentences: "Sanctify Thy name upon them that sanctify it, yea, sanctify Thy name throughout

Matthew 6:9–13

9. Our Father which art in heaven Hallowed be Thy name.

10. Thy Kingdom come. Thy will be done in earth, as it is in heaven.

Thy world." Or: "Our Father who art in heaven, show mercy with us for the sake of Thy great name by which we are called; and fulfil unto us, O Lord our God, that which hath been written, "At that time will I bring you in, and at that time will I gather you." And again: "Our God who art in heaven, assert the unity of Thy name, and establish Thy kingdom continually, and reign over us for ever and ever."

11. . . . "Satisfy us with Thy goodness, and bless our year." (9th benediction of the *Amida.*) "Give me neither poverty nor riches; feed me with mine allotted bread. . . . " (Proverbs 30: 8.)

11. Give us this day our daily bread.

12. "Forgive us, our Father, for we have sinned; pardon us, O our King, for we have transgressed; for Thou art gracious, who dost forgive." (6th benediction of the *Amida.*)

12. And forgive us our debts, as we forgive our debtors.

13. "O Lead us not into sin, or transgression, iniquity, temptation, or shame. . . ." And "May it be Thy will . . . to deliver me this day, and every day, from arrogant men and from arrogance . . . and from any mishap, and from the adversary that destroyeth . . ." "For the kingdom is Thine, and to all eternity Thou wilt reign in glory." (*Alenu.*) This last sentence is based upon I Chronicles 29: 11 — "Thine, O Lord, is the greatness, and the power, and the glory, and the victory, and the majesty; for all that is in the heaven and in the earth is Thine. . . ."

13. And lead us not into temptation, but deliver us from evil: For Thine is the kingdom, and the power, and the glory, for ever. Amen.

APPENDIX II

RABBANITE ELEMENTS IN THE KARAITIC LITURGY

In the eighth century a group in Babylonia under the leadership of Anan, renounced the *Talmud* and the "Oral Law" and established a sect in Judaism called "Karaism," i.e., adherents to the Bible only. There were two underlying motives for this uprising against the Talmudic teachings which were hitherto unanimously accepted by all Jews. The one came from without, influenced by a similar movement among the Mohammedans of that time which sought to abide by the written word of the Koran without interpolations. The other motive was a personal one: Anan was rejected by the heads of the academies as successor to the post of his uncle who was Resh-Galutha, Exilarch. Soon Anan learned that without interpolations it was impossible to extract laws and regulations from the Bible; and while rejecting the Talmudic interpretations, he adopted his methods. In his work of *Laws* (*Sefer Hamitzvoth*)[1] he developed a "new *Talmud*." Correctly did Natronai Gaon make the statement that Anan said: "Abandon the *Mishna* and the *Talmud* and I will prepare a *Talmud* of my own." [2] Together with all Talmudic institutions he abolished the prayers as they were arranged by the sages in the long period of over a thousand years and substituted them with biblical verses.[3] Yet in the course of time the Karaites realized that they had to draw from the fountain of traditional Judaism, for their sect lacked vitality. After a few centuries the movement started to decay until it dwindled away to but a few thousand adherents.[4] Very little has been retained of Anan's liturgy.[5] For five hundred years no unified liturgy existed among the Karaites, until Ahron b. Joseph (1260–1320) in Constantinople compiled a code of prayers for the whole year. This compilation became the standard liturgy for that sect, though some additions, prayers and poetry, were inserted after him. The latest additions date back to but a hundred years ago. This ritual was first printed in Venice, 1528–9, and with additions in Chukut-Kale in 1734. The latest edition was published in Wilna, 1890, in accord with the Vienna edition of 1854, in four volumes, by Jacob Shishman. Volume I contains weekdays and Sabbath services. Volume II — Services for the festivals. Volume III — Services for the Day of Atonement and for the Ten Days of Penitence, and Volume IV, contains benedictions, home services and miscellanea for special occasions as well as two hundred and thirty poems and songs.

Anan abolished the evening service (Aravith), claiming that it has no source in the biblical daily sacrifices. The Karaitic liturgy has consequently a morning and an evening (Minha) service. The first chapter of Genesis is read at every service; it is divided into seven parts for the seven days of the week, and was taken over from the *Maamadoth* service (see Chapter IV). The invocation "Barechu" was replaced by Nehemiah 9:5 and a collection of biblical verses which contain invocations. The portion Numbers 28:1f., dealing with the daily offering, is read. The Psalms 145–50 are read, on each day a psalm. The "Widdui" has to be recited at every service during the year. This is composed of biblical verses. However, at some services the rabbanite "Ashamnu" (Vol. I, p. 217) and some other passages are adopted. In the confession the Destruction is always mentioned as having been caused by our sins.

The principle of "Kedusha" was taken over with three responses, "Kadosh," "Baruch," and "Shema." The Karaite liturgy has an abundant number of "Kedushoth" for different occasions. They all have these three responses, interspersed with various scriptural verses. The "Shema" in its rabbanite form, i.e., the three paragraphs, were also taken over, after which the following creed is read: "JHWH is our God. He is one true God. His perfect Law is true. His sanctuary, the house of worship is true. His prophets are true. The new month according to seeing the new moon [6] is true. His commandments . . . and all His sayings are true. . . ."

The idea of silent prayer was likewise retained. Its language, style and contents are similar to the Talmudic prayers. In the morning service the idea of "Yotzer" is kept by giving the verse of Isaiah 45:7, plus several biblical passages containing the idea of creation.

In every service Psalm 136, the "big Hallel" as it is called in the *Talmud*, is incorporated. The morning service has also the Song of the Sea. The sentence from Psalm 99:2 "The Lord is great in Zion; and He is high above all the peoples," which, according to Anan, should precede every benediction,[7] has been retained. The morning service has also the last part of Hallel Psalms 117–118, and the passage from I Chronicles 29:10–13.

The formula of the benediction (see Introductory notes) was replaced by the sentence "Blessed be the Lord for ever, amen and amen," though the Talmudic formula is frequently employed. In the silent prayer for the morning service (Vol. I, p. 87) the phraseology of the "Kaddish" is reflected. The counting of the "Omer" is observed in the morning service in a somewhat varied wording.

The benediction for New Month day, Volume I, p. 91, has been compiled of "Mi sheberach" and "Hannothen teshua" of the Sabbath service; of the "Yaale Weyavo;" "Roshe hodoshim" with the seal of that intermediary benediction of Rosh Hodesh Musaf service; and concludes with the Priestly benediction with its introduction. A collection of private prayers — *Bakashoth* (Vol. I, pp. 153f.), each beginning with *yehi ratzon* are imitations of rabbanite meditations. They finish with the traditional seal, "Praised be thou, O Lord, who hearest prayer."

The evening service for Sabbath has also Psalm 92. Only one biblical verse, I Kings 8 : 56 is given as an allusion to Sabbath.

For the Sabbath morning service Psalm 104 is read. The fourth commandment Exodus 20 : 8–11, Exodus 31 : 16–17; 35 : 1–3; and several other passages are inserted as references to Sabbath.

A special Widdui is read in the Sabbath morning service. On Sabbaths between the fasts of Tammuz and Av parts of the Lamentations are inserted in the Sabbath morning service. Before "Kedusha" a long benediction is recited, beginning with "Praised be Thou O Lord our God and God of our fathers Who hast chosen, loved and sanctified and redeemed Thy people Israel from all peoples . . . and Thou causest to inherit Thy holy Sabbaths to observe and rest on the day of rest. . . ." "Hannothen teshua" — the prayer for the royal family has been adopted and expanded. For the taking out of the Tora to read the scriptural portion, the verses which constitute "Uvnuho yomar" are utilized; "Ashre" is also recited. At the conclusion "En Kelohenu" is chanted.

For taking out the Tora "Shema" and "Wayhi binsoa" were retained. The Cohen who is called to read the first portion recites the formula "The Lord is great in Zion," etc., coined by Anan.[8]

On "Shabbath B'reshith" there is a special benediction. "Praised . . . that Thou hast caused us to live and to reach in peace the time to begin the reading of the Tora. So may we merit to finish it in Jerusalem the Holy city, amen." Style and structure are rabbinic.

During the seven Sabbaths between Pessach and Shavuoth Psalms 119 and 120–131 are recited. There is also a special service for rain (pp. 446f.), and for travelers on the sea (p. 450).

The "Haggada" relating the Exodus is called "Hallel Haggadol" — the big Hallel, and is recited in the synagogue. It consists of several psalms and scriptural verses, among which is Psalm 136. Psalm 105 is divided into half verses; after the first half a refrain : "Hallel wehodoth ladonai," and after the second half a refrain : "Hodu lo Ki tov" are inserted. The narrative is compiled of various biblical passages relating the Exodus. For the ten plagues the passages from Exodus are recited. This order of the Karaites was known at the time of Natronai Gaon (ninth century), because he says that whoever recites the biblical narrative without the Midrashic interpolations, as the followers of Anan do, should be excommunicated.[9]

For the home on Passover night a "minor Hallel," i.e., abridged Haggada, was composed. The benediction for Matza includes Maror. An additional benediction reads ". . . Who bringest bread of affliction out of the earth." There are special "Kiddush" and "Grace" texts for each holiday. The idea and partly the text of "Havdala" was borrowed.

The Sabbath before Pessah is called "Shabbath Haggadol," and the Sabbath after the Fasts in Av, "Shabbath Nahmu!"

The Festivals are: Pessah, Shavuoth,[10] Terua (for Rosh Hashana, because this is the name by which the day is called in the Bible), and Succoth. On Pessah and Shavuoth the whole "Hallel" is recited; on Terua and Succoth only Psalms 117 and 118 are read. "Simhath Tora" has been retained, or rather borrowed later with the poem "Sisu wesimhu," likewise the hymn "Yigdal." All biblical references to the four Festivals are collected and arranged to be recited on those days, but there are no newly composed prayers. Terua is a festival like the others, not a day of Judgment or a "day of memory," as in rabbinic conception. Terua does not mean to blow the Shofar, but to give praises. Therefore the Shofar blowing was abolished.

The Day of Atonement and the ten days of Penitence occupy the whole of Volume III. There we find the 13 attributes, and "Wayehal," sentences like "Our God and God of our fathers, wipe out transgressions like a cloud as Thou hast said: I, even I, will blot out your transgressions for My sake. . . ."

In connection with the destruction of the Temple several lamentations and compilations of scriptural verses are recited.

A poem by Juda Meruli (Vol. III, pp. 85f.) seems to be a rather poor substitute for Gabirol's "Crown of Royalty." The hymn "Ki Anu Amecha" (p. 108) was taken over, omitting the first line. The confession "Al het," and R. Nissim's Widdui have been paraphrased on pp. 112f. The "Ashamnu" occurs on p. 119 while other paragraphs have been digested (*l.c*). "Yaale weyavo" is given with some variants (p. 167), likewise the "half" Hallel, and that against the Talmudic decision of reciting Hallel on this day (see b. Rosh Hash. 32b; Chapters XV, XVI). "Anenu" and other responsive petitions are partly rendered in full, partly reworked and elaborated.

The Karaites retained but one date of the Fast-days, this is the 10th of Teveth, because this is in agreement with II Kings 25:1. The 17th of Tammuz they changed to the ninth, following Jeremiah 39:2. The 9th of Av was changed to the 7th, according to the date given in II Kings 25:8–9. To these fasts the 10th of Av was added as a Fast-day, because according to Jeremiah 52:12, the Babylonians destroyed the Temple on the tenth of Av. The tenth of Av is given instead of the *seventh* (II Kings 25:8–9), so the Karaites keep both days. On the Sabbaths between the ninth of Tammuz and the 7th of Av the Book of Lamentations, Deuteronomy 32 and several biblical paragraphs, the contents of which reprimand, "Kinoth" and the Book of Job are read. The Karaites, in addition, have introduced a Fast-day on the 24th of Tishre, in accordance with Nehemiah 9:1.

The "Kiddush" over wine on Friday with its eulogy and the benediction over wine and bread were retained.

While Hanucca was discarded because it was not Biblical, Purim is highly regarded. For this day a number of biblical paragraphs and the book of Esther are read. There is also a special table service for Purim.

For circumcision there is a service with a benediction by the Mohel, "Blessed . . . and who hast commanded us to circumcise on the eighth day," and another one for the naming of the child.

The Wedding service is very impressive. The bridegroom takes an oath as follows: "According to the covenant on Mt. Sinai, and in agreement with the laws on Mt. Horeb, and following the regulations of God, our elders and prominent men I . . . betrothe and sanctify . . . to become my wife in purity and sanctity, by dowry, by written agreement, and by cohabitation, according to the law of Moses and Israel." And while putting on the ring the groom recites Hosea 2:21–22. The "Kethuba" is then read. It follows the rabbanite text but in Hebrew instead of in Aramaic. The essence of the "seven benedictions" have been retained. The ceremony is interspersed with several delightful songs.

The greatest part of *birchoth hannehenin* has been taken over (see Chapter IX). So also the prayer before reclining.

The morning benedictions (Chapter VIII) Volume IV, pp. 73–76, were carried over almost verbatim with but one addition: "Blessed . . . who createst me in a human image, O (I) worm of Jacob."

The Karaite services are much longer than those of the rabbanites; therefore, here too, provision was made for short services in Volume IV, pp. 89f.

The services are embellished with an abundant number of poetical insertions, in spite of Anan's antagonism to piyyut. A considerable part of the piyyutim was composed by the compiler of the liturgy, Ahron b. Joseph. The others are mostly by Karaite payetanim. But also poems by Solomon b. Gabirol, Jehuda Halevi, Abraham b. Ezra, Israel Najara, Solomon b. Mazal-tov, and some others were incorporated. Some poems of rabbanite origin were attributed to Karaites, such as *bath ahuvath êl kama*, by Benjamin,[11] used partly for Bakkashoth and partly for the second evening of New Year's day, according to the Sephardic-oriental ritual, is ascribed to Benjamin Nahawandi (Vol. III, p. 312). Besides "Adon Olam" and "Yigdal," the following popular rabbanite poems are found in the Karaite liturgy: *Eth shaare ratzon* from Sephardic ritual, *ode laêl levav hoker*, *hammavdil*, *tzur mishello achalnu*, *yom ze leyisrael*, *ki eshmera shabbath* from Sabbath "Zemiroth," for circumcision, according to Sephardic ritual, *yehi shalom* and others. Several poems were imitated: *bor'chi atzula* Volume III, p. 273, from Hallevi's poem for Ne'ila, Ashk. ritual *yetzaw haêl*, *ibid.*, *yëiruni*, *ibid.*, p. 235, *asher lecha yom ibid.*, p. 241 from Abraham b. Ezra's *lecha êli* for Col Nidré service.[12]

Anan adopted the rabbinic principle of substituting prayer for sacrifice.[13] He also "accepted the Talmudic principle that after the destruction of the Temple the actual sacrifices are substituted by the reading of the Biblical passages about them." [14] He likewise "followed the rabbinic tradition of reading the portion about Amalek's attack upon Israel, evidently because he regarded Haman the Agagite as the descendant of Agag, Amalek's King, in Saul's time"[15] (see Chapter XII, 4).

Finally, the custom of calling up first Cohen, then Levi, then Israelites to read the portion from the Pentateuch (Vol. I, p. 408), is also borrowed from the Talmudic practice.

Among their customs some are of rabbinic origin, as abstaining from meat on the ten days of Av, walking without shoes on the fast of Av, and refraining from building a house or from preparing new things on these fast days.

The Karaites discarded the structure of the rabbinic liturgy, but did not succeed in creating a structure of their own. In fact, their liturgy lacks all structure and form. It rather gives one the impression of an accumulation of Biblical paragraphs and verses. There seems to be no beginning, middle, or end, but a formless mass of scriptural passages in which the main ideas of Praise, Petition, Israel, Zion, Temple, Sin and Forgiveness are thrown together.

APPENDIX III

TO CHAPTERS VIII–X

1. To Chapter VIII

Yotzer. It is suggested that the original wording of the first benediction read as follows: בא"י אמ"ה יוצר אור ובורא חושך עושה שלום ובורא את הכל. המאיר לארץ ולדרים עליה ברחמים, טובו מחדש בכליום תמיד מעשה בראשית. בא"י יוצר המאורות.

This is the version given in S.R.A. for the private Yotzer [1] (4b). The other parts were inserted by the "Yordei Mercava" sometimes during the eighth century; they also insisted upon having the "Kedusha" recited in the Yotzer.[2]

These mystics have also influenced the second and third benedictions.[3] The opinion is prevalent among scholars that those passages indulging in the exaltation of the glory of God and His heavenly hosts, that alphabetic acrostics as "אל ברוך", and that occasional rhymes as "פועל... גבורות... הנפלאות", "ומברכים... וממליכים", "רחם עלינו... משגב בעדנו" and others are the creations of the mystic school. Parts of "Baruch Sheamar" and "Yishtabah" are attributed to that school for the same reason [4] (see Chapters IV, VI).

Avoth. Its Palestinian version is: בא"י... אל עליון קונה שמים וארץ. מגיננו ומגן אבותינו מבטחינו בכל דור ודור. ברוך...

This version has been retained in part in the Friday evening service (see Chapter X).

Kedushath hashem. S.R.A., 8a, gives the version of the first sentence: "לדור ודור המליכו לאל כי לבדו מרום וקדוש" which sentence is also in the Roman ritual; while the Sephardic ritual has this sentence for the High Holydays only.

For the third benediction of the daily Amida, the old Palestinian ritual had the version as it is retained for the High Holydays, namely: "קדוש אתה ונורא שמך ואין אלוה מבלעדיך. ברוך..".[5]

The Palestinian version of the fourth benediction is as follows: "חנינו אבינו דיעה מאתך ובינה והשכל מתורתך. ברוך...".

The Palestinian version of the 5th benediction is as follows: "השיבנו' אליך ונשובה חדש ימינו כקדם. ברוך..."; it is taken from Lamentations 5:21.

The Palestinian version of the 6th benediction is as follows: סלח לנו אבינו כי חטאנו לך, מחה פשעינו מנגד עיניך, כי רבים רחמיך. ברוך...

This sentence occurs also in the Amida of the Day of Atonement and is based upon Micah 7:18.

In the Palestinian version of the 9th benediction there is the phrase:

"For a speedy redemption" — „וקרב מהרה שנת קץ גאולתינו"; while an old version to which that of Saadya agrees is very short, reading: ברך עלינו ה' את השנה הזאת לטובה בכל מיני תבואתה. ברוך...

The Palestinian version of the 10th benediction is rather short[6]: „תקע בשופר גדול לחירותינו ושא נס לקיבוץ גאליותינו. ברוך...

The oldest version of the 12th benediction retained reads:[7] „למשומדים אל תהי תקוה ומלכות זדון תעקר בימינו. בא"י מכניע זדים.

The Palestinian version reads:[8] „למשומדים אל תהי תקוה ומלכות זדון מהרה תעקר והנוצרים והמינים כרגע יאבדו ימחו מספר החיים ועם צדיקים אל יכתבו. בא"י..."

Another version reads:[9] „למשומדים אל תהי תקוה אם לא ישובו לבריתך..."

It is strange, however, that old versions of the 13th benediction read: „על גרי הצדק יהמו רחמיך ותן לנו שכר טוב עם עושי רצונך..." so that the above mentioned terms are missing.[10]

That the benediction *sim shalom* was originally recited before the Destruction is evident from the old Palestinian version which reads as follows:[11] „שים שלומך על ישראל עמך ועל עירך ועל נחלתך וברכנו כלנו כאחד. בא"י עושה השלום."

This version presupposes the existence of the *city* and the *inheritance*.

Beginning with 1370, attacks on the Alenu from Christians did not cease,[12] especially on account of the passage: "For they bow down to vanity and emptiness and pray to a god who saveth not" — „שהם משתחוים להבל וריק ומתפללים אל אל לא יושיע". It was claimed the Jews refer to Jesus, because the word „וריק" equals numerically to the word „ישו" — both being 316. Consequently, the passage was deleted from the Ashkenazic ritual. Yet in 1702, the Prussian government in Berlin started an investigation into the true meaning of the Text of Alenu, and on the 28th of August 1703 the government issued a verdict prohibiting the recitation of the above mentioned passage and the custom of spitting during the Alenu. Special officials were posted in the synagogue to watch that the order be obeyed.[13]

In the Italian ritual, the word „שהם" is changed to the past form „שהיו", and „להבל וריק" are changed to „לאלילים" — meaning, idols, so that the passage refers to the ancient pagan worship.

2. To Chapter IX

The oldest version of the benediction was very short. In all likelihood, the first benediction read: „בא"י אמ"ה הזן את העולם כולו בטוב בחסד וברחמים. בא"י הזן את הכל.", or even without the eulogy.[14]

The second benediction originally read „נודה לך ה' אלהינו כי הנחלתנו ארץ חמדה. בא"י על הארץ ועל המזון."

Later the two words „ברית ותורה" were inserted (b. Ber. 49a) probably due to the prohibition of both by Roman authorities.

The earliest formula for the third benediction seems to have been: „רחם ה׳ אלהינו על ישראל עמך ועל ירושלים עירך ועל ציון משכן כבודך ועל מזבחך ועל היכלך. בא״י בונה ירושלם.״

To that „מלכות בית דוד״ was urgently recommended (b. Ber. *l.c.*).[15]

The fourth benediction which is now quite long was originally very short, reading „בא״י הטוב והמטיב״.

In the rituals the benedictions were greatly elaborated.[16] The first three benedictions were regarded in the *Talmud* as Biblical, while the fourth was a rabbinic addition (b. Ber. 46a).

3. To Chapter X

(To p. 176). In the sentence "by the mouth of the upright . . . etc. . . . ", we find in the words „ישרים, צדיקים, חסידים, קדושים״ the acrostic of „יצחק״, and according to the Sephardic ritual, the acrostic of „רבקה״ is found in the words „תתרומם, תתברך, תתקדש, תתהלל״.

(To p. 181). The following portions are read together occasionally: „בהר-בחקותי, חקת-בלק, תרומה-תצוה, ויקהל-פקודי, תזריע-מצרע, אחרי-קדושים, מטות-מסעי, נצבים-וילך.״

APPENDIX IV

THE POETICAL INSERTIONS FOR SPECIAL OR DISTINGUISHED SABBATHS

Here we shall present a description of the poetical insertions in the Ashkenazic and Italian rituals. These insertions are still recited in some orthodox congregations.

1. *Sabbath and New Moon*. The Ashkenazic ritual has the following insertions in the Yotzer:

"אלהינו אלהים אמת„ is a poem by Benjamin b. Zerah (tenth–eleventh centuries). It is an alphabetic acrostic with three lines to the stanza. The author describes the solar and lunar calendar; it is interwoven with Midrashic elements. The Italian ritual has this poem for *Sabbath "Bereshith."*

"לך אלים„, *Ofan*, describes the singing of the Kedusha by the heavenly hosts; it is based upon Wayikra Rabba 2; b. Hagiga 14a; and Bereshith Rabba 78. The end words are *Kadosh* and *Baruch*. The alphabetic acrostic goes up to *Yod* only and seems to be abbreviated. This poem is mentioned by Maharil.

In his *Siddur — Safah Berurah* — Roedelheim, 1812, Heidenheim gives the following "piyyutim":

"אילת השחר„ in the *Yotzer* by Meyir b. Isaac.

"אביר הגביר„, *Ofan*, by Abraham b. Ezra (?); it is in Hazağ meter.

"אמונתך אמתי„ — a poem by Meyir b. Isaac, the precentor in Worms (eleventh century). It is an alphabetic acrostic with the name of the author at the end. The author praises the creation of the world, utilizing several Scriptural and Talmudic phrases.

The Italian ritual has the following insertion in the Yotzer:

"תאמת אור בקדש„ — an alphabetic acrostic by an unknown Italian poet. It is a praise for the creation of light, of Sabbath, of the spiritual light which radiates from it and from the Sanctuary which is to be restored.

2. *Sabbath Bereshith*. The Ashkenazic ritual has the following insertions in the Yotzer:

"אמונתך אמתי„, *Zulath*, by the above mentioned Meyir b. Isaac. Maharil gives other "piyyutim."

"אל נשא„, also in the *Yotzer*, is a poem by Solomon b. Juda of Rome (tenth century).

"לבעל התפארת„, *Ofan*, is a poem by Benjamin mentioned above.[1] It describes the singing of the angels, giving several angelic names and the name "אדירי רון„ — the mighty.

"שאלו שחקים„, *Ofan*, a poem by the above mentioned Solomon.

3. *Sabbath Wayera.* The Ashkenazic ritual (Heidenheim) has: "שננו לשונם„, *Ahava*, a poem by Samuel, describing the *Akeda* and the troubles Ishmael caused Israel.

"אחשבה לדעת„, *Zulath*, is a poem by the above mentioned Solomon. It is an alphabetical acrostic, and the meter has five words to the line. It is a meditation.

The last three "piyyutim" are also mentioned in Maharil.

4. *Sabbath-Hanucca I.* "אודך כי אנפת„, Yotzer, is a poem by Joseph b. Solomon of Carcassonne [2] of the tenth century. This "piyyut" is based upon the Megilath Antiachus, and the books of Judith and Maccabees. The rhyme consists of four words to the line in alphabetic acrostics. This poem is also in the Italian ritual for the same day.

"כבודו אור יזריח„, *Ofan*, is a poem with an alphabetic acrostic.

"שני זיתים„, *Mĕora*, is a poem by the above mentioned Solomon. The author draws from Zachariah 4 : 3, 14. This poem is a fervent prayer for the re-establishment of Zion, the Sanctuary, and the priestly service. It used to be sung in a tune which is a variation of the tune of *Maoz Tzur.*[3]

"אין צור חלף„, *Zulath*, is a poem by the same poet. Its style is obscure, and its meter is three words to the line.

These poems are also given in Maharil.

5. *Sabbath-Hanucca II.* When two Sabbaths occur during the eight days of Hanucca, the following poems are recited:

"אודך כי עניתני„, *Yotzer*, is a poem by Menahem b. Machir of Regensburg of the eleventh century. It describes the Jewish troubles which came as a result of the combats and wars between Antiachus and the Maccabees. In the days of Maharil no "piyyut" was recited on the second Sabbath of Hanucca.

"אמצו בתופף„, *Ofan*, is a poem by Abraham.

"אשר יצר„, *Mĕora*, is a poem by Ephraim b. Isaac; it is in Hazağ meter. It is an expression of the hope for the restoration of the Temple.

"אין מושיע„, *Zulath*, is a poem by Menahem b. Machir. It consists of three words to the line, and describes the cruelties of the Greeks.

The *Gĕula* is the same as in 6.

The Italian ritual has the following:

"אזכור מעללי יה„, *Yotzer*, is a poem by Moses.

"יתנו צדקות ה׳„, *Ose Shalom*, is a poem by Isaac b. Samuel. It is recited before Kaddish Tithkabbal; it is also found in the Maaravoth for New Year in the Roumanian ritual.[4]

Heidenheim gives also the following:

"אשר יצר„, *Mĕora*, a poem by Ephraim b. Isaac.

"אין מושיע וגואל„, *Zulath*, a poem by Menahem b. Isaac mentioned above; it consists of three words to the line.

6. *Sabbath Beshalah* (Heidenheim). "יום ליבשה", *Geula*, a poem by Jehuda Halevi. This poem is also recited on the second Sabbath of Hanucca and on the seventh day of Passover. Its refrain is from the prayer: "שירה חדשה שבחו גאולים".

7. *Sabbath Yithro*, and whenever the Ten Commandments are read (Heidenheim). "אמרות האל טהורות", *Meora*, a poem by the same poet. It is in the shortened Ramal meter: – ᴗ – –, repeated twice. The content of the poem has no bearing whatsoever on the portion *Yithro*.

8. *Sabbath Shekalim*. Maharil writes that from this Sabbath on to Succoth *Haccol Yoducha* is sung with a *long-stretched* tune.[5]

Yotzer:

"אל מתנשא", *Yotzer*, is also in the Italian ritual. It is an alphabetical acrostic. It has several Scriptural phrases. According to *Tanhuma*, *Ki thisa*, God showed Moses a *Shekel* of fire — which coin was to be donated to the sanctuary.

"כבודו יתרומם", *Ofan*, is a poem consisting of only four lines.

"אתה אהבת", *Zulath*, is an alphabetical acrostic.

Kerova:

"מסוד חכמים" is the introduction, "Reshuth", used at the beginning of all *Kerova*.

"אז מאז זמות", a poem by Eleazar Kallir.[6]

"מעתיק פלוסים" is a continuation of the previous poem. This poem, as well as the following poem, speak of the idea of counting the people for the donation of the *Shekel*.

"מי יוכל לשער" is a poem probably by the same author.

"אומן בשמעו" is also by the same author. It is based upon *Yalkut*, *Ki thisa*, *beginning*, and explains the way Moses counted the people Israel (see Baer, p. 651).

"אל נא" is used in many *Kerovoth* and seems to be a remnant of an old *Kerova*, older even than Yannai.[7] It is based upon the introductory passage of the *Kedusha*.

Then follow the two verses from Psalms 146 : 10 and 22 : 4. The first verse is taken from the last response of the *Kedusha*, and the second verse is a reminder of the beginning of the third benediction.

The phrase "חי וקים" was probably first used by Kallir.[8]

"אלה אזכרה" is a poem by the same author. It is an alphabetical acrostic and has five words to the line. The poet complains, saying that due to the fact we failed to observe the laws pertaining to just trading we are now deprived of the law of *Shekel*.

"אז ראית", *Silluk*, is a poem by the same author. It has five words to the line.

The Kerova for Musaf is known as "Shiv'atha" because there are poetical insertions for all the seven benedictions of the Amida. The "piyyut" is also found in the Roumanian ritual; the author is probably Kallir. Each paragraph starts with a word from Canticles 1 : 14, and each paragraph has six lines with five words to each line. A refrain — "אור פניך" — runs through all seven stanzas. This has four lines in the same meter. The fourth line, however, is changed to afford a fitting link to each of the seven benedictions. The author utilizes the Midrashic interpretation of the Biblical verse (b. Shabbath 88b), which is as follows: The Perfect One will forgive the sin of him who covered his hands with kidskins (Jacob) committed in the vineyard (Zion).[9]

9. *Sabbath after Shekalim* — "הפסקה ראשונה". "אור זרוע", *Yotzer*, is a poem by Menahem b. Machir. It has four words to the line. The piyyut is based upon Bereshith Rabba 8 which maintains that God took counsel with the souls of the righteous concerning the creation of the world. The author describes the laws appertaining to the fixing of the holidays.

"מלאכי צבאות", *Ofan*, is a poem by the same author. It has three words to the line.

"אחור וקדם צרת", *Zulath*, also by the same author. It too has three words to the line. The last line of each stanza is Biblical. These "piyyutim" are quoted in Maharil.

10. *Sabbath Zachor.* "זכור את אשר עשה", *Yotzer*, is a poem probably by Kallir.[10] It describes the misdeeds of Amalek. It is also found in the Italian ritual.

"כבודו יתרומם בפי", *Ofan*, is similar to the *Ofan* for Shekalim.

"אתה מלא רחמים", *Zulath*, is an alphabetical acrostic. It is a petition for Israel's redemption.

Kerova for Shaharith. "אזכיר סלה" is a poem by E. Kallir.[11] It is an alphabetical acrostic and consists of four words to the line. It describes the troubles which Haman the Amalekite caused unto Israel.

"תמימים בעודם" is probably the work of the same author. It is a reversed alphabetical acrostic.

"אצילי מרעי" is the work of Juda who is supposed to have been the brother of Kallir.[12] It has four words to the line, and has both the straight and reversed alphabetical acrostic.

Psalms 146:10 and 22:4 are recited here.

"בלשון אשר" is a petition. Then there follows the sentence "חי וקים" (see Chapter XV).

"אץ קוצץ" is a poem by Eleazar Kallir which describes the wickedness of Haman (see Chapter XI).

"אל נא" is recited here (see Chapter XV).

"זכור איש" is a piyyut mentioned in Tosafoth to b. Rosh Hashana 3a; there it is called "*Pizmon.*" It is a poem by Kallir.

This poem describes the evil deeds of Esau who shortened the life of his grandfathers by five years (*Yalkut*, ki thetze, end). From him Amalek descended.

"אלהים אל דמי", *Silluk*, is a poem by Kallir. It is a fervent prayer for the welfare of Israel.

Kerova for Musaf—[13] *Shiv'atha* (O.H., p. 177). This Kerova is ascribed to Kallir. Each of the seven stanzas starts with a word from Exodus 17 : 15. There are ten lines to the stanza, each stanza consisting of six words. The piyyut lacks the charm of the *Musaf Kerova* for *Shekalim*.

The Italian and Sephardic rituals have three piyyutim by Jehuda Halevi. They are given in two variants: one is in the Italian tradition and the other in the Sephardic.

"אדון חסדך", *Mi Chamocha*.

"אמר כל אלה הדברים".

"אלהים עדר".

"אכלו רעים".

These poems describe the story of Esther and Israel's salvation.

11. *Sabbath after Purim* — "הפסקה שניה". "את פני מלך", *Yotzer*, is a poem by Moses b. Habub.

"שמך לעד", *Ofan*, is a poem by Shalom who lived about 1200.[14] It is in the Hazağ meter. The author is probably not Ashkenazic, as seen from his style.

"ה׳ אלהים צבאות", *Zulath*, is a poem by Mose.

Baer, p. 682, brings another *Yotzer:*

"אורות מאפל" is attributed to M. Rothenburg; it is mentioned in Maharil.

12. *Sabbath Para.* "אם אשר בך דבוקה", *Yotzer*, is a poem with an alphabetic acrostic and with three words to the line. It deals with the law and idea of *Para Aduma* — Red Heifer. It is also in the Italian ritual. It is attributed to Kallir.[15]

"כבודו יתרומם", *Ofan*, is similar to those described above.

"אשרי כל חוסי בך", *Zulath*, is an alphabetical acrostic.

Kerova for Shaharith:

"אצולת אמן" is recited with the same Biblical verses treated in 8.

"אצורה ומפרשה" is a poem by E. Kallir with two words to the line.

"אמרה סנונה" is probably by the same author; it has three words to the line.

"אצילי עם" is also the work of the same author; it has four words to the line. All these piyyutim deal with the significance of *Para Aduma*.

"אין לשוחח", *Silluk*, is a poem with four words to the line. It explains the great value of the laws of cleanliness and spiritual purification.

Kerova for Musaf — *Shiv'atha* (O.H., p. 209f.). This has the same structure as the previous Kerova for Musaf. It is ascribed to Kallir. Each stanza starts with a word from Job 28 : 23. There are five words to the line. The content of this poem is similar to that of the *Shaharith Kerova*.

13. *Sabbath Hahodesh.* "אות זה החדש", *Yotzer*, is a poem with three words to the line. It speaks of the significance of the month *Nissan* in the history of Israel. It is also found in the Italian ritual.

"כבודו משבחים", *Ofan*, is a poem in the same style as the previous *Ofan*.

"אל עושה פלא„, *Zulath*, recounts the wonders of God which He performed for Israel.

Kerova for Shaharith. "אתית עת דודים„ is a poem with three words to the line and with the usual Biblical verses.

"רבות עשית„ has four words to the line.

"אבי כל חוזה„ is a poem by E. Kallir with three words to the line. The piyyut is based upon a Midrashic interpretation of Exodus 12:2 according to which God taught Moses the lunar calendar.

"אדון מקדם„ is the work of the same author; it speaks of the great value of *Nissan* to Israel.

"הוא נקרא ראש„, *Silluk*, is a poem with four words to the line. Its content is similar to that of the previous piyyut.

Kerova for Musaf — Shiv'atha. It is identical in structure to the previous Kerova for Musaf, especially to that of *Shekalim*. It has four words to the line. Each stanza starts with a word from Isaiah 41:27. The refrain beginning with "ארבעה„ has in each stanza another theme: Four New Years (*Mishna* Rosh Hashana), four seasons, four periods (b. Rosh Hashana 16a), four portions referring to the four distinguished Sabbaths on which special portions are read, four cups which God will give unto Israel (Bamidbar Rabba 88), four kingdoms (Dan. 11), and four craftsmen (Zach. 2:3). The second lines in the stanzas 1, 3, 5, 7 are identical, while in the third line the text alternates: 1, 3, 5, 7 and 2, 4, 6. The fourth line leads over to the benedictions of the *Amida.*[16]

14. *Sabbath Haggadol.* "אתי מלבנון„, *Yotzer*, is a poem by Benjamin b. Zerah. It is an alphabetical acrostic. The piyyut is based upon Canticles of which several phrases were inserted. This poem speaks of redemption.

"אאמיר מסתתר„, *Yotzer*, is the work of Joseph b. Samuel Tov-elem (Bonfils) of the tenth century. It has three lines to the stanza; the third line is Biblical.

"בלולי אש„, *Ofan*, is the work of the above mentioned Benjamin. It describes the nature of the angels.

"אז כארשת„, *Zulath*, is a poem by the above mentioned Joseph. It has five words to the line, and recounts the story of the Exodus.

"אומרת אני„, *Zulath*, is the work of the same Benjamin. The Book of Canticles is utilized in all these piyyutim as a love theme of Israel to God on the occasion of the people's redemption. Obviously, here we have two sets of *Yotzer* by the two authors. The same source we find also in the *Kerova for Shaharith.*

"אבא בחיל„. "יוצאי חפזון„. "ירדת להציל„. "כרם חמד„. "אלהים בצעדך„. "אין ערוך„. "אלהי הרוחות„.

All these poems are the works of Joseph b. Samuel.

"אוני פטרי רחמתים„ in which the poem "ויהי בחצי הלילה„ is generally recited in the *Haggada* in the Ashkenazic ritual is the work of Yannai (O.H., p. 234f.).[17]

"אדיר במרומים", *Seder*, is not by Yannai.[18]

The Italian ritual has the following:

"אני חומה", a poem by Juda. The alphabetic acrostic is interrupted after *Beth* with the acrostic of the author's name.

"כך גזרו רבותינו" is a poem by Benjamin. It is an alphabetic acrostic with the name of the author. It describes the laws of Passover.

15. *First Sabbath after Passover.* "ויושע אור ישראל", *Yotzer*, is a poem by Meyir b. Isaac. This piyyut is based upon the Song of the Sea beginning with Exodus 14:30. The stanzas start with the first words of the verses of the Biblical song.

"ארוני עוז", *Ofan*, is a poem whose author is unknown. It is based upon the Hazağ meter and comes probably from Provence.[19] It is a description of the songs of the angels.

"אראלים", *Ofan*, is a poem by Joseph Sabara of the twelfth century. It is recited in Bohemia, and is similar in style and meter to the previous poem.[20]

"אלוהי, ימי שנותי", *Ahava*, is a poem by Joseph Shabbathai b. Isaac. Several stanzas are missing at the end of the poem.[21] The piyyut expresses Israel yearnings.

"אין כמוך באלהים", *Zulath*, is a poem by Isaac b. Shalom of the twelfth century.[22] In this piyyut, the author describes the persecutions which took place on the twentieth of the first month of the year 1147, as indicated in the text.

"שביה עניה", *Gĕula*, is a poem by Solomon b. Gabirol; it has the Mutakarib meter. This poem is an outburst of Israel's longing for redemption.

16. *Second Sabbath after Passover.* "ארנן חסדך", *Yotzer*, is a poem by Joseph b. Samuel Bonfils. It has four words to the line. It is an alphabetical acrostic, and praises creation.

"יחיד ערץ", *Ofan*, is a poem by Jacob (probably of Spain). It has the Hazağ meter. The poem has a Scriptural refrain and describes the Kedusha singing of the heavenly hosts.

"איומתי שמתי", *Mĕora*, is the work of Samuel Cohen. It is a cheerful song of love to Israel. Some of the end lines are phrases from Isaiah 60.

"אל אל חי ארנן", *Zulath*, is a poem by Simon b. Isaac. It has three words to the line with a refrain. It speaks of Israel's complaint over his troubles.

This Zulath is also used for the first Sabbath after the Seventeenth of Tammuz.

"שנותינו ספו", *Gĕula*, is a poem by Solomon (Habavli?). It is the same as the previous poem in content.

17. *Third Sabbath after Passover.* "אמיץ דר חזקים", *Yotzer*, is a poem by Solomon. It has three words to the line. The author's name is in an acrostic in the last line of every stanza.

"לבעל התפארת", *Ofan*, is the work of Benjamin b. Zarah. This piyyut is also used for Sabbath *Bereshith*.

"סגולתי מלוכה", *Ahava*, is a poem by Meshullam b. Moshe of the eleventh century. It has seven two-word lines to the stanza. The seventh line is Biblical. The poem is a dialogue between God and Israel. The stanzas alternate by beginning and ending with "סגולתי" or with "דודי". Israel complains over his fate, and God consoles him.

"אריות הדיחו", *Zulath*, is a poem by the above mentioned Joseph b. Samuel. It has three words to the line with a short refrain. It is used also for the second Sabbath after the Seventeenth of Tammuz.

"שדודים נדודים", *Gĕula*, is a poem by Solomon (b. Gabirol?). It has the Mutakarib meter and a refrain from Lamentations 5:20. Several other Scriptural phrases are used. The poem is a song of hope for redemption. It is also found in Avignon ritual.

18. *Fourth Sabbath after Passover.* "אשיחה בדברי", *Yotzer*, is the work of Amittai b. Shefatya of the eighth century. It describes the creation.

"ידודון", *Ofan*, is a poem by Jacob, probably of Spain.

"סגולתי איומה", *Ahava*, is the work of Eleazar bar Dan(iel). This poem is evidently confused with another poem. The meter, structure, and content are identical to the Ahava of 17.

"אלהי בך אחבק", *Zulath*, is a poem by Ephraim b. Isaac of Regensburg of the twelfth century.[23]

In Heidenheim's Siddur, four lines are missing in this poem, due to the censor. Three of these lines are given in *Otzar Hatefilloth*, p. 265, while the verse with the letter "Pe" of the acrostic is missing. It has three words to the line and three lines to each half stanza. The poet complains of Israel's suffering in bitter words.

"שכולה אכולה", *Gĕula*, is a poem by Solomon (b. Gabirol?). It is similar to the previous *Gĕula* in style, meter, and content.

19. *Fifth Sabbath after Passover.* "אגורה", *Yotzer*, is the work of Elija b. Menahem of le Mans of the eleventh century.[24] Each stanza has an ending stanza with the author's name in the acrostic and with *Kadosh* at the end.

"יקודי אש", *Ofan*, a poem by Jacob, is similar in meter, structure, and content to the previous *Ofan*.

"סגולתי, משכתיך", *Ahava*, a poem by Menahem b. Jacob b. Solomon of Worms who died in 1203.[25] It is similar in structure and content to the previous *Ahavas*.

"אלהים לא אדע", *Zulath*, is a poem by the above mentioned Ephraim b. Isaac. It has three lines to the stanza with the refrain "עד מתי ה'". It is similar to the previous *Zulath* in both content and form.

"יקוש בעניו", *Gĕula*, is the work of Isaac. It is similar in both meter and content to the previous *Gĕula*.

20. *Sabbath before Shavuoth.* "אהלל בצלצלי", *Yotzer*, is a poem by Benjamin b. Zarah. In accordance with Kabbalistic conceptions, it describes the powers of the Hebrew alphabet which appear as initial letters of words.

"ארחות אראלים", *Ofan*, appears with a refrain from Isaiah 6:3. This piyyut is also found in the Roumanian ritual. In its alphabetic acrostic it describes the revelation on Mount Sinai. It is also used for Shavuoth.

"אשר יחדיו", *Mĕora*, a poem by Abraham b. Samuel. Zunz suggests that he is the brother of Juda the Pious (*Ltg.*, p. 284). It has two words to the line, or the Hazağ meter. It speaks of revenge and redemption.

"אימתי, יונה", *Ahava*, is a poem by Isaac b. Rava, or Reuven, as the last stanzas vary.[26] The initial and closing words alternate in the stanzas "איומתי" and "אילותי". The poem is in the form of a dialogue between God "אילותי" and Israel "איומתי".

"אלהי אקראך", *Zulath*, is the work of Samuel b. Juda. It is an alphabetic acrostic with the author's name in the second line. It has three words to the line. The author describes the horrors of the First Crusade in 1096 which took place before Shavuoth. The date (8)56 — 1096 — is indicated in the last stanza.[27]

"יונה נשאת", *Gĕula*, is a poem by Jehuda Halevi.

The Italian ritual has only one piyyut for this Sabbath: "אמונת עתים" by Abraham, probably of Oriental origin.

The *Mĕoras*, *Ahavas*, *and Gĕulas* of the piyyut for the six Sabbaths between Passover and Shavuoth, or the *Sefira Sabbaths* as they are commonly called, became favorite texts with the East European Hazzanim. Many of them composed fine musical selections for these poems which used to touch the Jewish hearts, especially so the musical selections of Solomon Kashtan and Joseph Altshul.[28]

In his *Siddur*, p. 713f., S. Baer gives five *Zulath piyyutim* for five Sabbaths only, and no piyyut at all for the first Sabbath. These poems are different from the ones described above. They are as follows:

"אזכרך דודי" by Meshullam b. Kalonymos of the eleventh century with five words to the line.

"אלהים אל דמי", by Benjamin b. Zarah; it has the same meter.

"אתה אלהים", by the above mentioned Meshullam and in the same meter.

"אחרי נמכר", by Baruch b. Samuel of Mayence who died in 1221; it too has the same meter.

"אותך כל היום קוינו", *Ahava*, a poem by Ephraim b. Isaac with three words to the line.

"אלהים באזנינו", *Zulath*, a poem by Eliezer b. Nathan of Mayence of the twelfth century. In this piyyut, too, the year 1096 is indicated.

All these piyyutim recount the sufferings of the Jewish communities in Germany during the Crusades.

These *Zulath* piyyutim are also given by Maharil.

21. *Sabbath after Shavuoth.* "אדיר ונאה בקדש", *Yotzer*, a poem by the above mentioned Meyir b. Isaac. It has five accentuated words

to the line. After every three stanzas, a stanza ends with the word "Kadosh." The piyyut is based upon Midrashic themes.

"כבודו אות", *Ofan*, a poem by Abraham, belongs to the earliest piyyut. It is based on the mystic interpretation of the heavenly realm.

The *Meora* is the same as in 20.

"אור ישראל וקדושו", *Zulath*, is the work of Joseph b. Samuel Bonfils. It has three words to the line and four lines to the stanza. The fourth stanza is Biblical. It is a description of the receiving of the Tora on Mount Sinai.

"אשר יצר" for the Sabbath of *Bhaalothcha*.

The Meora is the same as in 5.

22. *Sabbath of Shelah lecha.* "שש מאות", *Ahava*, is a poem by Solomon (b. Juda?) in the Hazağ meter. The author describes the Kabbalistic laws of the fringes (Tzitzith), because the last paragraph of this portion is the third paragraph of the Shema which deals with the fringes. The refrain is from Numbers 37 : 38.

23. *Sabbath of Hukkath.* "אל מחוללי", *Ahava*, a poem in the above mentioned meter. The content is culled from the portion Numbers 21, and the refrain is taken from Numbers 21 : 17.

24. *Sabbath before the Ninth of Av* (Italian ritual). "הכל אנחו", *Yotzer* and "איך לזמר" are based upon Lamentations.

25. *Sabbath Nahmu* (Ashkenazic ritual). "אל אל שדי", Yotzer, is a poem by Menahem b. Machir with six words to the line. It is based upon Isaiah 40 — the Haftara for that week. This Yotzer is given by Heidenheim, while Baer has

"ארוממך אל חי", a poem by Meyir b. Isaac. It has three words to the line in an alphabetic acrostic. Each stanza has an additional stanza with four words to the line, ending with *Kadosh*. These ending stanzas have the name of the author in an acrostic. This poem praises the creation, and is interspersed with Midrashic elements.

"שאו מנחה", *Ofan*, is a poem by Menahem b. Machir in the Hazağ meter. It is based upon Isaiah 40 : 26 the words of which are used as initial words of the stanzas. The last two poems are cited in Maharil.

"שתי פעמים", *Ahava*, is a poem by Solomon b. Juda in the above mentioned meter. It is didactic in content, describing the Rabbinical laws concerning the recitation of the Shema and its benedictions.

"אמת משל", *Zulath*, a poem by Meyir b. Isaac with three words to the line. Phrases of Isaiah 40 are utilized in this poem, while the theme is taken from *Pesikta* § 29 (Maharil).

The Italian ritual has "את יום פדותכם", a poem by Juda b. Menahem, probably of Rome of the twelfth century. It has three words to the line, and three lines to the stanza, the third of which is taken from Isaiah 40.

"ארחמך מרחמי" has four words to the line and four lines to the stanza, the fourth of which is Biblical. Both piyyutim have alphabetic acrostics.

26. *Sabbath of Ekev.* "ידיד עליון", *Ahava*, a poem by Juda in the Hazağ meter. It describes the Rabbinical laws pertaining to *Tefillin*, because in this portion the second paragraph of Shema is included, and that indicates the commandments concerning the Phylacteries (Deut. 11 : 18). The refrain is taken from Canticles 8 : 6.

27. *Sabbath before Rosh Hashana.* "אל אלהים", *Yotzer*, a poem by Isaac b. Moses of the eleventh century. It has three lines to the stanza, the third of which is Biblical with an alphabetic acrostic. It is based upon *Hechaloth*,[29] and describes the seven heavens.

"שאו לבבכם", *Ofan*, a poem by the same author in the Hazağ meter. It has five lines to the stanza with a refrain from Psalm 99 : 9. In this poem, the angels join in the prayer of Israel.

"אלהים אלי אתה", *Zulath*, is an alphabetical acrostic by the same author. It is followed by the name of the author. It is a supplication.

28. *Sabbath Teshuva* (*Shuva*) (Heidenheim and O.H.). "אל אל אשחר", *Yotzer*, is a poem by Menahem b. Machir. It has three lines to the stanza, the third of which is from the *Haftara* of the day (Hosea 14 : 2–10). After each three stanzas, an additional stanza follows which contains the name of the author and which ends with *Kadosh*.

"האזינו", *Ofan*, is a poem by the same author. It is an alphabetic acrostic and has six words to the line. The acrostic runs only up to *Samech*. The author's name is in the initial letters of the fourth word in each first line of each stanza.[30] There are four lines to the stanza, the fourth of which is Biblical. The first word of each stanza is taken from the portion of the day, Deuteronomy 32.

"אדעה כי אין", *Zulath*, a poem by the same author and in the same meter. The motive of repentance runs through all these piyyutim.

S. Baer gives the following piyyutim: "אור עולם", *Yotzer*, a poem by Eliezer b. Nathan. The ending of each stanza is from Isaiah 55 : 6f. and other Scriptural phrases.

"כי אם שם", *Ofan*, a poem by the same author. Each stanza begins with a word from Deuteronomy 32 : 3.

"אל אלהינו נשוב", *Zulath*, likewise by the same author. It speaks of repentance.[31]

The Italian ritual has for this Sabbath. "אלי שובה" — an alphabetic acrostic. It is the same as the previous piyyutim in content.

29. *Sabbath before Succoth.* "את השם הנכבד", *Yotzer*, a poem by Meyir b. Isaac. It has three lines to the stanza, the third of which is Biblical. The content consists of the motive of the approaching holiday in its Midrashic interpretation.

"יחו לשון", *Ofan*, a poem by Jacob; it is in accordance with the Bohemian tradition. It has the same meter as the previous poem. The poet describes the singing of the angels, and concludes with a prayer for redemption.

"אזכרה מקדם", *Zulath*, a poem by Isaac consisting of six words to the line in an alphabetic acrostic which runs only up to *Yod*.

"אליך תשוקתי", *Yotzer*, is a poem by Meyir of Rothenburg. It is found neither in Heidenheim nor in Baer.[32]

The Italian ritual has for this Sabbath:

"שולמית הנבחרת", a poem with three lines to the stanza, the third of which is Biblical. *Succa* and the four species make up its content.

On those Sabbaths on which *Ofan* is recited a short poetical passage is inserted before the last response of the *Kedusha* in Musaf. This passage starts with the last word of the previous response; "אלהיכם". The passages now in use (see Heidenheim, p. 103 and Baer, p. 243), are by Juda b. Samuel the Pious and some by his father.

APPENDIX V

POETICAL INSERTIONS FOR THE THREE FESTIVALS

A. Maaravoth.

For Pesah. 1. The first evening service of Passover has one poem divided into five parts for the 1, 2, 3, 4, and 6th insertions. Each part begins with "A night of Watching" (Exod. 12:42), "ליל שמורים". It is an alphabetical acrostic with the letters "ט—נ" missing. This poem is attributed to Rashi.[1] However, it is also found in the old Roman ritual [2] in the same incomplete form. Each stanza has four lines and its own rhyme.

The author expresses the hope that just as God redeemed Israel from Egypt at midnight so will He in the future deliver His people at the same time.

For the third part another "piyyut" is given: "פסח אכלו". It is likewise an alphabetical acrostic, but its author is unknown.

The seventh poetical insertion is found in M.V., p. 569: "אזכרה שנות עולמים". The poem is not generally used; its author is Jehuda b. Isaac according to Heidenheim. Landshuth holds that M.V. is correct in ascribing it to Meyir b. Yitzchak. M.V., however, has an insertion which the Ashkenazic ritual does not contain. In this insertion Brody finds the acrostic Isaac ben Isaac — "משואבי מים" — who, according to Zunz (*Ltg.*, p. 331) lived in France in the fifteenth century. Zunz (*o.c.*, p. 149) is of the opinion that "אזכרה" is by Meyir b. Isaac — the famous Hazzan in Worms in the eleventh century.

The poem starts with "I shall remember years of old" and describes the sacrificing of the Pascal lamb in Jerusalem. It has an alphabetical acrostic.[3]

2. For the second evening the following poem is inserted: "A night of watching, when Israel's light, the Holy One, fulfilled His servant's word in Egypt" — a poem by Meyir b. Isaac.[4] This poem is divided into five parts and has the alphabetical acrostic with "א—ז" "ט—ש", "ת" and "ח" are missing. The poem is given in M.V., pp. 570–1, where the two letters are also missing.

Before the third part, a poem by the same author is inserted: "ליל שמורים, אדיר" — "A night of watching, the mighty and glorious in praises created a memorial to his wonders on the night of Pesah." It is an alphabetical acrostic in which Israel's historic events are reviewed.

The seventh part is by the same author [5] — "אור יום הנף". It deals with the sacrifice of the "Sheaf" — *Omer*.

3. In M.V., p. 572, there are poetical insertions for Friday evening of the Passover week. They begin with "The Sabbath is a true emblem for the beloved children" — a poem by Abraham Nathan.

4. M.V. has a poem by Solomon for the seventh evening. The first words of each line are taken from Exodus 14:30–31 and 15; it describes the scene on the Red Sea.

The Ashkenazic ritual now has for the seventh evening the poem: "The Lord saved the people, saved of yore . . ." — "ויושע ה' אום" — a poem by Joseph b. Jacob of the eleventh century.[6] It is in the same style as the previous one (M.V., p. 573). It is divided into five parts. There is another poem for part three; it is: "On Passover the faithful sang a song . . . " — "פסח אמונים שיר". This poem is an alphabetical acrostic.

M.V. assigns this poem for the eighth evening.

5. A poem by Yekuthiel b. Joseph is used for the eighth evening. It is an alphabetic acrostic and is divided into three parts, there being an insertion before the third part. The poem begins with "He saved whoever cherisheth His holy boughs, His flower of praise . . ." — "ויושע אומן". The words are from Exodus 14:30–31 and 15, and are used as in the previous ones. In the insertion to part three — "פסח אשרי" — whole sentences of the Song of the Sea change off with sentences from the Prophets and Psalms.

In the Sephardic and Yemenite rituals, Psalm 107 is recited on the first two evenings before the evening service, and after the service Hallel is chanted. The Italian ritual has this Psalm before the reading of the Tora in the morning service.

For Shavuoth. 1. On the first evening of Shavuoth there is a poem by Joseph b. Samuel Tov-elem (Bonfils) of Limoges (France) who flourished in the eleventh century. The poem — "וירד אביר יעקב" — describes the contents of the Ten Commandments in an alphabetical acrostic. The insertion to paragraph 3 "טוביה למרום עלה" continues the acrostic, but has another rhyme. The first words of the Ten Commandments are utilized.

M.V. gives this poem and an additional poem — "Days of yore, years of old" — by Isaac b. Isaac of the eleventh century; it describes the offering of the "ripe-fruit." The Ashkenazic ritual does not have this poem.

2. For the second evening, the Ashkenazic ritual uses a poem by Isaac b. Moshe of the eleventh century.[7] It is full of praise of the Ten Commandments. It is similar to the previous in both form and structure. M.V., p. 575, gives another poem for the occasion by Joseph b. Jacob:[8] "I am, once He in His holiness spoke."
"וירד אלהים על הר סיני" by Isaac b. Moshe in the eleventh century.

This last poem is given in the Polish ritual, while the Ashkenazic ritual has "אל אלהים ה'" — a poem by Eliezer ben Nathan (Rabban) who lived at the end of the eleventh century in Mayence.[9] The author tries to prove that the Ten Commandments contain the six hundred and thirteen laws.

The Sephardic and Yemenite rituals recite Psalm 68 before the service; the Italian ritual has it before the reading of the Tora-portion.

For Succoth. 1. On the first evening of Tabernacles, a poem — "אוחזי בידם" — by Joseph Tov-elem is used. The poem praises Israel who glorifies God with the four plants. The form and structure are the same as the previous poems.

2. For the second evening "ישמחו בחגיהם" — a poem by Yehiel b. Isaac [10] is read. It is a glorification and a description of the "Booth" — *Succa.*

3. M.V., p. 579, has poetical insertions for Friday evening of the Succoth week too.

4. For the eighth evening — (Shemini Atzereth) — the Polish ritual has a poem by Daniel b. Jacob of the twelfth or the thirteenth centuries; it is "אעניד לך" — "I will crown Thee with glory and praise on the eve of this Eighth Day of Assembly." The author tells of the place the number eight occupies in Jewish tradition. In form and structure this poem resembles the others.

M.V. gives this selection for the *last* day. The Ashkenazic ritual has another poem for this evening; it is "שמיני אותותיו" — by Joseph b. Nathan Hazzan who migrated to Würzburg in the twelfth century.[11] The poem is similar in content, form, and structure to the previous one. There is an additional seventh part — "אודות באר" — by the same author which relates the important rôle which water played in Jewish history and describes the celebration of water libation which was observed during the Succoth Festival.

5. For the eve of Simhath Tora — the Rejoicing in the Law — there is "את יום השמיני" — a poem by Isaac of the thirteenth century (?). It has the same form as the previous ones. It begins with "On the eighth day Thou wilt prepare blessings for me and with songs of deliverance wilt compass me about." [12]

In the Ashkenazic communities, the evening services have a special mode in which they are chanted.[13]

The Sephardic and Yemenite rituals recite Psalms 42 and 43 before the services of the first and second evenings, and on the eighth evening they have Psalm 12.

B. SHAHARITH.

For Pesach. Ashkenazic ritual for the first morning of Passover:

1. *Yotzer:* "אור ישע" — a poem by Solomon b. Juda of Rome who is called "Habavli" (tenth or eleventh centuries); it is quoted in Maharil. The Italian ritual has the same poem for the second day before "Barechu." The poem has the alphabetical acrostic and the name of the author in alternating lines. The language is hard and obscure. The poem has four lines to the stanza. The last line is always taken

from the Song of Songs. In accordance with Midrashic interpretation, Canticles is supposed to be a love-song between Israel and God.[14]

2. "צאינה וראינה„ — a poem by Mordechai. In this poem too phrases of the Song of Songs are utilized. It is found in the Italian ritual. In a heavy style, the quality of Israel's religious laws is praised.

3. *Ofan.* "ראשו כתם פז„ is a poem in a reversed alphabetical acrostic by Solomon b. Juda.

4. *Zulath.* "אהבוך נפש„ seems to be a continuation of the previous poem in content. It too has phrases from Canticles; it is an alphabetical acrostic by Mordechai.

5. "שחורה ונאוה„ is in the same style by Solomon b. Juda.

6. *Gĕula.* "ברח דודי עד שתחפץ„ — "Flee my beloved, till our love shall please Thee"; it is probably by the same author. The poem consist of three stanzas with phrases from Canticles. It is a prayer for redemption (quoted in Maharil).

At the end of the "Gĕula piyyutim" there occurs the passage "בגלל אבות„ — "For the fathers' sake Thou wilt save the children, and bring redemption unto their children's children."

S.R.A. 6b forbids the use of this phrase; M.V., p. 66, is of the same opinion. The idea is that nothing ought to be inserted between "Gĕula" and "Tefilla" (b. Ber. 9b).

The ITALIAN ritual has for the first day:

1. *Reshuth.* "בקר אערך אקראך„ — a poem by Benjamin b. Joab de synagoga of Montalcino (fourteenth century);[15] it is to be recited before "נשמת„. The name of the author is in the acrostic.

2. "יה שמך„ — a poem by Jehuda Halevi; it is to be recited before half Kaddish.

3. "אנעים חדושי שירים„ — a poem by Shabbathai b. Moshe of Rome of the eleventh century; it is an alphabetical acrostic in the first and third lines. The acrostic of the author's name is in the second line, while the fourth line is taken from Canticles.

4. "צאינה וראינה שמחת„ — a poem by the same author; it has the same style.

5. "גן נעול אושר„ — likewise by the same author and in the same style.

6. "יעידון„ — a poem by Isaac; it closes with "Barechu."

7. "אפתח נא שפתי„ — a poem recited before opening the ark; it is the work of Mattathya b. Isaac of Bologna.

For the second morning the Ashkenazic ritual has:

1. *Yotzer.* "אפיק רנן„ — a poem by Meshullam b. Kalonymos of Lucca of the tenth century. The poem has the same structure and content as that for the first morning.

2. "צאינה וראינה„ — by the same author.

3. *Ofan.* "גן נעול„ — by the same author.

4. *Zulath.* "אודך כי„ — by the same poet.

5. *Gĕula.* "ברח דודי אל מכון„ — by the same poet.

This poet probably created the form of the five poems which became the model for others given in the service of the first morning.

6. *Kerova.* The service of the second morning has also insertions in the first two introductory benedictions of the Amida; they are by Eleazar Kallir. The poem has an alphabetical acrostic and is divided in four parts: Part one closes the first benediction; part two closes the second benediction; part three closes with Psalms 146: 10 and 22: 4; and the fourth part closes with the sentence: "Living and existing, revered, exulted and holy (God)!"

This poem deals with the laws pertaining to Passover offerings and with God's providence and protection of Israel.

7. "אז כל חיתו יער„ — a poem by the same author. In this "piyyut," the significance which the sacrifice of the oil has had in the Bible is discussed.

8. "אל נא, לעולם תערץ„ — "O God, forever, shalt Thou be revered and forever hallowed." This passage is usually recited here whenever poetry is inserted in the Amida. This is a short Kedusha (see Appendix IV).

9. "שור אשר מאז„ has the same content as 7; it utilizes the portion of Leviticus 32: 26–33, 44 which is read on this day.

10. "אומץ גבורותיך„ — a poem by E. Kallir; it is the same as in the Haggada (see Chapter XIV).

11. *Silluk.* "בעשר מכות„ is probably by the same author as 1–5. Here the poet relates with Midrashic interpretations the causes and effects of the ten plagues.

Whenever there are *Kerova* insertions, they are preceded by the passage "מסוד חכמים„ (see Appendix IV).

For the Sabbath morning service during the Passover week:

1. *Yotzer.* "אהוביך אהבוך„.
2. "צאינה וראינה„.
3. *Ofan.* "דודי שליט„.
4. *Zulath.* "אלה וכאלה הראיתני„.
5. "מים רבים„.
6. *Gĕula.* "ברח דודי אל שאנן„. All these six "piyyutim" are by Simon b. Isaac b. Abun of Mayence of the eleventh century. In content, structure, and form they are similar to those of the first and second days.

For the seventh morning. 1. *Yotzer.* "ויושע שושני פרח„ (Maharil) is a poem by Simon b. Abun. Each stanza begins with a word from the Song of the Sea and ends with a phrase from Psalms 114–115. The poem closes with a prayer for redemption: "As Thou didst wondrously show Thy many miracles to the generations of old."

2. *Ofan.* "ידועי שם„ — a poem by Jacob which name is in an acrostic. Each line has a separate rhyme. After four or five lines a refrain recurs: "The God of Gods and Lord of Lords is He." The poem describes the heavenly hosts.

3. *Zulath.* "אי פתרום" — a poem by Simon b. Abun. In content it is similar to 1; it too utilizes the Song of the Sea.

4. *Gĕula.* "יום ליבשה" by Jehuda Halevi. It is a praise for crossing the sea, and embodies a plea for redemption.

5. *Kerova.* "אותותיך ראינו אז" — a poem with an alphabetical acrostic.

6. "מגלת עמוסים" — also an alphabetical acrostic but in reversed order.

7. "שבטי יה" — a poem with Biblical phrases.

8. "אמרו לאלהים אדירים".

9. "אילי הצדק" — a poem with sentences from the Song of the Sea after each stanza. There are twenty stanzas.

10. "שם יקרא ככתיבתו".

11. *Silluk.* "חסדי ה׳ אזכיר".

All these are the compositions of Simon b. Abun. They all speak of the wonders of the Exodus as explained in Talmudic literature.

The Italian ritual has for the seventh morning: 1. *Reshuth.* "אתה הארת" — (Anonymous). It is an alphabetical acrostic relating the events at the Red Sea.

2. "ותען להם מרים" — a poem by Azaria Rossi who died in Mantua in 1577. In both poems there are phrases from the Song of the Sea.

3. "ארוממך אלהים" — a poem by the same author.

For the eighth day the Ashkenazic ritual has: 1. *Yotzer.* (Maharil) is the same "piyyut" which the Italian ritual has for the seventh day (1).

2. *Ofan.* "מחוללת, מהוללת" — a poem by Moshe b. Isaac of the thirteenth century. It has the same poetical form as 2 of the seventh day.

3. *Zulath.* The poem is the same as on the seventh day.

4. *Kerova.* "אימת נוראותיך".

5. *Kerova.* "תחבולות עש".

6. *Kerova.* "איום ונורא" — a poem by Hananel and Kalonymos of the eleventh century.

7. *Kerova.* "מה מועיל" — a poem by Moshed and Kalonymos of the eleventh century.

8. *Kerova.* "אדני חלד", by the same poet.

9. *Kerova.* "אצולים מפרך" — by Moshe b. Kalonymos. In structure and form it is the same as 9 of the seventh day.

10. *Silluk.* "אומץ גבורותיך מי ימלל" — a poem in which phrases from "Nishmath" are used; it relates the chase of the Egyptians after Israel at the Red Sea.

For the eighth morning the Italian ritual has: 1. *Reshuth.* "אופל המוני נגלו לעיני" — a poem by Elijah in which phrases from the Song of the Sea are used.

Shavuoth. For the first morning of Shavuoth the poetical insertions in the Ashkenazic ritual are all by Simon b. Abun.

1. *Yotzer.* "אדון אמנני" (Maharil) is an alphabetical acrostic; it is in praise of the Tora which is the beginning and end of all wisdom. The author takes Proverbs 8 : 22–32; 22 : 20 as a theme and weaves around it Midrashic interpretations.

2. *Ofan.* "ועתה בנים" (Maharil). In this poem Proverbs 8 : 33 is divided into five parts and used as first words for the five stanzas. The language is plain, but sublime in describing the song of the heavenly hosts, according to b. Hagiga 13b and Hullin 91b.

3. *Zulath.* "אנכי שמעת". In this poem every stanza starts with the first word of the Ten Commandments and concludes with Proverbs 8 : 33–36; 9 : 1. The author explains the ethical value of the Ten Commandments.

4. *Kerova.* "אורח חיים".

5. *Kerova.* "תמכו כבוד".

6. *Kerova.* "שלמים בחנוהם".

7. *Kerova.* "אם לא אמריך".

All these relate the revelation on Mount Sinai and interpret the Ten Commandments as laws given to man for his benefit.

8. *Kerova.* "אל נא לעולם תוערץ" (Maharil).

9. *Kerova.* "שעשוע יום יום". Here the poet again takes up Proverbs 8 as his theme and recounts the Biblical story from creation up to the revelation.

10. *Seder.* "אלוף מסובל". In this long poem the author tries to explain the Ten Commandments according to the Talmudic and mystic interpretations.

11. *Silluk.* Here the author describes the effect the revelation had upon the people, according to *Mechilta* (Yalkut § 300).

The Italian ritual has: 1. *Reshuth* to "Nishmath." "אזכור מקדם" — a poem by Joab b. Yehiel of Rome of the thirteenth century. His name is in an acrostic. It recounts in brief the revelation.

2. "יה שמך" — a poem by Jehuda Halevi.

3. *Reshuth* to *Barechu.* "אור ישראל" — a poem by Jehuda b. Menahem of the twelfth century who lived in Rome. The author uses the portion of the Pentateuch for the day: Exodus 19, each stanza ending with a sentence of the portion. The poem is an alphabetical acrostic, and the last two lines carry the name of the author.

For the second morning the Ashkenazic ritual has again poetical insertions by Simon b. Isaac b. Abun. His "piyyutim" for this day run along the same lines as those on the previous day.

1. *Yotzer.* "אילת אהבים" — (Maharil).

2. *Ofan.* In Eastern Europe the insertion here is like on the first day: "ועתה בנים"; in Germany it is "ארחות אראלים" (Anonymous, Maharil).

3. *Zulath.* "אנכי שמעת" for Eastern European communities; "אנכי גדול במעדים" for German communities. This last poem is an alphabetical acrostic, and it is anonymous.

4. *Kerova.* "ארץ מטה ורעשה„ (Maharil) — a poem by Eleazer Kallir; it is based upon b. Shabbath 88a. according to which God created the world on the condition that Israel accept the Law, else he would destroy it. Therefore, the earth trembled, doubting whether Israel will accept the Law willingly.

5. *Kerova.* "מן ההר למעוניו„ — a poem which describes the fight of Moses with the angels who, according to the *Talmud* (*l.c.*) opposed the idea of giving the Tora to man.

6. *Kerova.* "קדוש הופיע מפארן„. This paragraph too is based upon Midrashic interpretations (*Yalkut*, Tehillim § 796).

7. *Kerova.* "אנכי בשם אל שדי„ — This poem too has a Midrashic theme: "I, God, set a limit to the expansion of the world." It contains a brief extract from the Ten Commandments.

8. *Kerova.* "אז בכתב אשורית„ — gives the mystic interpretations of the letters of "אנכי„.

9. *Kerova.* "אל נא לעולם„ (Maharil).

10. *Kerova.* "ה׳ קנני ראשית דרכו„ is similar in content and structure to 9 of the first day.

11. *Seder.* "אתו מצות„ is similar to the *Seder* of the first day.

12. *Silluk.* "אלה העדות„ is similar to the *Silluk* of the first day.

For the second day the Italian ritual has: 1. "אלהים בהנחילך„ — a poem by Leonte b. Abraham in which the high value of the Ten Commandments is eulogized.

Succoth. For Succoth morning the Ashkenazic ritual has: 1. *Yotzer.* "אכתיר זר„ — a poem probably by E. Kallir; [16] it is an alphabetical acrostic. The author explains the significance of the four plants according to Midrashic lore.

2. *Ofan.* "אאמיר אותך סלה„ — probably by the same author. It is a beautiful hymn and was rendered into English by Alice Lucas: "Thy praise, O Lord, will I proclaim in hymns unto Thy glorious Name." [17]

3. *Zulath.* "אנא הושיעה נא„ — is a prayer for the restoration of the Temple and for Israel's redemption.

4. *Kerova.* "אימתי בחיל כפור„ (Maharil for the second day) is by Eleazer Kallir.

5. *Kerova.* „מאלמי מגדים".

6. *Kerova.* "קושט שעינת עץ„.

These three sections which Maharil has for the second day belong to one "piyyut" with an alphabetical acrostic. The author works into his poem the Midrashic conception of the booth and the four plants and the Talmudic laws concerning them.

7. *Kerova.* "אקחה פרי עץ הדר„ — is a poem by the same author and has the same contents as the previous one.

8. *Kerova.* "אל נא„.

9. *Kerova.* "אז היתה חנית סכו„ is likewise by the same author. The form of this poem will be found often in the Synagogal poetry

for the High Holydays. Each stanza has six short lines (two accentuated words) and has as the first line two alternating refrains: the passage cited and "וחן בשלם סכו" in the closing lines "בספיר וסכות" and "והיא סכתו". There are six stanzas, in which the idea is developed that before the Temple was built God dwelt among the angels "o'er the sapphire space," but after Israel erected the sanctuary God preferred to dwell "with them of earth He fashioned." This poem has a beautiful English rendition by Elsie Davis.[18]

10. *Silluk.* "אקחה בראשון" — a poem by the same author and along the same lines as 4–8.

The Italian ritual has for this day: 1. *Reshuth* to *Nishmath.* "שירו לאל הודו" — a poem by Mattathya b. Isaac of Bologna; it is in glorification of the creation, the booth and the four plants.

2. *Reshuth* to *Kaddish.* "יה מלכי" — a poem by Joab b. Benjamin; it is a prayer for redemption.

3. *Reshuth* to *Barechu.* "אכתיר זר" — the same as 1–3 in the Ashkenazic ritual. The last two stanzas are changed.

For the Second morning the Ashkenazic ritual has: 1. *Yotzer.* "אאמיץ לנורא" (Anonymous). The poem is interwoven with phrases from Leviticus 23 : 39–44 and Deuteronomy 16 : 13–17. It is an alphabetical acrostic.

2. *Ofan.* The same as on the first day.

3. *Zulath.* According to the Ashkenazic ritual, it is the same as on the first day, but according to the Polish ritual the anonymous poem "אנא תרב עליצותיך" is recited. It is a prayer for deliverance; it has a reversed alphabetical acrostic.

4. *Kerova.* "ארחץ בנקיון כפי".

5. *Kerova.* "תשורת שי".

6. *Kerova.* "אווי סכת הנופלת".

7. *Kerova.* "אלים כהשעין אב".

All these are given in Maharil for the first day; they are by E. Kallir. They follow the same ideas as the *Kerovoth* of the first day.

8. "אל נא".

9. "אמנם מצוה" — a poem by E. Kallir.

10. *Silluk.* "כי אקח מועד". The author speaks of the Temple to be rebuilt in the future, according to the vision of Midrashic literature.

For the second day the Italian ritual has: 1. "אומץ קצות דרכך" — an alphabetical acrostic to "Kaf" without rhyme. The stanzas end with "סכה" and belong probably to the period before Kallir — before the eighth century.[19]

For the Sabbath morning of the Succoth week the Ashkenazic ritual has:

1. *Yotzer.* "את השם הנכבד" — a poem by Meyir b. Isaac; it is an alphabetical acrostic (Maharil). Each stanza consists of three triplet lines, and to each stanza there is an additional triplet with the closing

"קדוש". The "piyyut" is interspersed with Biblical phrases, and recounts the wonders of the creation and His providence with regard to Israel, and closes with the hope of redemption.

The Polish ritual has another *Yotzer*. "אפאר לאלהי מערכה" by Jehuda; it is along the same lines as the previous.

2. *Ofan*. The Polish ritual has "ירוצצו כברקים" by Isaac; it describes the activities of the heavenly hosts.

3. *Zulath*. Though Maharil says that on this day neither *Ofan* nor *Zulath* is said, the Ashkenazic ritual still has the *Zulath* "אזכרה מקדם" by Isaac. It is alphabetical acrostic running up to "Kaf." It has six words to the line. The author uses Midrashic elements.

The Polish ritual has a *Zulath* "יפה וברה" by Jehuda, probably the same author as in the Yotzer.[20] The poem deals with the Exodus, with the plagues, with the Succa, and with the four plants.

The Italian ritual has for this day: 1. *Reshuth* to *Barechu*. "את עמי טובות אבשר" (Anonymous); it utilizes Malachi 3:10; Deuteronomy 28:12; Genesis 27:28; Psalm 29:11. It is an alphabetical acrostic. The poem is full of hope concerning the future of Israel.

For the eighth morning, the Ashkenazic ritual has: 1. *Yotzer*. "אום כאישון" (Maharil). It is an alphabetical acrostic, being a prayer for the forgiveness of Israel's sins and for redemption.

2. *Ofan*. The Polish ritual has: "אראלים ומלאכים" by Amittai b. Shefatya of the eleventh century.[21] The author's name is in an acrostic. It describes the activities of the chief angels as given in the Midrash.

3. *Zulath*. "אמונים אשר נאספו" is a soulful prayer for the welfare of the congregation. It was rendered into English by Nina Salaman:[22] "Thy faithful souls assembled, That long for blessing, bend Their stature down before Thee."

The Italian ritual has for this day: 1. *Reshuth* to *Nishmath*. "צמאה נפשי לאלהים" — a poem by Abraham b. Ezra.

2. In the Kaddish. "אום כאישון" as in the Ashkenazic ritual (see 1).

For the Simhath Tora morning the Ashkenazic ritual has: 1. *Reshuth* to *Nishmath*. "נשמת מלמדי" — a poem by Menahem b. Machir, according to the Polish ritual. It is a prayer for those who occupy themselves with the study of the Tora. Psalm 19:8–10 is used as closing lines for six stanzas.

2. *Yotzer*. "אשרי העם שלו ככה" (Maharil) — a poem by Moshe b. Abshalom Hazzan of the twelfth century. The author employs phrases from Deuteronomy 33 as closing lines for each stanza. In similar manner, phrases from Genesis 49 are used. The idea running through the poem is the selection of Israel to receive the Tora. The name of the author is in an acrostic running through the third lines, while an alphabetical acrostic runs through the beginnings of the first lines.

3. "אשריך... אשר כל סתום" — a poem which speaks of the revelation of the secrets of God's teachings to Israel. It is an alphabetical acrostic.

4. *Ofan*. "אשריך אום קדוש" — a poem by Menahem b. Abitur b. Levi. The verse of Deuteronomy 33 : 29 is used as beginnings of each line. The acrostic indicates the author's name; in the acrostic several lines are missing. It is a glorification of the Tora and of those who observe it.

The Polish ritual has another *Ofan*. "אשנבי שחקים" by Amittai mentioned above in 1 to which poem this *Ofan* is similar in style.

5. *Zulath*. "אז בקשוב עניו" — a poem by Moshe b. Shemuel (see 2). It relates the struggles of Moses when God ordered him to go up on Mount Nebo and die (Deut. 32 : 48–49). The author employs Midrashic elements (Devarim Rabba 32–33).

The Italian ritual has for this day: "אמרת רנן ערוכה" — in the *Kaddish* before *Barechu*. It is a double alphabetical acrostic. Phrases from Deuteronomy 32–33 are used. It recounts Israel's history up to the death of Moses.

C. Insertions before and after Scriptural Readings:

On Passover. On the first day: In the Italian ritual, before the ark is opened the passage "אפתח נא שפתי ואענה ברון" by Mattathya b. Isaac of Bologna is read. The author utilizes Biblical phrases and prays for the redemption of Israel.

Then the Scroll is taken out and Psalm 105 is recited.

On the second day, Psalm 106 is read; on the seventh, Psalm 18.

On the eighth day, "אין כמוך" is read. In addition to the text used, several verses from the Psalms are recited in the Italian ritual.

Then there follows "תאיר נוגה". This is a glorification of the Tora and a prayer in which parts of the texts for the "Hakafoth" of *Simhath Tora* are used. It is followed by "מי כמוך" Exodus 15 : 11 which is continued in an alphabetical acrostic running up to "Mem." Then follows "על הכל" and "ותגלה", as in the Ashkenazic ritual on weekdays. A prayer for the teachers and leaders "ועל מרי רבותינו" in an alphabetical acrostic closes the selection.

The Sephardic-Oriental Synagogue has a Kedusha for the seventh day by David Pardo (1719–92). The selection is in poetical form with three lines to the stanza, the closing lines being verses from the Song of the Sea.

For the second day of Passover, the Polish ritual has a hymn "יה אלי" by Juda which is recited after the Scriptural reading. It is an introduction to Musaf.

On Shavuoth. On the first day, before taking out the Scroll, the Italian ritual has Psalm 68.

The Sephardic-Oriental ritual has a "Kedusha" by Israel Najara for the first day: "ירד דודי לגנו"; it utilizes phrases from the Song of Songs. This poem is translated into Ladino. Then the "Azharoth" —

Warnings — by Solomon b. Gabirol which precede the poem "אמון יום זה" by David b. Eleazar Bekoda are chanted. They deal with the warning to observe the commandments and laws of the Tora.

On the second day, "Azharoth": "בצל שדי" by Solomon is recited; it is along the same lines as those of the first day. The Yemenite ritual has the same, but before the Scriptural reading the poem "אצולה לפנים" by Abraham b. Ezra is chanted.

The Italian ritual has the "Azharoth" for the Sabbath before Shavuoth and adds "אז שש מאות", a very old piyyut, which in the Ashkenazic ritual is recited on Shavuoth at the Musaf service.

The Sephardic ritual gives the "Azharoth" to be read in two parts before the Minha service on Shavuoth.

On the first day before the Scriptural reading the Ashkenazic ritual has an Aramaic "piyyut": "אקדמות מלין" by Meyir b. Isaac. It is a poem in praise of creation and God Who has given the Tora.[23] In some congregations, another "piyyut" is recited before the reading of the Ten Commandments; it is "ארכין ה' שמיא" an alphabetical acrostic based on Midrashic elements. It describes the excitement of the angels when Moses ascended to the heavens to receive the Tora. "Piyyutim" in Aramaic of a similar mystical character are to be found in M.V., pp. 305–308, 310–344.

On the second day, "יציב פתגם" an Aramaic poem by Jacob b. Meyir is chanted before the Haftara.

On Succoth the Italian ritual has:

a. "בת ברורה" — a poem by Eleazar Elijah in honor of the "Hathan Tora."

b. "אשריכם ישראל" — is an alphabetical acrostic running up to "ח"; it is in praise of Israel who was chosen to receive the Tora.

c. "אשריך ישראל" — likewise an alphabetical acrostic; it explains the high value of the Tora to Israel.

d. "מי עלה למרום" — a poem in praise of Moses who ascended on high to receive the Tora in which the Ten Commandments and several other important laws are written.

e. "אז מרחם אמי". In this poem Moses asks why he should die. The answer is that he should not be considered a deity, but only a mortal being.

f. "אז כל בריות" — a poem with same content as the previous one. In addition, God promises Moses that his death will not be similar to that of other men, for nobody will know his grave, that the gates of paradise will be open to him, and that his soul will be immortal.

g. "לא אמות" — Moses pleads: "I shall not die"; and God replies that he has to die because he is a mortal being.

h. "שח ציר נאמן" — Moses recounts all the works he did at the command of God.

i. "איש אשר הקרן לו אורה" — Moses' mother, Jochebed, pleads for her son.

k. "אורח זו אלך" — Moses bids farewell to his people: "My people, peace be with you"; and the people respond: "Our shepherd, go to peace." Whereupon the last sentences of Deuteronomy are read.

l. "אזלת יוכבד" — a poem in Aramaic. Jochebed runs to Egypt, to the Nile, to the Sea, to the desert, to Sinai, to the rock — asking whether they saw Moses.

m. "ויהושע בן נון פתח" — Joshua laments the death of Moses. The last sentences of the Scriptural reading are translated into Aramaic."

The Sephardic ritual has a short introduction for the "Hathan Tora": "חתן נעים עלה" — "O sweet groom rise," and for the "Hathan Bereshith": "בסימנא טבא" — "May it be a happy augury."

The Sephardic-Oriental ritual has: "אל רם בכל נודעת" and "יה השב לבצרון" by Isaac; and "קומה ה׳ למנוחתיך".

These three short poems are built upon Numbers 10:35.

For the "Hathan Tora" — "ישמח חתני" — a blessing is chanted.

After his Scriptural reading, the congregation says: "Return in peace to thy place; may God favor thy deeds; blessed be in thy coming and blessed in thy going."

In addition to these, the Sephardic-Oriental and Italian rituals have a large group of songs to be sung ad libidum.

In the Yemenite ritual, 1. the poem "אצולה לפנים" by Abraham b. Ezra is sung. Then there follows "מברך רחמנא" in Aramaic; it is the work of Benjamin Cohen, and is a prayer for the well-being of the community.

2. "אמונה יצרה" by Yahya Aldahari; it is a poem in praise of the Tora and closes with a prayer for deliverance. The poem is an alphabetical acrostic.

3. "אשר בגלל אבות בנים גדל" — a poem which recounts the making of the tablets as described in Midrashic interpretations. This poem is found in M.V., p. 459, with slight variations.[24]

For the second day, the Polish ritual has the same "יה אלי" as on the second day of Passover. On the eighth day the memorial service is recited.

On Simhath Tora, the Ashkenazic ritual has the same service for the "Hakafoth" as on the previous evening. When the "Hathan Tora" is called upon, the prayer "מרשות האל" is recited; it is the same as in the Italian ritual with but slight variations. It is also found in M.V., p. 457.

Another "Reshuth" is recited for the "Hathan Bereshith": "מרשות מרומם" by Menahem b. Machir; both are praises of the Tora and blessings on the persons called upon. The poem for "Hathan Tora" seems to be older than that for the "Hathan Bereshith."

In some congregations, "אשריך הר העברים" by Abraham b. Ezra is recited before the Haftara; it is in praise of Moses (M.V., p. 460).

"אשר בגלל אבות" is recited before replacing the Scroll, as given in the Italian ritual.

E. INSERTIONS FOR MUSAF. *On Passover.* For the first day, the Sephardic and Yemenite rituals have "תקון הטל" — Prayer for Dew.[25]

1. In the "Avoth" benediction: "שזופת שמש" — by Solomon — "The people tainted by the scorching sun . . . cheer her affliction with showers of dew. . . ."

2. In the "Gevuroth" benediction: "שלח רוחך" — by Solomon.

3. "מבטח כל היצור" — both are prayers for the fertilization of the earth and resurrection.

4. "לשוני בוננת" — a thanksgiving.

5. "לך לשלום גשם" — "Farewell, O rain, in peace; and be welcome, O dew!"

6. "בטללי אורה" — is a double acrostic running up to "Kaf." Each line begins with "בטללי" and closes with "אדמה".

All these poems have a delightful style.

At the conclusion the following passage is recited: "For Thou, O Lord, our God . . . causest the dew to descend for a blessing. We beseech Thee, cause it to descend for light, for blessing, for joy . . . for benefit, for salvation, and sustenance."

After the Musaf of the Three Festivals the Italian ritual has an alphabetic poem: "ה' ישפות לנו שלום" — by Benjamin b. Abraham;[26] it is an acrostic. It deals with the redemption of Israel through the Messiah.

For the second day, "היום תאמצנו" is recited in the last benediction; it is an alphabetical acrostic. This hymn is used in an abbreviated form in the Ashkenazic ritual for the High Holydays.

For "תפלת טל", the Ashkenazic ritual has the following insertions:

1. In the "Avoth" benediction "בדעתו אביעה חידות" (M.V., p. 370).

2. In the "Gevuroth" benediction: "תהומות הדום".

Both these poems express the hope for the fertilization of the earth and the resurrection; they are alphabetical acrostics running up to "ט" only.

3. "ארשה ארוש" — a doubly alphabetic acrostic.

4. "אאגרה בני איש".

5. "תחת אילת עופר" — a reversed alphabetical acrostic. In the second lines, the acrostic of Eleazar Kallir of *Kiriath Sepher* is given.

6. "אלים ביום מחסון" — an alphabetical acrostic. Here the author worked into his poem the twelve months, the twelve tribes, the twelve constellations, the twelve fathers of the tribes. Each stanza describes the "Mazzal" of the month and the righteous hero through whose merits the month is blessed. The idea is taken from Soferim XIX, 10.

7. "טל תן לרצות ארצך" — a reversed alphabetical acrostic. Each of the six stanzas begin and close with "טל". This is a prayer for the fertilization of the soil and for the salvation of the people.

All poems mentioned above are by Eleazar Kallir.[27]

At the conclusion, the ark is opened and the following passages are read: "For a blessing and not for a curse. For life and not for death. For plenty and not for famine." After each phrase, the congregation responds with "Amen."

On Shavuoth. On the first day, in the fourth benediction, the Italian ritual has "אזהרת ראשית". This poem belongs to the oldest poetical elements of the Synagogue. It is an explanation of the six hundred and thirteen laws,[28] and closes with "אז שש מאות" in three stanzas. This insertion is to be found in the Musaf of the second day in the Ashkenazic ritual.

For the second day, the Italian ritual has "אתה הנחלת" which in the Ashkenazic ritual appears on the first day. The content of this "Azharoth" is similar to that of the first day, and also belongs to the earliest poetical products.[29] Following this number, "אז שש מאות" is recited.

The Ashkenazic ritual has the same insertions as the Italian ritual has on the second day. In addition, however, it has seven more numbers in the same form and content.[30]

On Succoth. The Sephardic and Yemenite rituals have insertions for the Musaf of the *Shemini Atzereth*.

"תקון הגשם" — Prayer for Rain.

1. In the "Avoth" benediction. "שפעת רביבים" — by Solomon.
2. "מכסה שמים".
3. "לשוני בוננת" — the same poem as in the Prayer for Dew.
4. In the "Gevuroth" benediction. "אלהי יפתח אוצרות" — an alphabetical acrostic in which Biblical phrases are used.
5. "בגשמי אורה" — the same litany as in the Prayer for Dew, save that "בטללי" is changed for "בגשמי". The closing passage is here also repeated.

All these poems have the poetical style, even as the poems for the Prayer for Dew. They are prayers for rain and speak of the benefits of rain to man.

For the same occasion, the Italian ritual has a poem — "אלהי יפתח השמים" — which is similar to that in the Sephardic ritual in content and in phraseology; it is the work of Abraham.[31]

For the Prayer of Rain the Ashkenazic ritual has:

1. In the "Avoth" benediction. "אף ברי אתת".
2. In the "Gevuroth" benediction. "יטריח לפלג".

"אף ברי" is the name of the angel who is in charge of rain (Job 37 : 1).

3. "אפיק מען" — an alphabetical acrostic.
4. "אקשטה כסל" — a four-fold alphabetical acrostic.
5. "תקום לארץ" — a reversed alphabetical acrostic by Eleazar Kallir.
6. "יפתח ארץ" is similar to 6 in the Prayer for Dew in its content.

In this poem too the twelve months, the twelve "מזלות", and the twelve fathers of the tribes and the Biblical heroes are praised; the heroes are: Abraham, Isaac, Jacob, Moses, Levi, Simeon, Juda, Issachar, Zebulun, Gad, Dan, Naftali, Asher, Joseph, Benjamin, Joshua, David and Solomon.

The beginnings of the stanzas are furnished with words from Deuteronomy 28 : 12. For the beginnings of the third lines the word "מים" is used, and for the beginnings of the fifth lines words from Isaiah 55 : 10 are used.

7a. "איום זכור נא" — an alphabetical acrostic which speaks of the deeds of the patriarchs, Moses and Aaron, in connection with water.

7b. The Polish ritual has "זכור אב" — an alphabetical acrostic recounting the deeds of Abraham, Isaac, Jacob, Moses, Aaron, and the twelve tribes, and their devotion, and the many miracles God showed them on water. The poem has two refrains alternating: "For his sake do not refuse water" and "For his sake favor us with a spray of water."

APPENDIX VI

SELIHOTH AND KINOTH

A. SELIHOTH. For the Fast of Gedaliah: The Sephardic and Yemenite rituals have “אבלה נפשי„ and “יוקם דם עבדיך„, both lamenting the murder of that hero.

For the Tenth of Teveth: “וארץ שפל רומי„, “בחדש העשירי„, „אז בבוא יום“, “שעה עליון„ by Yechiel Mondolfo of the seventeenth century; they are in Hazağ meter, and “יושב בשמים„.

For the Fast of Esther: “אנגי בהעמיקו„ by Yosef, “יחלת עבדיך„ by Isaac, “יהירים קמו„, “איך זרים, אכזרים„ in the Hazağ meter with the refrain from Psalm 124: 1–3.

For the Seventeenth of Tammuz: “וארץ שפל רומי„, “בחדש הרביעי„, “אז בבגדי„, “שעה נאסר„ by Solomon b. Gabirol in Hazağ meter, and “אלהי ישועתי„.

There are also short Selihoth for the Minha service of these fast-days; they consist of Psalm-verses and responses.

The Italian ritual has Kerova for all the nineteen benedictions; the Selihoth are inserted in the sixth benediction. This consists of the Thirteen Attributes, the Widdui, three Psalms and three poetical Selihoth.

For the Fast of Gedaliah, the Ashkenazic ritual has:

1. “אבלה נפשי„ as in the Sephardic ritual.
2. “אמנת מאז ארשת„ by Benjamin.
3. “את צום העשירי„ by Menahem b. Jacob (died 1203 in Worms).
4. “ארח צדקה„ by Solomon with five words to the line. This is called "Shalmonith" (see Chapter V).
5. “שוממתי ברוב יגוני„ by Solomon b. Gabirol;[1] it has six syllables to the meter and three lines to the strophe; it is called "Shalmonith."
6. “אזרחי מעבר הנהר„ — "Akeda" — three words to the line and two lines to the strophe.
7. “הורית דרך תשובה„ — by Benjamin. This is a Pizmon, i.e., a song to be chanted according to a fixed tune (see Chapter V).
8. “כסא כונן„ — by Samuel. This is the second part of a Seliha beginning “אדון משפט„. It has three words to the line and four lines to the stanza. The last line is taken from the Scriptures.
9. “תורה הקדושה„ — by Simon b. Isaac b. Abun. Here the Tora is asked to plead in behalf of those who observe it.

The Polish ritual has a different set of poetical Selihoth:

1. “אז טרם נמתחו„ is the opening (Pethiha) by Solomon b. Isaac "Rashi."[2] It has five words to the line, and is an alphabetical

acrostic. The name of the author is at the end where he describes the Paradise as being situated in the south and Hell in the north.

2. "את ה׳ בהמצאו" by Elijah b. Shemaya.

3–4. Are the same as the numbers 1–2 in the Ashkenazic ritual.

5. "אורך ואמתך" by Shemaya; it has three words to the line.

6. "תשוב תרחמנו" Shalmonith, utilizing Biblical passages.

7. Is the same as 7 in the Ashkenazic ritual.

8. "Akeda": "אז בהר המור".

9. "זכור ברית אברהם" Pizmon cited often in the Selihoth for the Day of Atonement.

10. The same as 9 in the Ashkenazic ritual.

For the Tenth of Teveth, the Ashkenazic ritual has:

1. "אדברה וירוח לי" by Benjamin.

2. "אבן הראשה" by Abraham b. Menahem [3] of the thirteenth century; it has five syllables to the meter.

3. "אם קרואה" four words to the line.

4. "אבותי כי בטחו" by Ephraim b. Isaac of Regensburg of the twelfth century. This "Pizmon" is retained in full in the Polish ritual where it consists of fourteen stanzas of which only the first three are retained in the Ashkenazic ritual. This has only six stanzas, the last three of which are not found in the Polish ritual.[4] In the latter, the author complains concerning the fall of Jerusalem at the hands of the Crusaders.[5]

5. "אריד בשיחי" by Isaac b. Yakar of the twelfth or the thirteenth centuries. This poem has the ring-form, i.e., the last of the short two-word lines is repeated as the first word in the next line; for example, "אריד בשיחי", "בשיחי לגוחי", "לגוחי בהשיחי". The repetition adds only metrical sound, but does not improve the content. In translating that sentence, the repetitions are left out. It is as follows: "I am distraught in my complaint to my Creator, when I am bowed down."

6. "גרוני נחר זועק" by Gershom b. Juda.

The Polish ritual has only three insertions: 3, 4, and "אזכרה מצוק" by Joseph.

For the Fast of Esther the Ashkenazic ritual has:

1. "אתה האל עושה פלאות" by Simon b. Isaac b. Abun; it has four lines to the stanza.

2. "אתה האל עושה פלא" by Samuel.

3. "אדם בקום עלינו" by Menahem b. Machir; it has six words to the line. The fourth line of the stanza is taken from the Bible.

4. "במתי מספר" by Meshullam. It is a Pizmon with four words to the line.

5. "פניך האר" by Simon b. Isaac; it has three words to the line. The last word of the fourth line is repeated at the beginning of the first line of the next stanza. The last line is taken from the Scriptures.

The Polish ritual has only 1, 3, and 4.

For the Seventeenth of Tammuz the Ashkenazic ritual has:

1. "אתאנו לך יוצר".
2. "אפפוני מצוקות" by Kalonymos b. Juda of the tenth or eleventh centuries.
3. "אדאג מחטאתי" by Jacob b. Hezekiah; it has four words to the line.
4. "שעה נאסר" the same as in the Sephardic ritual.
5. "אודה עלי פשעי" by Moses b. Samuel of the twelfth century.[6] The poem has three words to the line; the last word of the fourth line is repeated at the beginning of the next line.
6. "איך מכל אומות" by Amittai; it has three words to the line.

The Polish ritual has for this fast-day also only three poems: 1, 4 and "אמרר בבכי" by Menahem b. Machir.

For the other fast-days the Ashkenazic ritual has:

For the first Monday of "בה"ב":

1. "תבוא לפניך" by Solomon.
2. "ישראל עמך" by Isaac b. Meyir; it has four words to the line.
3. "אין מי יקרא בצדק" by Solomon.
4. "ישראל נושע בה'" Pizmon by Shefatya mentioned in the Ne'ila service.
5. "אדון בינה הגיגנו" has three words to the line.

The Polish ritual has 2 and "אלהים בישראל", "מלאכי רחמים" by Samuel Cohen.

For Thursday:

1. "אך בך מקוה".
2. "אם עונינו רבו" by Solomon.
3. "איה כל נפלאותיך" by Gershom b. Juda.
4. "רועה ישראל" Pizmon by Meshullam mentioned in the Ne'ila service.
5. "גדול עוני" by Gershom b. Juda; it has four words to the line and has the ring-form as explained above.

The Polish ritual has 4 from the Monday Selihoth and "אנשי אמונה" and "תענית צבור" by Meyir Hatzair.

For the last Monday:

1. "אליך נשואות עינינו".
2. "אין כמדת בשר"; it has four words to the line.
3. "אזון תחן"; it has four words to the line.
4. "אזכרה אלהים" a Pizmon by Amittai mentioned in the Ne'ila service (Chapter XVI).
5. "אל נא רפא נא" mentioned in the Minha service of the Day of Atonement (Chapter XVI).

The Polish ritual has 2, 4, and 2 from the Seventeenth of Tammuz.

B. Kinoth. The Sephardic ritual has sixty-five Kinoth: thirteen for the evening and fifty-two for the morning service. Only a few Kinoth are common to both the Sephardic and Ashkenazic rituals;

they are: "שכורה ולא מיין, אש תוקד בקרבי, שומרון קול תתן, בליל זה יבכיון, אז בחטאינו חרב, יום אכפי הכבדתי" and they, too, vary greatly. Furthermore, "אלה אזכרה" which is recited in the Ashkenazic ritual in the Musaf of the Day of Atonement is read in the Sephardic ritual on the Ninth of Av.

"שומרון קול תתן" is the work of Solomon b. Gabirol. It is a dialogue between Zion and Samaria, i.e., Juda and the Northern kingdom; each of the kingdoms relates the sins which she committed and for which she was punished. Zion is called Oholiva and Samaria Ohola (Ezek. 23:4).

"שכורה ולא מיין" is by the same poet. Speaking to Zion, the poet says: "O thou intoxicated one, but not with wine, cast away thy tambourines, cut off thy hair and disguise thy face, and raise lamentations . . . and cry to God concerning the destruction of thy Temple. . . . When the enemy penetrated the sanctuary, he found the priests at their holy duties which they did not abandon until they were killed."

"יום אכפי" by Jehuda Halevi recounts the story of the assassination of the prophet Zechariah (Lam. 2:20; II Chron. 24:20–21; b. Gittin 57b).

His blood, the legend says, was not accepted by the earth and was rustling for revenge, until Nabuzaradon came and made inquiry concerning the reason for the restlessness of this blood. When told the story, he ordered that the blood of the priests be shed, but Zechariah's blood still did not rest. He then ordered that innumerable elders, women, and children be slaughtered, but the blood still did not quiet down. In his rage, the enemy continued to shed blood, until it turned into a river of blood, but Zechariah's blood seethed and did not rest. Finally, the enemy raised his eyes toward heaven and cried out: "Dost thou want me to spill the last drop of Israel's blood?" Whereupon the blood calmed down.[7]

Psalm 79 is chanted in the Mode of Lamentations.

In "אש תוקד בקרבי" the two exits from Egypt and Jerusalem are set against one another.

In "איך נוי חטאתי" the story of a brother and sister is told. The children of the High Priest Yishmael were taken into captivity by two Romans who decided to marry them to each other by force. The unfortunate children finally escaped this shameful mating by death (b. Gittin 58a).

In the Sephardic, Italian, and Yemenite rituals there is the following custom: In the evening, after the Kinoth are recited, all lights in the synagogue are extinguished, and the precentor sitting on the floor cries out: "O brethren, house of Israel, hearken. Today is one thousand, eight-hundred and . . . years since our Sanctuary was destroyed and the crown of our head fell. Woe unto us, for we have sinned!"

The Sephardic Kinoth have a simpler language and a clearer style than those of the other rituals. They all concentrate on the theme of the Destruction, with the exception of two poems: "אבינו הגמול הזה" and "מי האב ייסר בנו" in which the expulsion from Spain is told in the following manner: "Your brethren were expelled from Serece and Seville; then I saw their stiffneckedness, so I brought upon them the expulsion from Castile, Sicily, Aragon, Granada."

Besides the poets already mentioned, the Sephardic Kinoth have several anonymous poems. The latest compositions are by Moses Zacut (1623–97): "דודי נהפך", and "ארים בקול בכיה".

The Haftara is translated and interpreted in Ladino. Each verse is recited in Ladino and in Hebrew. Whereupon the whole book of Job is chanted.[8]

At Minha, two poems of consolation, each beginning with "נחמו, נחמו עמי" (Isa. 40:1) are chanted.

The Ashkenazic ritual has sixty-one Kinoth: four for the evening and fifty-seven for the morning service. The Polish ritual has forty for the morning and five for the evening service. Of these twenty-three Kinoth are from the Ashkenazic ritual, and seven do not appear in that ritual. Seven are from the Sephardic ritual and were treated above. Besides, the Polish does not have the Kerova by E. Kallir mentioned above.

One number consists of Lamentations V, each verse being divided into two parts. After the first part, "אוי" — "Woe" is exclaimed; and after the second part, "אוי מה היה לנו" is repeated. The arrangement is mentioned in Maharil (Tisha Be'av). The latter gives only twenty-one numbers, and adds that in some places three more Kinoth are recited. Maharil testified that seventeen of them were composed by E. Kallir. These Kinoth are the same as in the Italian ritual mentioned above. However, only twelve of the Kinoth given in the Italian ritual are found in the Ashkenazic ritual.

In many of the Kinoth verses from Lamentations have been utilized. Seven numbers start with "איכה" — the first word of the first three chapters of Lamentations. Some have Bible verses as refrains. They have alphabetical acrostics and rhyme. The Kina "אם תאכלנה נשים" takes Lamentations 2:20 as its theme: "When mothers ate their fruit . . . woe unto me. . . . When their hair was cut off and they were bound to running horses. . . . When thousands young priests hid in the Temple to be burned (b. Taanith 29a). . . . When three hundred sucklings were hanged on one tree. . . . But the holy spirit says: O, they lament only over that which happened to them, but keep silent of the transgressions they have committed."

In "אי כה אמר" the complaint is voiced concerning the unfulfilled promises to the patriarchs. The last line of every stanza is taken from Psalm 74.

In "אז במלאת ספק" the prophet Jeremiah is described as having met a beautiful woman in ugly disguise. He called to her to return to the right path. She is willing to repent, but urges him to pray for her, to call the patriarchs and Moses and Aaron.

In "אז בהלוך ירמיהו" the poet relates how the prophet went to the graves of the patriarchs that they may plead for their children. But the holy spirit replies: Your children have transgressed; they have polluted the Sanctuary by shedding innocent blood. Finally, Jeremiah turns to Leah and Rachel whose pleadings God can no longer withstand and promises to bring back their exiled children.

The first twenty Kinoth are recited by the precentor; the others are divided among the prominent members of the congregation (Maharil). In these numbers, names of several Ashkenazic authors are found, as Kalonymos Hakatan, Isaac, Abraham b. Meyer who describes in "אבל אעורר" the terror of an attack on some Jewish communities in the twelfth century. Baruch, Menahem b. Machir of Regensburg of the eleventh century who describes in "אשאג מנהמת לבי" the bloodshed of the first Crusaders, David Halevi, and David b. Alexander of the twelfth century. His Kina "אזכרה נגינותי" has the alternate refrain "בצאתי מצען" — "When I left Zoan (Egypt)" — and "בצאתי מכנען" — "When I left Canaan." "אסירים בשיר" by Yehiel b. Jacob of the thirteenth century has a similar refrain: "בלכתי להר חורב" — "When I went to Mount Horeb" and "והר ציון חרב" — "Mount Zion is destroyed." In "מי יתן ראשי מים" Kalonymos b. Juda laments over the Crusades of 1096. Joel Halevi recounts the same sad event in "יבכיון מר מלאכי שלום". The congregation in Cologne was asked to abandon its faith and to embrace Christianity, but was slaughtered upon refusal. In his "ואתאונן ואקונן" Juda b. Moses Cohen of the thirteenth century describes the attack on the Jewish community in Frankfort a/m where one hundred and seventy-three souls were killed and synagogues and academies ruined. Meyir b. Yehiel of the thirteenth century gives a description of the Ten Martyrs in his "ארזי הלבנון".[9]

The first forty-five of the sixty-five Kinoth in the Ashkenazic ritual are called Kinoth, while the last sixteen are designated as "ציונים" — "Zionides" — because they start with the word "ציון" and are addressed to the holy Mount. Jehuda Halevi was the first poet to create this pattern with his well-known "ציון הלא תשאלי". He took his motives from Isaiah 49:14–26; 51:17–23; 52:1–2; 54; 60; 62. This poem is found in the Carpentras ritual,[10] but strange to say, the Sephardic ritual does not have this wonderful poem.

This poem of Halevi's has been translated into English several times. The translations are by Nina Salaman (I), Alice Lucas (II), Maurice Samuel (III) in verse, and by B. Halper (IV) in prose.[11]

The other elegies of that type are by Eleazar Hakatan, Elijah the old, Eleazar b. Moshe Hadarshan of Würzburg, Michael b. Perez of the fifteenth century, Menahem Zion b. Meyir of the fifteenth century, Yakar b. Samuel Halevi of the thirteenth century, Moses b. Jacob. Meyer Rothenburg's "שאלי שרופה באש" over the burning of the Talmud in Paris in 1242 is also inserted in the Zionides.

The last number is "אלי ציון" which is also found in the Roumanian ritual; it is chanted according to a traditional tune.[12]

In the Yemenite ritual, the Kinoth are mostly the same as in the Sephardic ritual, with the addition of a few numbers by local authors and with some additions by Abraham b. Ezra and Jehuda Halevi.

NOTES

NOTES TO INTRODUCTORY NOTES

1. *Mishna* Ber. IV, 5; b. Ber. 32a; *o.c.* 26b, 34a; Jer. Ber. IV; b. Megilla 17b; b. Ber. 28b; Jer. Ber. II, 4; b. Ber. 4b, 27b, 60b; 47b, 48b.

PART I

NOTES TO CHAPTER I

1. Friedrich Heiler, *Das Gebet*, München, 1920, p. 237.
2. Such prayers are: Exodus 32: 1–13, 31–32; 33: 12–16; and especially 34: 6–7, 9; Numbers 6: 22–27; 10: 35–36; 12: 13; and Aaron's entreaty: 12: 11; 14: 17–20; Deuteronomy 3: 23–25; 9: 18–20, 25–29; and 26: 5–10. The last one is a prayer which everyone is to utter who offers his first ripe fruit; the prayer Deuteronomy 26: 13–15 serves the same purpose.
3. *Ibid.*, p. 221f.
4. See M. Jastrow, *Die Religion der Assyriens und Babylonien* I–III. Saul's reform evidently brought about the law in Exodus 22: 17; Leviticus 19: 31; 20: 6; and others.
5. *Das Gebet*, München, 1920, pp. 43–44, 46–47.
6. R. Kittel, *Die Psalmen*, Leipzig, 1914, p. xxxvii.

NOTES TO CHAPTER II

1. On the nature of the music in the First and Second Temple see A. Z. Idelsohn, *Jewish Music*, Chapter 1.
2. The same we hear in II Kings 3: 20 concerning the sacrifice of the morning offering which is also called Minha.
3. *Otzar Hagĕonim*, Ber. ed. B. Lewin, Haifa, 1928, p. 77.
4. The following are petitional in character: # 3, 4, 5, 6, 7, 10, 12, 13, 20, 22, 25, 26, 28, 32, 35, 38, 42, 43, 51, 54, 55, 56, 57, 59, 61, 62, 63, 64, 69, 70, 71, 74, 77, 79, 83, 85, 86, 88, 102, 109, 120, 123, 130, 137, 140, 141, 142, and 143.

The following are meditations: # 1, 2, 8, 9, 11, 14, 15, 16, 23, 27, 30, 31, 36, 37, 39, 40, 41, 44, 45, 46, 49, 50, 52, 53, 58, 60, 65, 68, 73, 75, 76, 78, 80, 81, 82, 84, 87, 89, 90, 91, 94, 101, 105, 106, 107, 110, 112, 116, 119, 121, 124, 125, 127, 129, 131, 132, 138, 139. The following are laudations: # 18, 19, 21, 24, 29, 33, 34, 47, 48, 66, 67, 72, 92, 93, 95, 96, 97, 98, 99, 100, 103, 104, 108, 111, 113, 115, 117, 118, 122, 126, 128, 133, 134, 135, 136, 144, 145, 146, 147, 148, 149, 150.

5. *Das Gebet*, p. 238.

NOTES TO CHAPTER III

1. B. Lewin, *o.c.*, p. 23.
2. b. Berachoth 33a; Maimonides, Yad, Hilchoth T'fillah IV.
3. From Assyr. and Babyl. Literature, translated by Robert F. Harper, New York, 1904.
4. *Ibid.*, p. 134.
5. *Ibid.*, p. 151.
6. *Ibid.*, p. 378.
7. *Ibid.*, p. 420.
8. *Ibid.*, p. 422.
9. *Ibid.*, p. 424.
10. *Ibid.*, p. 430.
11. *Ibid.*, p. 433.
12. *Ibid.*, p. 439.
13. The Hebrew Text of the Book of Ecclesiasticus, etc., edited by Israel Levi, Leiden, 1904.
14. *Ibid.*
15. The numbers refer to the order of the benediction in the ritual.
16. We use the New Apocrypha, etc., translated by R. H. Charles, Oxford, 1919.

    See also Oesterley, E. O. E., *The Jewish Background of the Christian Liturgy*, Oxford, 1925, Chapter I.
17. b. Kethuvoth 105 gives the number 394, while Jer. Meg. III, 1 has 480 synagogues in Jerusalem. Josephus recounts of synagogues built by Agrippa I, *Ant.* XIX 6 : 3.
18. See *Jewish Music*, Chapter VI, p. 105.

NOTES TO CHAPTER IV

1. The MS. of the hundred benedictions by Rabbi Natronai was recently discovered in the Geniza fragments and was published by L. Ginzberg, Geonica II, pp. 114–117. The text is almost identical with that in S.R.A. In M.V., p. 3f., a detailed account of the hundred benedictions is given.
2. Though the sources quote only passages from the *Zichronoth*, none the less the other two introductions are also considered Rav's compositions due to the similarity in the style.
3. In *Jewish Music*, Chapter VI, a survey of the "precentor" is given.
4. I. Miller, "חלוף מנהגים", p. 42, Vienna, 1878. According to Miller, the completion of the reading took three and a half years. The Pentateuch was divided into 175 portions.
5. *O.c.*, or rather every three and a half years.
6. *O.c.*, p. 41.
7. *O.c.*, p. 46; T. Soferim XX, 7; Tosafoth to b. Sanhedrin 37b; L. Ginzberg, Geonica II, p. 52; *ibid.* I, p. 131 and II, p. 42—doubts whether the Babylonians had the *Kedusha* in Talmudic times. Ginzberg is of the opinion that the *Kedusha* was introduced in the Amida by the Babylonian mystics, especially the *Kedusha* beginning with "Kether." The Palestinians, he asserts, had a short *Kedusha* in the *Yotzer*.
8. *O.c.* On the variations of the prayer-texts several studies have been published. Concerning the Amida see L. Finkelstein, "The Development of the Amida," *J.Q.R.*, 1925–6, pp. 1–43, 127–170; concerning Grace see the same author, *J.Q.R.*, 1929, pp. 211–262.
9. See Chapter VIII, III.
10. L. Ginzberg, *Geonica* I, p. 142, is of the opinion that the Aramaic Col Nidré text was not used in Babylonia. In *Ginze Kedem* IV, by B. Lewin, Jerusalem, 1930, p. 65ff., some old Selihoth from Gaonic times were published.
11. A. Berliner, *Randbemerkungen* I, 1909, p. 19.

NOTES TO CHAPTER V

1. B. Gittin 7a; see *Jewish Music*, pp. 92–93ff.
2. Alphabetical acrostics are found in Psalm 9 — "א—פ" in every second verse; in Psalms 25, 34, 37, 111–112 in every half verse; in Psalm 119 the acrostic is eightfold; also in Psalm 145.
3. "א"ת ב"ש", or also "אי"ק בכ"ר" and the like.
4. *O.c.*, in the name of Elisha b. Abuya it is related that at the occasion of a festivity the guests sang alphabetical acrostics.
5. *Cf.* H. Burgess, Select. *Metrical Hymns*, etc., London, 1853.
6. *O.c.*, p. 41.
7. *Mahzor Yannai* by I. Davidson, New York, 1919, pp. xviiiff. Yannai's piyyut was also called "Hazanuth" (Harkavy, *Studien*, VIII, pp. 128, 131). This term was later applied to the musical rendition of the liturgy. See *Jewish Music*, pp. 125, 182.
8. *O.c.*, p. xixff.
9. *O.c.*, p. xxiv.
10. Only one poem "אז רב נסים" (see Chapters X, XIV), which is a part of the "Krova" for the "Great Sabbath" (*cf.* Baer, p. 707; O.H., p. 134f.), "אוני פטרי רחמתים" has been retained in the Ashkenazic ritual of the "Haggada" service. (*Cf.* O.H., p. 240; Davidson, *o.c.*, p. xxiv.) Some fragments of his poetry have been discovered and published by Prof. I. Davidson, *o.c.*
11. Landshuth, *Amude Haavoda*, p. 103.
12. See Chapter X.
13. As in his poems "אל דר, אדירי איומה", of the New Year Musaf service, and in his lamentation (Kina) "איכה אצת".
14. As in "אץ קוצץ" of Sabbath *Zachor*, or as in "אשר אימתך" and "באראלי אמן" of the Musaf service for the Day of Atonement.
15. One such poem is the lamentation (Kina) "אם תאכלנה נשים".
16. Some of his innovations are listed by Zunz, *Ltg.* Chapter III. A. b. Ezra in his commentary to Eccl. V, 1 accused Kallir of having corrupted the Hebrew classical language, i.e., that of the Bible; he also claims that his rhymes are not perfect.

17. Zunz, *Ltg.*, p. 523ff.
18. In spite of the fact that A. b. Ezra, in the above-mentioned place, praises his style and the correctness of his forms, his style is much heavier than Kallir's. See Chapter VII on Saadya's *Siddur*.
19. Elbogen, *Studien*, pp. 122ff.
20. Two of his prayers are printed in the *Otzar Hatefilloth*, pp. 91–96, and 1096–1101.
21. *Cf.* "תשובות מנחם".
22. On the Spanish religious poetry *cf.* M. Sachs, *Religiöse Poesie der Juden in Spanien*, 2 Vols., Berlin, 1845.
23. Maharil (38b) says that Maaravoth used to be recited only in Worms, because according to Rokeah the fast had to be completed after sunset and the service was therefore prolonged with poetical insertions; while in other congregations the completion of the fast was not required.
24. J. Berachoth IV, 8b. The name is likewise used in Syrian Liturgy; see M. Sachs, *o.c.*, p. 178.
25. See Aruch ed. Kohut, *ad loc.*
26. Suggested by S. L. Rappaport.
27. See *Jewish Music*, pp. 169–170; Table XXI, 6b.
28. I. Davidson, *o.c.*
29. Elbogen, *Studien*, etc., pp. 56, 76.
30. *O.c.*, pp. 103ff.
31. These works are described and printed in part by Elbogen, *Studien*, etc., pp. 74–190.
32. The number thirteen is thus derived: 1. "יהוה" the Merciful One before the sin; 2. "יהוה" the Merciful One after the sin (R. Tam to b. R.H., 17b); 3. "אל" the Mighty One; 4. "רחום" the Compassionate One; 5. "וחנון" the Donner; 6. "ארך אפים" the Long-Sufferer; 7. "ורב חסד" He Who is inclined toward lovingkindness; 8. "ואמת" the Truthful One; 9. "נוצר חסד לאלפים" Who preserveth mercy to the descendants; 10. "נושא עון" Who forgiveth iniquity; 11. "ופשע" and transgression; 12. "וחטאה" and unwilling sins; 13. "ונקה" and cleanseth. *Cf. Otzar Hatefilloth*, p. 391.
33. See *Jewish Music*, Chapters VII and VIII.
34. *O.c.*, Chapter IV.

35. *Otzar Hagĕonim*, Ber. ed. B. M. Lewin, Haifa, 1928, p. 70.
36. *Sefer Haitim*, p. 250, Cracow, 1902.
37. More I, § 59, Rsps. Pe'er Hador, 64, 129, 130.
38. *Cf. Shibolê Halleket* ed. S. Buber, Wilna, 1887, § 28.
39. *Otzar Hageonim*, Ber. ed. B. M. Lewin, p. 70, Haifa, 1928.
40. *Hapardes* ed. Ehrlich, p. 227f.

NOTES TO CHAPTER VI

1. Friedrich Heiler, *Das Gebet*, p. 250f.
2. *O.c.*, p. 258.
3. *Cf. Jewish Encl.*, Vol. III, "Cabala."
4. Shir Rabba 8 end; *Jewish Music*, p. 359.
5. F. Heiler, *o.c.*, p. 331.
6. *O.c.*, p. 333.
7. Translation by Prof. S. S. Cohon.
8. From F. Heiler, *o.c.*, pp. 339–340.
9. William B. Seabrook in his recent book, *Jungle Ways*, New York, 1931, p. 305f., relating his experiences on his travels among the West African tribes gives the explanation he received from the Hagoun — the chief saint of the Habbe cliff dwellers, with regard to the nature of their deity Amma, which is in some way similar to the Kabbalistic conception of the masculine and feminine principles of the Creator of the universe. According to the explanation of the Hagoun, Amma is the universal invisible God. He is everywhere and manifests himself in everything. Amma who was first of all divided himself into two principles: the male principle, the fructifier, and the female principle, the bearer. From the combination of these two, which are opposites, yet one, all life — man, animal, plants — is born. " So Amma is life."
10. *Cf. J.E.*, *o.c.*; *Jewish Music*, p. 364.
11. See *Beth Oved*, Leghorn, 1922, p. 127; Zunz, *Ritus*, p. 150; Berliner, *o.c.*, p. 35.

    The desire to preserve the tetragrammaton in as concealed a manner as possible caused the mystics to invent new letters and substitute them for the letters of the Name of God. They would either take the next letters of the alphabet, as for example, "יהוה אלהינו יהוה„ would become “כוזו במוכסז כוזו„; or they would change the letters in accordance with the reverse letters of the alphabet, substituting “ת, ש, ר„ for “א, ב, ג„. According to this latter system, “יהוה„ was changed to “מצפץ„.

12. Berliner, *o.c.*, p. 45.
13. *Otzar Hatefilloth*, pp. 626–627.
14. Berliner, *o.c.*, p. 46.
15. Zunz, *o.c.*, p. 151.
16. Zunz, *o.c.*
17. *Jewish Music*, Chapter XIX.

NOTES TO CHAPTER VII

1. Published by L. Ginzberg, *Geonica*, Vol. II, pp. 115–119; see Chapter IV, above.
2. *O.c.*, pp. 119–123.
3. *O.c.*, p. 125.
4. *Untersuchungen zum Seder des Gaon R. Amram*, Frankfurt a/m, 1908.
5. *O.c.*, Vol. I, pp. 123–154.
6. The MS. is now in the Oxford Library (England) and was discovered by M. Steinschneider in 1851. Cat. Bod. 2203f.
7. *Cf.* Zunz, *Ritus*, Berlin, 1858, p. 55.
8. *Cf.* A. Berliner, *Aus Meiner Bibliothek*, the piyyutim were described by H. Brody in *o.c.*
9. On the struggles concerning the rituals *cf.* my *Thesaurus*, Volumes I–V in the Hebrew introductions, and in S. Rosanes, *History of the Jews in Turkey*, Volumes I–III.
10. *Cf.* S. Rosanes, *o.c.*, Vol. I, second edition, Tel Aviv, 1930, p. 206f.
11. *Cf.* A. I. Schechter, *Studies in Jewish Liturgy*, Philadelphia, 1930, p. 71.
12. Treated in *o.c.*
13. See *Thesaurus* (Hebrew Edition), Vol. I, pp. 9f.; on the Yemenite poetry compare my *Diwan of Hebrew and Arabic Poetry of the Yemenite Jews*, Tel-Aviv-Cincinnati H.U.C. Press, 1930.
14. See I. Toledano, *History of Jews in Morocco* (Hebrew), *Ner Hammarav*, Jerusalem, 1911, p. 69; my *Thesaurus*, Vol. V, p. 1.

15. *Cf.* Zunz, *Ritus*, p. 57f.
16. M. Gaster, introduction to the Mahzor *Shaar Hashamayim*, Oxford, 1904, p. xiii, claims that the Portuguese ritual used in London and Amsterdam is the original Castillian ritual.
17. *Cf.* details in S. Rosanes, *o.c.*, pp. 298, 305.
18. *Cf. o.c.*, pp. 308–311.
19. In 1540 there existed in Salonica fourteen congregations with different rituals: the German, Castillian, Aragonian, Catalonian, Portuguese; of Evora, Italy, Calabria, Apulia, Sicily; there were also the Greek, Provinçale, etc., rituals. See Zunz, *Ritus*, p. 146.
20. *Cf. Jewish Music*, Chapter XIX.
21. *O.c.*
22. *Cf. Beth Rabbi.*
23. *Cf.* Zunz, *Ritus*, pp. 187–189 and pp. 222–225; *Synagogale Poesie*, p. 437f.; A Berliner, *Randbemerkungen*, Vol. I, p. 47f.
24. See quoted sources in note 23.
25. In his preface he explains that "אלעזר" amounts to three hundred and eight, and the word "רקח" has the same numerical value; and every author, he maintains, ought to indicate his name in letter-numbers in the name of his book.

PART II

NOTES TO CHAPTER VIII

1. We use here S. Singer's *Daily Prayer-Book* and S. Baer's *Avodath Yisroel.*
2. A. Berliner, *Randbemerkungen* I, p. 11.
3. *Magen Abraham*, § 46.
4. A. Berliner, *o.c.*, p. 12.
5. A. Berliner, *o.c.*, I, p. 15.
6. See I. Bondi, p. 20.
7. The *Yalkut* quotes Jer, Ber. 9, 3, but in the Krotoshin edition that passage is missing.
8. For details concerning the Fringes and the Frontlets see my *Ceremonies*, etc., p. 57.

9. On these Kabbalististic Meditations compare A. Berliner, *o.c.*, p. 36f.
10. *Cf.* the variations given in *Otzar Hatefilloth*, p. 184f.
11. Rokeah, § 320; Tur, O.H., § 51, 1; *Hechaloth Gedoloth*, F. 22.
12. I. Bondi, *o.c.*, p. 20.
13. *Cf. Yuhasin*, Cracow, p. 122; *Seder Hadoroth*, Warsaw, 1889, p. 169.
14. See *Thesaurus*, Vol. III (Hebrew), p. 40.
15. I. Bondi, *o.c.*
16. B. Lewin, *o.c.*, p. 76; *cf.* also A. Schechter, *o.c.*, p. 54, where proof is given that the reading of the Song of the Sea was originally customary in Rome and was adopted from there in Germany. J. Mann, *Genizah Fragments*, etc., in H.U.C. *Annual* II, 1925, p. 282, holds that the custom to recite the Song in the daily service is of Palestinian origin. In Babylonia it was first said only on the Sabbath and Festivals.
17. *Cf.* A. Berliner, *o.c.* I, p. 4f.
18. *Cf.* De Sola Pool, *The Kaddish*, second edition, p. 20f.
19. From *Higayon Hanefesh*, quoted and translated by Pool, *o.c.*, p. 104.
20. Cited by A. Berliner, *o.c.*, Vol. I, p. 69.
21. A quotation from *Yesh Nohalin*, p. 35; Pool, *l.c.*
22. *O.c.*, p. 105.
23. *L.c.* The custom to recite the Kaddish less than 12 months is probably based on Eduyoth II : 10.
24. *O.c.*, p. 106; Zunz, *Zur Geschichte*, p. 319f.; *Nachtrag zur Ltg.*, p. 4. Concerning details of the Kaddish, i.e., language, origin, versions, etc., *cf.* De Sola Pool's painstaking book, mentioned above.
25. A. Marx, *Untersuchungen*, etc. . . ., p. 4.
26. *Cf.* Landshuth, *Hegyon Lev*, p. 45 and Baer, p. 79.
27. B. Lewin, *o.c.*, p. 29.
28. The third paragraph was read in the morning service only, according to Pal. r., *Halachoth Gedoloth*, ed. Hildesheimer, p. 23.
29. "אל מלך נאמן" has the initials "אמן" (b. Shabbath 119b) and "ברוך שם כבוד מלכותו לעולם ועד" which was the response in the Temple service (b. Yoma 35b, 39a; Taanith 16) was ordered to be recited silently (*Oholoth* I, 8; b. Pes. 56a).

30. *Cf. J.Q.R.*, 1903, pp. 392–408 and 1904, p. 561.
31. J. Mann, *o.c.*, p. 284.
32. *J. Enc.*, Vol. IV, p. 587.
33. I. Bondi, *o.c.*, p. 17.
34. See *J.Q.R.*, Vol. 16, p. 22.
35. *Cf.* B. Lewin, *o.c.*, p. 82.
36. Some scholars are of the opinion that the third benediction represented originally the Kedusha to which the verse Isaiah 6 : 3 was added. Compare L. Ginzberg, *Geonica* I, p. 131. The old sources, like T. Soferim, call the Kedusha "Kadosh" referring to the first sentence only.
37. In M.V., p. 711, the version of T. Soferim is "Nakdishach V'naaritzach."
38. L. Ginzberg, *o.c.*, Vol. II, pp. 50–51.
39. *Cf.* S. Baer, p. 237; O. Hat., p. 141.
40. *O.c.*, pp. 52–53.
41. G.V., p. 368.
42. *Hegyon Lev*, p. 57. See also I. Davidson, *Otzar*, etc., Vol. III, pp. 351ff.
43. L. Finkelstein in *J.Q.R.*, Vol. 16, p. 149.
44. K. Kohler, H.U.C. *Annual* I, 1923, p. 399.
45. L. Finkelstein, *o.c.*, pp. 151–153 gives many of these versions. Variants of the Pal. version of the Amida, *cf.* J. Mann, *o.c.*, p. 306f.
46. *O.c.*, p. 399.
47. *J.Q.R.*, Vol. 16, p. 15.
48. *O.c.*, p. 400.
49. *O.c.*, p. 401.
50. *L.c.* See also I. Davidson, *Otzar*, etc., Vol. II, p. 193.
51. For the derivation of "משועמד" *cf. Aruch of Parchon*, Pressburg, 1844, 2b and Zunz's note there, who quotes R. Hai Gaon and S. Hamlamed using the same term, and *ibid.* 66b, as well as M. b. Ezra, *Shire Israel.* See also S. Baer, p. 94, and Levy's *Dictionary* S. V. "שמד".
52. *J.Q.R.*, *l.c.*
53. *Ibid.*, *l.c.*
54. *Cf.* L. Landshuth, *o.c.*, p. 65 and S. Baer, p. 97. See also in *J.Q.R.*, Vol. 18, p. 37f. by A. Mishcon.
55. *Jüd. Gott.*, p. 40.

56. *Hegyon Lev*, p. 63.
57. *O.c.*, p. 404f. See also I. Davidson, *Otzar*, etc., *l.c.*
58. *J.Q.R.*, Vol. 16, p. 161.
59. *Ibid.*, p. 163.
60. *Ibid.*, p. 165.
61. *Tosefta* Ber. III, says that on Hanucca the event of the day should be mentioned in Hodaa.
62. *J.Q.R.*, Vol. 16, p. 21, notes 48 and 86.
63. On the variants compare *J.Q.R.*, *l.c.*, and O. Hat., p. 370f.
64. According to Hai Gaon; see B. Lewin, *o.c.*, p. 35.
65. *J.Q.R.*, Vol. 16, pp. 32, 168.
66. *Cf.* A. Schechter, *o.c.*, pp. 91, 97–99.
67. *Cf.* for example Elbogen, *Das Achtzehn-Gebet;* L. Finkelstein, "The Development of the Amida," in *J.Q.R.*, *o.c.*
68. *O.c.*, p. 405.
69. Maimonides, Tefilla 5, 13, speaks of prostration during Tahanun; compare *Hamanhig*, Vol. I, pp. 71–72, from which it is obvious that the spiritual leaders rejected the custom until it was finally abandoned.
70. Yavetz still does not have this psalm.
71. A. Berliner, *Randbemerkungen*, Vol. I, p. 24; Yavetz does not give this verse.
72. *Cf.* Zunz, *Ritus*, p. 131, and S. Baer, p. 118.
73. *Ritus*, p. 10; *Gottesd. Vortraege*, pp. 375–376 in which Zunz maintains that the text of this Tahanun was known to the compiler of *Midrash Tehillim*. Compare also Landshuth, p. 84f. and *Tzeda Laderech*, 1554, Chapter 51. The existence of the long Tahanun in S.R.A., p. 20 seems to be of a late insertion, since it is missing in some MSS.; see A. Marx, *o.c.*, p. 11.
74. A. Berliner, *o.c.*, Vol. I, p. 29.
75. In modern times in some synagogues the people are called upon by numbers only, as first — "Rishon," second — "Sheni," etc.
76. This is in accordance with T. Soferim XIV, 14.
77. See Elbogen, *o.c.*, p. 79. There was no "Kedusha desidra" in the Pal. r., J. Mann, *o.c.*, p. 300.
78. See I. Davidson, *Thesaurus* . . ., Vol. I, p. 142. The old form of "En Kelohenu" is found in a fragment of the Pal. r., J. Mann, *o.c.*, p. 324.

79. *Jewish Music*, Chapter III.
80. *Cf. J.Q.R.*, Vol. X, p. 656.
81. A. Berliner, *o.c.*, Vol. I, p. 26. J. Mann, *o.c.*, p. 305.
82. J. Mann, *l.c.*

NOTES TO CHAPTER IX

1. See Eduyoth V, 6–7; b. Hullin 100a; Eisenstein, *Otzar Dinim Uminhagim*, p. 267. Later on, however, the Christian Church adopted this custom to be observed, at least, before divine service. See *J. Enc.*, Vol. I, p. 70.
2. A. Berliner, *o.c.*, Vol. I, p. 27.
3. L. Finkelstein, in *J.Q.R.*, Vol. 19, pp. 218–219.
4. *O.c.*, pp. 215ff.; see Appendix I.

NOTES TO CHAPTER X

1. More about this custom see my *Ceremonies of Judaism*, pp. 3–6.

1a. See O.H., p. 584f.

2. *Cf. Seder Hayyom* by Moses b. Machir, 1599.
3. See J. Eisenstein, *Dinim Uminhagim*, S. V. Lechu Neranena.
4. According to R. Shalom Gaon, B. Lewin, *o.c.*, pp. 8–9.
5. *L.c.*
6. *O.c.*, pp. 7–9.
7. *Thesaurus*, Vol. III, p. 39.
8. Bondi, *o.c.*, p. 28.
9. *Cf.* Landshuth, p. 260.
10. *Cf. Jewish Music*, Chapter IV.
11. On the tunes for Yigdal compare *Jewish Music*, pp. 221–223.
12. The Sephardic and Oriental rituals start with I Samuel 2:1–10 and with several other Biblical verses. Whereas the Yemenite ritual starts with the concluding paragraphs of *Malchuyoth* and *Zichronoth* of the New Year Musaf.
13. The Sephardic ritual has a different order of these psalms. It adds Psalms 98, 121–124. Baruch Sheamar is placed after Psalm 136 with variations in the wording. The Yemenite ritual has the same order, while the Roman ritual again shows variations.
14. The Persian ritual has "נשמת" before "ויושע". The Song of the Sea is extended to Exodus 15:26, whereupon the

Song of Deborah (Judges 5:3 on) is recited. Davidson, *Otzar*, etc., Vol. III, p. 231, holds that the "Nishmath" is a composite poem, compiled of three parts. The original text known in Mishnaic times closes with „לך לבדך אנחנו "מודים, the second part up to "תשתחוה„ was composed in Talmudic times, and the third, concluding part was added in Saboraic or Gaonic times.

15. *Shekalim* (M. Shekalim I, 1; b. Meg. 13b). On the first of Adar or when the New Moon is announced, messengers are sent out to remind the people of their duty to give the *Shekel* for the Temple (see Exod. 30:11–16).

    Zachor — Remember. According to Rabbinic tradition, Haman was descendant of *Amalek* (Josephus, *Ant.* 11, 6, 5; Targum Esther I:16; III:1; Esther Rabba 7). For this reason, the cited passage of the Pentateuch is read to remind the people of the command to exterminate Amalek.

    Para deals with the sacrifice of the "Red Cow." This portion is read to call the people's attention to purification before Passover (Rashi to M. Meg.; b. Meg. 29a).

    Hahodesh — The announcement of the month of *Nissan* which the Pentateuch calls the first month of the year. The cited portion is read in order to call attention to the approaching festival of Passover.

16. See I. D. Eisenstein, *o.c.*, p. 102. On contents of the Haftaras and their connections to the Pentateuchal portions compare "The Pentateuch and Haftara," etc., edited by the Chief Rabbi J. H. Hertz, Oxford, 1930.
17. A. Schechter, *Studien*, etc. . . ., p. 61. Schechter entertains the opinion that the presence of this passage in the S.R.A. is a later addition, since it is supposed to be of Palestinian origin.
18. See Chapter V, 8.
19. *Jewish Music*, p. 156.
20. *Cf.* I. D. Eisenstein, *Otzar Dinim*, etc., p. 103; J. Mann, H.U.C. *Annual* IV, pp. 183ff.; I. Elbogen, *Der jüdische Gottesdienst*, 3rd ed., p. 591.
21. M.V., p. 175, gives a special poetical paragraph in V of Musaf Kedusha for the festivals.

22. Elbogen, p. 119 says that the Sephardic and Italian rituals read the Avoth before Minha.
23. See *Jewish Music*, p. 170, concerning this tune which is similar in its character among all the congregations, with the exception of Yemen and Persia. See also *Thesaurus*, Vol. II, p. 75f.
24. See Berliner, *o.c.*, Vol. I, p. 27.

NOTES TO CHAPTER XI

1. On the Sabbath ceremonies compare my *Ceremonies of Judaism*, *o.c.*
2. In the *Adonoi Moloch* Mode; *cf. Jewish Music*, Chapter III, and the *Jewish Song Book*, pp. 123–126.
3. *Cf. Jewish Music*, Chapter IV; on p. 389 the music for this song is given in both modes.
4. The tune is given in *Jewish Music*, p. 390.
5. *O.c.*, p. 385.
6. On Najara's life and work compare *Jewish Music*, pp. 362–363; *Thesaurus*, Vol. IV (Hebrew) p. 18f.
7. *Jewish Song Book*, p. 128. There are two tunes traditional in Germany and only one in England.
8. On the dishes see my *Ceremonies of Judaism*, Sabbath.
9. Some non-Biblical words are used, as:
   "סוכה„ — the seer (b. Meg. 14).
   "הלומים„ — fitting (b. Sanhedrin 21b).
   "למשחה„ — to be proud of (Rashi to Exodus 29:29).
10. Zunz, *Ltg.*, p. 511.
11. See *Jewish Music*, Chapter XIX; *Thesaurus*, Vol. X.
12. See also Zunz, *Ltg.*, S.P., p. 554.
   "המנטל„ — the exalted, from "נטל„ to lift.
   "נטל„ — be rejected, from "נטל„ to cast away. M.V. has "אבטל„, also five more stanzas. Baer gives three additional stanzas.
13. M. Gaster I, Musical sup. XLIV.
14. *Jewish Music*, pp. 360–361.
15. *O.c.*, p. 401, 1–2.
16. *O.c.*, p. 372, 2; Sefer Hashirim, # 54.
17. *Cf.* also Rokeah § 53; Col-Bo § 37.

NOTES TO CHAPTER XII

1. See *Jewish Music*, pp. 20–21 for details; B. Sota 30b; Jer. Sota V, 4; *Mechilta* ed. I. H. Weiss, p. 42; *Tosefta* ed. Zuckerm. p. 303; S.R.A., ed. Kornell 33a.
2. Another benediction is given in Soferim XIX: 9.
3. See *Jewish Music*, pp. 168, 171, 173.
4. See *Jewish Music*, Chapter IV. With regard to the congregation reciting the verses aloud: 1 : 5; 8 : 15–16; 9 : 4–9; 10 : 3 — M.V., p. 210, says that it is only a custom to interest the children. The German congregations chant the last phrase of 1 : 22; 2 : 17; 7 : 10 in joyous tunes. The phrases: 1 : 7 “וכלים מכלים שונים„; 2 : 6 “והעיר שושן נבוכה„; 4 : 1; 4 : 16 “וכאשר אבדתי אבדתי„; 8 : 6 are chanted by the Ashkenazim according to the Mode of Lamentation. See *o.c.*, p. 65 for details.
5. *Cf. Thesaurus*, Vol. III, p. 61.
6. M.V., p. 583, brings poetical insertions for the eve of Purim. Judging from the frivolous tone, they could not have been intended for services. See Zunz, *o.c.*, p. 485.
7. M.V., p. 301, gives the formula thus: "This is the first day" without the phrase "of the Omer." *Pardes*, p. 46, says that the word "Omer" should be mentioned.

NOTES TO CHAPTER XIII

1. See my *Ceremonies of Judaism*, p. 119.
2. *Cf. Pirke de R. Eliezer*, Chapter 29, and Tosafoth to b. Shabbath 130a. *Cf.* the meal which the father of Elisha ben Abuya made.
3. The marriage-canopy is still customary among the Arabic Bedouins. In this canopy the couple live for seven days.
4. *Cf. Thesaurus*, Vol. I.
5. *Cf. o.c.*, Vols. II, III, and IV.
6. *O.c.*, Vol. IV, pp. 36–37.
7. It is recorded in *Yore Dea*, 338 : 2 in the name of Nachmanides. *Mabar Yabok* and *Totzoth Hayyim* have also the confession of the Day of Atonement.
8. Rabbi Akiva's soul departed as he pronounced the word "Ehad" — "One" (b. Ber. 61b).
9. About three English miles.

NOTES TO CHAPTER XIV

1. From the Union Haggada.
2. *Ibid.*
3. *Ibid.*
4. Moritz Lazarus, *The Ethics of Judaism*, Part I.
5. *Ant.* XVII, 9:3; b. Pes. 64b gives exaggerated numbers of the pilgrims for Passover during the time of Agrippa I.
6. *Cf. Jewish Music*, Chapter I, p. 20f.
7. On the ceremonies of the "Seder" see my *Ceremonies of Judaism*, pp. 38–44.
8. Jer. Pes. II gives a Hebrew version.
9. Was known already to Joseph Tov-elem; see L. Landshuth, *Haggada*, etc., Berlin, 1855, p. XXI.
10. b. Pes. 109a: "Now that the Sanctuary is destroyed there is no joy without wine." See Chapter X, I, 4.
11. See also Abudraham and Maharil with regard to a fifth cup.
12. "He was pleased with us and beautified us; separated us as a holy gift from every nation, made us inherit a precious land, sanctified His Name in the world for the sake of the fathers who did His will. . . . He called us the community of the saints, a precious vineyard . . . took them from all the nations of the earth; for they are compared to the host of heaven . . . the beaming of their faces is like the radiance of the sun . . . kings look at them and rise; princes bow low, on account of the Lord of Hosts Who has chosen them. . . . He brought us near Mount Sinai . . . and made us inherit the words of life. . . ." It closes in the same version as the regular Kiddush discussed above. The Aleppo ritual has this Kiddush for all Three Festivals. *Cf. Thesaurus*, Vol. IV (Hebrew), p. 36.
13. The Talmudic ruling is: Whatever is dipped in liquid requires the washing of the hands (b. Pes. 115a; S.R.A. 38a).
14. Similarity to the first sentence is found in b. Taanith 20b.
15. There is no other reference to that story in the Talmudic literature. See M.V., p. 295 note. Tosafoth b. Kethuvoth 105a gives the Haggada as a source. However, there is a similar story told in *Tosefta* Pes. X, 12 about Rabbi Gamaliel and the elders who celebrated the *Seder* in Lydda the whole night.

16. The Persian ritual has: "And the atheist, blunt his teeth and thus say to him: Exodus 13:8. Regarding the Wise man *Mechilta*, Bo, reads: אותנו... את פתח לו בהלכות הפסח (עד) אין מפטירין *Cf.* Friedman's ed.
17. דצך עדש באחב — A. De Sola in the Sephardic ritual, Oxford, 1906, p. 28, translates the three words: "the scorpion stung the uncle."
18. See Chapters VIII, IX.
19. M. Pes. *l.c.;* b. Pes. 118a; see Chapter III, II.
20. Tashbez § 99.
21. *Cf. Jewish Music*, p. 188:13, 191. The oldest tune was printed in the Haggada, Koenigsberg, 1644, ed. Rittangel. See W. Bäumker II, No. 59.
22. The text is printed in the Prague Haggada, 1527. It seems that the author utilized Psalm 74:16 and Bereshith Rabba 6, 3. Here are abbreviations of the verses:
    לך ולך from Psalm 65:2 ...לך דומיה... ולך ישולם
    לך כי לך from I Chron. 29:11 ...לך ה' הגדולה... כי כל... לך ה' הממלכה
    לך אף לך from Psalm 89:12 לך שמים אף לך ארץ
23. *Jewish Music*, p. 174. The tune occurs first in Rittangel's Haggada, *l.c.; cf. ibid.*, pp. 168–169.
24. *O.c.*, p. 380.
25. *Cf. J.Enc.*, Vol. VI, p. 127.
26. With this passage, Rabbi Shalom of Austria used to conclude the Pesah service (fourteenth century, Maharil); it is printed in the Prague Haggada, 1527. This Haggada has been reprinted in Berlin, 1925.

NOTES TO CHAPTER XV

1. Probably taken from "Shaare Tzion," section 3, p. 115, Wilna, 1859, which was first printed in Prague, 1662. Still Hayim M. Margoliouth *Shaare Teshuva* in Or. Ha. § 488 doubts its appropriateness.
2. S. London in his *Siddur*, Sulzbach, 1786, 61b, however, gives it as an established custom. S. Geiger in *Divre Kehilloth*, p. 178, 1862, speaks of this custom for the High Holydays only and says that it is of late date.
3. For an old variation of the intermediate benediction for

Musaf compare I. Elbogen, "Die Tefilla der Festtage," MS. 1911, pp. 426–446, 586–599, where fragments of the Geniza are given — a separate version for each festival.

4. Joseph Caro on O.H., § 128, 44.
5. In the Sephardic and Yemenite rituals the Cohanim say the first words by themselves.
6. Joseph Caro, on O.H., § 128.
7. In the Orient, they say the first word by themselves. The reader starts with the second word.
8. The formula of this benediction is mentioned in Rashi to b. Yoma 68b as having been the prayer of the High Priest with the variation: May our service (offerings) be acceptable to Thee. After the Destruction, this was changed to the present version (see Chapter VIII; Baer, p. 98).
9. The old Roman and French rituals carry this poetry too; compare Landshuth, *Amude Ha'avoda*, p. 68.
10. In the thirteenth century it was still not generally used, for *Sefer Hamahkim*, p. 32 (Ed. J. Freiman, Cracow, 1909) speaks of some Hazzanim who insert "piyyutim" in the evening service. However, Maharil, Pesah, gives the poems as they are now used in the Ashkenazic ritual. Obviously, this custom was well established in that ritual in the fourteenth century.
11. See O.H., § 669 the note of *RMA*. Already Isaac Luria used to perform this custom after the service of the outgoing *Simhath Tora* only. At this occasion he used to dance and sing, and would go from one synagogue to another to do it (Minhage Ari). From this we may deduce that this custom was well established in his days.
12. See Rabbi Shneur Zalman's *Siddur*.
13. *Jewish Music*, p. 140: 10.
14. Tashbetz § 245.
15. *L.c.*
16. *Jewish Music*, pp. 137–138: 2.
17. *Cf. Thesaurus*, Vol. IV, Nos. 65–71; Vol. V, Nos. 93–98; *Mahzor*, Ed. Gaster, Vol. IV, XVII–XIX.
18. This reading was not known in Talmudic times. Neither S.R.A. nor M.V. nor Maimonides mention this custom. Juda Barcelona was the first to mention it (Sefer Haitim);

after him Abudraham. The idea is explained according to the *Sifré*, Wa'eth'hanan, that as soon as the reading of the Tora is finished it shall be begun anew.

19. *Cf.* S.R.A., 50, and M.V., pp. 416f., 424f. The benediction occurs in b. Succa 46a; Pes. 76b, and in *Tosefta* Ber. ed. Zuckerm, p. 15.
20. *Cf.* my *Ceremonies of Judaism*, pp. 23–25.
21. At the time of Rabbi Saadya Gaon the circuits were conducted after the Scriptural readings and just before Musaf; compare S.R.A. 51. This custom still prevails among the Hasidim.
22. *Cf.* M.V., p. 444. Religious processions and circuits were customary and still are among all cults and organized religions, both primitive and civilized.
23. See O.H., § 664 : 4. The custom of using the willow is ascribed in the *Talmud* (b. Succa 43b–44a) as having been instituted by the Prophets, and is therefore not Pentateuchal.
24. Isaac Luria prescribes five beats.
25. *Cf.* the Italian ritual, edition S. D. Luzzatto, Leghorn, 1856, Vol. 2, 178b.

NOTES TO CHAPTER XVI

1. *Cf.* b. Eruvin 39b, Betza 4–5, Rosh Hashana 30b. Jer. Eruvin III end refers the institution of two days to the prophets. M.V., p. 357 § 320.
2. An opposition arose against these insertions, but M.V., p. 364 quotes a decision in their favor.
3. *J.Q.R.*, Vol. X, p. 656; Finkelstein, *o.c.*, pp. 29, 145.
4. Responsa by Hai Gaon quoted in M.V., p. 367, note. Also *Zohar*, Shemoth. Some ascribe them to R. Johanan ben Nuri. M.R.H. IV, 3. See I. Davidson, *Otzar*, etc., Vol. II, p. 182.
5. There was a difference of opinion as to whether New Year was called Festival: the one quote Nehemiah 8 : 10–12 to prove the joyous nature of the day, while the others insist on its serious character and maintain it to be a day of Judgment on which even Hallel is not recited; see b. Rosh Hashana 32b. The three sentences beginning with *uv'chen*

is reminiscent of *Malchuyoth*, *Zichronoth*, and *Shoferoth*, Abudraham, p. 141.

6. *Cf.* I. Elbogen, *o.c.*, p. 143.
7. *J.Q.R.*, Vol. X, p. 651; Finkelstein, *o.c.*, p. 169. Hai Gaon reads "המלך עושה השלום"; see B. Lewin, *o.c.*, p. 35.
8. *Cf. Jewish Music*, pp. 157, 158 : 2.
9. *O.c.*, Chapters IV, VII, and VIII. The Ashkenazic ritual especially created an abundant number of tunes and modes for the High Holydays.
10. In the Yemenite ritual, no silent Amida is recited. This is a remnant of the old ways of worship at the time when the people could not recite the Amida by themselves and had consequently to follow the recitation of the precentor. *Mishna* Rosh Hashana IV end; b. Rosh Hashana 34–35. Maimonides, Tefilla § 9, 2; Elbogen, *o.c.*, p. 28.
11. On the differences in Midrashic sources compare M.V., p. 384, note b.
12. See *Jewish Music*, Chapter III, pp. 56–59.
13. See L. Dukes, *Zur Kenntnis d. Neuhebr. Poesie*, Frankfort, 1842, p. 53.
14. Through the blowing of the Shofar, Israel influences the Judgment in its favor.
15. See Elbogen, *o.c.*, p. 143.
16. On variations of Malchuyoth, Zichronoth, and Shoferoth according to the Palestinian ritual *cf.* J. Mann, *o.c.*, p. 326.
17. See Be'er hetev on O.H., 692. The custom was endorsed by I. Luria.
18. In the Troyes ritual "Maarivim" were inserted on both evenings. Sefer Troyes, M. Weisz, Budapest, 1905, p. 22. M. Roumania has "Maarovoth" for both evenings, and also for the evening of the Day of Atonement. M.V., p. 576, has poetical insertions for the evenings of New Year also. For the first evening it has: "My faithful ones are ready when they blow (the Shofar) in the month of the mighty": "אמוני נכונים בתקעם". For the second evening it has a poem by Joseph Tov-elem: "מלך אמיץ כח" — "O King, powerful and great of deeds"; Zunz, *o.c.*, p. 136.
19. See *Thesaurus*, Vol. I, 93; IV, 185.

20. *Jewish Music*, pp. 118–119: 10–12.
21. *O.c.*, p. 121: 6.
22. *O.c.*, pp. 122–123.
23. *Taklall*, Vol. II, F, 63 note.
24. Comprising the mystic name of God which consist of 72 letters (see Chapter VI).
25. *Jewish Music*, p. 140: 7b.
26. *O.c.*, p. 166: 4.
27. *L.c.*, 3.
28. Zunz, *o.c.*, p. 115.
29. *Or Zarua* § 276. The author says that he found the story in MS. of Ephraim of Bonn who lived in the latter part of the twelfth century.
30. For studies regarding this selection, see *J.Enc.*, Vol. I, p. 525.
31. See Adler's *Mahzor*, New Year, p. 151. Enelow, in his introduction to Menorat Ha-maor, Vol. II, New York, 1930, p. 17 attributes this poem to Yose b. Yose, without evidence.
32. *Jewish Music*, p. 148: 1. M.V., p. 387, does not quote the first paragraph of Alenu.
33. The custom of "Tashlich," i.e., casting away the sins into floating waters, is of a late date, probably about the thirteenth or fourteenth centuries. Maharil was the first to mention it. The custom was first used by the Ashkenazim. *Cf. J.Enc.*, Vol. XII, p. 66. The Oriental-Sephardim practice it also since I. Luria.
34. Similar to *Jewish Music*, p. 167, 6.
35. See my *Ceremonies*, etc., p. 18.
36. M. Gaster in his preface to *Mahzor Sepharad*, Vol. III, London, 1904.
37. Out of consideration that he may not be able to carry them out. Due to that, pious people arranged a formula to annul vows during the year without waiting for the Day of Atonement. This formula is called "התרת נדרים" and is found in the Ashkenazic ritual (O.H., p. 1028f.) and in the Sephardic-Oriental ritual for the eve of the Day of Atonement.
38. There was no Col Nidré in the Palestinian ritual. Instead, Psalms 130 and 103: 2–22 used to be recited as given in

Soferim 19, 2; J. Mann, *o.c.*, p. 327. Nor was "ובכן תן פחדך" said on the evening of the Day of Atonement, *l.c.*

39. The Aleppo ritual has the custom of repeating Col Nidré seven times, whereas in Worms Meyir b. Isaac used to repeat it only twice.
40. See *Thesaurus*, Vol. IV, Hebrew ed., p. 35.
41. *Jewish Music*, p. 159. *Thesaurus*, Vol. I, No. 116; IV, No. 259.
42. In the Sephardic and Italian ritual before "Barechu" "והוא רחום" is said (S.R.A.).
43. She'iltoth Rav Ahai, § 167.
44. The Italian ritual gives in addition Chapter 17.
45. For the beginning of the Haftara S.R.A. gives Isaiah 57:15.
46. Worshipping the dead and sacrificing to them in order to make them favorable to the living was an ancient cult among all ancients and is still done among primitive people today. William B. Seabrook, in his book *Jungle Ways*, New York, 1931, p. 112f., explaining the belief in immortality of the soul of the Yafouba tribes in French Africa, submits the following interpretation of a witch-doctor: "When the spark burns out, the mechanical doll (body) is junk and the soul goes free, a disembodied sentient personality. While a man's soul is in his body . . . is he not worthy of worshipping, of altars or sacrifices, be the man ever so good or seemingly powerful, for the most of his time is taken up selfishly with his own busy mechanical doll job. When it goes free, the soul has not only more power but also more to occupy itself with the affairs of others, for helping or harming. Therefore it is wise to keep on favorable terms with such disembodied spirits, and thus simply is derived the cult of the Dead."
47. Jacob Weil of the fifteenth century; see Eisenstein, *Otzar Dinim Uminhagim*, p. 97.
48. Salfeld, *Martyrologium*, 1896–8, cited in the *Rabbi's Manual*, revised edition, Cincinnati, 1928, p. 202f. The Nuremberg *Memor-book* contains a summary of the persecution of 1096–1298, and the names of the martyred who died between 1096 and 1349, and a list of cities and

villages in which massacres took place under Rindfleisch (1298) and Armleder (1336–1339) and at the time of the Black Death (1348–9). Several other Memor-books are of a similar character. The Memor-book of Worms gives a list of communities which suffered during the Chmelnitzki pogroms. See *J.Enc.*, art. *Memor-book*, Vol. VIII, p. 456; *Manual*, etc., *l.c.*

49. See L. Landshuth, *o.c.*, Appendix, p. xff. See also *Manual*, *o.c.*
50. See D. de Sola Pool, *o.c.*, p. 104.
51. S.R.A. 48b.
52. I. Elbogen, *Studien*, p. 56f. where in *Anhang* I the text of that Avoda is given.
53. M.V., p. 395, says that in all places, with the exception of Cologne only, tekia is sounded. In the latter congregation and in Palestine the four sounds are blown.
54. On the traditional tunes of these poems *cf.* *Jewish Music*, pp. 117:2, 118:6.
55. *Thesaurus*, Vol. IV, Nos. 262, 265.
56. Zunz, *o.c.*, p. 17.
57. Tur O.H. § 620 says that on this day the Thirteen Attributes used to be recited twenty-six times in the academies of Babylonia.
58. *Thesaurus*, Vol. IV, No. 92.
59. *Cf.* Zunz, *o.c.*, pp. 17, 23.
60. Mahzor Adler, Part I, p. 31.
61. Zunz, *o.c.*, p. 18.
62. *O.c.*, p. 240.
63. *Jewish Music*, p. 167:7.
64. Mahzor, *o.c.*, p. 38.
65. Zunz, *o.c.*, p. 228.
66. *Jewish Music*, p. 166:1.
67. Mentioned in M. Taanith II, 4.
68. D. A. de Sola, in Mahzor, ed. Gaster, *o.c.*, p. 45.
69. It is doubtful whether Solomon b. Gabirol is the author; compare Zunz, *o.c.*, pp. 311–312 where Solomon b. Abun of France of the twelfth century is quoted as the author.
70. Compare *J.Enc.*, Vol. IX, p. 316.
71. S.R.A. 47b.
72. The same tune as in *Jewish Music*, Table XXV, 4.

73. *L.c.*, 3.
74. Zunz, *o.c.*, p. 109 ascribes only five of them to this poet.
75. Zunz, *o.c.*, pp. 164, 257.
76. *O.c.*, p. 256.
77. Though tradition ascribed it to Yose, this Avoda seems to be even earlier than Yose; compare Elbogen, *Studien*, p. 77.
78. Zunz, *o.c.*, p. 503.
79. W. Heidenheim in his commentary answers Abraham b. Ezra's criticism, that since "שושן עמק" is masculine the feminine form "איומה" is a grammatical error, and besides, how can the fearful rose of the valley be frightened? But the poet refers to Israel which is referred to as "איומה" — "the fearful one" and is compared to the lily of the valley. Thus the prophet Hosea (7 : 8) compares Ephraim to a cake not turned, by omitting "כ" — as. So also here, instead of "כשושן עמק איומה" "כ" is omitted.
80. S. D. Luzzatto in his introduction to the Italian Mahzor, Vol. II.
81. *Jewish Music*, p. 153.
82. Elbogen, *o.c.*, p. 84.
83. The fourth line has four feet sometimes.
84. See Chapter V.
85. However, Zunz, *o.c.*, p. 483 ascribes this poem to Solomon b. Isaac Girundi of the thirteenth century.
86. Zunz, *Zur Geschichte*, etc., p. 425.
87. Luzzatto, *o.c.*, says that only the refrain is by Kallir, whereas the poem is by Eleazar b. Mordechai who imitated a similar poem by Kallir.
88. *Thesaurus*, Vol. IV, Nos. 308–310.
89. Some are of the opinion that both pieces are by Abraham b. Ezra. The first is an imitation of Kallir's poems which have the same wording in the morning and Minha services.
90. The reasons for reciting the first stanzas may be either to cut the insertions short, on account of the late hour, or also to repeat at least the headlines of some of the popular Selihoth with their tunes. Natronai Gaon ordered that at Shaharith five Selihoth, at Musaf seven, at Minha three, and at Ne'ila three should be recited, but if there is time, then five should be recited (S.R.A. 48b).

NOTES TO CHAPTER XVII

1. "בה"ב", "ב" the second — Monday; "ה" the fifth — Thursday; and "ב" the second — Monday. In Hebrew the weekdays are called according to their numerical order.
2. For a long time the Twentieth of Siwan was a Fast-day in commemoration of the Chmelnitzky pogroms in Ukraine (1648–9).
3. Some people used to fast on New Year, or on the evening of New Year. Abudraham, p. 140.
4. *Cf. Jewish Music*, pp. 58–59; *Thesaurus*, Vol. II, pp. 16, 71–72.
5. An additional sixth number is found in some.
6. The order of the Selihoth and their names for the four Fast-days are already mentioned by Maharil. He gives the reason for reciting "Akeda" during the Ten Days of Penitence for which the order should be: one opening (Pethiha), three Selihoth, one Shalmonith, one Akeda, one Pizmon, Hatanu and Tahanun.
7. According to M. Taanith IV, 6, the fall of Bettar also took place on this day.
8. *Cf.* b. Megilla 31b and Tosafoth.
9. This custom is mentioned already in Soferim XVIII, 3.
10. Amram orders its recitation in the three services, but M.V., p. 229, demands its recitation once only at Minha.
11. Zunz, *Syn. Poesie*, pp. 71–72, maintains that Kallir wrote one for the morning and the other for the Minha service.

NOTES TO CHAPTER XVIII

1. On Maamadoth *cf.* S. Freehof in C.C.A.R., Year Book, Vol. 33, pp. 410ff.
2. A full text of the Maamadoth is given in Baer, pp. 495–546. In his *Siddur* (Altona, 1743), Jacob Emden disagreed with the existing text and introduced some other selections.
3. Eshkol I, § 4; O.H. § 1–2. Moses b. Machir in *Seder Hayyom* describes a midnight meditation which is a combination of Tikkun Hatzoth and Maamadoth.
4. Many of them are printed in the *Otzar Hatefilloth.*
5. So was Rabbi Nahman of Bratzlaw's published under the title *Likkute Tefilloth* by his disciple Rabbi Nathan.

6. *Ibid.; Shivhè Horan*, p. 4b, Lemberg, 1909.
7. *Likkute Moharan*, Part I, p. 42b.
8. *Ibid.*, Part II, p. 43b; *Shivhè Horan*, p. 75b.
9. *Ibid.*
10. See his *Likkute Tefilloth; Shivhei Horan*, p. 4b.
11. Rabbi Levi-Yitzhok in particular.
12. A. Kahana, *Sefer Ha'Hasiduth*, pp. 256–266, Warsaw, 1922.
13. See *Tzavoath Ri'Bash*, pp. 43–48, Zolkiev, 1795; *Kether Shem Tov*, pp. 43–46, 56–67, Slavita, 1912.
14. A. Kahana, *o.c.*, p. 203.
15. *Ibid.*, p. 258. Translated by Fred. A. Doppelt, by whom also are some of the explanations in the preceding pages.
16. In my *Jewish Music*, a meditation — "The Dudule" — by Levi-Yitzhok is given both in translation (p. 420) and in the original with its tune (p. 422).
17. E. Z. Zweifel, *Shalom Al Yisrael*, p. 8, Žytomir, 1868. Translated by F. A. Doppelt.
18. *Likkute Tefilloth*, prayer 105. See A. Kahana, *Sefer Hahasiduth*, p. 380f., translated by A. Z. Idelsohn.
19. Many of these collections remained unpublished and are described by E. Shulman in his book in Hebrew on the Yiddish language and literature, Riga, 1913, pp. 55–71.
20. *O.c.*, p. 68. *Cf.* also *J.Enc.*, Vol. IV, p. 551.
21. *Cf.* S. Freehof, "Devotional Literature in the Vernacular," in C.C.A.R. *Yearbook*, Vol. 33, pp. 375–415, where a detailed description of character and contents of these meditations are given.
22. *O.c.*, pp. 382–383.
23. Translation by S. Freehof, *o.c.*, p. 382.
24. E. Schulman, *o.c.*, pp. 69–71.
25. The English by S. Freehof, *o.c.*, p. 399.
26. *O.c.*, p. 400.

NOTES TO CHAPTER XIX

1. On the development of preaching see L. Zunz, *Gottesdienstl. Vorträge;* S. Maybaum, *Jüdische Homiletik*, etc., Berlin, 1890.
2. *Jewish Music*, Chapter XII.
3. "אלה דברי הברית", Dessau, 1818.

4. Theologische Gutachten ueber das Gebetbuch . . . des neuen Israel Tempelvereins in Hamburg, 1842, p. 6. (Translated from the Judeo-German): "The rabbinical court of our community herewith makes it public, that a few days ago a *Siddur* (prayer-book) for Sabbath has come forth which contains different versions from those composed and arranged by our sages and the 'Great Assembly.' Many parts of the benedictions of Shema and of the Shaharith and Musaf services for Sabbath were omitted altogether and many of them were changed. Therefore, the rabbinate warns and informs every Israelite that it is prohibited to pray from this book; and whoever uses it, does not fulfill his devotional obligation."
5. *O.c.*, pp. 10–12.
6. Their decisions are printed in *o.c.* The rabbi who issued the prohibition was Isaac Barnays. He renewed the old interdiction and based it on the ground that prayers concerning Israel's aspirations, as Redemption, Messiah and Resurrection, have been abolished in the new prayer-book; and concludes: "ואסור להתפלל... מתוך הסדור הלז" — "It is prohibited to pray from this book obligatory prayers and benedictions."
7. I have used the second edition, Berlin, 1851–2.
8. S. S. Cohon, *Christianity and Judaism Compare Notes*, New York, 1927, p. 84; Elbogen, *o.c.*, p. 424.
9. Elbogen, *o.c.*, p. 425.
10. D. Philipson, *History of the Reform Movement*, first edition, pp. 357–359.
11. Philipson, *Journal of Jewish Philosophy and Lore*, Cincinnati, 1919, p. 79.
12. *O.c.*, p. 80.
13. "The Reform Prayer Book," in the *Journal of Jewish Philosophy and Lore*, Vol. I, p. 211, Cincinnati, 1919. S. S. Cohon, *o.c.*, p. 82.
14. See D. Philipson, *o.c.*, p. 222.
15. *Yearbook* of the C.C.A.R., Vol. XIX, pp. 253ff.
16. Compare Philipson, *o.c.*, pp. 215, 220f.
17. The idea and style of the "Anthem" is Christian and was especially developed in the English Church. *Cf.* Grove's *Dictionary*, Vol. I, p. 89f.; *Jewish Music*, p. 321.

18. אתה בחרתנו מכל העמים להיות לך לעם סגולה
19. שמחה לארצך וששון לעירך וצמיחת קרן לדוד עבדך is changed to שמחה לכל יושבי תבל וצמיחת קרן למיחדי שמך
20. See *Second Conference of the World Union of Progressive Judaism*, London, 1930, p. 178.
21. *Aspects of Judaism*, second edition, p. 46.

NOTES TO APPENDIX I

1. Oesterley, W. O. E., *The Jewish Background of the Christian Liturgy*, Oxford, 1925, p. 125.
2. *O.c.*, p. 120f.
3. *O.c.*, p. 126.
4. *J.Enc.*, Vol. IV, *s.v.*, Didache, Didascalia.
5. *O.c.*, p. 127f.
6. In *J.Q.R.*, Vol. XIX, p. 215f.
7. Oesterley, *o.c.*, p. 114.
8. *O.c.*, pp. 120–121.
9. *L.c.*
10. *O.c.*, p. 147.
11. *O.c.*, p. 148.
12. *O.c.*, p. 149.
13. *O.c.*, p. 150.
14. *J.Enc.*, Vol. IV, p. 587.
15. Finkelstein, L., in *J.Q.R.*, Vol. XIX, p. 215f.; *J.Enc.*, *l.c.*
16. *Cf. J.Enc.*, Vol. IV, p. 593f., and in the H.U.C. *Annual*, Vol. I, p. 410f., where he gives a translation of the whole text.
17. Kohler, K., *The Origins of Synagogue and Church*, New York, 1929, p. 240; H.U.C. *Annual*, I, p. 387f.
18. See Oesterley, *o.c.*, p. 151f.; De Sola Pool, *o.c.*, pp. 21, 111.

NOTES TO APPENDIX II

1. In Harkavy's *Studien und Mitteilungen*, VIII, Petersburg, 1903.
2. Seder Amram, ed. Koronell, 38a.
3. Harkavy, *o.c.*, p. 158; L. Ginzberg, *Genizah Studies*, 1929, p. 439f.

4. Before the World War there were about 12,000 Karaites in the world.
5. In addition to the fragments published by Harkavy, *o.c.*, J. Mann published another fragment of Anan's liturgy in the *Journal of Jewish Philosophy and Lore*, 1919, p. 329f. The fragment of the evening service published by Ginzberg, *o.c.*, p. 437f., has only some elements in common with that of the present Karaitic liturgy.
6. Anan abolished the fixed calendar and reintroduced the sanctification of the month according to the appearance of the new moon.
7. Harkavy, *o.c.*, p. 18.
8. See previous note.
9. S. R. Amram, *o.c.*, 37b–38a.
10. Pentecost falls on the 50th day after the first Saturday in the Passover week. Because they understand the passage in Leviticus 23:15, "And ye shall count unto you from the morrow after the day of rest" in the literal sense.
11. Zunz, *Ltg.*, p. 393.
12. On the Karaitic Liturgy compare also Zunz, *Ritus*, p. 158f., and J. M. Jost, *Ges. D. Judenthums u. seiner Sekten*, Vol. II, Leipzig, 1858, p. 307f.
13. Harkavy, *o.c.*, p. 36.
14. J. Mann, *o.c.*, p. 330.
15. *O.c.*, p. 338.

NOTES TO APPENDIX III

I.

1. *Cf.* Zunz, *Gottesdienstliche Vortraege*, p. 369f.; L. Landshuth, *Hegyon Lev*, p. 42f.; Elbogen, *Studien*, p. 20f. This was also the old Palestinian ritual; see S. Schechter in *J.Q.R.*, Vol. X, pp. 654–655.
2. Ph. Bloch in *Monatsschrift*, etc., Vol. 37, p. 305f. Kedusha in Yotzer was not customary in the Pal. r., J. Mann, *o.c.*, p. 290.
3. *L.c.*
4. Ph. Bloch, *o.c.*, p. 263.
5. S. Schechter in *J.Q.R.*, Vol. X, p. 656.

6. L. Finkelstein, *o.c.*, p. 151.
7. See S. Mendelsohn, *Journal of Jewish Philosophy and Lore*, Vol. I, p. 355f.; L. Finkelstein, *o.c.*, p. 155.
8. *J.Q.R.*, Vol. 16, p. 157.
9. *Ibid.*, Vol. 10, p. 657. Compare M.V., p. 18, where it is stated that this benediction was arranged after Jesus the son of Pandera. See S. Krauss, *Lehnwörter*, p. 464; S. S. Cohon, *Jesus*, etc., p. 88, and note 10 *ibid.* (reprint from *Journal of Bibl. Exeg.*, 1929).
10. A. Marx, *o.c.*, p. 5.
11. *J.Q.R.*, Vol. 16, p. 169.
12. Zunz, *Ritus*, p. 147f.
13. L. Geiger, *Geshichte d. Juden in Berlin*, Vol. II, p. 27f.

2.

14. *J.Q.R.*, Vol. 19, p. 227.
15. *O.c.*, p. 233.
16. *O.c.*, pp. 243ff., gives a comparative study of the texts.

NOTES TO APPENDIX IV

1. Zunz, *Ltg.*, p. 122.
2. S. D. Luzzatto, *o.c.*, p. 21.
3. *Jewish Music*, pp. 168, 171; *Thesaurus*, Vol. VII.
4. Luzzatto, *l.c.*
5. *Jewish Music*, p. 160; *Thesaurus*, Vol. VII.
6. Zunz, *Ltg.*, p. 96.
7. I. Davidson, *Mahzor Yannai*, p. XXXII.
8. *L.c.*
9. This Musaf Kerova was one of the favorite texts of the Hazzanim for musical settings. Compare H. Weintraub, Shire Beth Adonai, and *Thesaurus*, Vols. VI–VIII.
10. Luzzatto, *o.c.*, p. 22.
11. Zunz, *o.c.*, p. 44.
12. Compare O.H., p. 168, and Davidson, *Otzar*, etc., Vol. I, p. 330.
13. This Kerova and that for Para was lately discovered. See O. Hat., p. 117f.
14. Zunz, *Ltg.*, p. 705.
15. Luzzatto, *o.c.*, p. 23.

16. This Kerova too was set to music by many Hazzanim. See work cited in note 9.
17. I. Davidson, *Mahzor Yannai*, p. 32f.
18. *O.c.*, p. xxxvii.
19. According to Zunz, *Ltg.*, p. 679.
20. *L.c.*
21. Davidson, *o.c.*, Vol. I, p. 203.
22. Zunz, *Ltg.*, p. 458.
23. Zunz, *o.c.*, p. 274.
24. *O.c.*, p. 128.
25. *O.c.*, pp. 294–295.
26. *O.c.*, p. 719; Davidson, *o.c.*, p. 128; O.H., p. 270.
27. Zunz, *o.c.*, p. 163.
28. *Jewish Music*, pp. 266f., 299; *Thesaurus*, Vol. VIII.
29. Zunz, *o.c.*, p. 155.
30. *O.c.*, p. 159.
31. Maharil gives other piyyutim. See Mahzor Sabioneta, 1517.
32. Compare I. Davidson, *o.c.*, Vol. I, p. 235.

NOTES TO APPENDIX V

1. Zunz, *Ltg.*, p. 73, quotes Solomon Duran, but adds that there is no evidence.
2. *L.c.*
3. The name of the author is to be found in the acrostic of the last stanza.
4. Zunz, *o.c.*, p. 149.
5. *L.c.*
6. Zunz, *o.c.*, pp. 172–173. However, only the insertion for paragraph 3 has this name in the last stanza. Maharil quotes other poems for the seventh and eighth evenings.
7. Zunz, *o.c.*, p. 154; mentioned by Maharil.
8. *O.c.*, p. 173.
9. *O.c.*, p. 485; Landshuth, p. 20.
10. Called Michelmann of Zulpich and lived in the thirteenth century. Zunz, *o.c.*, p. 484.
11. Zunz, *o.c.*, p. 271.
12. Maharil quotes the poem according to the Ashkenazic ritual.

13. Compare *Jewish Music*, p. 138 : 1.
14. *Cf.* Shir Hashirim Rabba, Chapter 6 end; Chapter VI.
15. S. D. Luzzatto, however, holds that the author is Benjamin b. Abraham Delli Mansi, *o.c.*, p. 24.
16. Zunz, *o.c.*, p. 70.
17. Adler's *Mahzor*, Tabernacles, p. 208. See musical setting in *Jewish Songbook*, p. 163.
18. *O.c.*, p. 212.
19. Zunz, *o.c.*, p. 70.
20. *Ibid.*, p. 91.
21. *Ibid.*, p. 166. But according to the Chronicle "Achimaatz" he lived toward the end of the eighth and at the beginning of the ninth centuries. It may be that there were two "Payetanim" with the same name.
22. Adler's *Mahzor*, p. 241.
23. This text has a traditional tune; see *Jewish Music*, pp. 156 : 7, 160.
24. Mentioned in S.R.A. 52. Furthermore:
    4. "שמחו בשמחת תורה" — an alphabetical acrostic.
    5. "אנא משה רחימא" — a poem in Aramaic in praise of Moses.
    6. "שמחו אהובים" — a poem in the order of 4.
    7. "חדו חדו רבנן" — an alphabetical acrostic in Aramaic.
    8. "הללויה.... אשמחה".
    9. "סימן טוב.... מתי".
    10. "כי בשמחה תצאון".
    11. "מפי אל.... יתברך".

    All these are popular songs in folk-style and in alphabetical acrostics, praising the Tora and Israel.
25. According to the Palestinian climate, dew starts to fall with the spring season, and rain with autumn.
26. S. D. Luzzatto in his introduction to the Italian ritual, Vol. I, p. 24.
27. Zunz, *Ltg.*, p. 45. This last poem is also found in the old Roman ritual, A. Schechter, *o.c.*, p. 121.
28. *O.c.*, p. 21.
29. *O.c.*, p. 23; Luzzatto, *o.c.*, p. 26.
30. Luzzatto, *l.c.*, is of the opinion that these numbers are a

continuation of "אתה הנחלת" and are so found in the old Roman and Roumanian rituals.

31. Zunz, *o.c.*, p. 717, b. Moses, or b. Mahadib, or b. Ezra; *cf.* Luzzatto, Vol. I, pp. 15–16.

NOTES TO APPENDIX VI

1. Zunz, *o.c.*, p. 412.
2. Zunz, *o.c.*, p. 252.
3. *O.c.*, p. 349.
4. Baer, p. 613, is of the opinion that after composing the poem the author made a revised and abridged edition.
5. Zunz, *o.c.*, p. 277.
6. *Ibid.*, p. 263.
7. This was not the prophet, but the son of the priest Jehoiada. The story in the *Talmud* (*l.c.*) concludes that as soon as Nabuzaradon saw how difficult it is to atone for the killing of one soul, he reflected upon his own deeds and, abandoning the army, he embraced Judaism.
8. On the Mode of Job compare *Jewish Music*, p. 59.
9. Zunz, *o.c.*, p. 488 doubts his authorship.
10. It is reported that Maharil used to recite this poem, (Maharil, Tisha Be'ab).
11. I. *Jewish Classical Series I*, p. 151 (Jewish Publication Society).
    II. *Standard Book of Jewish Verse*, Ed. Joseph Friedlander, p. 371.
    III. E. Fleg's *Jewish Anthology*, p. 218.
    IV. *Anthology of Post-Biblical Poetry*, Vol. II, p. 106.
12. *Jewish Music*, pp. 168: 9, 172–3: 5–7.

GENERAL INDEX

GENERAL INDEX

INDEX TO THE HEBREW PRAYERS AND POETRY

INDEX TO THE HEBREW PRAYERS AND POETRY